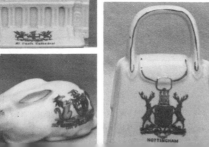

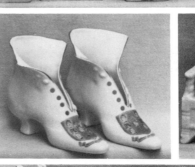

The 1989
Price Guide to
Crested China

The 1989
Price Guide
to Crested China

Nicholas Pine

Milestone Publications

Original listings taken from
Crested China by Sandy Andrews

Published by Milestone Publications
Goss & Crested China Ltd,
62 Murray Road,
Horndean, Portsmouth, Hants. PO8 9JL.

Edited by Lynda Pine, Sandy Andrews and Vanessa Amis
Photography Michael Edwards Studio
Typeset by Barbara James Typesetting, Hayling Island
Printed and bound in Great Britain by
Richard Clay, Industrial Estate, Chichester, Sussex

British Library Cataloguing in Publication Data

The Price guide to crested china. —— 1989-
  1. Crested porcelain. Prices - Lists
  338.4'37382

  ISBN 1-85265-101-6

Contents

Acknowledgements 9
Preface 11
Manufacturers and
  Trademarks 16
Introduction to Trademarks and
  Recorded Models 19

Crested China Manufacturers

Abbey China 21
W M Adams & Sons 21
Adderleys 22
Alba Pottery 22
Albion China 23
Albion China (R & B) 23
Albion China (T.C. & P.) 24
Aldwych (B.R. & Co) 25
Aldwych China 25
Aldwych (W & R) 26
Alexandra China 26
Alexandra 28
Amber China 29
Anglo Heraldic Co 29
Arcadian China 30
Argonauta Porcelain 52
Argosy China 53
Asbury 53
Asbury China 54
Atlas 54
Atlas China 55
Atlas Heraldic China 55
Aurelian China 56
Avon China 57
Aynsley 57
B 58
Balmoral China 58
Bell China 59
Belleek 59
Birks Crest China 60
Birks China 60

Blairs China 61
Boots 61
Botolph China 62
Bow China 64
Bramwell China 65
British Manufacture 316
Bute China 65
Cable China 66
Caledonia China 66
Caledonia China 67
Caledonia Heraldic China 68
Cambrian China 69
Carlton China 70
Carmen China 87
Cascade China 88
Cauldon China 88
Celtic Porcelain 89
Ceramic China 89
Challenge China 90
Chelson China 90
Christop China 91
Civic 91
CJB & Co. 92
Clarence China 92
Clarence Crest China 93
Clays 94
Clifton 94
Clifton China 97
Colleen China 98
Collingwood 99
Columbia China 99
Coral Porcelain 100
The Corona China 100
Coronet Ware 102
Craven China 105
Crown China 105
Crown Derby 106
Crown Devon 107
The Crown Duchy English
  China 108

C & SC   108
Crown Staffordshire   108
Curzon Art   109
C W and Co.   109
Cyclone   110
The Dainty Ware   111
Derwent China   113
Devonia Art China   113
Diamond China   115
Disa Art China   116
Do! Do! Crest China   116
Doric Herald   117
Dougall's "Castle" Series   117
DRGM   118
The Duchess China   118
Eglinton China   119
Elite China Series   120
Empire China   120
Empire Gem   121
Empress China   121
Endor China   122
English Emporium China   122
English Herald China   123
English Souvenir China   123
Erin China   124
Esbeco   124
Etruscan China   125
Exceller   125
Excelsior   126
Fairyware   126
Famous Henley China   127
Fenton China   128
Filey China   128
F.L.   129
Florentine China   129
The Foley China   132
Fords China   133
F.P. and S.   133
Furstenberg   134
The Garnion Ware   134
Gemma   135
W.H. Goss   139
Gladstone China   139
Gothic China   140

Grafton China   140
Granic China   152
Grays Sports China   152
The Griffin China   153
Grimwades   154
Grosvenor Series   155
Grosvenor Ware   155
Gwalia Ware   156
H & L   157
H & S   157
Hamilton China   158
Heathcote China   158
Herald China   159
Heraldic China   159
Heraldic China   160
Herald Series   160
E. Hughes and Co. China   161
Iceni Crest China   161
Imperial   162
Impero   163
Ionic Heraldic   163
Ivora Ware   164
JBC   164
JBM   165
JP   165
JW   166
Kangaroo Art China   166
Kangaroo Brand   167
Keltic   167
Kensington China   168
King China   169
Kingsway Art or Crest China   169
Kyle Series   171
LAB   172
Lawrence Sheriffe Ware   172
Leadbeater Art China   173
Lion China   174
Limoges   175
Liverpool Rd. Pottery   175
Lochinvar   176
Locke and Co.   176
Lynton China   178
M   178

Macintyre 179
C. McDMann & Co. 179
Marine Art China 180
Maxim China 180
Mayfair Ware 181
Meir Arms China 181
Melba Bone China 182
Melba China 182
Mermaid 183
The Milton China 183
Moore Bros. 185
Mosanic 186
Moschendorf 188
Mother Shipton China 188
Nautilus Porcelain 189
Nelson China 190
Ness 191
Niagara Art China 191
Norfolk Crest China 192
Noritaké 193
Nornesford China 193
One and All 194
Oxford Art China 194
P 195
Palatine China 195
Palmer 196
P.A.L.T. 196
Panorama 197
Paragon China 198
Park for the People China 198
Patriotic China 199
Pearl Arms China 199
Pheonix China 201
Podmore China 201
Poppyland China 204
Porcelle 204
Premier 206
Princess China 207
Queen China 207
Queens China or Ware 208
Queens Crest China 209
Queeny China 210
Raleigh China 211
R & M 211

Raphael China 212
Regency Ware 212
Regis 213
Registry Ware 214
C.L. Reis 214
Rex China 215
Rialto China 215
Ribblesdale China 216
Eugene Rimmel 216
Rita China Series 217
Robinson & Leadbeater 218
Roman Bath China 219
Rosina Queens China 219
Rowena China 220
Royal Albert Crown China 221
Royal Arms China 221
Royal China 222
Royal China Works,
  Worcester 222
Royal Coburg 223
Royal Doulton 223
Royal Ivory Porcelain 224
Royal Stafford China 224
Royal 'Vale' China 225
Royal Worcester 225
Ryecroft China Series 226
S 226
St. George China 227
St. Pauls 228
Sandifords Ceramic China 228
San Juan 229
Savoy China 229
Saxony 235
Scotch Porcelain 237
Shamrock China 237
Shamrock Crest China 238
J. Shaw 238
Shell China 239
Shelley China 239
Signal 247
Skarab China 248
Snowdon China 248
Souvenir Series 249
S.P. Co. Ltd. 249

Spencer Art China   250
Sphinx   250
Sporting Series   251
SR   251
Stanley China   252
Star Bazaar Art China   252
Strand China   253
Success (Art) China   253
Sussex China   254
Sussex China S.P. Co.   255
Sussex Ware   256
Swan China   256
Sylvan China   262
Syren China   263
Talbot China   264
Taylor and Kent   264
Temple Porcelain   265
Thistle China   265
T.M.W. and Co. Ltd./
  and S. Ltd.   266
Tourist Art China   266
Towy China   267
Tre-Pol-Pen Series   267
Triood   268
Tudor Arms China   269
Tuscan China   269
Tuskar Rock China   271
Union Crest China   272
Union K   272
Unity China   273
Universal Series   273
Vale China   274
Venetia China   274
Vectis/Vectis Models   275
Victoria Arms China   276
Victoria China   276
Victoria (China)   279
Victorian Porcelain   279
Vignaud   280
W   280
W & Sons   281
Wade   281
Warwick China   281
Waterfall Heraldic China   282

Waterloo Ware   284
Waverley China   284
W.C.G.   285
Wedgwood   285
Wembley China   285
White Horse China   286
The White House   287
W.H.H. and S.   287
Wilco Series   288
Williamsons   288
Willow Art and
  Willow China   289
Willper Heraldic China   301
Wilton China   302
Wil-Wat China   304
W and R   304
W.R. and S.   305
Wy Not? Crest China   306
Unmarked Models   307
Country of Origin Marks   314

Illustrated Section

Unglazed/Parian busts   323
Buildings   325
Monuments   330
National/Traditional
  Souvenirs   332
Seaside Souvenirs   336
Animals and Birds   340
Great War   349
Home/Nostalgic   358
Comic/Novelty   363
Alcohol   366
Ancient Artefacts   367
Sport   368
Musical Instruments   370
Transport   371
Footwear   373
Miscellaneous   374
Miniature Domestic   375

Acknowledgements

This catalogue could not appear without several hundred thoughtful collectors taking the trouble to notify us of pieces not listed in *Crested China*, published in 1980, or *The Price Guide to Crested China*.

The original compilation of these listings and continual updating has been undertaken by Sandy Andrews who I gratefully thank.

My wife Lynda and co-director Vanessa Amis have also added to the listings, verified prices and carefully checked entries for which I thank them.

In particular, I would like to thank Len Harris for his work on Locke & Co., Worcester and for tirelessly supplying lists of unrecorded pieces for many years. Len has methodically checked every piece that has passed through his hands and the authors and collectors everywhere owe him a debt of graditude.

Special thanks also to P.D. Williams who has collected examples of every different crested china factory mark and has for many years especially given us full details in order to update this book.

We also wish to thank Stephen Godly, Norman Pratten, Michael Shears and Graham Flett who have also greatly assisted.

The following collectors have all forwarded lists, new information, photographs, further information when asked, and we are extremely grateful to each and every one.

S.E. Aymes, N.A. Ball, Mrs C. Barnes, Mr & Mrs J. Barnes, Mrs M. Barton, Mrs R.C. Beere, J. Birch, J.F. Bishop, Mrs B. Bowker, N.A. Bown, Mrs A. Brain, Mrs M. Briggs, Mrs C.V. Bright, Crd L. Brokenshire, Mrs J.M. Brown, Mrs P. Bullock, A.G. Bunce, Mrs L. Chantry, B.L. Clark, M.G. Cook, W. Cover, Mrs J. Dadds, Mrs E.M. Davies, N. Dewsey, P.W. Dodds, Mrs S. Edwards, Mrs V. Elkington, J.R. Emerson, Mrs W. Eveleigh, R.T. Evley, P. Finch, A. Ford, Mrs Fowler, Mrs B. Gay, M.B. Geddes, J. Gilbert, Mrs J. Gill, Mrs J. Gorlick, Mrs Griffiths, P. Hacker, D.A. Halfacre, H. Hall, S.J. Harker, A.T. Higgins, B. Holmes, Mrs A. Hopton, F.J. How, Miss J.M. Hurrell, D. Jackson, Mrs A.C. Jones, Mrs H. Jones, M.W. Jones, S.H. Jones, Mrs V. Juniper, G. Karon, C. Keane, Mrs D. Kyle, Mr & Mrs R. Latham, D. Leach, M. Lee, W.S. Loader, R. McIntyre, L. Macham, Mr & Mrs S. Maidment, Mrs B. Malin, D. Millar,

S.R. Morgan, A.M. Munday, K. Nelson-Tomsen, H.C. Newman, R. Nichols, P.J. Osborne, Mrs A. Palmer, C.J. Parker, H. Parker, S.D. Phelps, Mrs S.J. Piper, P.H. Platt, Canon C.F. Pollard, B. Prindeville, R. Radcliffe, A. Ramsden, Mrs J. Reeves, M. Regnard, Mrs K.M. Richardson, Mrs. R. Riley, Mrs J. Robinson, J. Sanders, M. Du Sautoy, N. Sharp, M. Shears, J. Simpson, A.P. Sisley, R. Smith, Miss V. Soudain, D. Staff, J. Stevens, Mrs K. Stewart, Mrs J. Stonelake, M. Stuart, Mrs P Swinnerton, Mrs D. Tatton, T.B. Terry, D. Thomas, N. Tzimus, Mrs C. Waller, M.J. Walton, R. Ward, Mrs V.A. Waterman, I.G. Watson, Mrs Webb, Mrs S. Westbrook, J. Wheeler, Mr & Mrs J. Whipp, P. Wilks, S. Williams, Mrs P. Wilson, B. Windmill, J.E. Wright, H.J. Yallop.

Please continue to send details of any new models to Milestone Publications for inclusion in future editions of *The Price Guide to Crested China*.

Preface

The Price Guide to Crested China should be read in conjunction with *Crested China* by Sandy Andrews, the standard work on the subject. The prices of W.H. Goss china models will be found in *The Concise Encyclopaedia and Price Guide to Goss China* by Nicholas Pine, published as the companion volume to this guide.

This price guide is essentially a listing of all the pieces in *Crested China* without the full descriptions given in that volume, to which have been added some two thousand pieces which have been notified since 1980 and over 1000 since 1983. The total number of recorded pieces is now in excess of 7000. A number of pieces has been omitted from this edition that are not now believed to exist. If you have accurate information on any piece that cannot be located in this Guide, please inform the publishers in order that it may be included in a future edition.

To find the value of any piece first look up the correct manufacturer; this will be found by reference to the mark on the base of the piece in question. All items are listed in the order of the headings given on Page 19.

This guide is designed to represent average prices that one would expect to pay from a dealer. As a matter of editorial policy, prices in previous editions were not set on the high side as it is considered more important that a collector should not pay too much for a piece rather than he miss the odd bargain.

The market has continued to rise strongly during the three years since publication of the 1985 edition. Rarer items have usually doubled and more common items have risen by approximately one-third.

As the years go by, it is becoming clearer which pieces are scarce and which are not, so we are able to set prices more accurately, or rather, the market sets the prices for we can only respond to supply and demand, reflecting the 'collectibility' of a piece.

We constantly assess and discuss prices and alter our master listings every working day.

In order to assist the reader, we have included a section where almost 1000 pieces are illustrated and valued including items in every theme and price range. This section should allow one to quickly obtain the approximate value of any item and will be of use to market traders and dealers who do not specialize but need to value pieces rapidly when buying or selling.

They represent the prices charged by Goss and Crested China Ltd. in 1988 and are, in our opinion, fair and true values of the current retail selling price, net of any Value Added Tax.

Goss & Crested China Ltd. are the leading dealers in heraldic porcelain and whilst we do not have every piece we do have a constantly changing stock of several thousand pieces to interest the collector. We produce *Goss & Crested China* an illustrated monthly catalogue containing 32 pages of items for sale. This is available by subscription, please enquire for details of this and our range of publications on the subject of heraldic china, a full list of which will be found at the back of this book. Visitors are welcome to view our stock at any time, but preferably by prior appointment please.

Full details of all the listed factories, their histories, downfalls and details of their numbering systems, if any, may be found in *Crested China* and are not repeated here.

Any notable decorations will add value to a piece, i.e. transfer printed scenes, views, birds, animals or floral decorations or indeed some pieces may be found solely coloured in blue, red or yellow. A premium of between £3 and £15 should be added for any piece having an unusual or attractive decoration or verse. Inscriptions have been omitted from the guide unless they are essential in determining the nature of the piece. Some models have military inscriptions, i.e. details of particular engagements during the Great War. For such pieces, usually produced by Savoy, £8—£12 should be added. Matching crests are very few and far between on models produced by factories other than W.H. Goss and may be disregarded. In the case of buildings, monuments and the like a small premium should be paid for the correct arms although most items will be found to display local crests as they were usually sold in those areas.

Much domestic ware was produced, often carrying coats of arms as an afterthought as much as by design. Such pieces, including cups and saucers, plates, milk jugs, large pots and vases, are only worth around £2—£5 each but tend to be the most overpriced items at fairs, markets etc. Such ware is not very collectable. Ordinary small vases, jugs, pots, ewers, etc. from any factory are worth £1—£2 and named models £3—£5.

Many similar pieces carry different factory marks on their bases, for example Arcadian, Swan and Clifton were all made by Arkinstall & Son Ltd. Where the same piece could have been produced with several different marks the reader's attention is drawn in such cases to the names of the factories and chapters under which one should look if the piece cannot be found listed under the factory or mark shown on the base. To aid the reader a table of the principal manufacturers of crested china and their trademarks, subsidiaries and firms using their products will be found on page 16. Manufacturers were constantly merging, being taken over, ceasing production and selling their designs and moulds to other potters so similar pieces constantly appear with different marks. Many items which are normally found coloured can also be found white, either with or without gilding; and sometimes having no factory mark. All these variations are individually listed and priced, but in general, such items would normally be worth approximately ½ to ⅔ of the value of the coloured version. Likewise, a piece normally found white glazed only would be increased in value by ½ to ¾ should a coloured variety be found.

New items are constantly coming to light but after assuming that a piece is a new model as it is not listed under the appropriate heading in this guide, one must refer to *Crested China* or the table of principal manufacturers on page 16 and check under all other relevant factory headings. Many known models are now being seen with different factory marks, these are all worth the same as identical pieces listed everywhere.

One point that needs to be clearly made is that pieces from one pottery are not worth more than those from another. For example, Savoy is not worth any more than Swan or for that matter Carlton, Grafton or Shelley etc. Over the years one has often been told by amateur dealers and stallholders that Arcadian is worth more than other factories. This is not so. The only reasons for the constant uttering of this myth I would venture are that firstly Arkinstall & Son Ltd. were more prolific than most and that there are hundreds of Arcadian pieces to be found, dealers therefore would usually have a number in stock and these would be preferred to items with no factory mark or a lesser known — in fact little-known marks are definitely rarer, but, alas they are not worth a premium either. Secondly, this fallacy has been passed on over the years and in this vacuum of knowledge, such gems as this have thrived. I am pleased to say that I have heard it little during recent years.

The value of crested china may be determined by three factors: theme, rarity and condition — in that order. The most popular themes are: Great War; Buildings; Animals (including birds); Transport; Memorials; Monuments; Statues; Cartoon/Comedy Characters; Comic/Novelty; Sport; Alcohol and Musical Instruments. This list is by no means ex-haustive but it does cover the main spheres of interest among collectors. Rarity is self explanatory; a 'Bomb Thrower' is rarer than a 'Cenotaph' and therefore it is worth more. These two factors may be summed up as 'Collectability', for example a common animal would be worth far more than, say, a unique billiken because there is far more demand for the animal from theme collectors. Thus supply and demand play an important part. It should always be borne in mind that even the most attractive and rare crested cup and saucer will never be worth more than a few pounds whereas a rare military piece could command as much as £400.00.

Condition is another factor which affects price. Whilst not as important as with Goss china, it still affects the value of an item considerably and the following remarks should be noted. Crested china produced by other manufacturers was never as fine as that of the Goss factory. William Henry Goss conducted over one thousand experiments which took many years before he perfected the parian body which he used as his medium. The other producers were not interested in the high standards that Goss set himself, they were only concerned with jumping on the crested china bandwagon and producing wares as quickly and as cheaply as possible for the profitable souvenir trade which was rapidly developing. Some factories were better than others and Grafton in particular produced some very detailed and delicate models. Most foreign ware (mainly German or Czechoslovakian) is of poor quality, tending to be rather crude and heavy, therefore worth less as a general rule than English china.

Having made the point that crested china factories were not that particular about the quality of their products it follows that many pieces were substandard even before leaving the factory. The producers were not usually too concerned about this and many pieces were sold having firing cracks, chips (under the glaze) or other flaws; rubbed, poorly applied or non-existent gilding, imperfect transfers, crooked coats of arms and inscriptions as well as having indifferent glazing. This was sometimes incomplete and often heavy and too liberally coated, leading to a green-grey tinge in grooves and internal corners where the glaze has built up. This latter occurrence often leads to minor glazing cracks appearing in such build ups of glaze. These do not affect value. In addition, pieces were often wrongly named on the base, or not named at all.

Minor defects such as those given above are commonplace and do not affect value although naturally a piece completely free of such manufacturers' imperfections would be preferable. Such items however number less than 10% of all crested china produced so to restrict a collection to these pristine items only would be frustrating if not impossible. If one seeks perfection then W.H. Goss is the only factory that can be considered by the serious collector, indeed, many if not most Goss collectors consider other crested china to be inferior and would not dream of collecting it themselves. It does however have charms other than those of complete perfection to commend it. Pieces with particularly bad factory defects were often sold off without factory mark, crest or inscription, such items are worth around ⅔ of the price of a normal item.

Damage occuring in the period subsequent to manufacture such as cracks or chips affect value considerably and any piece so damaged would only be worth between ¼ to ½ of the perfect price. The same applies with restoration, whilst a restored item looks better than a damaged one it is worth little more and if the restoration is bad then it is worth less. These points should be borne in mind when buying from market stalls, antique fairs and shops where dealers seem to disregard damage when endeavouring to sell their wares. Damaged items are usually overpriced, if indeed the damage has even been noticed by the dealer concerned; it must be fully allowed for in the price when buying. It is only when one comes to sell that the wisdom of this advice will become apparent.

No forecast can be made as to whether prices will rise or fall in the future, that will depend upon economic factors which cannot be discussed here. During the last decade however, prices have multiplied approximately ten times with the rarer items increasing many times faster than the smaller pots and vases and the more common shapes. Over the years crested china has been a very good investment with all the fun of collecting thrown in. The publication of *Crested China* by Sandy Andrews has substantially increased interest in the subject and this price guide now in its third edition can only further that interest. Two major London auction houses now include crested china in with their sales of Goss and overseas interest is on the increase.

Goss & Crested China Ltd. would be pleased to hear of any pieces or unusual or notable crests or decorations (apart from non-models and domestic ware) that are not mentioned in the listings in this guide or in the main book for inclusion in future editions.

Should you wish to sell please note that the prices in this guide are used as a basis for purchasing and that we will pay good, fair market prices for all items offered. Please send us a list of the pieces that are for sale or exchange stating in each case the factory, height, crest and condition in order to receive our individual offers.

Nicholas Pine

Manufacturers and Trade Marks

The plethora of different manufacturers, wholesalers, retailers, marks and names found on the bases of crested china is confusing even to the author, who has only in recent years been able to work out with some reasonable degree of accuracy who made what and for whom. I now feel with this edition that I know the manufacturers of most trade marks which appear on the bases of crested china.

There are perhaps only eight major and a further two important manufacturers who accounted for the bulk of crested china made. These are followed by some eighty to one hundred very minor firms, which are usually only responsible for the production of a handful of pieces, and often only then as a sideline to their main areas of manufacture.

In order that the original manufacturer of a piece may be ascertained more easily, the following table has been included to aid identification. Under the name of the manufacturer that firm's main trade name has been given in bold in each case. Under this name will be found all known trade marks that can be attributed to that firm.

Therefore, if you have a piece that does not appear in the listings for that particular mark, try looking it up in the following table and check under firstly, the main and then under the subsidiary marks until it is located, you can then note the value of the item. Please do not forget to let the authors know about any models which are not listed under their own factory mark in order that they might be included in future editions.

Table of the principal manufacturers of Crested China and their Trade Marks, Subsidiaries and other firms using their products

Arkinstall & Son
Arcadian China
Albion China
Aldwych China
Amber China
Avon China
Birks Crest China
Botolph
Boots
Bute China
Carmen China

Christop China
C.J.B. & Co
Clifton
Coronet Ware
Ford & Pointon
Fords China
FL
FP & S
The Griffin China
Grosvenor Series
Iceni Crest China

JW
Kensington China
Nelson China
One and All
Palatine China
Queens Crest China
R & L
Robinson & Beresford
Robinson & Leadbeater
Raphael China
Snowdon China
Sporting Series
Sussex China S.P. Co.
Swan China
Vectis
Victis
Warwick China
Waverley China
Wembley China

Belleek Pottery
Belleek Pottery
Shamrock China

Wiltshaw & Robinson Ltd.
Carlton Ware
Aldwych China
Caledonia Heraldic China
Cambrian China
Craven China
Crown China
Cyclone
Kangaroo Brand
Lion China
Mother Shipton
Eugene Rimmel
Syren China

Sampson, Hancock & Sons
Corona
Alexandra
Anglo-Heraldic Co.
C.J.B. & Co
The Duchess China
Exceller
Granic China
Grosvenor Ware
Heraldic China
JBM
Mayfair Ware
Raleigh China
Regency Ware
Sussex China
Talbot China
Triood
Tudor Arms China
Waterloo Ware
Victoria China
Willper Heraldic China

E. Hughes & Co.
Fenton
E. Hughes & Co.
Royal China

Taylor & Kent
Florentine
Albion China
Atlas Heraldic China
Bell China
Bute China
C & SC
Caledonia China
Cascade China
Challenge China
Civic
Coronet Ware
Cyclone
The Dainty Ware
Doric Herald
Filey China
Gladstone China
Griffin China
Hamilton China
Ionic Heraldic
Keltic
Poppyland China
Premier
Royal Vale China
Taylor & Kent

Charles Schmidt & Co.
Gemma
Alexandre
Empire Gem
Empress China
Fairyware
Ness

Alfred B. Jones & Sons Ltd.
Grafton China
Argosy
C.L. Reis
Diamond China
English Herald China
Herald China
Herald Series
King China
Wil-Wat China

Wm. Kutzscher & Co.
Impero
Princess China
St. George China
W.H.H. and S.
Unmarked
Saxony
Made in Saxony

Edwin Leadbeater
Leadbeater Art China
Marine Art China
Nornesford China
Panorama

James MacIntyre
J. MacIntyre
Argonauta Porcelain
Caledonia China

Max Emanuel & Co.
Mosanic
Maxim China
Unity China
Austria
Czechoslovakia
Foreign
Germany

Nautilus Porcelain Co.
Nautilus Porcelain
Celtic Porcelain

Podmore China Co.
Podmore
Strand China

William Ritchie & Son Ltd.
Porcelle
Empire China
Ivora Ware
Mermaid
W.R. and S

Robinson & Leadbeater
R & L
Royal Ivory Porcelain
Victoria Porcelain

Birks, Rawlins & Co.
Savoy China
Aldwych China
Birks China
Bow China
Caledonia Heraldic China
Diamond China
Empire China
Endor China
Mermaid
Niagara Art China
Patriotic China
Porcelle
Queens China

Wileman & Co
Shelley China
The Foley China

R.H. & S.L. Plant Ltd.
Tuscan China
Nornesford China

Rowena
Shamrock Crest China

Charles Waine & Co.
Venetia China
CW & Co.
Etruscan China
Kyle Series

James Reeves
Victoria China
Botolph China
English Emporium China
Gothic

Hewitt and Leadbeater
Willow Art China
Abbey China
Alexandra
Asbury China
Balmoral China
Cable China
Caledonia Heraldic China
Clays
Curzon Art
Devonia Art China
Diamond China
Disa Art China
Elite China Series
Famous Henley China
H & L
H & S
JBC
Kingsway Art China
Kingsway Crest China
Lochinvar
Marine Art China
The Milton China
Norfolk Crest China
Oxford Art China
Palmer
Pearl Arms China
Regis
Roman Bath China
Signal China
St. Pauls
Star Bazaar Art China
Sussex Ware
Thistle China
Tourist Art China
Waterfall Heraldic
Wilco Series
Willow China
W and R
Wy Knot
Wy Not

Introduction to Trademarks and Recorded Models

These have been arranged by marks in alphabetical order, with manufacturer's name, if known, and recorded models after each mark.

The models have been grouped into types of souvenirs and have been arranged for the most part in the order in which they would have been made. Two themes are now listed under their own heading, namely hats and footwear, formerly included under Miscellaneous. The headings are as follows:

Unglazed/Parian
Parian busts are also found under this heading.

Ancient Artefacts
Models of historic interest as produced by W.H. Goss.

Buildings — Coloured

Buildings — White
Including bridges

Monuments (including crosses)

Historical/Folklore

Traditional/National Souvenirs
These have been listed in the following order: British, England, Ireland, Scotland, Wales, other countries.

Seaside Souvenirs
These have been listed in the following order: Bathing Machines, Crafts, Fishermen/Lifeboatmen, Lighthouses, Shells, Luggage, People and Punches.

Countryside

Animals
These listings include animals which are really regional symbols as the Sussex Pig. Most collectors would include these in an animal collection.

Birds (including Eggs)
These listings also include regional or national emblems such as the Kiwi.

Great War
These models have been grouped as follows:
Personnel, Aeroplanes/Airships/Zeppelins, Ships/Submarines, Armoured Cars/Red Cross Vans/Tanks, Guns/Mortars, Small arms, Shells, Bombs, Grenades, Mines, Torpedoes, Personal Equipment, Memorabilia and Memorials. (Florence Nightingale statues are always included in Great War collections although she died before 1914. Certainly the statue was offered for sale at the same time, so it is listed under this heading).

Home/Nostalgic

Comic/Novelty

Alcohol

Sport

Musical Instruments

Transport

'Modern' Equipment
'Modern', that is, at the time it was made.

Hats

Footwear

Miscellaneous

Miniature Domestic

Domestic

Under these headings models are listed alphabetically, if that is possible. all inscriptions and verses are printed in *italics*.

If a model is best described by its inscription this will be placed at the beginning of an entry in *italics*.

Sizes are height unless otherwise stated.

All values are given in £ and p in Sterling currency.

The 1989 Price Guide to Crested China has been designed and produced as a revision to **Crested China,** the base reference work. This Price Guide contains additional information which has come to light since 1980.

Crested China Manufacturers

Abbey China

For mark see *Crested China*, p. 19.

Trademark used by Hewitt & Leadbeater for a fancy goods retailer or wholesaler in Tewkesbury.
Hewitt & Leadbeater usually used the trademarks Willow or Willow Art. Stock numbers where known as Willow Art.

Seaside Souvenirs
Lighthouse pepper pot. 110mm.   5.50
(There is almost certainly a
matching salt pot.)

Animals
Cat, sitting, one ear down.
102mm.   10.50

Birds
Peewit posy holder. 78mm long.   6.50

Home/Nostalgic
Grandfather Clock, inscribed:
*Make use of time let not advantage
slip. Shakespeare.* No. 149.
140mm.   10.50

Cartoon/Comedy Characters
Baby with arms outstretched,
 inscribed: *Cheerio.* Some
 colouring on face. 125mm.   30.00

Hats
Schoolboy's Cap. 62mm long.   22.00

Wm. Adams & Sons

W Adams & Sons, Tunstall produced some ornamental ware and domestic china with crests for Langhams China Shop, Bury St Edmunds.

Adderleys

Alba Pottery

For marks see *Crested China, p. 19.*

Trademark used by Adderleys Ltd. Daisy Bank Pottery, Longton.

Range of 'smalls' to commemorate the Great War — inscribed: 1914 WAR EDITION.   from 5.00

ALBA POTTERY ENGLAND

Trademark used by a British pottery for exported goods. The only model found has an Honduras crest.

Monuments
Iona Cross. 110mm.   7.50

Albion China

This mark originally thought to be a variation of the Albion China T.C. & P. mark now appears clearly to be a mark used by J.A. Robinson Ltd. (Usual mark Arcadian). As they took over Robinson & Beresford (see below) they presumably went on using the 'Albion China' trademark.

Ancient Artefacts
Shrewsbury Salopian Ewer, inscribed: *Roman Salopian Ewer found at Uriconium now in Shrewsbury museum.*
No. 613. 75mm   3.00

Albion China (Robinson & Beresford)

For marks see *Crested China*, p.21.

Trademark used by Robinson and Beresford, Baltimore Works, Longton. Subsequently a branch of J.A. Robinson Ltd.

Ancient Artefacts
Glastonbury Bowl, No. 55. 50mm.   2.25
Lincoln Jack, inscribed: *Model of the Lincoln Jack from original in museum.* No. 50. 63mm.   3.00
Loving Cup originated by Henry of Navarre King of France. 2 or 3 handled. No. 579. 40mm.   3.00
Newbury Leather Bottle. No. 83. 65mm.   2.25
Silchester Vase. No. 54. 60mm.   2.25

Historical/Folklore
Ancient Coaching Hat, model of.
No. 687. 65mm long.   7.50

Albion China
(T.C. & P)

For marks see *Crested China*, p. 21.

Trademark used on china made for a Scottish wholesaler by Taylor and Kent (Ltd.), Florence Works, Longton. (Usual trademark Florentine.)

Ancient Artefacts

Irish Bronze Pot. No. 62. 42mm.	2.25
Puzzle Jug. 67mm.	5.50

Buildings — White

Blackpool Tower. 120mm.	10.00

Historical/Folklore

Mother Shipton. 72mm.	13.00

Traditional/National Souvenirs

Lancashire Clog. 88mm long.	4.75
Welsh Hat with blue band. 62mm.	4.75

Seaside Souvenirs

Lighthouse on rocky base. 100mm.	5.50
Portmanteau. 60mm long.	4.00
Yacht. 130mm.	10.50

Animals

Camel, kneeling. 100mm long.	13.00
Cat sitting, very furry coat. 90mm.	10.00
Cat, Manx. 90mm long.	16.00
Dolphin Jug. 100mm.	5.50
Elephant kneeling. 88mm long.	15.00
Frog Jug. 80mm long.	5.50
Hare. 95mm long.	8.50
Pig standing. Can be found with the inscription: *The Pig that won't go.* 90mm long.	10.00
Toad. 35mm.	10.50

Birds

(Giant) Hen, brooding. 91mm long.	6.50
Pelican Jug. 83mm long.	5.50
Swan posy holder. 80mm.	4.75

Great War

Bust of Sailor. 85mm.	30.00
Monoplane with roundels and 4-bladed movable propeller. 170mm long.	75.00
Tank, (wide Botolph mould with side guns standing proud). 125mm long.	21.50
Shell. 75mm.	3.00
Bury St. Edmunds Bomb.	11.00

Home/Nostalgic

Firebucket. 65mm.	3.50
Old Armchair, The with verse. 85mm.	7.50
Lamp. 69mm.	4.75
Pillar Box. 76mm.	8.25

Comic/Novelty

Negro Minstrel, bust, some colouring. 100mm.	30.00

Miscellaneous

Carboy. 76mm.	3.00

Footwear

Boot with gold buckle. 95mm long.	4.75
Oriental Slipper. 100mm long.	4.00

Miniature Domestic

Candle Stick and holder with snake curled around stem. 105mm.	5.50
Coffee Pot with lid. 76mm.	7.50
Dish, circular with 3 handles. 80mm.	2.00
Tea Pot with lid. 60mm.	7.50
Tea Pot with lid, squat. 35mm.	7.50

Aldwych China

For marks see *Crested China*, p. 23.

Trade name used by the retailer, Samuels, The Strand, London on crested china manufactured by Arkinstall and Son Ltd. (usual trademark Arcadian), Birks, Rawlins and Co. (usual trademark Savoy) and Wiltshaw and Robinson Ltd. (usual trademark Carlton).

Stock numbers where known coincide with those used on other models made by above firms.

Aldwych (A and S) Models
Mark used on wares manufactured by Arcadian. See *Crested China*, pp. 26/27.

Parian/unglazed
Bust of George V. 130mm.   35.00
Bust of Queen Mary. 130mm.   35.00

Monument
Nelson's Column. 169mm.   45.00

Animals
Elephant. 75mm long.   13.00
Tortoise. 72mm long.   6.50

Birds
Cock, standing, inscribed: *Cock o'*
   *the South.*100mm.   14.50
Swan. 50mm long.   6.50

Great War
Tommy in Sentry Box, not named.
   105mm.   75.00
Cannon Shell, inscribed: *Jack*
   Johnson. 90mm.   8.50
Steel Helmet with EP on side.
   70mm long and only 24mm
   high.   22.50

Home/Nostalgic
Grandfather clock, inscribed.
   108mm.   10.50

Miscellaneous
Horseshoe. 55mm long.   3.00

Aldwych (BR and Co) Models

BR & Co. mark as used by Savoy. See *Crested China*, p. 216.

Most pieces found with this mark are small vases etc. Only one model has been recorded.

Countryside
Acorn, *model of.* No. 110. 56mm.   5.50

Aldwych (W & R) Models

W & R mark as used by Carlton Ware. See *Crested China*, p. 76.

Monuments

Nelson's Column with four lions
at base. 165mm.   45.00

Great War

Tank inscribed: *HMLS Creme de Menthe*. 135mm long.   25.00

Alexandra China

For further marks see *Crested China*, p. 23.

Trademark used by a wholesaler, china manufactured by several leading producers of crested china, particularly Sampson Hancock (Corona Pottery).

Ancient Artefacts

Aberdeen Bronze Pot.   2.25
Bronze Bowl. 50mm.   2.25

Buildings — White

Marble Arch. 75mm.   13.00
Bottle Oven. No. 233. 82mm.   15.00
St Pauls Cathedral. 2 sizes:
  90mm.   15.50
  135mm.   21.50
Tower Bridge. 140mm long.   29.00
Westminster Abbey, West Front.
3 sizes:
  90mm.   16.00
  114mm.   16.00
  130mm.   21.50

Monuments

Cleopatra's Needle. 130mm.   65.00
Monument, The. 159mm.   65.00
Nelson's Monument. Trafalgar
  Square. 165mm.   45.00
Peter Pan Statue. 144mm.   60.00

Historical/Folklore

Ark. 85mm long.   4.75
Burns and Highland Mary (also
  impressed WILLOW). 117mm.   30.00
Man in the Moon. 35mm.   19.50

Traditional/National Souvenirs

Welsh Harp. No. 292. 95mm.	5.50

Seaside Souvenirs

Bathing Machine. 73mm.	7.50
Canoe. 106mm long.	5.50
Shell. No. 56. 83mm long.	3.00

Animals

Black Cat in Boot. 93mm long.	14.50
Cat, sitting, with ruff of fur. 100mm.	17.50
Cat, sitting, very long neck. 68mm.	6.50
Cat, Manx, 75mm long.	16.00
Dog, Bulldog, standing. 63mm. Can be found inscribed *'Duggie Haig'* with Union Jack on back. 63mm.	15.00
	145.00
Dog, Scottie with glengarry. 88mm.	10.50
Fish, 120mm long.	4.00
Fish Vase, 63mm.	5.00
Monkey holding coconut. 75mm.	22.00
Pig, standing, 80mm long.	10.00
Polar Bear. 185mm long.	47.50
Rabbit, crouching, ears back. 67mm long.	5.50
Shetland Pony. 110mm long.	22.00
Teddy Bear sitting upright.	8.50

Birds

Swan, 51mm.	6.50
Swan posy holder. 78mm.	4.75
Wise Owl with verse. 110mm.	12.50

Great War

Monoplane, with movable prop. 145mm long.	65.00
British Airship on stand. 130mm long.	20.00
Battleship with 2 guns forward and 1 aft. 120mm long.	16.00
Lusitania. 163mm long.	75.00
Submarine, inscribed: E4 110mm long.	16.00
Red Cross Van. 98mm long.	23.00
Tank with inset trailing wheels. 100mm long.	17.50
Renault Tank. 115mm long.	65.00
Field Gun. 130mm long.	13.00
Howitzer. 120mm long.	16.00
Torpedo. 150mm long.	47.50
Bell Tent. 85mm.	10.50

Flash Light, flat. 90mm.	10.50
Gurkha Knife. 140mm long.	20.00
Ad Astra, RAF Memorial with inscription: *Unveiled by HRH Prince of Wales July 16th* 1923. 170mm.	85.00
Cenotaph, inscribed: *The Glorious Dead* MCMXLV—MCMXLX, with green wreaths. 3 sizes:	
105mm.	4.00
145mm.	5.50
184mm.	7.50
Edith Cavell Memorial, London. 2 sizes: 115mm.	16.00
155mm.	16.00
Florence Nightingale Statue. 146mm.	16.00

Home/Nostalgic

Anvil. 48mm.	5.50
The Old Armchair, with inscription. 95mm.	7.50
Baby in Bootee. 76mm.	11.00
Basket, 1 handle. 58mm.	4.00
Hip Bath. 95mm long.	7.00
Chair, high backed. 105mm.	6.50
Desk, with inkwells. 58mm wide.	7.50
Grandfather Clock. 138mm.	9.50
Sundial with verse. 112mm.	7.50
Tobacco Pouch. 75mm long.	9.50
Watering Can. 70mm.	5.50

Alcohol

Barrel on Stand. 65mm.	4.00
Hand holding a beaker. 50mm.	6.50
Spirit Flask. 89mm.	13.00

Musical Instruments

Upright Piano. 62mm.	12.50

Transport

Petrol Can. No. 249. 66mm.	13.00

Modern Equipment

Gas Cooker. 70mm.	8.25

Miscellaneous

Castle, chess piece. 67mm.	4.00
King chess piece. 2 sizes: 82mm.	19.50
110mm.	19.50
Queen chess piece. 84mm.	24.50

Footwear

Ladies' Button Boot. 65mm.	8.25

Ladies' 18th Century Shoe. 2 sizes:
70mm & 85mm long.   7.50
Ladies' lace-up Walking Shoe,
scalloped edge, button up.
114mm long.   14.50
Sabot. 102mm long.   4.75

Miniature Domestic
Cheese Dish, 1 piece. 2 sizes:
70mm long.   5.50
82mm long.   5.50
Cheese Dish and cover. 2 sizes:
50mm.   5.50
60mm.   5.50
Coffee Pot with lid. 75mm.   7.50
Tea Pot with lid, bagware. 70mm.   7.50

Alexandra

Trademark used by C. Schmidt and Co.,
Carlsbad (Bohemia).

A wide range of small domestic shapes
coloured beige with maroon or
green trim and a heavy emboss-
ment of gold around the coat
of arms is found with this mark,
together with similar ware marked
Durbar, Gemma, Rococco, Victoria
and Empire. Some also have gold
bows painted above the arms, and
numbers painted on the bases in
gold. An important feature of this
ware is the sprays of pink roses
and rosebuds.

Domestic
Pepper Pot. 75mm,   8.00

Amber China

Trademark used by a retailer or wholesaler probably in Manchester on china manufactured by Arkinstall & Son Ltd. (usual trademark Arcadian).

Great War
Tank with inset steering wheels.
110mm long.   15.00
Peaked Cap, amber coloured.
72mm long.   14.00

Anglo Heraldic Co

For mark see *Crested China*, p. 26.

Trademark used by Sampson Hancock (& Sons), Bridge Works, Stoke (usual trademark Corona).

Ancient Artefacts
Canterbury Leather Bottle.
No. 156.   2.25
Glastonbury Bowl. 40mm.   2.25
Loving Cup, 3 handled. No. 135.
50mm.   3.00
Puzzle Jug with verse. No.148.
70mm.   5.50

Animals
Teddy Bear, sitting. 80mm.   8.50
Bulldog, standing. 112mm long.   15.00
Cheshire Cat always smiling, The.
95mm.   6.50
Pig, standing. 84mm long.   10.00

Home/Nostalgic
Coal Scuttle. 64mm.   4.00
Milk Churn. No. 168. 70mm.   4.00
Shaving Mug. 58mm.   5.50
Watering Can. 70mm.   5.50

Footwear
Ladies' Button Boot. 65mm.   8.00
Ladies' 18th Century Shoe.
No. 146. 90mm long.   7.50

Miniature Domestic
Cheese Dish and cover. 50mm.   5.50
Tea Pot with lid, frilled top.
No. 122. 65mm.   7.50
Tea Pot with lid. 65mm.   7.50

Arcadian China

For marks see *Crested China*, p. 26/27.

Trademark used by Arkinstall & Son Ltd., Arcadian Works, Stoke on Trent, subsequently a branch of J.A. Robinson & Sons, later Cauldon Ltd., and finally Coalport China Co. (John Rose & Co.) Ltd.

Parian/unglazed

Busts

Bust of King Edward VII in military uniform, later models found with inscriptions. On circular glazed base.

2 sizes: 130mm.	35.00
140mm.	35.00

Bust of King Edward VII wearing trilby, overcoat and suit, on circular glazed base. 125mm. — 56.50

Bust of Queen Alexandra, on circular glazed base, 2 sizes:

120mm.	35.00
140mm.	35.00

Smaller size can be found named in blue lettering.

Bust of King George V, can be found with circular glazed or keyhole base. With inscription. 135mm. — 35.00

Bust of Queen Mary, can be found with a glazed circular or keyhole base, with inscription. 135mm. — 35.00

Bust of Prince of Wales (later Edward VIII) in midshipman's uniform, inscription in red and blue. On glazed circular base. 135mm. — 65.00

(Any of the above can be found with matching crests on their glazed bases, for which £10.00 may be added).

Bust of *Burns*, found with poem by Wordsworth. On circular glazed base. 120mm. — 20.00

Bust of *Napoleon*, on square glazed base. 125mm. — 55.00

Bust of *Nelson*, on square glazed base.

2 sizes: 120mm.	55.00
140mm.	55.00

Bust of *John Peel*, with verse. 120mm. — 21.50

Bust of *Scott*, on circular glazed base. 120mm. — 17.50

Bust of Duke of Wellington on glazed base. 130mm. — 56.50

Bust of *King of the Belgians* on square glazed base, sculpted by W.C. Lawton.

2 sizes: 155mm.	60.00
175mm.	65.00

Bust of *Sir Douglas Haig* on square glazed base, sculpted by S.R. Sanders. 150mm. — 56.00

Bust of *Sir John French* on square glazed base, sculpted by W.C. Lawton. 155mm. — 55.00

Bust of *Sir John Jellicoe* on square glazed base, sculpted by W.C. Lawton. 170mm. — 65.00

Bust of *General Joffre* on square glazed base, sculpted by W.C. Lawton.

2 sizes: 155mm.	55.00
175mm.	65.00

Bust of *Lord Kitchener* on circular glazed base. 119mm. — 55.00

Bust of *Lord Kitchener* on square glazed base, sculpted by W.C. Lawton.

2 sizes: 155mm.	55.00
175mm.	65.00

Bust of Chamberlain on circular glazed base. 115mm. — 40.00

Bust of David Lloyd George on circular glazed base. 130mm. — 40.00

Bust of *Lord Roberts* on square glazed base. Sculpted by W.C. Lawton. 155mm. — 56.50

Bust of Rt. Hon. W.S. Churchill on square glazed base, sculpted by W.C. Lawton. 160mm. — 110.00

Ancient Artefacts

Most inscriptions begin *model of*, so this will not be repeated throughout the listing. These models are sometimes found not named and numbered.

Aberdeen Bronze Pot. 74mm. ... 3.00
Ancient Bronze British Pot.
  No. 618. 68mm. ... 3.00
Ancient Roman Vase now
  in Wedgwood Museum, Burslem.
  No. 202. 65mm. ... 3.00
Ancient Tyg, 1 or 2 handles.
  No. 58. 70mm. ... 3.00
Ancient Urn. No. 85. 35mm. ... 3.00
Ashbourne Bushel, with
  inscription. No. 99. 67mm dia. ... 4.50
Butterpot, old, of 17th Century.
  45mm. ... 3.00
Cadogan teapot, working model of. ... 10.50
Cambridge Roman Jug. No. 67.
  2 sizes: 60mm. ... 3.00
    75mm. ... 3.00
Canterbury Roman Ewer. 2 shapes:
  No. 23. 60mm. ... 3.00
  No. 25. 75mm. ... 3.00
Canterbury Roman Vase,
  inscribed: *Roman Vase found near*
  Canterbury original in Canterbury
  museum. 8 different shapes:
  No. 21. 65mm. ... 3.50
  No. 22. 60mm. ... 3.50
  No. 24. 66mm. ... 3.50
  No. 27. 66mm. ... 3.50
  No. 28. 70mm. ... 3.50
  No. 29. 60mm. ... 3.50
  No. 30. 60mm. ... 3.50
  No. 32. 63mm. ... 3.50
Canterbury Leather Bottle. 40mm. ... 3.00
Chester Roman Vase, inscribed:
  Roman vase now in Chester Museum.
  2 different shapes:
  No. 131. 56mm. ... 3.00
  No. 136. 60mm. ... 3.00
Chester Roman Vase, inscribed:
  Roman vase found at Chester from
  original in Museum.
No. 2643. 58mm. ... 3.00
Chinese vase, original in Hanley
  Museum. No. 127. 38mm. ... 3.00
Colchester Vase. ... 3.00
Derby Roman Vase. No. 26.
  63mm. ... 3.00
Devon Oak Pitcher. No. 165.
  60mm. ... 3.00
Dogger Bank Bottle. No. 206.
  2 sizes: 50mm. ... 3.00
    70mm. ... 3.00
Dorchester Jug. No. 66, 55mm. ... 3.00

Dorset Ewer, inscribed: *Roman*
  Ewer in Dorset Museum found at
  Bath. No. 69. 70mm. ... 3.00
Eddystone Spanish Jug. No. 585.
  60mm. ... 3.00
Egyptian Urn. No. 130. ... 3.00
Egyptian Vase, ancient, about 230 BC.
  No. 155. 45mm. ... 3.00
Egyptian Water Bottle, 60mm. ... 3.00
Exeter Vase from original in Museum.
  No. 70. 68mm. ... 3.00
Fountains Abbey Cup. 50mm. ... 3.00
Glastonbury Bowl.
  No. 55. 40mm. ... 3.00
Glastonbury Bronze Bowl.
  No. 74. 40mm. ... 3.00
Glastonbury Vase.
  No. 642. 55mm. ... 3.00
Grecian Bronze Pot found at Pompeii.
  No. 138. 50mm. ... 3.00
Greek Cauldron, Ancient. ... 3.00
Hastings Kettle. No. 237. 62mm. ... 3.00
Hereford Terracotta Kettle with lid. ... 6.50
Highland Whisky Jar.
  No. 679. 72mm. ... 3.00
Highland Quaich or Whisky Bowl.
  can be inscribed: *Scaub Asi.*
  134mm wide. ... 7.50
Horsham Vase, inscribed:
13th century vase found at
  Horsham. No. 201.
  2 sizes: 45mm. ... 3.00
    75mm. ... 3.00
Ipstones Jug. No. 73. 60mm. ... 3.00
Irish Bronze Pot, Ancient.
  No. 62. 50mm. ... 3.00
Irish Kettle. No. 95. 70mm. ... 4.00
Jersey Milk Can, Ancient, with lid.
  No. 523. 72mm. ... 5.25
Kendal Jug. No. 9. 75mm. ... 3.00
Lichfield Jug. No. 60. 70mm. ... 3.00
Lincoln Jack from original in
  museum. No. 50. 62mm. ... 3.00
Lincoln Vase from original in the
  museum. No. 80. 66mm. ... 3.00
Loving Cup originated by Henry of
  Navarre King of France.
  2 or 3 handled. No. 579. 40mm. ... 3.00
Newbury Leather Bottle,
  inscribed: *Leather bottle found on*
  battlefield of Newbury 1044 now in
  museum. No. 83.
  2 sizes: 45mm. ... 3.00
    65mm. ... 3.00

Norwich Cinerary Urn. 50mm.	3.00
Phoenician Vase original in Stoke-on-Trent museum. No. 25. 60mm.	3.00
Pompeian Vessel. No. 208. 55mm.	4.75
Pompeii Lamp. No. 603. 90mm long.	4.75
Portland Vase now in British Museum. No. 52. 60mm.	3.00
Puzzle Jug original in South Kensington Museum. No. 147. 70mm.	5.50
Puzzle Teapot. 50mm.	10.50
Roman Urn. No. 305. 63mm.	3.00
Salisbury Jack.	3.00
Salisbury Kettle. No. 90. 107mm.	3.00
Salt Maller.	3.00
Scarborough Jug. No. 82. 52mm.	3.00
Shakespeare's Jug, 60mm.	3.00
Shrewsbury Salopian Ewer. No. 613. 75mm.	3.00
Silchester Vase. No. 54. 55mm.	3.00
Southwold Jar. No. 627. 95mm.	3.00
Toby Jug, inscribed: *This is an exact copy in miniature of the old toby jug.* No. 253. 75mm.	8.25
Tutankhamun's Cup, inscribed: *Kings wishing cup found in King Tutankhamuns tomb at Luxor.* 55mm.	27.50
West Malling Elizabethan Jug or stoup with lid. No. 152. 75mm.	5.50
Winchelsea Roman Cup. No. 137. 50mm.	3.00
Winchelsea Vase. 2 sizes: No. 68. 55mm.	3.00
No. 87. 75mm.	3.00
Winchester Bushel, blue feet and handle. 83mm dia.	13.00
Winchester Vase.	3.00
Windsor Roman Urn. No. 123. 50mm.	3.00
Wokingham Tankard. No. 88. 78mm.	4.00
York Roman Ewer. No. 57. 60mm.	3.00

Buildings — Coloured
These buildings are not normally found crested.

Ann Hathaway's Cottage. 50mm long.	17.50
Bridlington Priory Church, model of. Light brown colour. 68mm long.	75.00
Burns Cottage. 68mm long.	21.75

Dean Goodman's Birthplace. 85mm long.	110.00
First and Last House with annexe. 2 sizes: 100mm long:	65.00
136mm long:	75.00
Guildhall, Thaxted, 83mm.	175.00
Jean Mac Alpines Inn, Famous Inn in 'Rob Roy' where the scene of a fray between Bailie Nicol Jarrie and the Highlanders took place. Unglazed. 104mm long.	125.00
Old Blacksmith's Shop and Marriage Room, Gretna Green, 85mm long (late Willow mould).	30.00
Old Star Inn, Alfriston. 80mm.	130.00
Round House, Alton, inscribed: *The Ancient Lock Up.* Light brown colour. 86mm.	75.00
Shakespeare's House. 2 sizes: 63mm long.	16.00
127mm long.	30.00
Wells Cathedral. Stone coloured with some colouring on doors and windows. 110mm long.	65.00

Buildings — White

Aberystwyth University. 110mm long.	110.00
Alton, The Round House. 83mm.	56.50
Ann Hathaway's Cottage. 2 sizes: 83mm long:	11.00
100mm long.	13.00
Big Ben, also found inscribed: *City of London.* 3 sizes: 92mm.	13.00
130mm.	15.50
150mm.	17.50
Blackpool Tower. 144mm.	13.00
Blackpool Tower with Buildings. 107mm.	8.75
Blackpool Tower with Buildings on heavy base. 2 sizes: 135mm.	8.75
165mm.	10.50
Boston Stump. 2 sizes: 89mm long.	30.00
110mm long.	47.50
Bunyan's Cottage. 95mm.	16.00
Canterbury Cathedral. West front. 126mm.	25.00
Canterbury, Westgate. 93mm.	26.00
Chester Cathedral. 120mm long.	47.50
Chesterfield Parish Church AD 1037. Model of. 125mm.	40.00

Clifton Suspension Bridge.
175mm long. 40.00
Cottage, very detailed.
2 sizes: 50mm: 6.50
100mm: 10.50
Cottage on rectangular base
usually found with no
inscription. 80mm. 7.50
Can be found inscribed: *Model of
Highland cottage, Welsh cottage or
Irish Cottage.* 60mm. 21.50
Ely Cathedral. 140mm long. 47.50
Fair Maid's House, Perth. 84mm. 50.00
*Farringtons Girl School Chapel,
Chislehurst Kent.* 125mm long.
(very rare) 90.00
*First and Last Refreshment House in
England.* Often found without
'refreshment' inscription.
75mm long. 10.50
Also found with annexe.
2 sizes: 100mm long. 40.00
138mm long. 40.00
Forth Bridge. 158mm long. 30.00
Gloucester Cathedral.
128mm long. 47.50
God's Providence House. 82mm. 40.00
Grimsby Hydraulic Tower. 170mm. 25.75
Hastings Castle Ruins. 96mm. 22.00
Hastings, Clock Tower.
2 sizes: 135mm. 12.00
152mm. 14.00
Hop Kiln. 86mm. 20.50
Houses of Parliament. 73mm long. 30.00
Irish Round Tower. 106mm. 10.50
King Alfred's Tower. 92mm. 35.00
Lantern Hill Church. *Ilfracombe.*
98mm long. 17.50
Largs Tower. 104mm. 13.00
Launceston Castle. 112mm long. 40.00
Lincoln Cathedral, West Front.
115mm. 22.00
Lincoln Stonebow. 88mm long. 22.50
London Bridge. Ye olde.
2 sizes: 88mm. 18.00
170mm. 22.00
Marble Arch.
3 sizes: 45mm. 10.50
65mm. 13.00
80mm. 16.00
Martello Tower, with inscription:
'Erected for Coast Defence 1804'.
73mm dia. 30.00

Morpeth Clock Tower, not found
named. 122mm. 16.00
Mundesley-on-Sea Castle Ruins.
105mm. 47.50
Norwich Cathedral. 105mm long. 47.50
*Old Curiosity Shop. Immortalized
by Charles Dickens. No. 14
Portsmouth Street.* 95mm long. 24.50
Old Pete's Cottage (near Ramsey).
75mm long. 30.00
Pegwell Bay, Clock Tower, 135mm. 16.00
Plymouth, Clock Tower. 150mm. 12.00
Portsmouth, Guildhall.
60mm long. 40.00
Queen Mary's Dolls House.
3 sizes: 75mm. 17.00
95mm. 17.00
118mm. 21.50
Two smaller sizes are often
found as boxes with loose roof
lids. (These models can be
found with the 'Cauldon' mark
as well as 'Arcadian'.
Same price.)
Rochester Castle, dating from 1126.
70mm. 37.50
Rowton Tower, with inscription:
*King Charles 1st stood on this
tower, Sept. 24th 1645 and saw his
army defeated on Rowton Moor.*
88mm. 35.00
St Albans. The Clock Tower. 125mm. 40.00
St. Nicholas Chapel, Ilfracombe.
100mm long. 20.00
St. Pauls Cathedral.
No. 114.
3 sizes: 72mm. 14.50
95mm. 15.50
130mm. 21.50
St. Tudno's Church, Llandudno.
73mm. 47.50
Can sometimes be found as a
money box.
St. Winifred's Bath, Holywell.
75mm. 40.00
Salisbury Cathedral.
120mm long. 40.00
Salisbury Clock Tower, not found
named. 130mm. 13.00
Shakespeare's House.
3 sizes: 50mm long. 10.50
83mm long. 13.00
100mm long. 16.00
Skegness, Clock Tower, 125mm. 13.00

Smallest House in Great Britain.
(at Conway)

3 sizes: 88mm.	16.00
97mm.	16.00
115m.	21.50
Southampton, the Bargate. 66mm.	21.50

Temple Bar.

2 sizes: 60mm.	16.00
95mm.	21.50

Tom Tower, Christchurch, Oxford.

88mm.	21.75
Tower Bridge. 135mm long.	29.00

Tower of Refuge, Douglas I.O.M.

68mm.	30.00
Tudor House, L shaped. 80mm.	40.00

Tynwald Hill, Model of, with
lengthy inscription.

110mm dia.	110.00
Wembley Stadium. 136mm long.	35.00

Westminster Abbey.

2 sizes: 70mm.	30.00
115mm.	40.00

Westminster Abbey, West Front.

2 sizes: 72mm:	16.00
118mm:	21.50
Wimborne Minster. 127mm long.	47.50
Windmill with movable sails. 85mm.	19.50

Very rarely found inscribed:

Windmill, Woodhouse.	30.00

Windsor Castle.

2 sizes: 55mm:	21.50
80mm:	28.00

Windsor Round Tower.

2 sizes: 58mm.	14.00
90mm.	18.50

Worcester Cathedral.

2 sizes: 127mm long.	35.00
140mm long.	40.00
York Minster. 105mm.	56.50

Monuments (including Crosses)

Banbury Cross, with nursery
rhyme: Ride a cock horse.

160mm.	30.00

Bloody Corner, Ilfracombe with very
lengthy inscription of slaying
of King Hubba on all 3 sides.
Same mould as Rufus Stone.

100mm	60.00
Bunyan Statue. 140mm.	19.50

Burns, Monument with dog.

70mm	19.50

Caister on Sea Lifeboat Memorial.

150mm.	19.00

Castleton Village Cross. 140mm.	30.00
Celtic Cross. 125mm.	12.00

Conway Seven are we Grave, with
inscription: 'The Grave
immortalized by Wordsworth's
Poem' and 'Two of us in
the churchyard lie'. This is a
triangular tube shaped tomb
with seven small towers.

110mm long (rare).	52.50
Drake Statue. 160mm.	13.00

Douglas Jubilee Clock Tower.

125mm.	40.00
Ethelfreda Memorial. 150mm.	65.00

Gibbets Cross, Hindhead with

inscriptions. 136mm.	10.50

(The) Globe, Swanage, Model of.

80mm.	16.00

Hull Fisherman's Memorial, with

inscription. 155mm.	16.00
Iona Cross. 142mm.	12.00

Irish Monument, not named but
appears with Irish Crests.
Circular base with man
standing on top. 138mm. This

is the metal man at Tramore.	56.50

King Alfred the Great, Statue.
Winchester. Rd. No. 521701.

170mm.	30.00

Maiwand Memorial, Forbury
Gardens, Reading. (Lion on
base). Can be found with black

lion, add £5.00. 100mm.	14.50
Margate Clock Tower. 140mm.	10.50

Margate Surf Boat Memorial.

125mm.	21.50
Nelson's Column. 102mm.	45.00

Nelson Monument, Great

Yarmouth. 206mm.	65.00
Newton Monument. 165mm.	30.00

Plymouth Armada Memorial.

181mm.	30.00

Richmond, Yorks, Market Cross.

125mm.	16.00

(The Great) Rock of Ages, Burrington
Coombe, near Cheddar, Som. with

three verses of hymn. 83mm.	7.50
Rufus Stone. 100mm.	5.50
Sailor's Stone, Hindhead. 100mm.	10.50

Saxon Lady and Child, both with

swords, on glazed base. 153mm.	43.50

Series of at least three figures
standing on a square plinth.
(These are not easily identifiable
and could be statesmen,
industrialists or literary figures.
It is thought that one is Joseph
Chamberlain and another is
Charles Dickens); inscribed:
Industry is the parent of success.
Edged in green. 135mm. Each. 65.00
Toad Rock. Tunbridge Wells. 85mm. 14.50
*Tom Hughes Monument, Rugby
School.* 142mm. 30.00
Victorian Lady and Gentleman
figure group on base, inscribed:
He that is satisfied is rich. Found
with colour transfer of children.
115mm. 65.00
Statue found with York Crest,
Lion and three Imps or Satyrs
on a square pedestal. 115mm. 34.50
Wallace Statue Aberdeen. 117mm. 40.00
Weymouth Jubilee Clock. 128mm. 16.00

Historical/Folklore
Archbishop of Canterbury's Chair
95mm. 10.50
Bell, squashed appearance.
Inscription in red relief:
Campan Achgme. 63mm. 35.00
Burns with Plough on rectangular
base. 120mm. 75.00
Coaching Hat, can be found
inscribed: *Model of ancient
coaching hat.* No. 687. 65mm long. 7.50
Devil looking over Lincoln. 108mm. 12.00
Ducking Stool, 2 pieces, hinged
together. With long details of
its last employment in
Leominster in 1809 and 1817.
120mm long. 85.00
English Folksong Bride beside
chest. 93mm. 40.00
Execution Block with Axe. 50mm. 30.00
Henry V Cradle. 78mm. 40.00
Jenny Geddes Stool 1637, 3 legged.
More often found unnamed. 5.50
40mm named. 10.50
Judge Bust.
2 sizes: 55mm. 8.50
75mm. 14.00
Can be found inscribed: *Defend
the children of the poor and
punish the wrong doer.* Add £10.00

Lady Godiva, Coventry, on horseback, circular base.
3 sizes: 76mm. 26.00
85mm. 26.00
115mm. 26.00
Lady Godiva on heart shaped base.
80mm. 22.50
Miner's Lamp, inscribed: '1836'.
85mm. 16.00
Mother Shipton, can be found with
verse.
2 sizes: 76mm. 12.00
115mm. 15.00
Peeping Tom, bust. 110mm. 16.00
Man in the Sun. 94mm. 47.50
Man standing in Pillory, can be
found inscribed: *Time for
reflection. AD1600.* 190mm. 17.00
Man sitting in Stocks, can be found
inscribed as above and 19.00
very rarely: *Berkswell stocks* or
The stocks, Dartmouth. 88mm. 25.75
*Shakespeare's Desk from the original
in the museum,* model of. Can be
found in lustre. 62mm long. 50.00
Trusty Servant on ornate rectangular base, with verse. Fully
coloured and without crest.
137mm. 87.50
Trusty Servant on small square
base, can be found with verse.
Fully coloured with crest and
unglazed. 130mm. 110.00
Winton Imp. 133mm. 55.00
Wishing Chair, Giants Causeway.
75mm dia. 56.50
Witches Cauldron with inscription.
47mm. 5.50
Yorick's Skull, inscribed: *Alas poor
Yorick.* 57mm. 10.50

Traditional/National Souvenirs
John Bull, bust.
3 sizes: 65mm. 14.50
85mm. 19.50
100mm. 22.50
Largest 2 sizes found with a
black hat.
Blackpool Big Wheel.
2 sizes: 60mm. 8.75
110mm. 12.00
Cheddar Cheese, Prime. 60mm. 5.50
Cheddar Cheese, Prime, with slice
out. 60mm. 5.50
Cornish Pasty. 98mm long. 7.50

Devonshire Dumpling. 45mm.	10.50
Isle of Wight, relief map standing	
upright on pintray. Coloured.	
106mm long.	30.00
Lancashire Clog. 94mm long.	4.75
Lancashire Clog, high narrow type.	
2 sizes: 95mm long:	4.75
135mm long.	7.50
Lancashireman's Jug with verse.	
75mm.	10.00
Lincoln Imp. 110m.	6.50
Lincoln Imp, on square stand.	
125mm.	8.25
Manx Legs, flat. 85mm dia.	13.00
Manx Legs on stand, can be found	
in lustre. 101m.	16.00
Manx Legs on rock. 51mm.	13.00
Mill Lass, bust, shawl draped	
round head and shoulders.	
60mm.	26.00
Sometimes inscribed:	
Lancashire Lass.	30.00
Yorkshireman's Jug with verse.	
83mm.	10.00
Irish Colleen, fully coloured on	
ashtray base. 105mm. (One of a	
series of ashtrays, *see* **Comic**	
section).	56.50
Irish Harp with green shamrocks.	
108mm.	8.25
Irish jaunting car, Model of. With	
horse and driver. 120mm long.	95.00
Irish Lady, bust, inscribed: *My*	
simple graceful Nora Criena.	
85mm.	30.00
Pat the Irishman, bust. 80mm.	21.50
Irishman and pig on shamrock	
ashtray base. 100mm long.	
(One of a series of ashtrays,	
see **Comic** section).	56.50
Shamrock shaped dish. 80mm long.	4.00
Bagpipes. 110mm long.	16.00
Gretna Green, Anvil from and	
verse. 66mm.	6.50
Scotsman, bust of. 65mm.	21.75
If named *Harry Lauder.*	30.00
Souter Johnny, sitting figure on	
chair with verse. Some	
colouring. 130mm.	30.00
Tam o'Shanter (bonnet) inscribed:	
Tha can sit on the thistle noo.	
Coloured feather and pompom.	
95mm dia.	21.75
Thistle candlestick. 50mm.	4.75

Thistle on stalk base (Candlestick or	
Vase) inscribed: *Tha can sit on*	
the thistle noo. 85mm.	4.00
Thistle vase, wide necked.	
3 sizes: 45mm.	3.00
70mm.	3.00
85mm.	3.50
Welsh Harp. 80mm.	8.25
Welsh Hat, Model of. Often	
unnamed. Can be found with	
longest Welsh place name	
round brim, for which add	4.00
2 sizes: 52mm.	4.75
72mm.	5.50
Welsh Hat, much wider brim.	
49mm.	8.75
Welsh Lady Bust, can be found fully	
coloured, inscribed: *Wales! Wales!*	
My Mother's Sweet Home.	
3 sizes: 65mm.	16.00
85mm.	21.50
100mm.	26.00
Welsh Leek, can be found with	
inscription: *King Henry V. The*	
Welshmen did goot servace (at Crecy)	
in a garden where Leeks did grow.	
Shakespeare.	
2 sizes: 76mm.	4.00
98mm.	5.25
Welsh Tea Party, 3 Welsh ladies	
taking tea, can be found with	
hats and cloaks coloured.	
2 sizes: 50mm.	35.00
95mm.	40.00
Welsh Tea Party, as above, on	
ashtray base. 50mm.	50.00

Seaside Souvenirs

Bathing Machine.	
3 sizes: 50mm.	6.50
65mm.	7.50
85mm.	10.50
Lifebelt. 80mm dia.	8.75
Lifeboat with yellow and blue rope.	
110mm long.	8.25
Can be found inscribed	
with any of the following names:	
Brother & Sister; Bob Newson;	
Charles Arkcoll; Charles Medland;	
Charles Susanna Stephens; The Charlie	
and Adrian; Co-operator No 2 also	
Co-operative No 2; Eliza	
Aveus; Elizabeth Simpson; James	
Stevens No 5; Kentwell; Mark Lane;	

Nancy Lucy; Richard Coleman;
The William Earle. Add £7. 15.25
Paddlesteamer. 160mm long. 82.50
Rowing Boat. 83mm long. 5.50
Yacht. 125mm long. 12.50
Trawler. 125mm long. 19.50
Lifeboatman, bust.
  3 sizes: 65mm. 15.25
        70mm. 15.25
        85mm. 19.50
Fishing Basket, found inscribed:
A good catch. 50mm. 5.50
Fisherman's Creel, with separate
  lid. 60mm. 5.50
Lighthouse. 7.50
Beachy Head Lighthouse, with black
  band.
  2 sizes: 102m. 7.50
       140mm. 9.00
Bell Rock. Lighthouse. No. 14.
  108mm. 21.50
Cove Sea Lighthouse. 136mm. 28.00
Eddystone Lighthouse, often found
  unnamed.
  3 sizes: 70mm. 4.75
      105mm. 7.50
      No. 10. 140mm. 10.50
Flamborough Head Lighthouse
  145mm. 16.00
Manghold Head Lighthouse. 60.00
Pharos Lighthouse, Fleetwood,
Model of. No. 255.
  2 sizes: 100mm. 5.50
      140mm. 10.50
  Smaller size (fully inscribed)
  has been found as pepper pot.
Scurdyness Lighthouse, Montrose.
  Pepper pot 104mm. 21.50
Spurn Head Lighthouse. 110mm. 10.50
Withernsea Lighthouse. 105mm. 10.50
Crab, very detailed. No. 6 or 9.
  85mm long. 8.25
Crab Ashtray. 90mm long. 7.50
Oyster Shell dish. 72mm dia. 3.50
Oyster Shell dish on 3 tiny feet.
  90mm long. 3.50
Nautilus shell on three 3 legs.
  80mm long. 16.00
Scallop Shell.
  2 sizes: 70mm. 3.00
      92mm dia. 3.00
Scallop Shell dish, very ornate.
  83mm dia. 4.00
Scallop Shell on rock, *Menu*
  holder. 58mm. 10.50

Shell Ink Well, one open shell
  inverted on another, usually
  inscribed: *We are always glad to*
  hear from you. Can also be found
  inscribed: *We're aye prood to hear*
  fae ye or *pins.* 105mm. 10.50
Whelk Shell, can be found
  inscribed: *Listen to the sea*
  or *We are always glad to hear*
  from you. Size varies from
  80mm-100mm long. 4.00
Gladstone Bag. 82mm long. 7.50
Bathing Belle on trinket box.
  110mm. 16.00
  Can also be found in coloured
  lustre finish.
Bathing Belle on ashtray. Some
  colouring inscribed: *cum fra dip.*
  57mm. 20.00
Bathing Belle dipping feet in pool,
  with inscription: *Cumfradip.*
  98mm long. 50.00
Punch and Judy Show. Rd No.
  37083? 90mm. 50.00
Judy, bust, some colouring. 90mm. 21.50
Punch, bust, some colouring.
  2 sizes: 65mm. 20.00
      80mm. 26.50

Countryside

Acorn. 55m. 5.50
Beehive on table. 78mm. 7.50
Hay Stack, circular. 58mm. 4.75
Hay Stack, rectangular. 50mm. 5.50
Pinecone, curved. 88mm long. 4.00
Tree Trunk vase. 70mm. 3.50
Tree Trunk Hatpin Holder. 105mm. 10.50

Animals

Small models of 'pets' were
  obviously made in great numbers
  for many years so the moulds do
  vary. Large, more exotic animals
  were much more expensive at
  the time and so are consequently
  rare.
Bear and Ragged Staff. 80mm. 19.50
Bear sitting. No. 2. 85mm. 30.00
Bull, Highland. 130mm long. 56.50
Calf, inscribed: *Why the Natives*
  are called Isle of Wight calves.
  100mm long. 14.50
Camel, 2 humps — Bactrian.
  70mm. 24.50

Cat, angry, standing with arched back and green eyes, inscribed: *My word if you're not off.*

63mm long, no colouring.	10.50
with colouring.	12.50
Inscribed.	16.00

Cat, climbing into boot, which has a mouse peeping out of its toe. 100mm long.   40.00

Cat, Cheshire. No bow round neck, inscribed: *Keep smiling.* 90mm.   7.50

Cat, The Cheshire. With orange or red bow round neck, inscribed: *The smile that won't come off.*
95mm.   12.50

Cat, long necked and sitting.   8.75
Inscribed: *My word if you're not off.* 108mm.   13.00

Cat, Manx with coloured face.
70mm long, no colouring	16.00
with colouring.	24.75

Cat, playing flute. 75mm.   19.50

Cat with bow, sitting on plinth. Bow sometimes coloured blue. 123mm.   30.00

Cat sitting with tail curled round feet, red bow and green eyes. No. 77. 67mm.   12.50

Cat sitting and smiling (grotesque, rather similar to Cheshire Cat), bow round neck, sometimes coloured orange. 75mm.   7.50

Cat sitting with bow round neck. 56mm.   10.00

Arcadian Black Cat Registered Series

No. 1 Black Cat on Jug. 60mm.	45.00

No. 2. Black Cat on vertical horseshoe 76mm.   40.00

No. 3. Black Cat on pillar box posting letter. 56mm.   47.50
This cat has also been found in cobalt blue instead of black.   60.00

No. 4. Black Cat on telephone. 65mm.   65.00

No. 5. Black Cat in canoe. 80mm long.   75.00

No. 6. Black Cat on wall. 70mm.   40.00

No. 6. Black Manx Cat on wall, cat without tail. The model has a matching Douglas Crest.   50.00
(A different mould to the above).

No. 7. Black Cat in boot. 61mm.   45.00

No. 8. Black Cat with bottle, bottle can have solid or cork top, can be inscribed: *Cheerio from. . .* (can be found in lustre). 70mm.   40.00

No. 9. Black Cat on milk churn. *New Milk* moulded on churn.
70mm.   40.00

No. 10. Three Black Cats in bed.	70.00
No. 11. Black Cat on swing. 63mm.	65.00

No. 12. Black Cat in well. (Can be found in lustre). 63mm.   47.50

No. 13. Black Cat operating radio. 63mm.   70.00

No. 14. Black Cat in Pram. 70mm.   85.00

No. 15. Three Black Cats in basket, and one on top. 70mm.   75.00

No. 16. Black Cat on scooter. (Can be found in lustre.). 70mm.   85.00

No. 17. Black Cat with umbrella. 65mm.   80.00

No. 18. Black Cat on bicycle. 80mm long.   80.00

No. 19. Black Cat in yacht. 96mm long.   60.00

No. 20. Black Cat playing double bass. 70mm.   95.00

No. 21. Two Black Cats on seesaw. 85mm long.   82.50

No. 22. Five Black Cats on a house, their tails spell: *Good luck.* 65mm.   85.00

No. 23. Three Black Cats on sledge (very rare).   95.00

No. 24. Black Cat playing piano. 52mm (very rare).   95.00

There are also very similar black cats which are not part of the Registered Series:

Black Cat, wearing kilt and glengarry, playing golf standing on golf ball. 70mm.   75.00
(This is from a Willow mould.)

Black Cat, standing alongside Welsh leek wearing Welsh hat. 60mm.   75.00

Sitting Black Cats
Can be found on the following bases:
Armchair
2 sizes: 55mm.	21.75
90mm.	21.75

Ashtray, horseshoe shaped. 93mm long.   19.50

Pouffe, inscribed: *Good luck.*

2 sizes: 80mm.	19.50
95mm.	19.50

Trinket box, horseshoe shaped.

70mm.	27.50

(All of these cats have blue/
green eyes and usually red
bows, but yellow bows are
sometimes found.)

Chimpanzee, sitting. 70mm .	22.00
Cougar (or Panther).	
102mm long (rare).	75.00
Cow, Jersey. 125mm long.	65.00
Cow, some colour, sitting on lid of	
butter dish, inscribed: *Butter.*	
115mm dia.	21.50
Crocodile (or alligator).	
125mm long.	75.00

(Can be found with blue lustre
finish.)

Bill Sykes Dog, Model of, sitting.
Sometimes inscribed: *My word
if you're not off.* No. 300. 103mm.   12.50

Bill Sykes Dog. Model of, standing.
Sometimes inscribed: *My word
if you're not off.*

3 sizes: 88mm.	10.50
102mm.	12.50
118mm long.	17.00

Bulldog, black, emerging from
kennel inscribed: *The Black
Watch.*

2 sizes: 56mm.	8.75
96mm.	10.50

Bulldog, sitting, very thin face.	
52mm.	21.50

Bulldog, standing, sometimes
inscribed: *Who said Germans.*
No. 301.

2 sizes: 115mm.	12.50
130mm long.	12.50
If inscribed	add 10.00
Dog, Collie, lying down.	
78mm long.	12.50

Dog, Collie, standing. Sometimes

inscribed: *Shetland collie*	add	4.00
and larger size *Sheep Dog*	add	8.00
2 sizes: 60mm.		11.00
95mm long.		12.50
Dog, Dachshund. 90mm long.		35.00

Dog, King Charles Spaniel,
begging on cushion. 2 sizes:

68mm.	8.25
95mm.	12.50

Dog, Labrador Puppy, sitting,
sometimes inscribed: *Daddy
wouldn't buy me a bow wow.*   add 7.50

2 sizes: 65mm.	10.00
75mm.	10.00
Dog, Puppy, head on one side.	
115mm.	10.50
Dog (Pup), sitting with one ear	
raised. 68mm.	7.50
Dog, Scottie, standing. 60mm.	7.50

Dog, Scottie, sitting wearing blue

Glengarry. 60mm.	10.50

Dog, Scottie wearing Tam
o'Shanter. Hat can be found
coloured blue. 85mm.   10.50

Dog, Scottish Terrier, can be
found inscribed: *Scotch Terrier* or
*As old Mrs Terrier said to her pup,
in all life's adventures keep your
tail up.*   add 8.00

2 sizes: 66mm long.	11.00
85mm long.	12.50

Dog, standing, facing sideways,
curly tail and blue collar.

80mm long.	16.00
Dog, Staffordshire Bull Terrier.	
80mm.	10.50

Dog, walking, blue collar. with
Old Mrs Terrier inscription.

90mm long.	19.50

Dog, Terrier looking out of kennel.
Inscribed: *Beware of the Dog.*   9.00

Dog posy holder, some colouring.

103mm.	8.25
Donkey. 2 sizes: 80mm.	23.00
120mm long.	30.00

Smaller size has saddle. Large
size can have inscription:
Hee-haw.   add 4.00

Elephant, trunk attached to

body. 55mm.	15.00

Elephant, trunk modelled free
from body, sometimes
inscribed: *Baby Jumbo.*   add 5.00

50mm.	17.50
Fawn. 50mm.	30.00
Fish, fat. 98mm long.	4.00
Fish, open mouthed.	
2 sizes: 80mm.	4.00
108mm.	4.50
Fish, curved body. 110mm long.	6.50

Fish ashtray in shape of plaice,
usually inscribed: *A pla(i)ce for
ashes,* but can be inscribed:
Caught at. . . 125mm long. 7.50
Fox. 102mm long. 40.00
Fox on square plinth. 114mm. 40.00
Frog, closed mouth. 45mm. 10.50
Frog, open mouthed and green
eyes, inscribed: *Always croaking.*
3 sizes: 60mm — no inscription. 6.50
   80mm. 10.50
   100mm long. 12.50
Goat. 82mm long. 40.00
Hare. 73mm long. 9.00
Kangaroo. 75mm. 75.00
Hippopotamus. 88mm long. 56.50
Lion, roaring. 85mm long. 22.00
Lion, walking.
3 sizes: 85mm long. 12.50
   116mm long. 12.50
   140mm long. 14.50
Smallest sizes can be found
inscribed: *King of the forest,* for
which   add 2.00
Monkey, sitting hand to mouth.
65mm. 13.00
Monkey, sitting holding
coconut. No. 34. 85mm. 22.00
Monkey, wearing coat. 75mm. 12.50
Mouse, holding acorn. 60mm. 16.00
Otter, holding fish in mouth.
120mm long. 47.50
Pig, smiling and sitting.
63mm long. 10.50
Pig, short and standing, inscribed:
I won't be druv. 63mm long. 10.00
Pig, tall and standing, inscribed:
*You can push or you can shuv but
I'm hanged if I'll be druv.*
78mm. 63mm long. 10.50
Hampshire Hog. Model of, sitting.
No. 148C. 70mm long. 12.50
Hampshire Hog. Model of, standing
inscribed: *Wunt be draw* and
verse No. 145. 105mm long. 14.00
Sussex Pig. Model of, sitting,
inscribed: *Won't be druv.*
No. 148. 88mm long. 12.50
Sussex Pig, Model of. standing fat 12.50
pig, can be found inscribed:
Mochyn bad with Welsh crest.
No. 148. 80mm long, if named 19.50
Sussex Pig, Model of. standing thin

pig, inscribed: *You can push or
you can shuv but I'm hanged if
I'll be druv* or *Won't be druv.*
No. 148. 78mm long. 12.50
Wiltshire Pig, Model of, sitting up
on haunches, alert ears. No.
148. 60mm. 14.50
Wiltshire Pig, Model of, standing fat
pig with double chin, inscribed:
Wunt be druv. No. 148. 85mm. 14.50
Piglet, kneeling. 70mm long. 8.25
Polar Bear.
2 sizes: 100mm. 40.00
   135mm long. 47.50
Pony, New Forest, can be found
unnamed. 100mm long. 21.50
Pony, Shetland, often found
unnamed.
2 sizes: 105mm. 25.00
   120mm long. 30.00
Rabbit, ears lying along back.
Found numbered 22 and 23. sizes
vary between 65-80mm long. 6.50
Rabbit sitting, ears apart. No. 13.
Sizes vary between 50-68mm. 6.50
Rhinoceros. 90mm long. 56.50
Russian Bear, inscribed: *War Edition*
and carries Russian Imperial
crest. 70mm. 65.00
Seal. 102mm long. 16.00
Squirrel, holding nut, on base.
65mm. 15.00
Squirrel Jug. 80mm. 10.00
Teddy Bear, sitting. 90mm. 10.50
Smaller size, 68mm, not found
inscribed. 8.50
Terrapin, walking, erect head.
74mm long. 8.75
Tortoise. 72mm long. 6.50
Tortoise, standing upright,
wearing blue helmet. 75mm. 30.00
Welsh Goat, Model of, inscribed: *Yr
Afr Cymreig.* 100mm long. 47.50
Wembley Lion. 100m long.
(stylised symbol of the B.E.E.). 17.50
3 Wise Monkeys on wall inscribed:
*I see no evil, I speak no evil, I hear
no evil.* 76mm. 10.50
Isn't this Rabbit a Duck. On its base
a rabbit, turned on its side a
duck. (Can be found in lustre.)
75mm. 22.00

Birds (including Eggs)

Chick, breaking out of egg. Can be
found inscribed: *Just out.*   add 3.00
2 sizes: 63mm long.   5.50
        86mm long.   5.50
Larger size can be found
inscribed: *Easter egg*   12.50
Chick in Egg pepper or salt pot.
Can have yellow head. 58mm.   4.75
Chick, very tiny and completely
yellow, sitting on a white egg,
inscribed: *Every little helps
mother will be pleased.* 50mm long.   16.00
Egg salt and pepper pots. 58mm.
Each   2.50
Eggshell, broken open. 39mm.   3.00
Egg with flat base, can be found   4.00
inscribed: *Sparrows egg.* 44mm.   8.50
Cock, standing, legs modelled
separately, inscribed: *Cock o' th'
North* or *Cock o' th' South.* Some
colouring to head. 100mm.   14.50
Cock, standing, legs modelled
together. Some colouring to
head. 85mm.   14.50
Hen, standing, some colouring.
62mm (matches above).   14.50
Hen, roosting. 54mm.   5.00
Heron, on circular base. 83mm.   28.00
Bird perched on circular base.
(Reputedly a blackbird). 68mm.   16.00
Bird, perched on tree, wings
extended. 125mm.
(very impressive).   36.00
Bird salt and pepper pots. 70mm.
Each   4.75
Dove, Fantail on square base.
70mm.   21.50
Duck. 86mm.   19.00
Norwich Canary. 100mm.   7.50
If coloured yellow.   13.00
Norwich Warbler. Canary on rock,
with whistle and bubble blower
base, Often found unnamed.
126mm.   21.50
Owl, baby. 40mm.   12.50
Owl, Barn. 63mm.   10.50
Owl, Horned (long eared).
2 sizes: 74mm.   10.50
        95mm.   10.50
Owl (wise), one eye closed,
with verse. 98mm.   12.50
Parakeet.
2 sizes: 60mm.   7.50
        83mm.   9.00

Parrot, sometimes inscribed:
Pretty Polly. No. 751. 70mm.   10.50
Peacock, yellow beak and coloured
plume. Rd. 115mm.   23.00
Peacock on ashtray. (Can be
found in lustre.) 80mm long.   20.00
Pelican, with details of its stomach
capacity. 70mm.   30.00
Penguin. No details of size.   37.50
Seagull. 76mm (rare).   30.00
Seagull, colouring to tip of wings
and yellow beak. 100mm.   24.50
Stork. 80mm.   15.00
Swan, detailed plumage.
3 sizes: 50mm long.   6.50
        70mm long.   6.50
        85mm.   6.50
Swan posy bowl. 88mm.   4.75
Turkey, on round base. 60mm.   18.50
Turkey, on square base. 76mm.   18.50

Great War

Many of these models are found with
the inscription *War Edition AD 1914*
and a crest of 'one of the allied
countries', (add £8.00 for this).
Some of the soldiers, although sold
separately, were based on the same
design idea and form a set. They are
therefore grouped together in the
listings.
British Soldier, Model of, more often
than not unnamed. 135mm.   87.00
Two versions exist. The later
mould has the rifle touching the
hat, and rifle butt turned
sideways.
Colonial Soldier, Model of. 135mm.   135.00
French Soldier, Model of. 135mm.   135.00
Scots Soldier, Model of. 135mm.   135.00
Bugler Boy, Model of. 135mm.   135.00
Drummer Boy, Model of. 135mm.   135.00
Sailor, standing with hands on hips
2 sizes: 95mm.   82.50
        132mm.   75.00
(All these figures are standing to
attention on an oval domed base.)

British Cavalry Soldier, Model of. on
horseback. 122mm.   145.00
Russian Cossack, Model of, on
horseback. 122mm.   145.00
Belgian Soldier, bust, usually
found with Belgian crest.
80mm (rare).   140.00

Despatch Rider, Model of, on motorbike.
(Can be found in lustre).
120mm long.   43.50
*Nurse and Wounded Tommy, Model
of.* 108mm long.   85.00
Nurse, inscribed: *Soldier's friend.*
Red cross on chest. 132mm.   47.50
Sailor, bust, found with hatband
impressed: *HMS Queen Elizabeth*
or with plain hatband. Inscribed:
The Handyman, HMS Dreadnought.
92mm.   30.00
There are 2 moulds, one with
hat tilted to left and one tilted
to right. With verse.
Can be found with hat coloured
blue.   43.00
Sailor Winding Capstan, Model of.
105mm.   82.50
Soldier, bust, inscribed: *Tommy
Atkins,* or *Territorial,* either
found with verse 'Its the
Soldiers of the King my lads'.
Some colouring. 90mm.   30.00
with verse   40.00
Soldier with Respirator, bust,
inscribed: *Model of new gas mask.*
95mm. (rare)   195.00
*Tommy driving a Steam Roller over
the Kaiser,* inscribed: *To Berlin.*
120mm (very rare).   435.00
Tommy in Bayonet Attack, Model of.
130mm.   130.00
*Tommy and his Machine Gun,
Model of.* 72mm.   30.00
Tommy on Sentry Duty. Model of,
in sentry box. 110mm.   75.00
*Tommy throwing his Grenade,
Model of.* 130mm.   130.00
New Aeroplane, Model of. Biplane
with fixed prop, and roundels
in relief. 120mm long.   100.00
New Aeroplane, Model of. Mono-
plane with revolving propeller.
135mm long.   40.00
Monoplane, movable prop.
149mm long.   55.00
Monoplane, V winged, with fixed
prop. Propeller can be found
with 2 or 3 blades.
2 sizes: 118mm long.   75.00

140mm long (rare).   80.00
(This model has a circular portion
added for no other reason
than to carry the crest.)
Aeroplane Propeller.
150mm long.   21.75
RAF/RFC crest.   30.00
Rarely factory marked.
British Airship, Model of, with
suspended engine. 120mm long.   65.00
British Airship on stand.
128mm long.   20.00
*Observer or Sausage Balloon, Model
of.* 84mm.   47.50
Super Zeppelin, Model of.
127mm long.   20.00
N.B. The captions for the
Super Zeppelin and the
British airship have been trans-
posed on page 58 of *Crested China.*
Battleship: *HMS Queen Elizabeth.*
160mm long.   30.00
Battleship, 3 funnels and tiny gun
fore and aft. 120mm long.   15.50
Minesweeper, not found named.
126mm long.   16.00
RMS Lusitania, not found named.
180mm long.   75.00
Torpedo Boat Destroyer, Model of.
115mm long.
(Can be found in lustre).   19.50
Submarine, inscribed: *E4.*
95mm long.   16.00
New submarine, Model of, inscribed:
E5. 126mm long.   16.00
Armoured Car, Model of.
95mm long.   30.00
Red Cross Van, red cross on each
side and rear. 'EH 139' printed
on radiator.
3 sizes: 78mm.   25.00
          85mm.   23.00
         160mm long.   400.00
(The large size is extremely rare).
Tank, Model of; (without wheels).
4 sizes: 100mm long.   60.00
         115mm long.   13.00
115mm size can be found
inscribed: *Original made in
Lincoln.*   24.50
Also found inscribed *285.*   add £10.00
         160mm long.   22.00

325mm long.   450.00
The two largest sizes also exist with
green/brown camouflage markings.
The smallest size is quite rare
and the largest size is very rare,
being so enormous that it must
have been made for shop display.
It has also been seen in lustre.
Tank, Model of, with inset wheels.
115mm long.   15.00
Can be found inscribed: *Original
made in Lincoln.*   30.00
Tank, Model of, with trailing steering
wheels. 144mm long.   17.50
Tank, Model of, exactly as above
but with one trailing wheel.
144mm long (rare).   350.00
Tank, Model of, exactly as above
but with a second wheel attached to the one-wheeled tank.   56.00
Whippet Tank, large hexagonal
gun turret at rear.
172mm long (rare).   260.00
Field Gun.
3 sizes: 120mm.   17.00
          140mm long.   17.00
          175mm long.   22.50
New Field Gun with Screen, Model of.
105mm long.   18.50
German Howitzer, Model of.
2 sizes: 115mm long.   16.00
          150mm long.   19.50
Trench Mortar, Model of. Can be
found inscribed: *Roaring Meg.*
70mm long.   10.50
If inscribed   35.00
Mortar on square base. (Krupp).
70mm.   14.00
Revolver, Model of. 83mm long.   35.00
Anti-aircraft Shell, Model of. 98mm.   17.50
Cannon Shell.
3 sizes: 70mm.   3.00
          90mm.   3.50
          135mm.   12.50
The 90mm and 135mm sizes are
often inscribed: *Jack Johnson* add   5.00
or sometimes: *Hartlepool's
Bombardment Dec 16th 1914,*
for which £8.00 should be
added.
Cannon Shell Salt and Pepper
pots. 70mm. Each   4.00

Shell Case. 56mm.   5.00
Clip of Bullets, Model of. 57mm.   13.00
Trench Flying Pig, Model of. (Flying
pig is a nickname for a type of
Stokes bomb.)
95mm long. (rare).   117.50
There are two different versions.
One has a tail at the back and the
factory mark is on the side which
is used as a stand. A later version
has no tail and a factory mark on
base which is its stand.
*Bomb dropped from Zeppelin, Model
of.* Inscription sometimes
reads: *German Zeppelin* or *on
Bury St. Edmunds.* 75mm.   11.00
If inscribed   17.00
*Bomb dropped from Zeppelin upon
Sheringham during first raid on
England 8.30 Jany, 18th 1915,
Model of.* With movable three
bladed propeller. 115mm.   82.50
Also found with the following
inscription: *First bomb dropped
from Zeppelin at Loftus Sept 8th
1915 at 9.30* or *Model of first
bomb dropped from Zeppelin on
Skinningrove Ironworks Sept. 8th
1915 at 9.30p.m.*   95.00
British Aerial Bomb, Model of.
75mm.   30.00
Canister Bomb, Model of. 60mm.   13.00
Plum Pudding Bomb, Model of.
Often found unnamed.
72mm (rare).   80.00
German Hand Grenade, Model of.
92mm (very rare).   85.00
Hairbrush Grenade, Model of.
104mm long (rare).   130.00
Mills Hand Grenade, Model of.
62mm.   13.00
British Aerial Torpedo, Model of.
102mm long.   27.50
German Aerial Torpedo, Model of.
88mm long.   30.00
Bandsman's Drum. No. 226.
53mm.   5.00
(Probably made originally for
the S. African War.)
Bell Tent. 64mm dia.   10.50
If inscribed: *Camping out.*   14.50
Capstan. 56mm.   10.00

Gurkha Knife, Model of. 110mm long. 20.00
Pair of Field Glasses, Model of. Often
found not named. 78mm long. 13.00
Sandbag, Model of. 73mm long. 13.00
Tommy's Hut, Model of.
105mm long. 40.00
Trench Dagger, Model of.
102mm long. 40.00
Trench Lamp, Model of. 70mm. 10.50
Water Bottle, Model of. 65mm. 13.00
Colonial Hat, Model of, found
inscribed: *Anzacs.* 88mm wide. 10.50
Inscribed. 16.00
Glengarry. 90mm long. 16.00
New Zealand Hat. 71mm dia. 17.50
Officer's Peaked Cap, white or
more usually with coloured
badge and hatband. Can be
found inscribed: *Territorials cap*
65mm dia. 10.00
Inscribed 22.00
Solar Topee (Pith helmet). 60mm. 16.00
Steel Helmet, inscribed: *Tommy's*
Steel Helmet. 65mm dia. 22.50
Anti-Zeppelin Candle Holder.
65mm. 14.00
Fireplace, inscribed: *We've kept the*
home fires burning.
2 sizes: 90mm. 12.50
115mm. 14.50
Angel with raised arms, found
with R.A.F. crest (not named)
but must be R.A.F. Memorial.
No details of size. 82.50
Bishop's Stortford *War Memorial.*
132mm. 90.00
Brora War Memorial.
155mm (rare). 110.00
Burford War Memorial, with
inscription. 128mm (rare). 82.50
Burnham on Crouch *War Memorial.*
146mm (rare). 75.00
Carillon Tower, Loughborough.
162mm. 60.00
Cavell Statue, inscribed:
Nurse Cavell.
3 sizes: 110mm. 11.00
147mm. 12.50
160mm. 14.50
Cavell *Memorial Statue, Norwich,*
inscribed: *Edith Cavell — Nurse,*
Patriot and Martyr. 175mm. 19.00
Cenotaph, Model of, with green
wreaths.
4 sizes: 80mm. 4.00

100mm. 4.00
140mm. 5.50
180mm. 7.50
Three larger sizes with inscription
Cheltenham War Memorial.
2 sizes: 150mm. 65.00
185mm. 75.00
Chesham *War Memorial.* 159mm. 95.00
Dover Patrol Memorial. 130mm. 22.00
Dover *War Memorial.* 140mm. 65.00
Dovercourt War Memorial.
2 sizes: 120mm. 110.00
137mm. 110.00
East Dereham War Memorial,
with inscription (rare). 95.00
Florence Nightingale Statue,
inscribed: *The Lady of the Lamp.*
2 sizes: 147mm. 15.00
170mm. 19.00
(Different moulds)
Folkestone War Memorial
inscribed: *May their deeds be*
held in reverence.
2 sizes: 97mm long. 50.00
156mm long. 60.00
Fryatt Memorial, with inscription
(rare). 110.00
Great Yarmouth *War Memorial,*
with inscription. 146mm. 22.00
Invergordon *War Memorial.*
148mm (rare). 100.00
Killin War Memorial. 150mm. 87.50
Earl Kitchener Memorial, drowned
off Marwick Head, Orkney, 5th
June 1916. 110mm. 95.00
Lewisham War Memorial. 155mm. 110.00
Margate *War Memorial.* 160mm. 60.00
March War Memorial. 160mm. 82.50
Moffat War Memorial with ram
on a rock. (rare). 108mm. 95.00
Newhaven Mercantile Memorial,
with inscription. 65.00
Norwich *War Memorial.*
134mm. 87.50
Plymouth Naval *War Memorial,*
with inscription.
3 sizes: 125mm. 56.50
156mm. 60.00
178mm. 65.00
Plymouth Royal Naval Memorial,
on octagonal stepped base.
144mm. 65.00
Sheringham War Memorial, with
inscription. 165mm. 100.00

Southsea Naval War Memorial.
2 sizes: 140mm.	50.00
162mm.	55.00

Stowmarket Memorial Gates.
110mm long.	110.00

Woodhouse Eaves, War Memorial
with inscription. 130mm.   85.00

Most war memorials are relatively rare, possibly because they were ordered in small numbers by local shops, and were only made for a relatively short period.

Home/Nostalgic

Anvil on tree trunk base, horseshoe, tongs etc. against base. 70mm.	5.50
Armchair. 65mm.	7.50
Armchair, inscribed: *The old armchair*, with verse. 90mm.	7.50
Basket with twisted handle.	
73mm long.	4.00
If inscribed: *Fruit Basket*	6.50
Bellows. 95mm long.	5.50
Chair, highbacked. 90mm.	5.50
Child in long nightdress, for use as candlesnuffer. Some colouring.	
100mm.	16.00
Coal Scuttle. 65mm.	4.00
Coal Scuttle, sometimes found inscribed: *Coal scuttle.* 80mm.	5.50
Cradle. 48mm.	6.00
Dressing Table Swing Mirror, with drawer. 50mm.	8.00
Dust pan.	
2 sizes: 95mm long.	5.50
143mm long.	8.00
Firebucket. 55mm.	3.00

Fireplace, with teapot, cat etc. in bold relief. Inscribed: *There's no place like home.* Some colouring.
2 sizes: 90mm.	12.50
112mm.	14.50

Fireplace, with cauldron, teapot, etc. moulded in slight relief. Inscribed: *There's no place like home.* Some colouring.
2 sizes: 65mm.	12.50
110mm.	14.50
Flat Iron. 77mm long.	7.50
Frying Pan. 120mm long.	6.50

Grandfather Clock, narrow.
2 sizes: 105mm.	10.50
145mm.	16.00

Grandfather Clock, Model of.
Usually inscribed: *Make use of time let not advantage slip.* Shakespeare. Can be found inscribed: *Top o' the morn.*
No. 209. 108mm (Two moulds, one with ornate moulding at top). 10.50
Invalid Cup. 50mm.	5.50
Jardiniere on fixed base. 95mm.	3.00

Kennel, can be found inscribed:
Beware of the dog. 50mm.	6.50

Lantern.
2 sizes: 70mm.	5.50
90mm.	5.50

Lantern, horn, not found named but sometimes inscribed: *Watchman what of the night.*
85mm.	6.50
Lantern, with open sides. 125mm.	20.00
Milk Churn, with lid. 63mm.	3.00

Pillar Box, with inscription: *If you haven't time to post a line here's the pillar box.* 63mm.
	10.00
Found marked *G.R.V.*	13.00
and very rarely *E.R. VII*	17.00
Saucepan with handle and separate lid. 45mm.	7.50
Shaving Mug. 60mm.	5.50
Spinning Wheel. 84mm.	16.00
Stool, 3 legs. 40mm.	5.50

Sundial, inscribed: *Life's but a walking shadow.*
2 sizes: No. 41. 86mm.	5.50
115mm.	7.50
Table, square with four legs. 40mm.	5.50
Thimble. 41mm.	10.50

Top Hat Match Striker and holder.
45mm.	6.50

Umbrella, open. 50mm dia.
(Usually not marked.)	14.50

Village Pump with trough. Can be found inscribed 90mm.   7.50

Old Warming Pan, Model of,
inscribed: *Polly warm the bed.*
No. 254. 125mm long.   10.00

Old Warming Pan, Model of, with ornate handle. No. 251.
120mm long.	14.00
Watering Can. 74mm.	5.50

Water Pitcher, inscribed: *Tak Hod An' sup lad.* 60mm.   7.00
Wheelbarrow. 100mm long.	9.00

Comic/Novelty

Alarm Clock, inscribed: *Many are
called but few get up!*
2 sizes: 40mm.   19.50
60mm.   21.50
Basket of Milk, six bottles, tops
can be gold or brown. 65mm.   19.50
Billiken, often found not named.
63mm.   4.00
Boy Scout, inscribed: *Be prepared.*
105mm.   40.00
Clown, bust. No inscription or
colouring. 65mm.   8.25
Clown, bust, inscribed: *Put me
amongst the girls.* Some
colouring. 80mm.   17.00
Clown, standing, hands on hips,
wearing baggy suit. 104mm.   40.00
Couple in Bed, inscribed: *John is
everything shut up for the night -
All but you darling.* 70mm long.   40.00
Couple in Bed, man sitting up,
woman with all the blankets,
inscribed: *They don't need many
clothes in the daytime but they want
'em all at night.* 70mm long.   47.50
Fat Lady on weighing scales, scale
registers 20 stone. Inscribed:
Adding weight. Blue bonnet.
90mm.   33.00
Japanese Girl, with fan and parasol.
No. 250. 64mm.   34.00
Jester, doubled faced bust, happy
with eyes open and sad with
eyes closed. Can be found inscribed: *Ye Jester awake. Ye Jester
asleep.* Some colouring.
2 sizes: 65mm.   8.25
90mm.   9.00
inscribed   12.50
Judge in his box reading a book.
82mm.   56.50
Lavatory Pan with brown seat,
inscribed: *Ashes.* Not found
crested. 69mm.   9.50
*Mister Gollywog, Now children
when I've tucked you safely in,
just say Mr Gollywog good-night.*
118mm.   65.00
Negro Minstrel, bust, verse by
Eugene Stratton. Some
colouring. 100mm.   24.50
Negro, standing with hands in
pockets as vase. 105mm.   30.00

Petrol Pump Attendant, body is
pump. Inscribed: *Petrol Sir.*
Some colouring. 95mm.   40.00
Policeman, smiling, with arms
behind back. 100mm.   24.50
Policeman, fat and jovial, with
raised hand. Inscribed (on
hand): *Stop.* 94mm.   28.00
Policeman on duty, with verse.
148mm.   25.00
Policeman, jovial holding large
truncheon. Uniform and
helmet blue. 106mm (rare).   60.00
Robinson Crusoe standing figure
with gun. 122mm.   75.00
Pierrot, standing. 100mm.   24.50
Sailor, standing, cap can be
found impressed: *Lion.* Blue
cap and coloured face. 95mm.   35.00
Sailor, as above, pepper pot.
85mm.
Sailor Toby Jug, blue hat and coat.
60mm.   47.50
65mm (fatter).   65.00
108mm.   75.00
Sailor Vase, pink face and some
colouring. 103mm.   56.50
Sailor, negro features, Vase.
100mm.   30.00
(Late also found marked
Goss England)
Suffragette double sided bust, front
sour old lady, inscribed: *Votes
for women,* back pretty young girl,
inscribed: *This one shall have the
vote.* 98mm.
Coloured features. 98mm.   30.00
A smaller version exists with no
colouring or inscriptions. 72mm.   18.00
Suffragette candle snuffer, double
faced as above. 72mm.   20.00
Suffragette hand bell, double
faced as above, with same
inscription and colouring. Also
found inscribed: *Nature has
endowed woman with so much power
that the law gives them very little.
Dr Johnson.* 110mm.   30.00
(All the suffragette items must be
considered scarce).
Teapot with eyes, mouth and
nose as spout. Some colouring.   22.00
A Truck of Coal from. . . Wagon of
black coal. 80mm long.   16.00

Comic Ashtrays: Coloured figures on white trays. (All are quite rare).

Flapper, sitting on bench on oval or heart shaped tray, yellow hat and dress. 105mm.	50.00
Bookmaker, with greyhound and hare on ashtray base. Some colouring. 90mm long.	46.50

For Irish Colleen & Irishman see: National Souvenirs.

Jester, sitting on heart or spade shaped tray, other card symbols are on tray. 65mm.	70.00
Puppy, coloured with hat, bow, cigar and beer! on ashtray. 90mm.	90.00
Racehorse and jockey, some colouring, on horseshoe ashtray. 100mm.	65.00
Scotsman, really grotesque, sitting on bench on round tray. 95mm.	55.00

Comic Cruet Sets: Rarely found as a set. They are all fully coloured.

Policeman salt pot. 80mm.	40.00
Regimental Sergeant Major pepper pot. 80mm.	30.00
Naval Petty Officer pepper pot. 80mm.	30.00
Sailor, comic figure in blue with green parrot on shoulder with white mustard barrel with lid. 63mm.	36.50

Little birds: these are fully coloured heads popping out of white eggs. They do not seem to match any other series of models, the black boy's face is much more carefully detailed than the black boys listed below.

Flapper's head hatching from egg, inscribed: *A little bird from* .... 50mm long.	20.00
Black Boy's head hatching from Egg, inscribed: *A blackbird from* .... 50mm long.	24.00

Black Boys — often found marked Rd. No. applied for. All the boys are fully coloured but sit on white boxes, baths and so on. Later models are very brightly and carefully coloured and lightly glazed. These are marked as late in the listing below. All these models, with the exception of *A little study in black and fright,* are uncommon.

Black Boy standing with hands in pocket, also found as salt pot. 94mm (late).	65.00
Black Girl, standing with hands on hips, also found as pepper pot. (Pair with above). 94mm.	65.00
Black Boy playing banjo, boy can be wearing red, yellow or blue striped pyjamas. 85mm.	85.00
Black Boy in bath of ink, towel hanging at side, inscribed: *How ink is made* 110mm long. (Probably Willow Art mould).	75.00
Black Boy in hip bath holding yellow soap. 90mm (late).	82.50
Black Boy in bed with spider, inscribed: *A little study in black and fright.* Boy can have red or blue striped pyjamas. 70mm long.	56.50
Black Boy in bed, face only peeping out from bedclothes, inscribed: *Just a little study in black and fright.* 70mm long.	60.00
No colouring.	40.00
Black Couple in bed, inscribed: *They don't need many. . .* 71mm long.	80.00
Black Boy being chased up a tree by a crocodile. 80mm.	110.00
Black Boy eating slice of melon, sitting on a soapbox. 80mm (late).	85.00
Black Boy eating melon slice, standing on corner of diamond shaped ashtray, inscribed: *I'se not melon-choly!* (Rare) 88mm.	110.00
Black Boy sitting at table eating a boiled egg which has a yellow chick popping out. 70mm.	90.00
Two Black Boys heads popping out of box, inscribed: *Box of chocolates.* 60mm.	30.00
Also found in white only.	22.00
Two Black Children, boy and girl sitting on a tree trunk. 80mm.	75.00

Black Boy holding container for
cigarettes. 100mm (late).   56.50
Black Boy holding container for
matches. 100mm (late).   56.50
Black Boy peering out of shower
(rare) 67mm.   120.00
Black Boy Toby Jug. 66mm.   45.00
Children: very late models,
beautifully coloured and
detailed children on white arm-
chairs, baths etc.. Usually found
marked Rd. No. applied for.
They are particularly appealing
and unfortunately rare.
Deduct £20 if not coloured.
Girl and Boy sitting in armchair.
Girl is wearing a frilly dress and
has a large bow on her head;
boy is dressed in top hat and
tails. 60mm.   95.00
Girl and Boy sitting in armchair.
Boy wears black jacket and hat.
75mm.   95.00
Girl and Boy as above sitting on
tree trunk. 87mm long.   50.00
Boy riding a Pig. Boy wearing a
coloured coat.   115.00
Girl standing by hip bath,
wearing towel. 75mm.   85.00
Girl, standing naked, red bow in
hair, beside circular bath.
Yellow face sponge attached.
62mm.   85.00
Baby in Washbowl with a coloured
transfer of an insect (variously
described as a wasp or a fly).
80mm long.   45.00

Cartoon/Comedy Characters
Ally Sloper, bust, with inscription.
85mm.   40.00
Baby, with arms outstretched,
inscribed: *Cheerio.* Some colouring
on face. 120mm.
(from Willow mould)   30.00
Bonzo dog sitting, hind legs out-
stretched in front, name
impressed on collar. 68mm.   37.00
Bonzo, sitting on feeding bowl.
65mm.   29.50
Bonzo and Felix sitting on bench,
coloured and not named.
76mm.   60.00

Harry Lauder, bust. Inscribed: *Stop
ye're tickling Jock.* Often found
not named. Some colouring   17.00
83mm, named   25.75
Mrs. Gummidge, standing figure
with inscription: *A lone lorn
creetur & everything goes contrairy
with her.* 112mm (rare).   40.00
Winkie the glad-eyed bird, not
named but can be found
inscribed: *Glad eyes.* 60mm.   14.00

Alcohol
Series of late models of a fully
coloured comic man (looks
rather like Mr. Pickwick, bald
with spectacles, wearing a green
suit, but probably was a
comedian or comic character
associated with heavy drinking)
on white models.
Man, as above, drinking beer
from tankard. 92mm. Can be
white, with silver tankard and
coloured face or   25.00
fully coloured.   35.00
Man, as above, holding tankard
on horseshoe ashtray, with
inscription: *The more we are
together the merrier we'll be.*   33.00
Man, as above, clinging to neck
of bottle. Fully coloured,
white bottle.
2 sizes: 80mm.   29.50
         95mm.   29.50
Man, as above, climbing into
large beaker. 75mm.   34.50
Beaker, fluted, with inscription:
*They speak o' my drinking, but
they dinna consider my drouth, or
Ye never ken the worth o' water
till the well not is dry.* 78mm.   7.50
Beer Barrel on stand, inscribed:
XXX on each end of barrel.
55mm.   5.50
Beer Bottle and tankard on
horseshoe ashtray, with
inscription: *The more we are
together the merrier we'll be.*   12.50
Beer Bottle and tankard on square
ashtray with inscription above.
90mm.   12.50

Bottle. 63mm. 4.75
can be found inscribed:
Special Scotch. 6.50
or more rarely *Lacon's fine ale.* 10.50
Bottle with cork. 76mm. 5.25
Carboy. 55mm and 85mm. 3.00
Drunk leaning against a statue on
an ashtray. Inscribed: *How cold
you are tonight dear.* Coloured
figure on white tray. 100mm. 56.50
Monk, jovial, and holding glass
with verse: *A jovial monk am I
contented with my lot. The world
without this gate. I flout nor care
for it one jot.*
2 sizes: 70mm. 12.50
112mm. 16.00
A Nap Hand, hand holding
coloured beer labels on heart
shaped dish. 62mm long. 45.00
Silver Tankard. 85mm. 11.00
Soda Syphon. 100mm. 10.00
Tankard, foaming, with verse:
'The more we are together'.
50mm. 4.75
Thistle Vase, with verse: *'Just a
wee deoch-an doris'.* 70mm. 4.00
Toby Jug, sometimes found with
verse: *No tongue can tell, No heart
can think, Oh how I love a drop of
drink.* 4 sizes:
45mm. Smallest size 8.25
can be found coloured 14.50
65mm. Middle size, is exactly
the same as Old Toby Jug. 6.50
75mm. 7.50
85mm. 8.25
Whiskey Bottle, can have solid or
cork top, inscribed: *One Special
Scotch.* 100mm. 7.50
Whiskey Bottle and Soda Syphon
on tray, inscribed: *Scotch and
Soda.* 88mm dia. 12.50

Sport
Billiard Table, cue and three balls.
100mm long. 95.00
Cricket Bag.
2 sizes: 80mm long. 7.00
100mm long. 8.00
Cricket Bat. 115mm long. 40.00
Curling Stone. 63mm dia. 13.00
Football. 50mm dia. 6.50

The F.A. Cup. 100mm. 10.00
named. 26.00
Golf Ball, often inscribed: *The
game of golf was first played in the
year 1448.* 42mm. 6.50
Golf Club Head. 94mm long. 10.50
Golf Bag and Clubs. 105mm. 75.00
Golfer, with clubs standing on
golf ball. 76mm. 35.00
Golfer standing on small golf ball
in centre of six-sided ashtray.
72mm. 47.50
Golfer's Caddie holding golf bag.
Figure coloured.
110mm (late model). 65.00
Golfer's Caddie, very tiny, holding huge bag of clubs. 88mm. 55.00
Jockey on Racehorse, oval base,
some colouring, unglazed.
115mm. 65.00
Tennis Racquet. 95mm long. 7.50

Musical Instruments
Banjo.
2 sizes: 125mm long. 8.50
150mm long. 8.50
Double Bass. 153mm long. 28.00
Guitar. 153mm long. 10.50
Harp. 104mm. 6.50
Piano, upright. 70mm long. 13.50
Tambourine. 50mm dia. 7.50
Violin with bow. 125mm long. 50.00

Transport
Car, open tourer (2 seater)
inscribed: *EH 139;* can be found
also inscribed: *HELL.*
110mm long. 30.00
Car, saloon, inscribed: *EH 139.*
76mm long. 30.00
Car, open 2 seater showing
exhaust pipes, curved boot, etc.
105mm long. 40.00
Car, taxi, inscribed: *EH 139.* Front
two seats open, hood over back
two. 85mm long. 56.50
Charabanc, 18 seater, inscribed:
*7734 which upside down reads
HELL.* 138mm long. 33.00
Can of Petrol, impressed: *Motor
Spirit.* 55mm. 13.00
Omnibus, Double decker bus with
stairs outside.
130mm long (rare). 165.00

Modern Equipment

Camera, folding. 60mm.   30.00
Gramophone in Cabinet.
  80mm long.   40.00
Horn Gramophone.
  2 sizes: 112mm.   19.50
            80mm.   19.50

Hats

Boy Scout's Hat. 73mm dia.   16.00
Luton Boater with coloured band.
  100mm long.   20.00
Bishop's Mitre. No. 19. 50mm long.   6.50
Straw Hat. 75mm long.   6.50
Top Hat. 40mm.   5.00

Shoes

Highboot.
  3 sizes: 73mm.   10.00
            85mm.   12.00
           104mm.   16.00
High backed narrow Shoe.
  2 sizes: 90mm.   7.50
           130mm long.   10.50
Hobnail Boot.
  2 sizes: 65mm long.   4.75
           80mm long.   5.50
Ladies Ankle Boot. 70mm long.   6.50
Dutch Clog. 102mm long.   4.50
Sabot, pointed toe. 60mm long.   4.75
Oriental Shoe.
  2 sizes: 85mm long.   4.00
           105mm long.   6.50
Riding Boot.73mm.   10.50
Shoe posy holder. 100mm long.   7.50
Slipper. 100m long.   7.50
Slipper wall pocket. 109mm long.   7.50

Miscellaneous

Ball of String. 55mm.   13.00
Ball of string match holder and
  striker. 55mm.   13.00
Bell, no clapper. 54mm.   5.50
Chess Set. Complete sets can be
  found but these are very rare. It
  is extremely difficult to collect a
  set with the same crests.
  Individual pieces are often
  found however, the rook being
  the most common, the pawn,
  strangely, is quite rare.
King. 88mm.   19.50
Queen. 84mm.   24.50
  also found in smaller size. 72mm.
Knight. 63mm.   9.00
Bishop. 60mm.   16.00
Rook. 55mm.   4.00

Pawn. 52mm.   20.00
Flower Bud Vase. 40mm.   3.00
Flower (Pansy?) shaped pin tray.
  80mm dia.   4.00
Handbell, no clapper. 53mm.   5.50
Horse's Hoof as inkwell. Inscribed:
  *We're aye prood tae hear
  frae ye.* 90mm.   12.50
Horse's Hoof on base
  No. 151. 30mm.   4.00
Horseshoe. 55mm long.   3.00
Horseshoe on stand.   5.50

Miniature Domestic

These models can be found with
  crests, views, black cats and
  other transfer decorations.
Amphora Vase on three red balls.
  90mm.   7.50
Beaker. 40mm.   2.50
Beaker, fluted with inscription: *Ye
  never ken the worth of water till
  the well gangs dry.* 50mm.   5.50
Chamberpot. 98mm.   3.50
Cheese Dish, one piece. 50mm.   7.50
Cheese Dish and cover. 50mm.   7.50
Cream Jug. 52mm.   2.50
Milk Jug with crinkle top. 38mm.   2.50
Tea Cup and saucer. 40mm.   5.50
Tea Pot with lid. 60mm.   7.50
Tea Pot, one piece. 48mm.   7.50
Vase with ram's head in relief.
  55mm.   2.50

Domestic

This is listed as it was made
  specifically to carry crests.
  Pieces can also be found with
  'Lucky Black Cat', 'Lucky
  White Heather' and other
  transfer decorations, but not
  usually views. Late pieces are
  found with the black cat
  Arcadian mark. Lettering is
  usually in blue.
Ashtrays, can be found inscribed:
  Ashtray. Various shapes:
  Club, diamond, heart and
  spade shaped with crinkle
  edges.   3.00
  Club shaped tray with match
  box stand. 105mm wide.   14.00
  Heart shaped bowl.   3.00
  Horseshoe.   3.00

Octagonal.	3.00
Trefoil.	3.00
Round tray with match holder.	10.00
Bulb bowl, hexagonal.	3.00
Candle Snuffer, cone. 63mm.	2.50
Candlesticks, various shapes:	
Column with ornate moulding.	3.00
Octagonal, fluted.	3.00
Short on oblong base with handle.	3.00
Short on fluted oblong base with handle.	3.00
Short on fluted leaf shaped base with handle.	3.00
Fern pots, fluted. 3 sizes:	3.50
Hexagonal. 3 sizes.	3.50
Flower bowl, octagonal.	3.50
Flower vase.	4.00
Hair pin box and lid, can be found inscribed: *Hairpins.* Fluted oblong or round.	5.50
Hair Tidy with lid, can be found inscribed: *Hair Tidy.* Various shapes:	
Hexagonal.	6.50
Octagonal with ornate moulding and blue bow.	8.50
Square, fluted. 65mm.	7.50
Hat Pin Holder, can be found inscribed: *Hat pins.* Various shapes:	
Octagonal.	9.00
Square fluted. 121mm.	8.50
Square with ornate moulding.	10.00
Fluted. 128mm.	8.50
Inkstand, with pen holder base.	7.50
Inkwell with lid. 68mm dia.	9.00
Match Holder, can be found inscribed: *Matches.* Various shapes:	
Hexagonal.	10.00
Round.	10.00
Round on base.	10.00
Pill Box and lid. 44mm dia.	7.00
50mm dia.	4.75
Pin Tray, can be found inscribed: *Pins.* Fluted round, diamond or oblong.	4.00
Pot Pourri, 2 shapes:	
Round vase shaped, lid with knob.	4.00
Round with domed lid (rather like a ginger jar).	4.00
Powder bowl, round.	3.50

Preserve jar with lid, round or tub shaped.	5.00
Puff Box, can be found inscribed: *Puff box,* hexagonal or round.	
2 sizes:.	6.00
Ring Stand.	6.00
Rose Bowl, fluted with brass fittings.	12.00
Tableware: Cups and saucers, coffee cans and saucers, and plates are all found in classic and simple shapes. Also the following:	
Beakers, plain and fluted.	2.25
Butter Tub.	5.50
Cream jugs and sugar bowls (matching) in various shapes:	
Hexagonal	5.25
Octagonal	5.25
Round, plain	3.00
Round, fluted	3.00
These can occasionally be found inscribed: *Help yourself to the crame/sugar* or *Be aisy wid the crame/sugar.* Add £6.00 with these inscriptions.	
Egg Cup.	5.00
Jugs, in a variety of sizes, also bagware.	2.50
Mugs. 2 sizes.	2.25
Mustard Pots. Various shapes:	
Round with pointed lid.	3.00
Round, fluted and ornate.	3.00
Round with silver lid.	10.00
Round, tall, with silver lid.	10.00
Pepper & Salt Pots, various shapes:	
Cone shaped, small.	3.50
Cone shaped, tall with silver lids.	10.00
Hexagonal.	3.50
Round, with silver lids.	10.00
Plate, with thistles and leeks moulded in relief.	4.50
Sugar Basin on stand.	3.50
Sugar Castor.	5.00
Sweet Dishes, various shapes:	
Octagonal.	2.25
Round, crinkle edges. 2 sizes.	2.25
Round, fluted, 2 sizes.	2.25
Teapots. 1, 2 & 3 cup sizes.	7.50
Tobacco Jar with lid, inscribed: *Tobacco.*	11.00

Trinket Boxes, can be found inscribed: *Trinkets*. Various shapes:

Heart shaped. 4 sizes.	4.00
Heart shaped with ribbon.	7.50
Hexagonal.	4.00
Horseshoe shaped.	4.00
Oblong.	4.00
Oval.	4.00
Round. 2 sizes.	4.00
Square.	4.00
Square with bevelled corners.	4.50
Square, fluted.	4.00

Argonauta Porcelain

For mark see *Crested China*, p. 64.

Trademark used by James Macintyre & Co Ltd, Washington China Works, Burslem.

Many rather heavy smalls found with this mark.

Ancient Artefacts
Mug, 1 handled. No. 17. 35mm.   2.25

Miscellaneous
Club shaped Dish. 75mm long.   3.00

Argosy China

Asbury China

For mark see *Crested China,* p. 65.

Trademark used by Grafton possibly using a retailer's mark. (Usual trademark Grafton).

Seaside Souvenirs
Bathing Machine with large
wooden wheels, and panelled
body. 55mm.   7.50

Animals
Elephant, comic, standing with
sandwich boards. 115mm.   100.00

Great War
Colonial Hat. 89mm long.   12.50

Footwear
Boot with laces.
No. 234. 80mm long.   7.50
Shoe with turned up toe.
80mm long.   4.75

Miniature Domestic
Tea Pot with lid. 90mm long.   7.50

For additional mark see *Crested China,* p. 65.

Trademark thought to have been used by Hewitt and Leadbeater, Willow Potteries, Longton. (Usual trademark Willow Art). Pieces were probably bought in for re-sale by Edward Asbury & Co., Prince of Wales Works, Longton, and marked with an Asbury trademark.

Buildings — White
Cottage. 55mm long.   6.50

Traditional/National Souvenirs
Welsh Hat. 57mm.   4.75

Animals
Lion walking. 110mm long.   12.50

Birds
Duck posy bowl. 70mm long.   7.50
Swan. 65mm long.   6.50

Great War
Monoplane, Bleriot type with
movable prop. 147mm long.   55.00
HMS Lion. 142mm long.   22.50
Tank. 85mm long.   30.00

Home/Nostalgic
Anvil. 56mm.   5.50

Novelty
Billiken, flat grotesque type.
68mm.   4.00

Miscellaneous

Hammer Head. 82mm long.	11.00
Toby Jug. 75mm.	6.50
Tree Trunk flower holder. 80mm.	6.50

Footwear
Sabot.

2 sizes:	60mm long.	4.00
	80mm long.	4.50

Hats

Top Hat. 40mm.	5.50

Atlas

Trademark used by unknown manfacturer.

The only piece recorded is a plain sugar bowl. 80mm.   3.00

Atlas China

Trademark used by Atlas China Co. Ltd., Atlas Works, Wolfe Street, Stoke. 1906-1910.

This company formerly Chapman & Sons Ltd was not thought to manufacture heraldic china. Obviously they did so during the early years when Goss historical models were so popular.

Ancient Artefacts
Newbury Leather Bottle,
not named. 67mm.   3.00

Miscellaneous
Cup and Saucer. 80mm.   4.50

Atlas Heraldic China

For mark see *Crested China*, p. 65.

Trademark thought to have been used by Taylor and Kent, Florence Works, Longton, for a wholesaler in Scotland. (Usual trademark Florentine).

Ancient/Artefacts
Salisbury Kettle, not named
100mm.   2.25

Monuments
Iona Cross. 108mm.   6.00
Statue: standing unglazed figure
of possibly a Saxon or Viking
Warrior with small oval shield in
left hand. Square glazed base.
130mm. (The one model recorded
has a Lanark Crest).   65.00

National Souvenirs
Welsh Hat with blue cord and
embossed tassels. 56mm.   4.75

Seaside Souvenirs
Whelk Shell. 100mm.   3.00
Portmanteau. 80mm long.   4.00

Animals
Elephant, kneeling. 67mm.   15.00
Fish, open mouth. 120mm long.   3.00

Birds
Kingfisher. 80mm.   20.50
Pelican cream jug. 83mm long.   5.50
Swan posy holder. 80mm long.   4.75

Home/Nostalgic
Baby in Hip Bath. 100mm long.   11.00
Sofa. 82mm long.   10.50
Napkin Ring. 38mm.   4.00
The Old Armchair, with verse.
85mm.   7.50

Sport
Cricket Bag. 110mm long.   8.00

Miscellaneous
Carboy. 76mm.   3.00
Thimble. 40mm.   10.50

Footwear
Oriental Shoe with turned up toe.
  95mm long.   4.00
Shoe, Ladies' 18th century.
  95mm long.   7.50

Miniature Domestic
Cheese Dish and cover. 55mm.   5.50
Coffee Pot with lid. 63mm.   7.50
Cup and Saucer.
  2 sizes: 40mm.   4.50
           55mm.   4.50
Tea Pot with lid. 70mm.   7.50

Aurelian China

Trademark used by an unknown English manufacturer.

Only one small jug known bearing the arms of Cheltenham.   3.00

Avon China

Aynsley

For mark see *Crested China*, p. 67.

For mark see *Crested China*, p. 67

Trademark used by Arkinstall & Son Ltd, Arcadian Works, Stoke-on-Trent. (Usual trademark Arcadian).

Many small pots and jugs etc. are found with this mark, probably an early Arkinstall mark.

Trademark used on china with military crests by John Aynsley and Sons, Portland Works, Longton. Aynsley models therefore almost always appear bearing military badges. Deduct £15 if no military badge.

South African War

Hand Grenade, with flames coming from the top. 88mm.	30.00
Cannon Shell. 104mm.	23.00
Empty Shell Case.	40.00
Bandsman's Drum. 55mm.	17.50
High Boot. 118mm.	22.00
Tent, with open flaps. 75mm.	23.00
Waterbottle.	
2 sizes: 80mm.	20.00
95mm.	22.00
Colonial Soldier's Hat.	
80mm long.	18.00
Forage Cap. 85mm long.	25.00
Glengarry. 90mm long.	25.00
Pickelhaube. 69mm long.	30.00
Pith Helmet.	21.00

Ancient Artefacts

Model of Loving Cup originated by Henry of Navarre, King of France, 3 handled. 39mm.	4.00

Traditional/National Souvenirs

John Bull, bust of. 85mm.	19.50

Animals

Hare. 80mm long.	9.00

Comic/Novelty

Suffragette Bust, double faced. 89mm.	25.00

Sport

Golf Ball. 43mm.	5.50

Footwear

Boot. 60mm.	30.00
Ladies Shoe. 92mm long.	13.00

Miscellaneous

Button, oval. 40mm.	8.00
Horse's Hoof posy bowl. 84mm long.	17.50
Horseshoe. 85mm long.	13.00
Circular Plaque. 75mm dia.	8.00
Circular Plaque with silver rim. 75m dia.	15.00
Shield Menu Holder.	
2 sizes: 63mm.	13.00
100mm.	17.50
Trinket Box, heart shaped, with lid.	11.00
Vase. 58mm.	7.00

B

Balmoral China

For mark see *Crested China*, p. 68.

For mark see *Crested China*, p. 69.

Trademark used by Blairs and Beaconsfield Pottery, Longton.

Trademark used by Redfern and Drakeford (Ltd), Balmoral Works, Longton.

Animals
Pig, standing. 80mm long.   10.00

Miniature Domestic
Cheese Dish, one piece. 50mm.   5.50

All china found with this mark has the British Empire Exhibition badge or an inscription *'Wembley 1925'* and was obviously made especially for this event. As some pieces are also seen with 'Willow Art' trademarks they could have been supplied for decoration by Hewitt & Leadbeater which had by then been purchased by Harold Taylor Robinson and was part of the J.A. Robinson Co.

Buildings — White
The Marble Arch, unglazed top.
    72mm.   16.00
Tower Bridge. 144mm long.   34.50

Birds
Goose, standing and very fat,
    with long slender neck.
    155mm.   33.50

Bell China

This mark has been found on pieces of domestic ware with EPNS tops. Taylor and Kent specialised in producing china for manufacturers to add metal lids etc. as did many other potteries.

Domestic
Sugar Sifter with EPNS top.
(Llandudno crest). 160mm.   6.50
Bottle for ink or perfume, screw top
made from an early version of
plastic. 80mm. (Birmingham crest)   7.50
Salt Pot with EPNS top. 100mm.   4.50

Belleek

For mark see *Crested China*, p. 69.

Trademark used by Belleek Pottery (David McBirney and Co.), Belleek, Co. Fermanagh, N. Ireland.

Ancient Artefacts
Irish Bronze Pot, not named,
with yellow interior, handles
and feet. (Ayr crest). 45mm.   22.50

National Souvenirs
Shamrock shaped loving cup, 3
handles. 50mm.   22.50

Animals
Pig, sitting, decorated with green
shamrocks.   40.00
Terrier, standing. 88mm.   26.50
Tortoise. 70mm long.   24.50

Home/Nostalgic
Milk Churn, with 2 handles. 60mm. 18.50

Alcohol
Barrel. 57mm.   18.50

Many very fine 'smalls' were
produced by this Pottery often
with the characteristic Belleek
lustre finish. These are valued
at £15.00 upwards.

Birks Crest China

Trademark used by Arkinstall & Son Ltd., Arcadian Works, Stoke-on-Trent. (Usual trademark Arcadian).

Animals
Crocodile (or Alligator).
127mm long.   75.00

Birks China

For mark see, *Crested China*, p. 69.

Trademark used by Birks, Rawlins & Co. (Ltd.), Vine Pottery, Stoke, previously L.A. Birks & Co., established in 1885. (Usual trademark Savoy).

Traditional/National Souvenirs
Thistle vase. 52mm.   3.00

Animals
Three wise Monkeys on diamond ashtray.
65mm.   13.00

Great War
Battleship with 3 funnels,
inscribed: *HMS Tiger.*
116mm long.   56.50
Cenotaph. 180mm.   7.50

Home/Nostalgic
Basket. 48mm.   3.00
Handbag. 88mm.   11.00

Novelty
Biscuit, impressed: *Huntley &
Palmers.* On stand.
Impressed: 399. 85mm.   26.00
With holes for hatpins.

Miniature Domestic
Tea Pot with lid. 110mm.   7.50

Blairs China

For mark see *Crested China*, p. 71.

Trademark used by Blairs Ltd, Beaconsfield
Pottery, Longton.

This trademark has only been
found on a range of 'smalls'
with Great War inscriptions
or commemorative prints.   from £5.00

Boots

For additional mark see *Crested China*, p. 71.

Trademark used for Boots The Chemist by
Arkinstall & Son Ltd, Arcadian Works,
Stoke-on-Trent. (Usual trademark
Arcadian).

Ancient Artefacts
Glastonbury Abbot's Cup, not
named. No. 238. 48mm.   2.25

Animal
Pig, standing, inscribed: *Wunt be
druv.* 85mm long.   11.00

Home/Nostalgic
Frying Pan. 108mm long.   6.50

Miscellaneous
3-handled Loving Cup. 38mm. Bears
the unusual combination of arms
of City of London, Arms of
Weymouth and Melcombe
Regis and Dorchester.   4.00

Many 'smalls' also produced not
of very good quality. These
often have Great War
inscriptions.   £2 - £10

Botolph China

For marks see *Crested China*, p. 71.

Trademark probably used by J. Wilson and Sons, Park Works, Fenton.
However, J W & Co Ltd, could be a china retailer or wholesaler. The china could have been made by several crested china manufacturers: probably Taylor & Kent (usual trademark Florentine) and J.A. Robinson Ltd. (Usual mark Arcadian and later Willow). This could well account for the three marks already recorded.

Buildings — White

Big Ben.	
2 sizes: 92mm.	13.00
130mm.	15.50
Blackpool Tower. 117mm.	13.00
Marble Arch, Model of.	
3 sizes: 48mm.	16.00
60mm.	13.00
80mm.	16.00
Nelson's Column. 124mm.	45.00
The Old Curiosity Shop, with inscription. 95mm long.	24.50
Old London Bridge, Ye. 86mm.	18.00
St. Pauls Cathedral.	
2 sizes: 76mm.	14.50
127mm.	21.50
Temple Bar. 96mm.	20.00
Tower Bridge.	
2 sizes: 118mm.	29.00
133mm long.	29.00
Wembley Sports Stadium. 134mm long.	35.00
Westminster Abbey, West Front.	
2 sizes: 80mm.	16.00
116mm.	21.50

Historic/Folklore

Man standing in Pillory. 105mm.	17.00
Mother Shipton. 73mm.	13.00

Traditional/National Souvenirs

John Bull, bust. 68mm.	14.50
Yarmouth Bloater. 100mm long.	6.50
Irish Harp. 106mm.	8.25

Seaside Souvenirs

Bathing Machine. 70mm.	6.50
Bathing Machine with bather wearing towel in doorway. 75mm.	14.50
Houseboat, square. 90mm long.	9.00
Yacht. 125mm long.	10.50
Lifebelt. 85mm dia.	8.75
Fisherman's Creel, fixed lid. 60mm.	4.00
Lighthouse. 95mm.	4.75
Suitcase. 58mm.	4.00
'The Glad Sea Waves'. 48mm.	18.50
Whelk Shell. 98mm long.	3.00

Countryside

Haystack, circular. 55mm.	4.75
Haystack, rectangular. 56mm.	5.50

Animals

Camel. 90mm long.	13.00
Angry Cat, arched back, coloured features. 82mm.	12.50
Cat, long neck. 106mm.	6.50
Cheshire Cat. 90mm.	6.50
Dog, Bulldog. 57mm.	13.00
Dog, Labrador puppy with curly tail, sitting. 90mm.	10.00
Dog, King Charles Spaniel, begging on a cushion. 70mm.	8.25
Dog, lying in cradle. 90mm long.	10.50
Dogs, King Charles Spaniels, two in Top Hat. 78mm.	16.00
Dolphin vase. 110mm.	5.00
Elephant, standing. 70mm.	13.00
Fish. 102mm long.	3.00
Hare. 93mm long.	9.00
Monkey, sitting, hands to mouth. 65mm.	13.00
Pig, lying. 68mm long.	8.25
Pig, standing, can be found with inscription: *The Pig that won't go.* 55mm.	10.00
Rabbit. 70mm long.	6.50
Rabbit, very fluffy. 100m long.	12.50
Seal with ball on nose. 75mm.	16.00
Tortoise. 70mm long.	6.50

Birds

Budgerigar. 100mm.	9.00
Canary on rock. 92mm.	7.50
Chicken in Egg. 63mm long.	5.50
Hen, roosting. 52mm.	5.50
Kingfisher. 76mm.	20.50

Owl, baby. 70mm.	12.50
Swan. 63mm.	6.50
Swan posy holder. 90mm long.	4.75

Great War

Nurse, inscribed: *A Soldier's Friend*. 125mm.	40.00
Sailor, bust of. 90mm.	30.00
Monoplane, with movable prop. 175mm long.	55.00
Observer Sausage Balloon. 80mm.	47.50
Zeppelin on stand. 130mm.	20.00
Battleship.	
2 sizes: 115mm.	15.50
165mm long.	30.00
Larger size found with inscription: *Great War 1914-18. The German Fleet surrendered 74 warships Nov 21st 1918.*	
Torpedo Boat Destroyer. 110mm long.	19.50
Submarine, inscribed: *E4*. 95mm long.	16.00
Submarine, inscribed: *E5*. 127mm long.	16.00
Red Cross Van. *EH139*, with 3 red crosses. 88mm long.	23.00
Ambulance. 100mm long.	23.00
Tank, Model of, (without wheels)	
2 sizes: 100mm long.	60.00
155mm long.	22.00
Tank with small integral steering wheels. 115mm long.	15.00
Tank, Model of (without wheels), wide version. There are at least two different moulds, possibly three. One has the side guns moulded flat to walls of tank, and the other has forward facing guns protruding from side turrets standing proud of sides.	
125mm long.	21.00
Field Gun. 120mm long.	17.00
Howitzer. 135mm long.	16.00
Trench Mortar. 70mm.	10.50
Cannon Shell, inscribed: *Jack Johnson*. 94mm.	8.50
Clip of Bullets. 85mm.	13.00
Revolver. 83mm long.	35.00
Bandsman's Drum. 58mm dia.	5.00
New Zealand Hat. 73mm long.	17.50
Fireplace, inscribed: *We've kept the home fires burning.* 110mm.	14.50

Cenotaph, Whitehall London, Model of. With green wreaths and inscription.	
4 sizes: 80mm.	4.00
100mm.	4.00
120mm.	5.50
145mm.	5.50
Cavell Memorial, London, inscribed: *Nurse Cavell*.	
2 sizes: 115mm.	11.00
160mm.	14.50

Home/Nostalgic

Armchair, inscribed: *The Old Armchair* and verse. 90mm.	7.50
Baby's Cradle. 45mm.	6.00
Baby in Hip Bath. 103mm long.	11.00
Coal Scuttle. 60mm.	4.50
Edwardian Boy and Girl cruet set. 90mm. Each	12.50
Flat Iron. 78mm long.	8.50
Garden Roller. 85mm long.	10.50
Grandfather Clock. 130mm.	10.50
Keys, on ring. 46mm.	24.50
Lantern. 70mm.	4.75
Pillar Box. 78mm.	8.00
Sofa. 80mm long.	10.50
Watering Can. 70mm.	5.50

Comic/Novelty

Boy on Scooter. 103mm.	16.00
Bust of smiling Boy, spill holder. 71mm.	7.50
Jack in the Box. 95mm.	16.00
Screw, inscribed: *A big fat screw.* This refers to a wage rise. 75mm.	20.00
Pierrot, sitting, playing banjo. Some colouring on hands and face. 120mm.	30.00

Sport

Cricket Bag,	
2 sizes: 80mm long.	7.00
110mm long.	8.00
Golf Club Head.	
2 sizes: 75mm.	10.50
95mm.	10.50
Snooker Table on 6 legs. With 3 balls and cue resting on top. 100mm long.	95.00
Tennis Racquet. 97mm long.	7.50

Musical Instruments

Grand Piano. 85mm.	14.50

Transport

Car Horn, inscribed: *Pip Pip.*
90mm long. 22.50
Charabanc, with driver.
115mm long. 33.00
Omnibus, double decker bus with
stairs outside. 130mm long. 165.00
Saloon Car, always found gilded
on one side only. 86mm long. 30.00

Modern Equipment

Radio Horn. 96mm. 18.00

Hats

Bishop's Mitre. 55mm. 6.50
Boater, hat. 75mm long. 8.75

Footwear

Oriental Shoe with pointed
turned up toe. 98mm long. 6.50
Shoe, Ladies, 18th century.
93mm long. 7.50
Thigh Boot, with scalloped rim.
100mm. 16.00

Miscellaneous

Horses Hoof vase. 64mm long. 4.00
Toby Jug. 65mm. 6.50

Miniature Domestic

Candlestick with snake
wrapped around it. 100mm. 7.50
Cheese Dish and sloped cover.
60mm. 7.50
Teapot with lid. 52mm. 7.50

Bow China

For mark see *Crested China*, p. 73.

Trademark used by Birks, Rawlins & Co
(Ltd.), Vine Pottery, Stoke (Usual trademark Savoy).

Ancient Artefacts

Carlisle Salt Pot (not named).
60mm. 2.25
*Celtic Vase in British Museum,
Model of.* No. 25. 45mm. 3.00
Greek Vase, inscribed: *Model of
Greek Vase from the collection of
Sir Henry Englefield.* No. 66.
72mm. 3.00
*Lincoln Jack from original in
museum. Model of.*
No. 39. 60mm. 3.00
Persian Vase. No. 144. 75mm. 3.00

Animals

Elephant and Howdah.
70mm (rare). 30.00

Great War

Battleship found inscribed with
one of the following: *HMS Lion* 56.50
or *HMS Ramilies.* 75.00
No. 524. 168mm long. 56.50
Submarine, inscribed: *E1,* usually
found with inscription.
150mm long. 40.00
Howitzer. 170mm long. 27.50
Cannon Shell, inscribed: *Iron
rations for Fritz.* 115mm. 8.25

Hats

Top Hat. No. 339. 44mm. 5.50

Bramwell China

Trademark used by an unknown manufacturer for a retailer probably in Sheffield. Only one model known with Sheffield crest.

Ancient Artefacts
Leather Jack, not named.
  No. 751. 62mm.   3.00
(This number does not occur for a model like this in other ranges — possibly the Stock No. should be 75 or 51. The other numeral being a paintresses mark).

Bute China

Trademark used by Taylor and Kent (Ltd), Florence Works, Longton. (Usual trademark Florentine).

Miniature Domestic
Coffee Pot with lid. 63mm.   7.50

Cable China

Trademark used by a branch of J.A. Robinson & Sons, probably Willow Potteries ltd. (Usual trademark Willow).

Seaside Souvenirs
Lighthouse, not named.
No. 135mm.   4.75

Home/Nostalgic
Anvil. 56mm.   5.50
Book, closed. 60mm.   5.00

Novelty
Minstrel bust, no colouring.
90mm.   9.00

Footwear
Shoe with blue bow. 113mm long.   13.00
Tulip in hand. 81mm.   4.00

Caledonia China

For mark see *Crested China*, p. 74.

Trademark used by Taylor and Kent (Ltd), Florence Works, Longton for the Glasgow wholesaler CR and Co. (Usual trademark Florentine). (See also Atlas Heraldic China).

Seaside Souvenirs
Yacht in full sail. 127mm long.   10.50

Animals
Dog, Bulldog, standing with verse:
Be Briton still to Britain
true, Among ourselves united.
For never by but British hands,
Maun wrongs be righted. Burns.
130mm long.   19.50
Camel, kneeling. 95mm long.   13.00
Manx Cat, wiry. 53mm.   16.00
Pig, standing. 80mm long.   9.50
Rabbit. 105mm long.   8.50

Great War
Highland Infantryman with pack,
rifle, on round plinth. 165mm.   110.00
Bust of Sailor, unglazed on glazed
base, inscribed: *HMS Queen*
Elizabeth on hat band. 140mm.   95.00
Monoplane. 127mm long.   55.00
Liner converted to troop ship,
inscribed. *HMS Lion*. 140mm long. 95.00
Submarine, inscribed: *E1*.
150mm long.   30.00
Glengarry. 90mm long.   16.00

Home/Nostalgic
Kennel, inscribed: *Beware of the*
Dog. 62mm long.   6.50
Policeman's Lamp. 70mm.   5.50
Shaving Mug. 55mm.   5.50
Sofa. 82mm long.   10.50

Comic/Novelty
Policeman, standing, hands
behind back, appears to be
holding shears. 105mm.   24.50

Modern Equipment
Box Gramophone. 55mm.   15.25

Alcohol
Barrel inscribed: *Real Scotch.*
   No. 405. 55mm.   7.50

Sport
Cricket Bag. 120mm long.   8.00

Footwear
Sabot. 90mm long.   5.50

Miniature Domestic
Cheese Dish and cover. 2 pieces.   5.50

Caledonia China

For mark see *Crested China*, p. 75.

Trademark used by James Macintyre and
   Co Ltd, Washington China Works,
   Burslem, for sale in Scotland.

Unglazed/Parian
Bust, *John Travers Cornwall, the boy
   hero aged 16, Hero of Jutland Battle.
   Faithful unto death.* On glazed
   base. *HMS Chester* impressed on
   hat band. 115mm.   250.00

Traditional/National
Welsh Hat. 56mm.   4.75

Animals
King Charles Spaniel begging on
   cushion. 70mm.   8.25
Two King Charles Spaniels
   sitting in top hat. 75mm.   16.00
Elephant posy bowl. 75mm.   7.50
Polar Bear, inscribed: *Sam.*
   88mm long.   47.50

Birds
Hen, roosting. 51mm.   5.50
Parrot. 92mm.   9.50

Great War
Red Cross Van. 87mm long.   23.00
Cenotaph inscribed: *The blood of
   heroes is the seed of freedom.*
   140mm.   5.50

Comic/Novelty
Screw inscribed *You could do with
   a big fat screw.* This means a
   wage rise. 75mm.   20.00

Miscellaneous
Dutch Sabot. 70mm long.   5.00
Policeman's lamp. 70mm.   5.50

Caledonia Heraldic China

For mark see *Crested China,* p. 75.

Trademark used by a Scottish wholesaler on crested china manufactured by leading arms ware firms including Birks, Rawlins and Co. (Savoy), Hewitt and Leadbeater (Willow Art) and Wiltshaw and Robinson Ltd. (Carlton).

Parian/Unglazed

Burns at the Plough, standing on rectangular base with a red flower on ground. Inscribed: *Wee, modest, crimson tipped flower thou's met me in an evil hour.* Also inscribed: *Wee sleekit cowrin tim'rous Beastie. . .* 105mm.	75.00
Bust of Burns on square glazed base. 160mm.	20.00
Bust of Scott on square glazed base. 160mm.	17.50

Buildings — Coloured

Model of House in Edinburgh where John Knox the Scottish Reformer died 24 Nov 1573. 93mm (Willow).	110.00

Buildings — White

Burns Cottage, Model of. 105mm long.	19.50
Carnegie's Birthplace. 70mm long.	30.00
Cottage, thatched. 60mm long.	6.50
Cottage, inscribed: *Tigh-na-gaat centre of Scotland.* 85mm.	30.00
First and Last House in England. 83mm long.	10.50
John Knox's House. 112mm.	30.00
Old Town House Dunbar, The. 135mm.	47.50

Monuments

The Black Watch Memorial, Edinburgh. 127mm.	65.00

Historical/Folklore

James V Chair. Stirling Castle. 100mm.	7.50
Mary Queen of Scots Chair. 80mm.	6.50
Mons Meg, Edinburgh Castle. 130mm long.	11.00

Traditional/National Souvenirs

Welsh Hat. 54mm.	4.75

Seaside

Bathing Machine. 80mm.	9.50
Grace Darlings Boat, Model of. Fully coloured boat on brown rocks. 108mm long, unglazed.	30.00
Longship's Lighthouse, *Lands End.* 118mm.	14.50
Lighthouse on rocky base. 115mm.	4.50
Suitcase, closed. 80mm long.	4.00

Animals

Angry Cat Pincushion. 78mm.	12.50
Cheshire cat posy holder, 2 sizes:	
80mm long.	16.00
90mm long.	16.00
Collie, standing. 110mm long.	12.50
Dog, Bulldog, sitting. 55mm.	10.00
Fish. 130mm long.	4.00
Lion, standing, with verse: *Be Briton Still. . .* 130mm long.	16.00
Pig, lying down. 80mm long.	10.00
Pig, sitting. 100mm long.	12.50
Pig, sitting, inscribed: *You may push me.* 75mm.	12.50
Pig, standing. 35mm.	16.00
Rabbit. 60mm long.	6.50

Birds

Clara Cluck candlesnuffer. (Savoy No. 324) 70mm.	19.00

Great War

Scottish Soldier on circular base. 160mm.	110.00
Monoplane with revolving prop. 178mm long.	55.00
Airship, (Observation Balloon) inscribed: *Beta.* 80mm long.	40.00
Liner converted to a troop carrier inscribed: *HMS Lion.* 140mm long.	95.00
Battleship impressed: *HMS Lion.* 140mm long.	22.50

Torpedo Boat Destroyer, Model of
103mm long.   87.50

Torpedo Boat Destroyer, Model of 140mm long.	87.50
Red Cross Van. 87mm long.	23.00
Armoured Car (Reputedly a Talbot, but not named). 125mm long.	80.00
British Motor Searchlight, Model of. 103mm long.	145.00
Tank with inset steering wheels, inscribed: *HMS Donner Blitzen* and *515* on side. 140mm long.	30.00
Tank, no steering wheels. Inscription exactly the same as above. 135mm long.	30.00
British Trench Mortar Gun. 100mm long.	47.50
Field gun, Model of. 150mm long.	17.00
Shell, inscribed: *Iron rations for Fritz.* 160mm.	9.50
French Trench Helmet. 82mm long.	40.00
Glengarry. 87mm long.	16.00

Home/Nostalgic

Book. 60mm.	5.00

Alcohol

Thistle with inscription: *A wee deoch an doris.* 44mm.	4.00
Toby Jug. 62mm.	8.25

Musical Instruments

Upright Piano. 83mm long.	12.50

Transport

Charabanc. 125mm long.	33.00
Open Tourer. 112mm long.	30.00

Hats

Top Hat. 44mm.	5.50

Miniature Domestic

Cheese Dish. 1 piece. 40mm.	9.00
Cheese Dish and cover. 50mm.	10.00

Cambrian China

For mark see *Crested China*, p. 74.

Trademark used for a Welsh retailer by Wiltshaw and Robinson Ltd, Carlton Works, Stoke-on-Trent. (Usual trademark Carlton).

National Souvenir

Welsh Hat, Model of, with longest Welsh place name round brim. No. 283. 56mm.	7.50

Carlton China

For mark see *Crested China*, p. 76.

Trademark used by Wiltshaw and Robinson Ltd, Carlton Works, Stoke-on-Trent.

Only one Carlton model found with this mark, the usual Carlton mark has been sandpapered off and this applied on top. The mark is indicative of a Scottish thistle and the only piece known bears the Edinburgh arms.

For other Carlton marks see *Crested China*, p. 76.

Parian/Unglazed
Unglazed models are mostly busts which are on circular glazed bases, normally carrying crests.

Busts
Bust of King Edward VII, later models inscribed. 135mm.	47.50
Bust of King Edward VII in trilby.	55.00
Bust of Queen Alexandra. 135mm.	35.00
Bust of King George V. 135mm.	30.00
Bust of Queen Mary. 135mm.	30.00
Bust of Burns, with verse by Wordsworth. 120mm.	20.00
Bust of *Sir Edward Carson KC, MP* on round glazed base with inscription: *Ulster will fight and Ulster will be right. Edward Carson.* 130mm.	75.00
Bust of Joseph Chamberlain. 115mm.	56.50
Bust of Lord Kitchener. Can be found inscribed: *In Memoriam Lord Kitchener of Khartoum went down in HMS Hampshire June 5th 1916 off the Orkney Islands. He did his duty.* 135mm.	85.00
Bust of Ruskin. 135mm.	30.00
Bust of Shakespeare. 120mm.	16.00
Bust of Sydney, inscribed: *Sir Philip Sydney. Thy necessity is greater than mine.* 135mm.	40.00
Bust of *Wordsworth*, no base. 77mm.	17.50
Bust of Wordsworth, on glazed base, impressed: *Wordsworth.* 3 sizes: 115mm.	23.00
125mm.	23.00
135mm.	23.00

Ancient Artefacts
These models are often found not named, named models usually have a printed number and this is given where known. Most inscriptions begin: *Model of* so this will not be repeated throughout the list.

Ancient Lampfeeder found at St Mary's in a marsh near Hythe. 2 sizes: No. 330. 46mm.	4.00
No. 829. 67mm.	4.00
Ancient Tyg, 1 handle. No. 184. 66mm.	3.00
Ancient Tyg, 2 handles. No. 245. 66mm.	3.00
Ancient Vase 1st Century AD, original in Wedgwood Museum, Burslem. No. 375. 60mm.	3.00
Ancient Roman Vase now in Wedgwood Museum, Burslem 1st Century AD. No. 369. Rd No. 489060. 62mm.	3.00
No. 378. 65mm.	3.00
Cambridge Jug. No. 332. 60mm.	3.00
Chester Ancient Vase.	3.00
Chester Roman Jug. No. 261. 70mm.	4.00
Chester Roman Vase. Found numbered 154, 286 and 288 (possibly different shapes). 60mm.	3.00
Christchurch Harvest Vase, inscribed: *Ancient Harvest Vase found at Christchurch, Hampshire.* No. 407. 44mm.	3.50
Cobham Bottle, inscribed; *Model of Leather Bottle at Cobham, immortalised by Charles Dickens.* 60mm.	3.00

Colchester Ancient Vase,
4 models: No. 349. 50mm.	3.00
No. 351. 66mm.	3.00
No. 352. 55mm.	3.00
No. 353. 68mm.	3.00

Colchester Famous Vase.
| No. 80. 50mm. | 3.00 |

Dogger Bank Bottle.
| No. 251. 65mm. | 3.00 |

Dorchester Jug, inscribed: *Old Jug found in North Square, Dorchester.* No. 177. 52mm. 3.00

Dorchester Roman Jug found in Bath. 70mm. 3.00

Eddystone Jug. No. 180. 58mm. 3.00

Elizabeth Jug or Stoup, inscribed: *Model of the West Malling Elizabethan Jug or stoup hallmarked London 1581, sold for 1450 guineas.*
| 2 sizes: No. 360. 74mm. | 4.50 |
| 90mm. | 4.50 |

Etruscan Vase, inscribed: *Model of 4th Century Etruscan Vase.*
| 2 models: No. 262. 89mm long. | 3.00 |
| No. 227. 42mm. | 2.25 |

Fountains Abbey Cup.
| No. 238. 50mm. | 3.00 |

Glastonbury Bowl.
| No. 172. 39mm. | 3.00 |

Grecian Vase. No. 257. 78mm. 4.00

Grecian Water Vessel, Ancient No. 264. 85mm. 3.00

Hampshire Roman Vase.
| No. 247. 65mm. | 3.00 |

Hanley Chinese Vase.
| No. 263. 62mm. | 3.00 |

Hanley Cyprus Vase.
| No. 374. 45mm. | 3.00 |

Hanley Egyptian Vase.
2 different models:
| No. 367. 64mm (2 large handles from neck to body). | 3.00 |
| No. 368. 63mm. (2 tiny handles on body only). | 3.00 |

Hanley Roman Jug.
| No. 370. 55mm. | 3.00 |

Hanley Roman Vase. 2 vases:
| No. 372. 63mm. | 3.00 |
| No. 373. 50mm. | 3.00 |

Hastings Kettle. No. 166. 60mm. 1.75

Heckmondwicke Saxon Jug.
| No. 240. 80mm. | 3.00 |

Hull Suffolk Palace Jug. No. 276. 3.00

(Ancient) Irish Bronze Pot.
| No. 183. 45mm. | 3.00 |

Irish Kettle. No. 346. 65mm. 4.00

Jersey Milk Can, with lid.
| No. 242. 70mm. | 4.75 |

Lichfield Jug. No. 181. 60mm. 3.00

Lincoln Jack (from original in museum). No. 156. 60mm. 3.00

Loving Cup. 2 handled. Not named. No. 97. 38mm & 47mm. 3.00

Loving Cup. 3 handled. Not named. 53mm. 3.00

Merthyr Tydfil Roman Pottery.
4 models: No. 288. 75mm.	3.00
No. 382. 50mm.	3.00
No. 383. 52mm.	3.00
No. 384. 75mm dia.	3.00

Newbury Leather Bottle.
| No. 229. 65mm. | 3.00 |

New Forest Roman vase found in Hampshire. No. 243. 76mm. 4.00

Old Bronze Porridge Pot. No. 221 3.00

Penmaenmawr Urn.
| No. 213. 50mm. | 3.00 |

Phoenician Vase (originally in Hanley Museum). No. 174. 70mm. 3.00
| No. 259. 80mm. | 3.00 |

Plymouth Jug. No. 180. 58mm. 3.00

Pompeian Vessel, not named.
| 60mm. | 3.00 |

Portland Vase (now in British Museum), often found not named.
| 2 sizes: No. 89. 58mm. | 3.00 |
| No. 117. 80mm. | 3.00 |

Puzzle Jug, can be found with verse.
| 2 sizes: 68mm. | 5.50 |
| 90mm. | 6.50 |

Larger size carries verse.
Puzzle Teapot with verse. 60mm. 10.50

Roman Pottery.
3 models: No. 376. 65mm.	3.00
No. 377. 70mm.	3.00
No. 378. 68mm.	3.00

Roman Urn found at Milborne Port.
| No. 265. 44mm and 50mm. | 3.00 |

St. David's Vase. No. 249. 62mm. 3.00

Salisbury Kettle,
| 2 models: No. 188. 100mm. | 3.00 |
| No. 281. 77mm. | 3.00 |

Salopian Ewer. No. 75. 76mm. 3.00

Shakespeare's Jug. 70mm. 4.00

Silchester Urn. No. 193. 54mm. 3.00

Silchester Vase, inscribed: *Vase
from Silchester in Reading
Museum.* No. 171. 50mm.   3.00
Southampton Pipkin.
No. 204. 54mm.   3.00
Spilsby Jug. No. 299. 75mm.   3.00
(Old) Swedish Kettle.
No. 344. 70mm.   3.00
Weston Super Mare Vase.
No. 300. 80mm.   4.00
Winchelsea Vase. No. 87. 77mm.   3.00
Winchester Bushel. No. 323.
80mm dia.   12.50
Windsor Urn. No. 284. 50mm.   3.00
Wokingham Tankard.
No. 217. 78mmm.   3.50
York Roman Ewer. No. 178. 57mm.   3.00

Buildings — Coloured
*Dove Cottage, the early home of
Wordsworth, Model of.* 50mm.   130.00
Grasmere Church, Model of. 90mm.   75.00
*(The) Transport and General Workers
Union Convalescent Home,
Littleport.* 112mm long.   175.00
Hop Kiln. 98mm.   65.00

Buildings — White
Arundel Castle, The Keep.
120mm long.   47.50
Bandstand, inscribed: *O listen to
the band.* 85mm.   14.00
Beach House, Canvey-on-Sea.
65mm.   55.00
Blackpool Tower. 125mm.   13.00
Blackpool Tower with base.
2 sizes: 100mm.   8.75
164mm.   10.50
Blackpool Tower and Big Wheel
on ashtray, inscribed: *Good old
Blackpool.*
2 sizes: 108mm.   19.00
130mm.   21.50
Burns Cottage, Ayr. 70mm long.   14.00
Carnarvon Castle, Eagle Tower.
100mm.   75.00
Conway Castle. 130mm long.   100.00
Cottage. 50mm (very delicate).   9.50
Cottage with coloured doors,
hedges and windows with a
removable roof lid, and
inscribed: *Ours is a nice house
ours is,* or with verse *A little wife
well willed, A little farm well*

*tilled, A little mouse well
filled and I am satisfied.* 70mm.   35.00
Dellar's Cafe, Paignton. 62mm.   55.00
Douglas Jubilee Clock. 127mm.   40.00
Douglas Tower of Refuge. 73mm.   30.00
Downham Clock 'Presented to the
town by James Scott 1878'.
150mm.   40.00
*Dutch Cottage, Canvey Island, dated
1621.* 75mm (scarce).   82.50
Fair Maid's House, Perth. 92mm.
found with inscription: *Fair Maids
House 1393* and verse *"loves
darts cleaves hearts. . ."* Scott.   50.00
Farnham Castle, pearl lustre.
98mm.   22.00
Fire Engine House, Leatherhead.
115mm (uncommon).   82.50
Forth Bridge. 166mm long.
Also found in lustre.   30.00
God's Providence House Chester,
inscribed: *Gods providence is
mine inheritace.* 108mm.   30.00
Grasmere Church. 65mm.   65.00
Grimsby Hydraulic Tower, with
details. 165mm.   27.00
Guildford Castle. Ruins, with
inscription. 75mm.   48.50
Harrogate *Pump House.* 75mm.
Inscribed: *A nip and a smell from
the old sulphur well.*   35.00
Hastings Castle Ruins. 88mm.   22.00
Hastings Clock Tower.
2 sizes: 127mm.   22.00
156mm.   25.00
Hop Kiln with coloured transfer
of hop. 96mm.   27.50
Irish Cabin found with coloured
shamrocks round base. No. 516.   16.00
75mm long. Inscribed   26.00
Irish Cabin, with woman and
spinning wheel outside, some
colouring. 82mm.   34.50
Irish Round Tower. No. 520. 126mm.   10.50
Keswick Town Hall and Clock
Tower.   50.00
King Charles Tower, Chester.
2 sizes: 85mm.   30.00
105mm.   42.50
Laxey Wheel. 92mm (not often
found).   35.00
Lincoln Cathedral. No. 156. 60mm.   40.00
Marble Arch.
2 sizes: 90mm long.   14.00
127mm long.   16.00

Martello Tower, inscribed: *The Wish Tower, Martello Tower erected in 1804, the date of Napoleons threatened invasion* and verse. 67mm dia.   30.00

Martello Tower, as above as a trinket box and lid. 67mm dia.   30.00

Moot Hall, Keswick. 102mm.   50.00

Old Bishops Tower, Paignton. 82mm (rare).   75.00

Oldest chemyste shop in England, Ye. Knaresborough. Coloured roof and door. 100mm long.   60.00

Old Pete's Cottage, with detail of origin of Old Pete. 72mm long.   30.00

Old Town House, Dunbar. 130mm.   47.50

Old Welsh Cottage, Model of. No. 400. 75mm long.   21.50

Pithead, Model of. 110mm (rare).   75.00

Rochester Castle Keep. 80mm.   30.00

Scarton Church. 90mm long.   50.00

St. Leonards Tower, Newtonabbey. 123mm.   43.50

St. Nicholas Church, Lantern Hill, Ilfracombe. 98mm.   30.00
Also found with some colouring.   47.50

St. Pauls Cathedral. 112mm.   15.50

Scarborough Castle, Model of. 80mm.   35.00

Skegness Clock Tower. 124mm.   13.00

Smallest House in Wales at Conway. 115mm.   20.00

Tintern Abbey, with green moss on walls. 105mm long.   56.50

Tom Tower, Christchurch, Oxford. 127mm.   28.00

Torquay Clock Tower. Inscribed: *Model of Mallock Memorial, Torquay.* 168mm.   30.00

Tower Bridge, Model of. 88mm.   29.00

Trinity Castle Clock Gate. 90mm.   47.50

Upleatham Old Church, the smallest church in England. 80mm.   30.00

Wallace Tower. 140mm.   27.00

Wembley Exhibition, British Hall. 88mm long.   47.50

Wembley Stadium, inscribed: *Model of British Stadium Wembley* and details of cost and size. 110mm long.   35.00

Westminster Abbey, West Front.   30.00

Wimborne Minster.   47.50

Windmill with revolving sails, can be found inscribed: *The Sussex Windmill.* Add £5.00. 103mm.   19.50

A Window in Thrums. 55mm.   30.00

Windsor Castle. 135mm long.   20.00

Windsor Round Tower. 95mm.   14.00

York, Bootham Bar. 114mm.   19.00

York, Cathedral, West Front. 112mm.   26.00

York, Micklegate Bar. 112mm.   19.00

York, Walmgate Bar. 95mm long.   26.50

Monuments (including crosses)

Barrow Memorial, Ulverston 135mm.   25.00

The Beacon, Alderley Edge 1799, with verse. 102mm.   50.00

Burns Statue, Burns holding a crimson tipped daisy, with verse. 160mm (not often found).   30.00

Cairn on Culloden Battlefield 1746. 65mm.   40.00

Caister-on-Sea, Lifeboat Memorial. 160mm.   16.00

Captain Cook's Monument on square glazed base. 145mm.   30.00

Cavell Memorial Statue. 165mm. See Great War.

Celtic Cross. 142mm.   12.00

Colne Market Cross 1822-1902. 125mm (rare).   60.00

Feltwell Cross. 142mm.   19.50

Flora MacDonald. Statue. 160mm (not common).   35.00

Florence Nightingale Memorial. See Great War.

Garstang Market Cross, inscribed: *Model of Market Cross.* 135mm.   40.00

Globe, Swanage, (Model of the) Unglazed globe on glazed base. 86mm.   19.50

Tom Hughes, Monument. Rugby School. 135mm.   30.00

Hull, Fishermans Memorial, with inscription. 170mm.   16.00

Hull South African War Memorial. 170mm.   20.50

Irish Cross. No. 519, 2 sizes: 115mm and 136mm.   13.50

Locke Tower, inscribed: *This tower was erected in memory of the donor of Locke Park by P. Locke, Joseph Locke MP, AD 1877.* 135mm.   35.00

Mallock Memorial, Torquay. See Torquay Clock Tower. 165mm.

Morecombe Clock Tower. 127mm.   65.00

Nelson's Column, not found
named. 163mm. 45.00
Queen Eleanor's Memorial Cross,
Northampton. 138mm. 56.50
Ripon Market Cross. 115mm. 13.00
Rufus Stone. 96mm. 4.75
Ruskin Cross, Model of, unglazed
cross on glazed base.
Rd No. 597960. 170mm. 13.50
(John) Ruskin Statue.
2 sizes: 120mm. 19.50
172mm. 22.50
Selby Market Cross. 130mm. 60.00
Toad Rock, Tunbridge Wells.
78mm. 18.50
*Toad Rock, Near Hathersage, Model
of.* 100mm long. 25.00
Sir William Wallace Statue,
Stirling, with long inscription.
130mm. 35.00
Wilberforce Statue, Hull. 155mm. 29.50

Historical/Folklore

Bardic Chair, in lustre. 105mm. 21.50
Biddenden Maids, inscribed: *The
Biddenden Maids were born joined
together at hips and shoulders in
year 1100 and a 34Y in 1100.*
105mm. 40.00
Bonnie Prince Charles Chair. 1745.
110mm. 21.50
Caveman, standing figure
holding club. Brown hair and
club. Can have inscription:
*Billie Bus, the man who called for
the empties BC umpteen.* 113mm. 82.50
Crown. 70mm. 21.50
Dropping Well, Knaresborough,
coloured details and water.
75mm. 27.50
Font, not named. 133mm. 8.00
Fox's chair, inscribed: *Model of
chair of George Fox the Quaker,
original at Swarthmoor Hall
Ulverston.* 96mm. 45.00
Grace Darling's Boat, Model of, and
description. Boat in blue, white
on brown rocks. 108mm long. 21.50
Great Peter, Bell with clapper.
10 tons 15 cwts. 55mm. 21.75
John Waterson's Clog. 100mm long. 15.00
Judge, bust, inscribed: *Defend the
children of the poor, Punish the*

*wrongdoer (inscription on New
Bailey Courts London).* 16.00
70mm. with inscription   add £10.00
Man in Pillory with some colouring, 21.75
can have inscription: *Ample time
for Reflection.* 100mm. If coloured,
add £10.00.
Mary Queen of Scots Chair,
Edinburgh Castle. 80mm. 6.50
Mary Queen of Scots Bed,
inscribed: *The Bed of Mary
Queen of Scots, Holyrood Palace,
Edinburgh.* 90mm long. 60.00
Mother Shipton. 110mm. and
115mm. 16.00
Miner's Lamp. 110mm. 16.00
Mother Shipton, coloured figure
on lustre oval base. 90mm. 30.00
Nose of Brasenose College Oxford.
94mm long. 11.00
Old Cromwell Cannon. 130mm long. 17.00
Sanctuary Knocker, Durham, on
vase or wall pocket. 10.00
*Scarborough Ducking Chair formerly
fixed on the Pier for the purpose of
ducking scolding women!! Last
used on Mrs Gamble. Now in
Museum. Period 1795.*
Chair 95mm. 80.00
Sedan Chair, inscribed: *Model of
17th century Sedan Chair.* 70mm. 22.00
Thomas A'Becket Shoe.
105mm long. 13.00
Ulphus Horn. (York) on base.
115mm long (quite rare). 27.00
(The) Wallace Sword, inscribed: *The
sword that seem'd fit for the
Archangel to wield was light in his
terrible hand.* 105mm long. 30.00
Watchman's Lamp, inscribed:
*Model of 16th century Watchman's
Lamp* and *Watchman what of the
night.* 2 sizes:
80mm and 115mm. 6.50
Witch's Cauldron with Macbeth
verse *Double, double, toyle and
trouble, fyer burns and cauldron
bubble.* 45mm. 4.75
Witch's Cauldron on Tripod
(rustic). 115mm. 11.00
Cauldron, unglazed. 72mm. 3.00
Xit, The Historical Dwarf with
inscription. Figure. 137mm. 65.00

Traditional/National Souvenirs

John Bull, bust. 100mm.	19.50

John Bull with Bulldog, standing figure on oval base. Union Jack waistcoat and black hat, dog has red, white and blue collar.

125mm.	130.00

Blackpool Big Wheel. Can be found in pearl lustre.

2 sizes: 80mm.	10.50
100mm.	12.50
Bolton Trotter. 105mm long.	7.00

Bolton Trotter, hand holding a trotter inscribed: *A good hold on a Bolton Trotter.* 110mm long. 8.25

Cheddar Cheese, inscribed: *Prime Cheddar Cheese.* Can be found in dark yellow and with slice

out. 50mm.	5.50
with colour.	9.00

Cotton Shuttle, Model of.

93mm long.	35.00

Lancashire Clog with verse: *There's many a factory lass wi' clogs on her feet.* 100mm long. 7.50

Lincoln Imp moulded in relief on Lincoln Jack, inscribed: *The Imp, Lincoln Cathedral.*

No. 156. 60mm.	9.50

Kelly from the Isle of Man. 3 legged man, holding Manx Kipper in

hand, fully coloured. 110mm.	80.00
Manx Legs on base. 95mm.	16.00

(The) *Ripon Horn* on rectangular base, inscribed.

2 sizes: 80mm.	12.50
120mm.	12.50

Ripon Hornblower, Model of with

verse. .120mm.	16.00

(The) Sheffield Grinding Stone.

80mm long (rare).	60.00

York Minster, The Fiddler of.

132mm.	70.00

Yorkshireman, standing figure holding tankard — often found not named. Found with inscription: *Take hod and sup lad*

and verses. 126mm.	30.00

Irish Cabin Trunk, more often found without this inscription.

58mm long. Inscribed add £8.00.	10.50

Irish Colleen, on circular base. Can have some colouring.

125mm.	56.50

Irishman, in black hat with yellow pig, standing on rectangular base, green edge, inscribed: *X miles to Belfast* and *Don't be radin milestones all the day Allana.*

90mm long.	95.00

Irish Harp, with green shamrocks.

90mm.	8.00

Irish Harp, Model of surmounted by crown. Decorated with

shamrocks. 105mm.	10.00

Irish Jaunting Car, with horse and driver, some colouring.

130mm long (This is quite rare).	110.00

Irish Spinning Wheel. Irish lady sitting by spinning wheel.

95mm.	65.00
Saint Patrick's Mitre. 70mm.	27.00
Bagpipes. 114mm.	16.00

Crown of Scotland, inscribed: *'The Crown of Scotland. Robert Bruce Crowned 1300, Buried Dunfermline 1329'.* 68mm. 30.00

Gretna Green, Model of Blacksmiths Anvil. This anvil is often found without inscription or verse.

70mm. With verse add £3.	4.50

Scotch Fisher Girl at Work, coloured

fish in barrel. 118mm.	40.00

Scotsman, standing figure, blue tam-o'-shanter with red bobble and brown walking stick. With verse *Just a wee deoch and doris.*

130mm. Harry Lauder.	80.00

Tam-o'shanter (bonnet) with coloured sprig of heather.

80mm dia.	24.50
Thistle hat pin holder. 80mm.	9.00

Thistle moulded Teapot with lid and coloured thistle handle,

can be found in lustre. 85mm.	12.50

Thistle Vase, can be found with verse.

2 sizes: 76mm and 115mm.	3.00
Prince of Wales Feathers. 95mm.	13.00

Pat's Hat and dudeen, green ribbon and black dudeen. With *Tipperary* inscription on

reverse. 45mm.	20.00

Welsh Hat, Model of, can be found with longest Welsh place name round brim. No. 283. for which

add £2.50. 56mm.	5.00

Welsh Hat, with orange band. Can
be found in lustre with a
coloured transfer 'Welsh
Teaparty'. for which add £6.00.
44mm. | 5.00

Welsh Leek, Model of, leaves
coloured green. 93mm. | 5.25

Welsh Leek, coloured black,
Lucky White Heather, 93mm. | 6.50

Jenny Jones, Welsh lady, standing
figure with black hat, brown
basket and red and green shawl.
147mm. Two varieties. | 35.00

Welsh Spinning Wheel, two Welsh
ladies with spinning wheel,
coloured hats and shawls.
95mm. | 50.00

Welsh Tea Party, three Welsh ladies
taking tea, coloured hats and
shawls, etc. 90mm. | 40.00

Bermuda Sailing Ship, can be found
with Bermuda crest.
127mm long. | 21.50

Gondola. 127mm long. | 14.50

Seaside Souvenirs

Bathing Machine, found
inscribed: *Morning dip.* Sizes
vary from 55mm. to 70mm. | 7.50

Lifebelt. 105mm dia. | 12.50

Lifeboat. Can be found inscribed:
Queensbury for which £8.00
should be added. 113mm long. | 12.50

Gondola. 127mm long. | 14.50

Motor Boat on waves.
120mm long. | 14.00

Motor Boat with Driver on waves.
120mm long. | 20.00

Punt with two women, some
colouring. 113mm long. | 75.00

Rowing Boat. (already covered in
historic) 108mm long. | 8.00

Trawler, inscribed on sail: *SM.*
115mm long. | 22.50

Yacht with billowing sail, some
colouring. 120mm long. | 20.00

Yacht, in full sail, found inscribed:
Saucy Sue. 110mm long. | 24.50

Fisherman on Rock, holding
brown net, inscribed: *Son of the
sea.* 117mm. | 30.00

Fisherman's Creel. 70mm long. | 5.50

Lifeboatman, bust with colouring
on face. 80mm. | 24.50

Lifeboatman in boat on sea, black
clothing. Lustre. 100mm. | 29.50

Lighthouse inscribed: *Sailor
Beware.* 140mm. | 10.50

Barness Lighthouse, Dunbar
116mm. | 40.00

Beachy Head Lighthouse, with
inscription. 148mm. | 9.00

Douglas Lighthouse. 128mm. | 75.00

Eddystone Lighthouse, Model of,
with probably just a Brixham
crest. 138mm. | 10.50

Flamborough Lighthouse, Model of.
Can be found as a hatpin
holder. 115mm. | 25.75

*Flamborough Head Fog Siren
Building.* 87mm long. | 47.50

Lighthouse Hatpin Holder
inscribed: *Girdleness.* 136mm. | 11.00

*Mumbles Lighthouse and Telegraph
Office.* 127mm. | 40.00

*Pharos Lighthouse Fleetwood,
Model of.* No. 409. 100mm
(Identical model, so named and
with same stock number can be
found as a pepper pot — same
price). | 5.50

Scarborough Lighthouse. 135mm. | 65.00

Scarborough Lighthouse, Model of,
with rectangular building
showing shell holes from Great
War. 98mm (rare). | 65.00

Withernsea Lighthouse. 134mm. | 12.00

Lighthouse pepper pot. 100mm. | 6.00

Limpet Shell with 3 feet. 23mm. | 5.00

Oyster Shell, found inscribed: *A
Whitstable native.* add £3.00. 70mm. | 4.50

Scallop Shell on 3 tiny feet.
80mm long. | 3.00

Shell Inkwell, inscribed: *We are
always glad to hear from you.*
95mm. | 10.50

Whelk Shell, inscribed: *Listen to
the sea.* 100mm long. | 4.25

Shell pin tray. | 3.00

Luggage Trolley inscribed: *Luggage
in Advance* and/or *LMS
Railway to Timbuktoo.* Can be
found in lustre. 76mm long. | 40.00

Valise (or travelling case) with
two straps.
2 sizes: 55m. | 4.00
70mm long. | 6.00

Bathing Beauty, reclining figure
with green or blue cap.
110mm long. | 50.00

Bathing Beauty lying on edge of lustre shell dish, bathing costume in several colours. Inscribed: *Washed up by the tide.* 110mm. 45.00

Boy on Donkey, can be found inscribed: *Gee up Neddy* or more occasionally: *This beats going to school.* Can be found without base. 98mm long. 65.00

Mr. Punch, bust. 82mm. 35.00

Punch and Judy Booth, with coloured Punch and Judy. Inscribed: *Good Morning Mr Punch.* 133mm. 56.50

Countryside

Beehive on square stand, with coloured transfer of bee. 64mm. 7.50

Campfire, cauldron inside three upright poles on triangular base. 122mm. 11.50

Pinecone, upright, closed. 79mm. 4.00

Tree Trunk candleholder. 113mm. 6.00

Tree Trunk vase, the Great Oak in Sherwood Forest, Nottingham. 115mm. 11.50

Farmer driving pig to market. Some colouring. Inscribed: *Don't be radin milestones all the day allana.* 88mm long. 125.00

Animals

Ape (Orang-utan) holding orange, brown face, 58mm. 19.50

Bear, looks like a Polar Bear, inscribed: *Russian Bear.* 130mm long. 45.00

Bear and Ragged staff. 85mm. 19.00

Bear wearing hat sitting on base. 104mm. 45.00

Bull, inscribed: *King of the Herd,* or much more rarely: *The Ox of Oxford.* 103mm long. 65.00

Cat, angry, with back up, inscribed: *My word if you're not off* or *The Midnight Rambler.* add £10.00. 80mm. 12.50

Cat, Cheshire, inscribed: *The Cheshire cat,* and *The smile that won't come off.* 90mm. 12.50

Cat, crouching. 81mm. 14.50

Cat lying down, tail curled up behind. 84mm long. 57.50

Cat (black), doing hand stand on oblong base, back legs up in air. Inscribed: *Well what about it.* 115mm (rare). 85.00

Cat, Manx. 75mm. 16.00

Manx Cat, back up, coloured face. Inscribed: *I am Rumpy* on forehead. 60mm. 23.50

Cat, long necked, inscribed: *My word* etc. 110mm. 8.75

Cat sitting, chubby and kittenish. 63mm. 10.00

Cat sitting on square cushion, impressed: *Good Luck.* 80mm. 10.50

Cat sitting, with red bow, salt pot or pepper pot. 70mm. 10.50

Cat sitting, wearing black topper with shamrock, bow tie can be found coloured red or green. Also found in lustre. 88mm. 13.00

Cat sitting, with blue bow (bow sometimes left uncoloured) 56mm. 12.00

Cat sitting, with Swastika round neck. 59mm. 10.00

This cat can also be found on a pouffe and inscribed: *Good Luck.* 85mm. 14.50

Black Cat, small, can be found with accompanying model coloured red or yellow, for which £20.00 should be added. Found on the following:

Armchair (upholstered) with green swastika and red horseshoe on arms, inscribed: *Jolly good luck.* 75mm. 26.00

(Old) Armchair with solid arms. 90mm. 24.50

Ashtray, circular, can be found with transfer of cigarette, inscribed: *Who burnt the cloth.* 110mm dia. 30.00

Ashtray, club shaped, lustre. 90mm long. 20.00

Ashtray, diamond shaped, lustre. 95mm long (It seems very likely that small black cats will be found on heart and spade shaped ashtrays as well and that all four were made in white and lustre. 20.00

Chair. 90mm. 24.50

Horseshoe ashtray, inscribed: *Jolly good luck.* 105mm long. 22.00

Piano. 95mm. 65.00

Pillar Box. Inscribed: *Good luck.* 110mm.	55.00
Rocking Chair, lustre. 100mm.	35.00
Sofa. Inscribed: *Jolly good luck.* 80mm.	28.00
Trinket box, inscribed: *Trinkets.* 93mm long.	22.00
Trinket Box, inscribed: *Hairpins.* 57mm long.	22.00

Black Cat, large, found on the following:

Oval base with coloured Swastika and horseshoe. Inscribed: *Good luck,* Base can be found in mother-of-pearl or blue lustre. 85mm.	21.50
Pouffe, the cat's bow is found blue instead of usual red. Inscribed: *Good luck.* 90mm.	22.50
Black Cat and Kitten on ashtray with match holder. Inscribed: *Don't scratch me, scratch mother.* Can be in maroon lustre. 70mm.	30.00
Chimpanzee. 84mm.	19.00
Doe on oval stand. 118mm.	65.00
Bulldog, sitting, inscribed: *Bill Sykes dog.* 95mm.	13.50
Bulldog, sitting, thin faced. Inscribed: *Model of Bill Sykes dog* and sometimes found also inscribed: *My word if your're not off.* 51mm.	19.50
Bulldog, standing, inscribed: *My word if you're not off;* can be found inscribed: *Slow to start, but what a hold.* Inscribed add £8.00. 120mm long.	13.00
Dog (French Bulldog), sitting with pricked-up ears and blue eyes. 57mm.	10.50
Dog (French Bulldog), inscribed: *My word if you're not off.* 100mm.	20.00
Dog, standing Collie. Inscribed: *Scotch Collie.* 110mm long.	40.00
Dog playing banjo, inscribed: *Some Band.* 83mm.	26.00
Dog looking out of kennel, inscribed: *The Blackwatch.* Dog's head is coloured black. 85mm.	15.00
Dog (Puppy) in slipper. Puppy coloured brown. 100mm long.	30.00
Dog (Puppy) sitting with one ear raised. Can be found painted blue, add £10.00. 83mm.	8.25
With painted spots.	11.50

This puppy can be found on a hand mirror (silvered) inscribed: *Me twice.* 105mm long.	32.50
Dog, Scottie, begging, pink ears and red collar. Can be found coloured red, add £10.00. 74mm.	17.00
Dog, Scottie, begging, wearing a glengarry, some colouring. 105mm.	11.00
Dog, Scottie, sitting, wearing a tartan tam-o'shanter with orange bobble. Also found in lustre. 2 sizes: 60mm.	11.00
80mm.	11.00
Dog, Scottish Terrier, standing with tail in the air. Found inscribed: *As old Mrs Terrier said to her pup in all lifes adversities keep your tail up.* 100mm long.	12.50
Dog, standing, impressed on collar: *Caesar* and inscribed: *I am the Kings dog.* Some colouring. 106mm long.	40.00
Donkey, inscribed: *Gee up Neddy.* 110mm long.	30.00
Elephant, walking. 51mm.	15.00
Elephant with raised trunk. 51mm.	16.00
Fawn. 70mm.	25.00
Field Mouse, on base. 54mm.	16.00
Fish (Salmon), 112mm long.	4.00
Fish ashtray, inscribed: *A plaice for the ashes.* 120mm long.	7.50
Flamborough Donkey, with orange and blue rosettes. 88mm (rare).	70.00
Monkey, sitting hands to mouth. 90mm.	39.50
Pig sitting on haunches, inscribed: *Wont be druv or You can push, you can shuv but I'm hanged if I'll be druv.* 60mm.	12.50
Pig, standing, found inscribed: *Wont be druv.* Also found entirely coloured blue. for which add £10.00. 65mm long.	10.00
Pig, fat and standing, found inscribed: *Wont be druv.* 80mm long.	14.50
Pig, standing, fat, found inscribed: *You can push, etc.* or *I'm the fellow who pays the rent.* for which add £20.00 94mm long.	12.50

Pig, sitting, wearing coloured German Pickelhaube and with Iron Cross on left breast. Pepper Pot. Reg. No. 642626. 90mm. Very rare. 150.00

Piglet, standing. 70mm long. 10.00

Rabbit, crouching with pricked ears. 65mm long. 6.50

Shetland Pony. 138mm long. 30.00

Stag with large antlers on oval stand. 146mm. Probably sold as a pair with doe, but less of them around, possibly because the antlers are fragile. 75.00

Teddy Bear. 85mm. 12.50

Terrapin. 75mm long. 11.00

Three Wise Monkeys on wall. Inscribed: *Speak no evil, see no evil, hear no evil.* Can be found coloured brown with red faces on white wall (add £8.00). 90mm. 10.50

These monkeys coloured brown can be found on an ashtray base with the same inscription. 90mm long. 12.00

Welsh Goat on rocky base, inscribed: *Yr Afr Cymreig* (The Welsh Goat). No. 391. 96mm. 56.50

Wembley Lion on ashtray base, some colouring. 60mm (This was the stylised lion symbol of the British Empire Exhibition and is usually found with BEE crest). 17.50

Birds (including eggs)

Hen roosting. 60mm long. 6.50

Hen and Cock, salt, pepper and mustard pots, some colouring. 70mm each 8.75

Chicken hatching from egg. 64mm long. 5.50

Egg cracked open, lying on side. 74mm long. 4.00

Owl, baby. 66mm. 12.50

Owl, wearing black mortar board with red tassel. (Models with Irish crests can be found with red mortar boards.) 75mm. 14.50

Models can also be found fully coloured. 22.50

Owl cream jug. 88mm. 10.50

Owl, pepper pot. 92mm. 15.25

Owl, fully coloured, on oval ashtray base. 70mm. 30.00

Parrot, inscribed: *Pretty Polly.* 74mm. 14.50

Peacock. Can be found coloured blue, add £10.00. 63mm. 14.50

Stork with pink beak, standing on one leg. 110mm. 20.00

Swan.
3 sizes: 55mm. 6.50
63mm. 6.50
76mm long. 6.50

Smallest can be found coloured red (add £10.00).

Swan pepper pot. 53mm. 6.00

Swan posy bowl. 78mm. 6.50

Woodpecker, comic, some colouring on wings, beak and feet. 60mm. 35.00

Carlton made a series of 5 birds on green bases and these are listed below:

Cock standing on green base, some colouring to head. 85mm long. 22.00

Duck standing on green base, yellow beak. Also found in lustre. 72mm. 21.50

Duck standing up, rather comic, on green base. 102mm. 28.00

Duck airing wings, green base, yellow beak. 80mm. 23.00

Turkey on green base, coloured beak and feet. 21.50

Can also be found in lustre and red or blue. 70mm. 30.00

Great War

Many Great War models are found with the following Victory inscriptions: *The Victory of Justice, Armistice of the Great War signed Nov 11th 1918* and *Victory of Justice. Peace signed at Versailles June 28th 1919.* These add interest but not value.

Munitions Worker, inscribed: *Doing her bit* and *Shells and more shells,* some colouring. 140mm. 80.00

Nurse with red cross, inscribed: *A friend in need.* 150mm. 40.00

Old Bill, standing figure of Bruce
Bairnsfather's cartoon character.
Inscribed: *Yours to a
cinder.* Can be found white   60.00
coloured. 138mm.   80.00
Sailor, bust. Inscribed: *The Handy
Man* and *HMS Dreadnought.*
85mm.   30.00
Sailor standing to attention with
blue trim. Inscribed: *Handy
Man.* 135mm.   75.00
Scottish Soldier with rifle, wearing
glengarry, some colouring.
148mm.   135.00
Scottish Soldier with bagpipes,
wearing bearskin, some
colouring. Very rare. 148mm.   175.00
Scottish Soldier with rifle,
wearing bearskin (busby) Some
colouring. Rare. 153mm.   175.00
Soldier standing to attention,
inscribed: *Are we downhearted
No!* and with verse *Its a long way
to Tipperary.* 153mm.   65.00
Soldier standing to attention with
ammunition belt worn over
shoulder. 125mm (rare).   125.00
Biplane with movable propellor.
145mm long.   95.00
Can be found with coloured
roundel and tail.   125.00
Also found with coloured
roundel and tail with skids instead of wheels. Very rare.
140mm long.   175.00
Biplane, with coloured roundels
and tailplane with movable
propellor. 165mm long.   145.00
Monoplane, rounded fuselage
and movable prop. 134mm long.   55.00
Monoplane, square fuselage and
movable prop. 140mm long.   55.00
Zeppelin or Airship with
moulded Iron Cross on side;
can be found with cross
painted black, or left white and
coloured roundels on nose.
118mm long.   40.00
with RAF roundels.   50.00
with French roundels.   60.00
*British mine sweeper whose splendid
work will live forever in the annals
of British history.* Can be found

inscribed: *HMS Gowan Lea,
HMS Peggy* or *HMS Mine-
sweeper.*   40.00
115mm long.   named 60.00
A very rare version exists in-
scribed: *HMD Indian Summer.*   95.00
Battleship, 2 funnels, 4 guns fore,
4 guns aft. 160mm long. Named:
*HMS Canada, HMS Australia,
HMS Marlborough*   65.00
Battleship, 3 funnels, 4 guns fore,
2 guns aft. 160mm long. Named:
*HMS Renown, HMS Iron Duke,
HMS Princess Royal, HMS
Warspite, HMS Inflexible.*   60.00
Battleship, 4 funnels, 2 guns fore,
4 guns aft. 160mm long.
Named: *HMS Lion, HMS Tiger.*   55.00
Battleship, 3 funnels, 4 guns fore,
2 guns midships, 2 guns aft.
Named: *HMS Lion, HMS Queen
Elizabeth.* 167mm long.   57.50
All the above can be found with
the following Victory inscription
only: *Great War 1914-18. The
German Fleet surrendered 74
warships Nov 21st 1918.*
Battleship, 3 funnels. Both bow
and stern rolled inwards.
120mm long.   22.50
Battleship with high prow,
inscribed: *HMS Humber, Model
of British Monitor.* Has also been
found with same Victory inscription as above and not named.
Inscribed: *Dreadnought.*   30.00
140mm long. Named.   56.50
Battleship with high prow, two
rear guns pointing upwards,
(not flat on deck). Rare.   60.00
HM Hospital Ship Anglia, Model of
with 2 funnels, often found
with further detailed inscription:
*Model of British Hospital
Ship whose voyage was disregarded
on three occasions by the
German Submarines.*
165mm long. (Has been found
wrongly named as *HMS Tiger*
and as *RMS Lusitania*).   70.00
RMS Lusitania, 4 funnels. Found
with details of sinking: *The
Lusitania was sunk by a German
Submarine May 7th 1915.
Lives lost 1198,* or the numerically
incorrect inscription: *Sunk*

*by German Submarine off the Irish
Coast, May 7th 1915. Lives lost
1275, Saved 703.* 168mm long.   75.00

British Submarine, Model of, blunt
nosed, often found without this
inscription but with E9 on side.
Submarines found unnamed
are found with the following
inscription: *Great War 1914-18.
150 German U Boats surrendered
Nov 20th 1918.* With or without
pinnacle. 140mm long.   30.00

*British submarine, Model of, half-
submerged,* inscribed: *E9.*
124mm long.   50.00

*Submarine, pointed nose and fish
tail,* inscribed: *E9.* 146mm long.
(Much rarer than blunt nosed
model).   43.00

Ambulance with 3 red crosses and
WD on radiator. 100mm long.   28.00

Armoured Car with Rolls-Royce
type front. 120mm long.   155.00
Difficult to find in perfect
condition.

Armoured Car with 3 guns on
turret, inscribed: *RNAS.*
116mm long.   82.50

British Anti-Aircraft Motor, Model of,
inscribed: *RNAS.* 121mm long.   90.00

Tank with trailing steering
wheels, inscribed: *HMLS Creme
de Menthe.*
130mm long.   25.00
Found with Victory inscription:
*The British Tank successfully used
against the Germans, Combles,
Sept 1916.*   30.00

Tank with no steering wheels,
inscribed: *HMLS.*
4 sizes: 80mm long.   110.00
        95mm long.   70.00
        134mm long.   26.00
        156mm long.   35.00
134mm & 156mm sizes are inscribed *HMLS Creme-de-Menthe*
and *130* and can be found with
Victory inscriptions. Also *The
British Tank gave them hell at
Marne 1918* and *Buy War Bonds.
The British Tank successfully used
against the Germans, Combles,
Sept. 1916.*

Tank Bank, as largest size tank
above but with slot for coins.
Two sizes of slot. Inscribed:
Buy War Bonds, and can be
found with *Combles* and
Marne inscriptions. 156mm long.   50.00

HM Whippet Tank. 121mm long.   95.00

Italian Fiat Tank, not named.
100mm long. (Very rare).   300.00

Vickers Tank, not named. 126mm
long (rare). The latest model
manufactured, approx. 1928-32.   215.00

British Machine Gun, Model of. MG
in green wreaths on barrel.
2 moulds, one with open
stand. 100mm long.   30.00

British Naval Gun, Model of.
88mm long (very rare).   175.00

British Trench Mortar, Model of.
Mounted on steps and barrel at
an angle. 66mm.   15.00

Trench Mortar, not named, with
horizontal barrel. 60mm.   13.00

Field Gun, found inscribed:
French 75. 2 sizes: 17.00
130mm & 148mm long.   named 22.00

Field Gun with screen and sight-
hole, inscribed: *French 75.*
145mm long.   28.00

British 15″ Shell. Model of. 90mm.   9.00

Cannon Shell, Model of. No. 606.
75mm.   5.00

German Incendiary Bomb, Model of.
75mm.   20.00

British Hand Grenade. 83mm.   16.00

Floating Mine. Model of. 83mm.   40.00

British Searchlight, Model of. Sometimes found inscribed: *The*   25.00
Zeppelin Finder. 68mm.   Inscribed 30.00

Capstan, Model of, with
brown rope. 70mm.   13.00

Bandsman's Drum, mustard pot,
found in lustre. 45mm.   7.50

Australian Hat, inscribed: *Anzacs*   12.00
for ever. 75mm long.   Inscribed 16.00

Colonial Hat, often found un
named. Also found inscribed.
Anzacs for ever.   10.50
95mm dia.   Inscribed 16.00

Forage Cap. 80mm long.   14.50

Glengarry with coloured thistle.
78mm long.   14.50

Officer's Peaked Cap, coloured
band. 78mm long.   10.00

Territorials Hat, coloured hat band.
85mm dia.   14.50

Kitbag, open neck, with verse. 72mm.	15.00
Kitbag, closed neck, with verse. 72mm.	15.00
Bell Tent. 66mm. Can be found	10.50
named *Tommies Bungalow*. 70mm.	17.00
Blighty. Map of England and Wales, with verse *Take me back to dear Old Blighty*. 115mm.	47.50
Kitchen Range, with black kettle but no teapot. Inscribed: *Keep the home fires burning till the boys come home*. 70mm.	13.00
Kitchen Range with black kettle and brown teapot. Inscribed: *We've kept the home fires burning till the boys came home*. 70mm.	16.00
Shrapnel Villa, Tommies Dugout somewhere in France. (From Bruce Bairnsfather's cartoons). 83mm long.	34.50
Blackpool War Memorial. 130mm.	56.50
Brighton War Memorial. 105mm long. (Building, not a statue).	100.00
Cenotaph, inscribed: *The Glorious Dead* with 2 green wreaths.	
2 sizes: 105mm.	6.00
146mm.	8.00
Clacton-on-Sea War Memorial. 148mm.	45.00
Cranbrook War Memorial. 130mm.	110.00
Douglas War Memorial. Can be found with lustre finish. 160mm.	75.00
Dunbar War Memorial. 123mm.	110.00
Edith Cavell, statue, inscribed: *Brussels dawn October 12th 1915. Sacrifice. Humanity.*	
2 sizes: 140mm.	10.50
163mm.	14.50
Elgin War Memorial. 165mm.	120.00
Feltwell War Memorial. 140mm.	110.00
Florence Nightingale, 1820-1910 The Lady of the Lamp. 175mm.	16.00
Northallerton War Memorial. 115mm.	82.50
Ripon War Memorial, found with Ripon Hornblower inscription. 115mm.	110.00 75.00

Tunbridge Wells War Memorial, soldier unglazed on glazed plinth carrying a rifle with fixed bayonet. With inscription: *Our Glorious Dead 1914-18. Honour, Gratitude, Praise.* 170mm.	90.00
Ulverston War Memorial. 140mm.	100.00

Home/Nostalgic

Anvil on tree stump base. 76mm.	5.50
Baby lying on side holding mug with dirty cheeks. Sometimes inscribed: *Mothers Darling*. Some colouring. 140mm long.	75.00
Basket of coloured fruit 88mm (Almost Art Deco).	21.50
Bellows. 95mm.	5.50
Book with lock. 66mm.	4.75
Clock, shaped. 83mm.	16.00
Coal Scuttle. 60mm.	4.00
Dog Kennel. 62mm.	4.50
Dust Pan, inscribed: *Who said dust.* 94mm long.	8.00
Inscribed	10.50
Fireplace, with a kettle and teapot in the hearth, and dogs and clock on the mantelpiece. Found inscribed: *By my Ain Fireside* or *East, West, Home is best*. 85mm.	19.00
Fireplace with clock and dogs on mantelpiece, cauldron on fire and black cat by side. Inscribed as above. 80mm.	17.00
Flat Iron, can be found in lustre. 60mm.	8.00
Frying Pan Rd. No. 537474. 110mm long.	6.50
Grandfather Clock, Model of. No. 389.	
2 sizes: 105mm.	10.50
135mm.	13.00
Grandmother Clock, inscribed: *Gude morn.*	
3 sizes: 88mm.	16.00
105mm and 135mm.	16.00
Kettle, fixed lid, inscribed: *Polly put the kettle on, we'll have some tea.* 80mm.	18.00

Lantern, inscribed: *Watchman what of the night?* 83mm.	7.50
Milk Can with lid. 55mm.	3.00
(The) Old Armchair, solid arms, with verse or inscribed: *Jolly Good Luck.* 88mm.	7.50
(The) Old armchair, open 'barley twist' arms, with verse. 120mm.	12.50
Pillar Box GVR, found inscribed: *If you haven't time to post a line here's the pillar box.* 73mm.	8.00
inscribed	10.00
Pillar Box *E VII R.* 72mm.	14.00
Rocking Chair. 98mm.	19.50
Saucepan with lid. 100mm long.	6.00
Shaving Mug. 58mm.	5.50
Sofa. 90mm long. (Lustre).	12.50
Spinning Wheel, found inscribed: *Model of ye olde spinning wheel* or more rarely: *The exact model of 14th Century spinning wheel.* 74mm.	17.50
Stool, three-legged. 40mm.	5.00
Sundial, round, inscribed: *Model of ye olde English sundial,* and *What' o'clock: lifes but a walking shadow.* No. 525.	
3 sizes: 80mm.	7.50
120mm.	12.50
140mm.	15.50
Sundial, square. Inscribed: *Let others tell of storms & showers, I'll only count the sunny hours.* 86mm.	7.50
Teapot, fixed lid. Inscribed: *Polly put the kettle on. . .* 80mm.	12.50
Time Glass. 60mm.	10.00
Thimble. 40mm.	10.50
Trug. 75mm.	4.75
Village Water Pump, round or square. 76mm.	11.00
Warming Pan, inscribed: *Sally warm the bed.* No. 392. 127mm long.	8.75
Wooden Basket. 50mm (rare).	10.50

Comic/Novelty

Altar Inkwell with two orange and black candle holders and Buddha-like figure as cover for inkwell. Rare complete, inscribed: *Sox Kik the god of luck and cheerfulness.* Can be found in lustre. 90mm long.	40.00

Baby Girl Handbell, with metal clapper. 100mm.	16.00
Beaver, man with very long beard on base, some colouring. 120mm.	60.00
Billiken, flat faced grotesque type. 63mm.	4.75
Billiken sitting on high backed chair with thumbs raised, inscribed: *Thumbs up.* 84mm.	7.50
Billiken without chair. 84mm.	7.50
Black Girl in hip bath, inscribed: *I'se making ink.* Can be lustre. 80mm long.	40.00
Black Girl in hip bath (different from above) same inscription. 85mm long.	40.00
Choir Boy Handbell. 88mm.	16.00
Cigarettes, matches and ash, container with cigarette on lid. 85mm long.	15.00
Clown, bust, inscribed: *Put me amongst the girls.* Some colouring. 75mm.	17.00
Girl, toddler, with outstetched arms on circular plinth, inscribed: *Diddle'ums.* Some colouring to face and bonnet. 125mm.	80.00
Humpty Dumpty: see sports.	
I'm forever blowing bubbles. Pears advert Blue Boy blowing bubbles. Clothes blue, bubble and bowl lustre. 110mm.	75.00
Ye Jester awake, Ye jester asleep double faced bust.	
2 sizes: 70mm.	7.50
84mm.	14.50
Larger size found inscribed: *John Citizen,* man carrying sack inscribed: *Housing, unemployment, taxes.* Hat and face coloured. 95mm.	82.50
Negro Minstrel, bust, verse by Eugene Stratton. 85mm.	
white.	16.00
coloured face.	34.50
Oval Rich Tea, brown biscuit on white base.	25.75
Policeman hailing: *From. . . . .* 138mm.	25.00
Policeman with raised hand, inscribed: *A policeman's lot is not a happy one.* 140mm.	22.00

Preserve Pot with coloured pear
and two leaves on lid.
Inscribed: *Preserve* (Lustre)
85mm.   10.50

Sack of Meal with mouse peeping out. Mouse can be coloured
grey. 75mm.   13.00

Suffragette Handbell inscribed:
Votes for Women and *She shall
have Votes.* 100mm.   35.00

Truck of Coal, *Black diamonds
from. . .* rarely inscribed
Brought down from Sunderland, add
£5.00. Can be found in lustre.
2 sizes: 60mm long, 95mm long   16.00

Weighing Machine inscribed: *Try
your weight.* 120mm.   26.00

Yes we have no bananas, oval Dish
with yellow bananas. 115mm.
Can be found in lustre.   13.00

Cartoon/Comedy Characters

Jackie Coogan, coloured figure of
boy film star, attached to white
tree trunk, ink well with lid.
73mm.   30.00

Harry Lauder, bust, with red
bobble on hat and coloured
thistle. 80mm.   30.00

Ally Sloper, bust, inscribed: *Vote
for Sloper etc.* Some colouring.
85mm.   40.00

Bonzo Dog, standing upright,
not named. Red tongue.
110mm.   30.00

Bonzo Dog, with fly on his tail.
Inscribed: *When yor're on a good
thing stick to it.* Can be found
unnamed.   40.00

Felix the Cat on oval base,
inscribed: *Felix kept on walking.*
Coloured Felix, swastika
and horseshoe on base. 75mm.   56.50

Felix the Cat on lustre armchair,
with Felix inscription.
Coloured Felix. 75mm.   52.50

Felix the Cat on ashtrays (various
shapes).   43.50

Felix the Cat on lustre pillar box,
with Felix inscription.
Coloured Felix. 115mm.   60.00

Felix the Cat on lustre sofa,
with Felix inscription.
Coloured Felix. 90mm.   56.50

Felix the Cat on *Hatpins* box and
lid. 80mm long.   43.00

Felix the Cat on Trinket box,
with Felix inscription.
Coloured Felix. 93mm long.   43.00

Felix the Cat on rectangular base,
a much larger and well
modelled Felix than the above,
with Felix inscription.
Cat is black. 82mm (very rare).   110.00

Winkie the Gladeye Bird, some
colouring. 68mm.   15.00

Woody Woodpecker, fully coloured.
63mm.   40.00

Alcohol

Beer barrel on stilts. XXX in red on
sides. 57mm.   5.50

Bottle with solid top. 92mm.   5.50

Bottle with cork. 2 sizes:
70mm and 94mm.   6.50
Can be found with Bass sign on
reverse and *Bass & Co.'s. Pale
Ale.*   10.00

Drunkard leaning on lamp-post,
fully coloured on ashtray. Inscribed: *Show me the way to go
home* and *Swat a night Boys Hic,
Snow Usse Hic.* (Lustre.) 112mm.   60.00

Gin bottle, inscribed: *Have a drop
of gin old dear.* 95mm.   20.00

Hand holding beaker, inscribed:
Good health. 88mm long.   7.50

Hip Flask.   7.50

Man sitting with beer barrel and
glass, some colouring.
Inscribed: *Beer Hic Beer Hic
Glorious Beer Hic.* 70mm.   55.00

Monk holding beaker with verse:
A Jovial Monk am I. 113mm.
Can be found with black cap.   16.00

Mr. Pussyfoot, holding umbrella
with one foot on bottle of
Scotch, inscribed: *No home in
Scotland.* 135mm.   30.00
(Mr. Pussyfoot was an
American Prohibitionist).

Soda Syphon. 100mm.   7.50

Toby Jug, with verse: *No tongue
can tell. No heart can sing How I
love a drop of drink.* Can be found
inscribed: *This jug is an exact
copy in miniature of the old
Toby jug* No. 413. 75mm.   8.25
Can be found coloured.   16.00

Whisky Bowl, inscribed *Scuab* and
As'i coloured cross and thistles
on handles. 123mm dia.   8.50

Sport
Five pieces have been found
labelled British Sports Series.
The ashtrays labelled in this
way have been listed
separately.

British Sports Series
Games Spinner and Match Holder
on shield ashtray, inscribed:
Put and take: yer ash: a match.
90mm long.   65.00
Goal with Keeper and Ball on
ashtray, inscribed: *League
Football first played 1888.* Some
colouring. 100mm long.   85.00
Golfer standing with Club on   75.00
ashtray. Coloured version.   85.00
94mm.
Humpty, Dumpty sat on a Wall.
Humpty on wall on ashtray,
some colouring. 97mm. Can be
found with an inkwell inset.   85.00
Tennis player holding Racquet
aloft in front of net. Inscribed:
40 Love. Some colouring.
83mm.   75.00

Other Sporting Items
Cricket Bag. 105mm long.   9.00
Cricketer carrying bat, flat
figurine on green base. Some
colouring. 115mm (rare).   95.00
Curling stone, inscribed: *Soop-up.*
61mm dia.   14.50
F.A. Cup. 100mm.   14.00
named   26.00
Footballer with football, arms
outstretched, some colouring.
110mm.   85.00
Golf Ball, can be found inscribed: 4.50
*The ancient game of golf was first
played in 1448.* 50mm.   6.50
Golf Club, can be found inscribed: 10.00
Fore, or as above or both. 95mm.   14.50
Jockey standing on base, silks can
be yellow/blue, red/black, green/
black or orange/black. 121mm.   75.00
Jockey on Racehorse, rectangular
base, silks can be blue/green,

blue/brown, green/yellow or
red/yellow. Very occasionally
the horse is found painted black.
Can also be found with inscription: for example: *Ala Baculia:
St Leger first run 1876.*
110mm long.   75.00
Jockey on Racehorse (comical)
with real hair tail (often missing)
on ashtray base, some colouring.
Inscribed: *Horsey keep your tail
up.* 102mm.   21.50
Racehorse on oval base.
2 sizes: 118mm long.   50.00
140mm long.   50.00
Roller Skate. 120mm long.   22.00
Tennis Racquet. 140mm long.   7.50
Trophy. 130mm.   14.00

Musical Instruments
Upright Piano, open keyboard,
Dolphin feet.
2 sizes: 64mm.   18.50
90mm.   20.00

Transport
Charabanc, inscribed: *Over the
hills and far away.* 'DN999' on
radiator. 148mm long. Found in
lustre.   33.00
Double Decker Bus, with driver
and outside staircase,
impressed: *Putney—Charing
Cross: Globe Theatre John Bull
Thursday: General.* 'DN999' on
radiator. 126mm long.   130.00
Motorbike and sidecar with rider.
112mm long.   75.00
Motorscooter on oval base
115mm long.   30.00
Open Sports Car, 'DN999' on
radiator. 106mm long.   40.00
Saloon Car, 'DN999' on radiator.
130mm long.   56.50
Stephenson Locomotive, with
detailed inscription:
*Locomotion 1825. This Engine was
built by Geo. Stephenson and Son,
and was used at the opening of the
S. and D. Rly. Sept 27th 1825.*
88mm.   85.00
Locomotive. 120mm long.   70.00

Modern Equipment

Gramophone in Cabinet, black
record on turntable, inscribed:
Music hath charms. Found in
lustre. 92mm. Can be found
coloured blue, add £10.00.   57.50

Gramophone, square with Horn,
inscribed: *HMV* or *His Masters
Voice,* with transfer of 'HMV'
dog and notes of music. 96mm.   25.00

Gramophone with dog listening
to horn, on oval base. Inscribed:
His Masters Voice. Some
colouring. 88mm long. Very
rarely found in lustre.   70.00

National cash register with '£.s.d.'
Found unnamed but with
'£.s.d.' (lustre). 70mm.   20.00

Radio Operator, inscribed:
Listening in. Some colouring.
85mm.   57.50

Radio Operator with
microphone, inscribed:
Listening in. Some colouring.
85mm.   75.00

Radio Operator with horn,
inscribed: *Listening in.* Some
colouring. 85mm.   75.00

Telephone, stick type, inscribed:
Hello, Hello or rarely *All alone
by the telephone.* 115mm.   16.00

Treadle sewing machine, found
inscribed: *Singer.* 80mm.   22.50

Footwear

Boot.

3 sizes: 50mm.	4.75
72mm long	4.75

Tall laced Boot. 85mm. Particularly
fine.   14.00
Riding Boot. 65mm.   10.50
Boot pin box.   8.25
Sabot. 100mm long.   7.50
Slipper wall pocket. 105mm long.   7.50

Hats

Bishop's Mitre. 70mm.   5.50
Boater Hat. 104mm long.   7.50
Boy Scouts Hat. 95mm dia.   16.00
Top Hat. 40mm.   5.50

Miscellaneous

Candleholder. 118mm.   3.00
Candlesnuffer. 65mm.   2.50

Dice pin box and lid. 50mm square. 13.00

Hand holding crinkle topped
flower vase (not a tulip as
usually found). 85mm.   4.75

Hand bell with porcelain clapper.
100mm.   7.50

Hatpin Holder Lighthouse,
inscribed: *Sailor Beware.*
136mm.   10.50

Hatpin Holder in shape of a
Thistle on leaves. 80mm.   10.50

Hatpin Holder, square base. 97mm.   8.50
Horseshoe. 115mm.   3.00

Horseshoe photo frame. Inscribed:
The Best of Luck. 125mm.   13.50

Horses Hoof pin box and lid.
98mm long.   4.00

Horses Hoof ink well with lid
Rd.No 538564. 95mm long.   12.50

Jug. Inscribed: *Measure for Measure.*
45mm.   5.50

Wall Pocket, very ornate with
Durham knocker. 84mm long.   5.50

Miniature Domestic

Barrel Jug. 47mm.   3.00
Cheese Dish (one piece). 45mm.   6.50

Cheese Dish, fluted with cover.
50mm.   7.50

Coffee Pot with lid. No. 271.
78mm.   6.50

Kettle. 60mm.   7.50
Tea set on tray. Tray 115mm long. 22.50
Teapot with lid. 50mm.   5.50

Teapot with lid with swan
shaped handle. 70mm.   12.50
Can be found inscribed *Polly
put the kettle on.*   16.00

Thistle Tea Pot with lid, lustre.
76mm.   12.50

Carlton also made a whole range
of pin or ashtrays, pill boxes
and trinket boxes in club,
diamond, heart and spade
shapes. They can be found
with crest or transfer views.
Very few articles for domestic
use, plates, cups etc. have
been found but this is probably
because they were used and
broken. Price range: 1.75 to 8.00.

Carmen China

For marks see *Crested China*, p. 105.

Trademark used for E.A. Green, Rugby by J.A. Robinson & Sons Ltd, Arcadian Works, Stoke-on-Trent (Usual trademark: Arcadian)

Ancient Artefacts
Model of Vase found near Winchelsea.
  75mm.   3.00

Monuments
*Tom Hughes Monument, Rugby
  School.* 135mm.   30.00

Seaside Souvenirs
Bathing Machine 'Morning Dip
  7 a.m.'. 65mm.   7.50
Eddystone Lighthouse. 125mm.   7.50

Animals
Dog, Scottish Terrier. 66mm long.   11.00
Tortoise. 69mm long.   6.50

Birds/Eggs
Egg with flat base. 44mm.   4.00
Hen roosting. 54mm.   5.50

Great War
Model of Tommy on Sentry Duty.
  105mm.   75.00
Standing Nurse *Soldiers Friend.*
  126mm.   47.50
Monoplane. 114mm long.   55.00
Battleship, 3 funnels and tiny
  gun fore and aft. 100mm long.   15.50
Torpedo Boat Destroyer, not
  named. 108mm long.   19.50
Jack Johnson. Shell. 90mm.   8.50
Tommy's Hut. 104mm long.   40.00
Bomb dropped from Zeppelin.
  80mm.   11.00
Bandsman's Drum. 53mm.   5.00
Officers Peaked Cap with
  coloured badge and hatband.
  65mm dia.   9.00

Home/Nostalgic
Grandfather Clock, with inscription:
  Make use of Time. 110mm.   10.50

Comic/Novelty
Clown, bust, inscribed: *Put me
  amongst the girls.* 85mm.   17.00

Sport
Golf Ball with inscription. 45mm.   6.50

Muscial Instruments
Banjo. 150mm long.   8.50

Miscellaneous
Candlesnuffer, conical. 65mm.   2.50
Circular Match Holder. 53mm.   10.00

Cascade China

Trademark used for a retailer on china manufactured probably by Taylor & Kent Ltd. Florence Works, Longton (Usual trademark Florentine)

Miscellaneous
Book.No.72. 57mm.   5.00

Cauldon China

For marks see *Crested China,* p. 105.

Trademark used by Cauldon Ltd, Stoke-on-Trent.

Buildings — White
Queen's Doll's House, found
   both glazed and unglazed.
4 sizes: 75mm (also with lid).   17.00
              95mm (also with lid).   17.00
              118mm.   21.50
              146mm.   24.50
Full inscriptions can be found on
   the base of these models.

Celtic Porcelain

For mark see *Crested China*, p. 106.

Trademark used by the Nautilus Porcelain Co., Possil Pottery, Glasgow.

Countryside
Log Vase. 32mm.   9.00

Miscellaneous
Carboy.   6.50

There is also a range of crested small vases.

Ceramic China

For mark see *Crested China*, p. 106.

Trademark thought to have been used by a German manufacturer for china imported into Scotland. Two smalls with St Andrews and Stornoway crests known.

Challenge China

Trademark used by an unknown manufacturer (But probably Taylor & Kent Ltd) for a retailer possibly in the Birmingham area.

Only two pieces known —
Jug. 83mm with Birmingham crest. 4.50
Lancashire Clog. 85mm long. 6.00

Chelson China

For mark see *Crested China*, p. 106.

Trademark used by New Chelsea Porcelain Co. (Ltd), Bagnall Street, Longton.

Range of Great War commemoratives on 'smalls' were produced. Value from £5.00 each.

Christop China

Civic

No details of mark available.

Trademark used by an unknown manufacturer for a retailer in the Colonies. Manufacturer possibly Sampson Hancock (and Sons), Bridge Works, Stoke (usual mark Corona) as this firm used the circle and buckle device in several of its trademarks.

This mark has only been found on one small flat sided vase, inscribed: *Souvenir, settler's centenary. Grahamstown.* and with a crest of Cape of Good Hope.   10.00

For mark see *Crested China,* p. 107.

Trademark used by Taylor and Kent (Ltd)., Florence Works, Longton. (Usual trademark Florentine)

Ancient Artefacts
Chester Roman Vase (not named).
62mm.   2.25

Seaside Souvenirs
Whelk Shell. 90mm long.   3.00

Animals
Cat sitting with long neck.
105mm. (This is a model of a
Destroyer's Ship's mascot
which became popular during
the Great War).   6.50
Manx Cat. 90mm.   13.00

Great War
Bandsman's Drum. 55mm dia.   5.00

Home/Nostaligic
Watering Can. 75mm.   5.50

Sport
Cricket Bag. 110mm long.   8.00

C.J.B. & Co

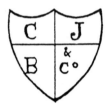

Trademark used by Sampson Hancock and Sons, Bridge Works, Stoke and later at the Garden Works, Hanley. (Usual trademark Corona).

The only pieces recorded are small vases.   3.00

Clarence China

Mark used by an unknown manufacturer and found only on a 57mm vase. No.291 with a Belfast crest. This would seem to be from one of the main manufacturers but the No.291 cannot at the moment be traced. It could possibly be Birks, Rawlins and Co (usual mark Savoy) as their range of ancient artefacts carry similar numbers.   3.00

Clarence Crest China

For mark see *Crested China*, p. 107.

Trademark used by Beresford Bros., Clarence Works, High Street, Longton. The models either bear a close resemblance to H & L (Willow Art) models or are the same. There must have been some connection between these two firms, both working in Longton. It is common to find firing flaws in this china.

Ancient Artefacts
Highland Whisky Bowl. Model of.
    90mm long.   4.00
Loving cup, 3 handled. 40mm.   3.00

Buildings — white
Windmill. 85mm.   30.00

Monuments
Baron Burton statue. 130mm.   20.50

Historical/Folklore
James V chair. 100mm.   7.50
Man in the Moon. 55mm.   19.50

Traditional/National Souvenirs
Welsh Hat with blue band. 55mm.   4.75

Animals
Cat, sitting. 78mm.   8.75
Dog, Dachsund, sitting.
    75mm long.   40.00
Elephant, standing. 78mm long.   13.00
Hare. 67mm long.   9.00

Birds
Swan. 57mm.   6.50

Great War
Soldier standing to attention,
    inscribed: *Our Brave Defender.*
    130mm.   40.00
Nurse, inscribed: *A friend in need.*
    130mm.   40.00
Monoplane with revolving
    prop. 150mm long.   55.00
Tank with trailing wheels.
    130mm long.   14.50

Field gun with screen.
    114mm long.   18.50
Bandsman's Drum. 58mm.   5.00
Kit Bag, with inscription: *Pack up
    your troubles in your old kit bag.*
    70mm.   15.00
Tommy's Steel Helmet.
    76mm long.   21.00
Kitchen Range, with pot on fire
    inscribed: *Keep the home fires
    burning.* No. 199. 78mm long.   9.00

Comic/Novelty
A Truck of Coal from. . Wagon of
    black coal. 70mm.   16.00

Alcohol
One Special Scotch, Bottle. 88mm.   7.50

Footwear
Ladies heeled Shoe, blue bow.
    115mm long.   10.50

Miscellaneous
Trump indicator ashtray.
    110mm dia.   50.00

A small range of domestic china
    was produced bearing colour
    transfers of good quality.
                 £5.00 upwards.

Clays

For mark see *Crested China*, p. 108.

Trademark used on crested china manufactured by Hewitt Bros. (Usual trademark Willow Art).

Buildings — White
Chesterfield Parish Church.
110mm long.   40.00

Historical/Folklore
Bell inscribed: *Curfew must not ring
tonight*. 72mm.   7.50

Animals
Elephant, walking. 70mm long.   13.00
Pig, standing. 96mm long.   10.00

Birds
Wise Owl, with verse. 98mm.   12.50

Great War
Soldier, with rifle, inscribed: *Our
brave defender*. 132mm.   40.00
Battleship, impressed:
HMS Lion. 140mm long.   22.50
Submarine, impressed:
E4. 116mm long.   16.00
British Tank, Model of, with
trailing wheels. No. 107.
125mm long.   14.50
Field Gun & Screen. 110mm long.   18.50
Officers Peaked Cap. No. 100.
75mm dia.   10.00

Cartoon/Comedy Characters
Baby, with arms outstretched,
inscribed: *Cheerio*. Some
colouring on face. 125mm.
(Great War cartoon character,
could be 'Pooksie'.)   30.00

Alcohol
Barrel, on stand. 52mm long.   5.50

Clifton

For mark see *Crested China*, p. 108.

Trademark used by a branch of J.A. Robinson Ltd, Stoke-on-Trent. Subsequently Cauldon Ltd. (Usual mark Arcadian).

Parian/Unglazed
Bust of King George V, glazed
circular base, with inscription:
*King George V born June 3rd 1865,
ascended the throne May 6th 1910.*
135mm.   30.00
Bust of Queen Mary, glazed
circular base, with inscription:
Queen Mary born May 26th 1867.
135mm.   30.00

Ancient Artefacts
Most inscriptions begin:*Model of,*
so this will not be repeated
throughout the list.
Ancient Tyg. No. 58. 70mm.   3.00
Ashbourne Bushel, inscribed: *His
Majesty King Charles 2nd's Royal
Standard Bushel fastened to the
Market Cross in the year 1677.*
95mm dia.   4.50
British Bronze Pot, Ancient. 71mm. 3.00
Canterbury Roman Vase,
2 shapes: No. 22. 63mm (with
handle); No. 29. 60mm (no
handle).   3.50
Carlisle Salt Pot. No. 110. 40mm.   3.50
Chester Roman Vase. No. 131.
60mm.   3.00
*Chinese Vase originally in Hanley
Museum*. 58mm.   3.00
Derby Roman Vase, inscribed:
*Roman Vase found at Little
Chester, Derby*. No. 26. 63mm.   3.00
Dorchester Jug, inscribed: *Old Jug
found in North Street, Dorchester.*
No. 17. 55mm.   3.00
*Egyptian Vase, Ancient, about
230BC*. No. 155. 45mm.   3.00
Exeter Vase. 65mm.   3.00

Fountains Abbey Cup. No. 94.
50mm. — 3.00

Glastonbury Bowl. No. 65.
40mm. — 3.00

Glastonbury Vase. No. 642.
55mm. — 3.00

Hastings Kettle. No. 237.
62mm. — 3.00

Irish Bronze Pot. No. 62
50mm. — 3.00

*Loving Cup originated by Henry
of Navarre King of France.*
3 handled.
40mm. — 3.00
50mm. — 3.00

Newbury Leather Bottle,
inscribed: *Leather bottle found on
battlefield of Newbury 1644 now in
museum.* No. 83. 65mm. — 3.00

New Forest Roman Jug, not
named. No. 174. 67mm. — 3.00

Nose of Brasenose College, Oxford
(not found numbered).
103mm long. — 8.25

Pompeian Vessel, not found
named. 43mm. — 2.25

*Portland Vase in
British Museum.*
No. 57. 60mm. — 3.00

*Puzzle Jug, original in South
Kensington Museum* with usual
verse. No. 147. 70mm. — 5.50

*Roman Salopian Ewer found at
Uriconium, now in Shrewsbury
Museum.* 75mm. — 3.00

Southwold Jar, (not found
numbered). 95mm. — 3.00

Winchelsea Roman Cup
(3 handles). — 3.00

Buildings — White
Highland Cottage, Model of. 60mm. — 21.50

Monuments
Baron Burton monument.
Inscribed: *Michael Arthur first
Baron Burton.* 130mm. — 30.00

Historical/Folklore
Ancient Coaching Hat, Model of.
No. 687. 68mm long. — 7.50

Jenny Geddes Stool, not named.
42mm. — 5.50

Witches Cauldron with verse.
47mm. — 5.50

Traditional/National Souvenirs
John Bull bust, eyes and mouth
coloured. 100mm. — 22.50

Luton Boater, not found named.
78mm dia. — 8.25

Melton Mowbray Pie, The, pie with
moulded pastry adornments,
with verse. 50mm. — 16.00

Thistle Vase. 93mm. — 3.50

Welsh Lady, bust, with
inscription: *Wales! Wales! My
Mother's sweet home in Wales* etc.
With black Welsh hat. 80mm. — 21.50

Welsh Leek. 95mm. — 5.25

Welsh Tea Party,
2 sizes: 55mm. — 35.00
95mm. — 40.00

Seaside Souvenirs
Lifeboat, inscribed: *Margate
Lifeboat, friend to all nations.*
118mm long. — 20.00

Clam shell menu holder. 62mm. — 10.50

Mr. Punch, bust, some colouring
—red hearts on cheeks.
Rd No.524786 80mm. — 26.50

Countryside
Acorn. 42mm. — 5.50

Haystack, circular. 58mm. — 4.75

Animals
Angry Cat, standing with arched
back, green eyes. 62mm. — 12.50

Cat, long necked and sitting, can
be inscribed: *My word if you're
not off.* 108mm. — 8.75

Elephant walking. Can be found
inscribed: *Baby Jumbo.* No. 237.
70mm. — 15.00

Frog, open mouth and green
eyes, inscribed: *Always croaking.*
80mm. — 10.50

Hare. No. 10. 73mm. — 9.00

Lion, walking. Inscribed:
King of the Forest.
110mm long. — 14.50

Sussex Pig, Model of, standing
inscribed: *You can push or you
can shuv but I'm hanged if I'll be
druv.* No. 148. 78mm long. — 12.50

Pony, Shetland.
2 sizes: 105mm long.	25.00
120mm long.	30.00
Teddy Bear, sitting. 90mm.	8.50

Birds

Chick emerging from egg. 72mm long.	5.50
Cockerel, standing. Inscribed: Cock O'th'North 100mm.	14.50
Owl. 69mm.	10.50

Great War

Despatch rider, Model of, on motorbike. 120mm long.	43.50
Sailor, bust, inscribed: HMS Dreadnought and The handy man. With verse: Hearts of Oak. 95mm.	30.00
With verse	35.00
Sailor, bust, impressed: HMS Queen Elizabeth. 86mm.	30.00
Soldier standing to attention with rifle over shoulder. 137mm.	87.00
Soldier, bust, inscribed: Territorial with verse 'It's the Soldiers of the King'. 95mm.	30.00
Monoplane, movable prop. 155mm long.	55.00
Battleship, impressed HMS Lion. 140mm long.	22.50
Tank, Model of. 116mm.	13.00
Tank with inset wheels. 127mm long.	15.00
Red Cross Van. 90mm long.	23.00
Howitzer (not found named). 115mm long.	16.00
Field Gun with Screen. 112mm long.	18.50
Trench Mortar. 70mm long.	10.50
Bomb dropped from Zeppelin, model of. 80mm.	11.00
Canister Bomb, Model of. 60mm.	13.00
Colonial Hat, Model of. 88mm wide.	10.50
Glengarry. 90mm long.	16.00
Kitbag with verse: Pack up your troubles. 75mm.	15.00
Anti Zeppelin Candle holder 62mm.	14.00
Sandbag. 73mm long.	13.00
Trench Lamp. 67mm.	10.50

Home/Nostalgic

Anvil on circular base. No. 25. 68mm.	5.50
Bucket. No. 92. 75mm.	3.00
Dustpan. 110mm long.	5.50
Flat Iron Stand. 70mm.	3.00
Grandfather Clock, Model of a, inscribed: Make use of time let not advantage slip. Shakespeare. No. 209. 108mm.	10.50
Pillar Box, inscribed: G V R if you haven't time to post a line here's the pillar box. 60mm.	10.00

Comic/Novelty

2 Black boys heads popping out of box, inscribed: Box of chocolates. Some colouring. 60mm.	30.00
Clown, bust, inscribed: Put me amongst the girls. Some colouring. No. 12. 80mm.	17.00
Policeman on duty, with verse. 148mm.	24.75

Cartoon/Comedy Characters

Ally Sloper, bust. Inscribed: Good Health Old Man. 90mm.	40.00

Alcohol

Barrel on stilts. 60mm.	5.50
Monk, holding glass with verse. 112mm.	16.00

Sport

Football. 50mm dia.	6.50

Transport

4 Seater Open Car, folded down hood. 140mm long.	30.00

Footwear

Oriental Slipper. No. 352. 105mm long.	6.50

Hats

Straw Boater, coloured ribbon. 95mm long.	20.00

Recorded Numbered Ornamental Wares

No. 16. Globe Vase. 46mm.	2.25
No. 37. Vase, wide mouth. 50mm.	2.25
No. 40. Trinket Box and lid, horseshoe shaped. 65mm long.	4.00

No. 45. Trinket Box and lid, spade
shaped.
40mm. 4.00
No. 63. Pot on 3 small feet. 41mm. 2.25
No. 72. Jug. 60mm. 2.25
No. 74. Jug. 82mm. 2.25
No. 100. Vase. 53mm. 2.25
No. 141. Vase. 47mm. 2.25
No. 144. Vase. 50mm. 2.25
No. 145. Vase. 53mm. 2.25
No. 146. Vase. 50mm. 2.25
No. 215. Vase. 60mm. 2.25
No. 216. Vase. 60mm. 2.25
No. 217. Vase. flat bottomed.
37mm. 2.25
No. 303. Vase. 52mm. 2.25
No. 305. Beaker. 34mm. 2.25
No. 532. Jug. 70mm. 2.25
No. 579. Loving Cup. 3.00
No. 587. Taper Vase. 60mm. 2.25
No. 666. Crinkle topped vase.
40mm. 2.25
Found not numbered. Trinket
Box and lid, heart shaped. 40mm. 4.00

Clifton China

For mark see *Crested China*, p. 111.

Trademark used by Wildblood, Heath and
Sons (Ltd), Peel Works, Longton. The
models show great resemblance to those
of H & L — Willow Art, also working in
Longton and later wares are identical to
Arcadian models.

Parian/Unglazed
Bust of Queen Alexandra on
round base. 137mm. 35.00

Ancient Artefacts
Loving Cup. 39mm. 3.00
Egyptian Urn, Model of. No. 130.
48mm. 3.00

Buildings — White
Wainhouse Tower. 135mm. 40.00

Monuments
Burton Statue, Burton on Trent.
Inscribed: *Michael Arthur first
Baron Burton, born 1837. Died
1909.* 130mm. 20.50

Historical/Folklore
Burns chair, Model of. No. 49.
90mm. 7.50

Traditional/National Souvenirs
John Bull, bust of. 90mm. 19.50

Seaside Souvenirs
Lighthouse. 110mm. 4.75

Animals
Cat in Boot. No. 65. 68mm. 14.50
Cheshire Cat, still smiling, green
right eye. 80mm. 7.50
Elephant, walking. 75mm. 13.00
Lion. 112mm long. 12.50

Birds
Canary on Rock, unnamed Norwich Warbler. No.23. 98mm. 13.00

Great War

Sailor, standing at attention.
Inscribed: *Our Brave Defender.*
130mm. 40.00

Monoplane with movable prop.
155mm long. 55.00

Battleship, impressed:
HMS Lion. 140mm long. 22.50

Liner converted to Troop Ship,
not named. 135mm long. 90.00

British Tank, Model of. 140mm long. 14.50

British Tank, Model of, with trailing
steering wheels. No. 120.
130mm long. 14.50

Field Gun with Screen. No. 214.
115mm long. 18.50

Shell. No. 114. 70mm. 3.00

Kit Bag with verse: *Pack up your
troubles.* 72mm. 15.00

Drum. 65mm dia. 5.00

Tommy's Steel Helmet.
75mm long. 21.00

Home/Nostalgic

Anvil. 88m long. 5.50
Shaving Mug. 65mm. 5.50
Watering Can. No. 126. 75mm. 5.50

Novelty

Billiken, The god of luck. 75mm. 4.00
inscribed 8.00

Cartoon/Comedy Characters

Standing Baby inscribed:
One of the B'Hoys. Saluting,
coloured face, 160mm.
Refers to the Alsager B'Hoys. 30.00

Alcohol

Barrel on legs. No. 85. 60mm. 4.00
Barrel on stand. No. 83.
63mm long. 5.50

Miscellaneous

Bell. No. 12. 55mm. 4.50
Hand holding Tulip. 80mm. 4.00

Miniature Domestic

Cream jug. 74mm. 2.25

Domestic Wares

Hexagonal and octagonal salt
pots can be found inscribed:
Salt. Jugs, beakers and small
vases can also be found. from £2.25

Colleen China

Trademark unidentified but could possibly
be Belleek.

National Souvenirs

Bust of *John Redmond MP 1914*
(The bust is hollow and has a
Wexford crest). 137mm. 50.00

Collingwood

For mark see *Crested China*, p. 113.

Trademark used by Collingwood Bros (Ltd.), St. George's Works, Longton.

This firm produced a range of 'smalls' to commemorate the British Empire Exhibition Wembley, 1924.   from £5.50

Columbia China

For mark see *Crested China*, p. 113.

Trademark used by an English manufacturer for export to British Columbia.

Only one small vase with this mark is known, it has a British Columbian crest.   4.00

Coral Porcelain

Trademark used by the Coral Porcelain Co. also known as the Scottish Porcelain Co.

A range of 'smalls' with Scottish crests was produced.   £3.00 upwards

The Corona China

For mark see *Crested China*, p. 113.

Trademark used by Sampson Hancock (& Sons), Bridge Works, Stoke and later at the Garden Works, Hanley (renamed Corona Pottery).

Ancient Artefacts

Aberdeen Bronze Pot. 58mm.	2.25
Canterbury Leather Bottle. No. 156.	2.25
Hastings Kettle. 57mm.	2.25
Newbury Leather Bottle, not named. 72mm.	2.25
Puzzle Jug. No. 148. 70mm.	5.50
Shrewsbury Roman Salopian Ewer. 60mm.	2.50

Buildings — White

Ann Hathaway's Cottage. 95mm long.	13.00
Blackpool Tower. 139mm.	9.50
Bottle Oven (inside of). 82mm.	15.50
Bridge, with grassy banks. 134mm long.	19.50
Canterbury Cathedral, West Front. 137mm.	40.00
Clifton Suspension Bridge. 115mm long.	40.00
Cottage. 60mm long. (This is identical to the model usually found marked British Manufacture.)	7.00
Crosthwaite Church, Keswick. 110mm long.	60.00

Monuments

Bunyan's Statue. 165mm.	18.00
Tom Hughes Monument, Rugby. 136mm.	30.00
John Ruskin Memorial. 105mm.	12.50

Historical/Folklore

Mary Queen of Scots Chair Edinburgh Castle. 80mm.	6.50
Noah's Ark. 95mm long.	4.75

Traditional/National Souvenirs

Lancashire Clog.

2 sizes: 70mm long. 4.75
102mm long. 6.50

Lancashire Clog. square toe and
gilded buckle. 80mm long. 5.50

Welsh Harp. 90mm. 7.50

Welsh Hat, can be found with
largest place name round brim.
45mm. 4.75
with wording 7.50

Seaside Souvenirs

Bathing Machine. 71mm. 8.25
Canoe. 102mm long. 5.50
Lighthouse, not named. 105mm. 5.50
Lighthouse, with steps. 115mm. 6.50
Beachy Head Lighthouse, black
band. 150mm. 7.50

Animals

Camel, 1 hump, kneeling.
114mm long. 13.00
Cat sitting with ruff around neck.
105mm. 17.50
Cheshire Cat. 95mm. 6.50
Manx Cat. 60mm. 16.00
Bulldog, standing. 112mm and
120mm long. 15.00
Bulldog, standing, with black
collar and Union Jack on back.
(Very rare). 130mm long. 145.00
Dog, King Charles Spaniel,
begging. 69mm. 10.50
Fish Vase. 60mm. 5.00
Lion, lying down. 140mm long. 19.00
Mouse, eating nut. 44mm. 19.00
Piglet, kneeling. 65mm long. 8.25
Pig, standing. 84mm long. 10.00
Pony, Shetland. 110mm long. 22.00
Rabbit with raised ears. No. 166.
63mm long. 6.50
Teddy Bear, sitting, can be found
completely brown with no
crest. No. 194. 85mm. 12.00
brown 30.00
Tortoise. 72mm long. 6.50

Birds

Swan. 85mm. 6.50
Swan, posy holder. 87mm long. 4.75

Great War

Monoplane, Bleriot type with
movable prop. 145mm long. 55.00
British Airship on base.
128mm long. 20.00
Zeppelin. 134mm long. 20.00

Battleship. 120mm long. 16.00
Lusitania. 163mm long. 75.00
Submarine, inscribed: *E4.* Size
varies. 102mm-120mm long. 16.00
New submarine, Model of. 146mm
long. (This is the submarine
usually named E5 by other
firms). 16.00
Red Cross Van. 98mm long. 23.00
Renault Tank. 100mm long. 65.00
Tank with inset trailing wheels.
100mm long. 17.50
Field Gun.
2 sizes: 120mm 13.00
140mm long. 15.00
Field Gun with Screen.
120mm long. 20.00
Cannon Shell. 100mm. 5.00
Torpedo, Model of. No. 285.
145mm long. 47.50
Bandsman's Drum. No. 208.
63mm dia. 5.00
Bell Tent, hexagonal tent with
open flaps. No. 209. 85mm. 10.50
Gurkha Knife. 140mm long. 20.00
Trench Lamp. 88mm. 10.50
Water Bottle. 68mm and 88mm. 13.00
Grandfather Clock, same mould
as usual Grandfather clock but
clockface transfer at 3.25, inscribed:
*World War 1914-1919. Peace signed
3.25pm June 28th 1919.* 128mm. 56.50
Cenotaph. Whitehall. 145mm. 5.50
Romsey War Memorial. 160mm 90.00
Rushden War Memorial. 158mm. 90.00
A small series of vases with
protraits General French, Lord
Kitchener and Admiral Jellico
set in the Union Jack or Royal
Standard flaf marked *1914* are
worth 17.50 to 30.00
A similar series of transfer prints of
soldiers in regimental uniforms
marked *1914* are worth 12.50 to 30.00

Home/Nostalgic

Alarm Clock, with detailed face.
85mm 30.00
Armchair. 60mm. 7.50
Baby in Bootee. 80mm long. 11.00
Baby's Cradle. 80mm long. 6.50
Grandfather Clock. 128mm. 9.00
Hip Bath. 95mm long. 7.00
Jardiniere, on fixed stand.
2 sizes: 82mm. 4.75
97mm. 4.75

Pillar Box. No. 171. 74mm.	8.00
Watering Can. 70mm.	5.50
Writing Slope/Desk top.	
No. 268. 53mm.	7.50

Comic/Novelty

Cigarette Case. 72mm long.	13.00
Man's Head cream jug. 76mm.	8.50

Sport

Tennis Racquet. 132mm long.	7.50

Musical Instruments

Banjo. 140mm long.	8.50
Double Bass. 150mm long.	32.50
Upright Piano. 63mm.	12.50

Modern Equipment

Gas Cooker. 70mm.	8.50
Gramophone, square with no horn, arm on middle of record. Crest is on the front edge. 57mm.	15.25

Miscellaneous

Horseshoe, on slope. 70mm long.	3.00
Horseshoe, wall plaque. 60mm long.	3.00
Bishop, Chess Piece. 61mm.	16.00
King Chess Piece. 115mm.	19.50
Knight Chess Piece. 70mm.	8.25
Pawn Chess Piece. 90mm.	19.00
Rook Chess Piece. 68mm.	4.00

Footwear

Ladies Button Boot. No. 149. 65mm.	8.00
Ladies 18th Century Shoe. No. 146. 90mm long.	7.50

Hats

Top Hat. 45mm.	5.50

Miniature Domestic

Candlestick square top and base. 83mm.	3.00
Candlestick round top and base. 85mm.	3.00
Cheese Dish. 1 piece. 60mm × 80mm.	5.50
Cheese Dish and cover. 60mm.	5.50
Cream Jug, ornate. 78mm.	4.00
Kettle with lid. 70mm & 87mm.	7.50
Tea Pot with lid. No. 122. 65mm.	7.50
Coffee Pot and lid. 75mm.	7.50

Coronet Ware

For marks see *Crested China*, p. 117.

A trademark used by Taylor and Kent (Ltd), Florence Works, Longton (usual trademark Florentine) and Ford & Pointon Ltd, Norfolk Works, Hanley. Subsequently, a branch of J.A. Robinson & Sons Ltd, and later Cauldon Ltd. Some late pieces are therefore from Arcadian moulds.

Ancient Artefacts

Fountains Abbey Cup, not found named. 48mm.	2.25
Puzzle Jug. 70mm.	5.50
Roman Oil Lamp. 100mm long.	3.50
Shrewsbury Roman Salopian Ewer. 60mm.	3.00

Buildings — White

Cottage. 50mm.	6.50

Monuments

Iona Cross, on square base. 108mm.	6.00
Wallace's Memorial at Stirling. 120mm.	40.00

Historical/Folklore

Judge, bust. 60mm.	12.50
Man in Pillory. 103mm.	17.00
Man in Stocks. 102mm.	19.00
Mother Shipton. 72mm.	13.00

National Souvenirs

Welsh Hat. 57mm.	4.75
Welsh Hat with blue band & gold tassles. 80mm.	6.50

Seaside Souvenirs

Bathing Machine with figure in doorway. 75mm.	14.50
Bermudan rigged Sailing Boat. 125mm.	17.00
Houseboat. 90mm long.	4.75
Whelk Shell. 95mm long.	3.00
Punch and Judy Booth, with Punch and dog Toby. (rare)	
2 sizes: 90mm.	50.00
110mm.	55.00

Punch, bust, with red nose.

83mm.	19.50
Portmanteau. 80mm long.	4.00

Animals

Camel with 1 hump, kneeling.	
56mm.	13.00
Cat, large and furry, snarling.	
93mm.	17.50
Cat, long necked. 103mm.	6.50
Cat, Manx. 64mm.	16.00
Cat, angry. 80mm.	10.50
Cat, sitting inscribed: *The Cheshire Cat, always smiling.*	
88mm.	7.50
Cat, sitting, bow round neck.	
70mm.	10.00
Dog, spaniel type, standing.	
76mm long.	10.50
Dolphin Vase. 102mm.	4.75
Elephant, kneeling. 60mm.	15.00
Fish, open mouthed.	
2 sizes: 102mm	4.00
120mm long.	5.00
Frog, open mouthed and green eyes. 60mm.	6.50
Monkey, wearing coat, sitting.	
75mm.	12.50
Mouse playing Mandolin, on base. 80mm.	21.50
Pig, standing, inscribed: *The pig that won't go.* 84mm long.	12.50
Pig, standing. 95mm long.	11.00
Pony, inscribed: *Shetland Pony.* 74mm.	25.00
Rabbit sitting, ears flat.	
74mm long.	6.50
Seal, with ball on nose.	
85mm long.	16.00
Teddy Bear. 96mm.	8.50
Toad with closed mouth.	
50mm.	10.50
Tortoise. 72mm long.	6.50

Birds

Hen, roosting. 55mm	5.50
Kingfisher. 80mm.	21.50
Kingfisher cream jug. 60mm.	5.50
Pelican cream jug. 80mm.	5.50
Swan posy holder. 90mm long.	4.75

Great War

Bust of Sailor. 90mm.	30.00
Tommy in Bayonet Attack. 130mm.	130.00

British Airship, on base.

130mm long.	20.00
Monoplane with movable prop and cross hatching.	
145mm long.	55.00
Monoplane with movable prop and no cross hatching.	
170mm long.	55.00
Battleship. 115mm long.	16.00
Torpedo Boat Destroyer, Model of.	
105mm long.	19.50
Submarine, inscribed: *E5.*	
130mm long.	16.00
Armoured Car with turret. 95mm.	30.00
Red Cross Van. 90mm long.	23.00
Tank. 110mm long.	13.00
Tank with large gun turrets.	
120mm long.	21.00
Tank with inset steering wheels.	
116mm long.	15.00
Field Gun. 145mm long.	17.00
German Aerial Torpedo.	
80mm long.	30.00
Cannon Shell. 76mm.	3.00
Zeppelin Bomb. 78mm.	11.00
Bandsman's Drum. 55mm dia.	5.00
Bell Tent.	10.50
Ghurka Knife. 110mm long.	20.00
Hand Grenade. 60mm.	13.00
Glengarry. 90mm long.	16.00
Peaked Cap. 63mm long.	8.75
Sandbag. 70mm.	13.00
Solar Topee. 60mm.	16.00
Telescope, folded. 70mm.	13.00
Tommy's Hut, unnamed.	
105mm long.	40.00
Shell. 130mm.	4.00
Water Bottle. 63mm.	13.00
Dartford War Memorial (rare).	
163mm.	85.00
Cenotaph. 100mm.	4.00

Home/Nostalgic

Anvil on wooden stump. 66mm.	5.50
The Old Armchair, with verse.	
86mm.	7.50
Broom head. 105mm long.	21.50
Coal Bucket. 63mm.	4.00
Coal Scuttle, ornate. 68mm.	4.50
Dustpan. 100mm long.	6.50
Flat Iron. 75mm long.	8.00
Frying Pan. 115mm long.	7.50
Garden Roller. 83mm long.	7.50
Grandfather Clock. 127mm.	10.50

Kennel. 52mm.	6.50
Milk Churn, 2 handles and lid.	
70mm.	4.50
Oil Lamp. 103mm long.	4.75
Pillar Box.	
2 sizes: 60mm.	7.50
78mm.	7.50
Shaving Mug. 58mm.	5.50
Sofa. 82mm.	10.50
Stool, 3 legged. 40mm.	5.50
Torch.	10.50
Watering Can. 70mm.	5.50
Wicker Chair. 92mm.	8.50

Comic/Novelty

Baby in Hip Bath. 100mm long.	11.00
Boy on Scooter. 95mm.	16.00
Bust of Mrs Gamp the suffragette, double faced smiling and fierce. 90mm.	25.00
Clown, bust. 65mm.	8.25
Truck of Coal. 90mm long.	15.00
Jack in the Box. 95mm.	16.00

Alcohol

Barrel on stand. 56mm.	5.50
Bottle of Champagne in Ice Bucket. 85mm.	7.50
Carboy. 75mm.	3.00
Drunkard, bust of (looks rather like Ally Sloper). 74mm.	19.50
Toby Jug. 63mm.	6.50

Sport

Cricket Bag. 110mm long.	9.00
Cricket Bat. 115mm long.	40.00
Football. 50mm.	6.50
Tennis Racquet. 95mm long.	7.50

Musical Instruments

Grand Piano. 82mm long.	16.00
Guitar. 152mm long.	12.00
Harp. 95mm.	5.50
Piano, upright. 65mm long.	12.50
Tambourine. 68mm dia.	3.50

Transport

Saloon Car. 85mm long.	30.00
Motor Horn: *Pip Pip.* 90mm long.	22.50

Sport

Golf Club head. 90mm long.	10.50
Cricket Bag. 113mm long.	9.00

Modern Equipment

Radio Horn. 93mm.	18.00
Square Gramophone. 55mm.	15.25

Miscellaneous

Boot. 70mm.	5.25
Castle chess piece. 67mm.	4.00

Footwear

Ladies Ankle Boot. 76mm long.	6.50
Ladies 18th Century Shoe. 95mm long.	7.50
Sabot with turned up toe. 90mm long.	4.75

Miniature Domestic

Cheese Dish. 2 pieces. 50mm.	5.50
Coffee Pot with lid. 80mm.	7.50
Cup and Saucer. 40mm.	4.50
Tea Pot with lid. 70mm.	7.50

Domestic

Salt Pot, octagonal. 85mm.	3.00
Serviette ring.	4.00

Craven China

For mark see *Crested China*, p. 119.

Trademark used by Wiltshaw and Robinson Ltd, Carlton Works, Stoke-on-Trent (usual trademark Carlton).

Animals
Cat sitting, blue bow.
56mm.   12.00
Rabbit, crouching. 60mm long.   6.50

Great War
Cannon Shell. 75mm.   5.00
British Searchlight. 70mm.   25.00
Glengarry, with coloured thistle.
78mm long.   14.50
Kitbag. 72mm.   15.00

Musical Instruments
Lute. 158mm long.   30.00

Footwear
Ankle Boot, laces undone.
78mm long.   4.75

Crown China

For mark see *Crested China*, p. 119.

Trademark used by Wiltshaw and Robinson Ltd, Carlton Works, Stoke-on-Trent (usual trademark Carlton).

Buildings — White
Cottage, two chimneys. 50mm.   9.50
Brick cottage, one chimney, on
rectangular base. 48mm.   12.00

Traditional/National Souvenirs
Blackpool Big Wheel. 82mm.   10.50
Jenny Jones, Welsh lady, standing
figure with black hat, brown
basket and red and green
shawl. 147mm.   35.00
Welsh Hat, with orange band.
44mm.   5.00

Seaside Souvenirs
Motorboat with driver on waves.
120mm long.   17.00
Lifeboat. 113mm long.   12.50
Luggage Trolley inscribed:
Luggage in Advance, etc.
80mm long.   40.00
Portmanteau. 55mm long.   4.00

Animals
Black Cat on oval base. 85mm.   21.50
Dog playing Banjo, inscribed:
Some band. 83mm.   26.00
Dog (puppy), sitting with one
ear raised. 83mm.   8.25
Dog, Scottie, wearing a Tam-
o'shanter, some colouring.
82mm.   11.00
Welsh Goat on rocky base,
inscribed: *Y afr Cymreig* 98mm.   56.50

Birds
Bird cream jug. 84mm.   5.50
Hen, roosting. 60mm long.   6.50
Owl, wearing black mortar board
with red tassel. 75mm.   14.50

Great War
HM Hospital Ship Anglia, Model of
with 2 funnels. 165mm long.   75.00

Home/Nostalgic

Bellows, ornate. 93mm long.	5.50
Grandfather Clock, inscribed: *Make use of time. Let not advantage slip.* 135mm.	10.50
Rocking Chair. 96mm.	19.50
Ornate Armchair with barley twist arms. 120mm.	12.50
Sundial square, inscribed: *Let others tell of storms and showers I'll count the sunny hours.* 90mm.	7.50
Sundial, circular. 76mm.	5.00
Village Pump, round. 76mm.	7.50
Water Pump with trough. 75mm.	11.00

Comic/Novelty

I'm forever blowing bubbles. Pears advert Blue Boy blowing bubbles. Clothes blue, bubble and bowl lustre. 110mm.	75.00
Truck of Coal, *Black diamonds from. . .* 95mm long.	16.00

Alcohol

Beer Barrel on stilts. XXX in red on sides. 57mm.	5.50
Bottle. 90mm.	5.50
Toby Jug, with verse. 79mm.	6.50

British Sports Series

Tennis Player holding Racquet in front of net, inscribed: *40 Love.* Some colouring. 83mm.	75.00

Transport

Motorbike and Sidecar with rider. 102mm long.	75.00
Open Sports Car, inscribed: *DN999.* 105mm long.	40.00

Modern Equipment

Gramophone in Cabinet, black record on turntable, inscribed: *Music hath charms.* 92mm.	57.50
Gramophone with dog, inscribed: *His Masters Voice.* 90mm long.	70.00
Telephone, stick type, inscribed: *Hello, hello.* 115mm.	16.00

Miscellaneous

Hair-pins, ornate box and lid. 100mm long.	5.50
Horseshoe. 105mm long.	3.00

Miniature Domestic

Tea Pot with lid. 90mm.	7.50

Crown Derby

Trademark used by Crown Derby Porcelain Company Ltd.

Footwear

Lady's Slipper. 98mm long.	20.00

Etruscan China

For mark see *Crested China*, p. 128.

Trademark used for a retailer or wholesaler AD, probably manufactured by Charles Waine, Longton. (Usual trademark Venetia).

This mark has only been found on a heavy small vase with a transfer print of H.M.S. Achilles. (A similar print occurs in the Arcadian range, but as print makers sold their wares to all manufacturers this provides no clue!)   12.00

Exceller

For mark see *Crested China*, p. 129.

Trademark used for a retailer in the south of England by Sampson Hancock (and Sons). (Usual trademark Corona).

Traditional/National Souvenirs
Laxey Wheel. 80mm.   40.00
Lancashire Clog. 80mm long.   5.50

Animals
Tortoise. 70mm long.   6.50

Birds
Swan Posy holder. 80mm.   4.75

Great War
Flash Light. 90mm.   10.50
Gurkha Knife. 140mm long.   20.00

Home/Nostalgic
Armchair. 60mm.   7.50
Tobacco Pouch. 75mm long.   9.50

Modern Equipment
Gas Cooker. 70mm.   8.50

Excelsior

For mark see *Crested China*, p. 129.

Trademark used by an unknown manufacturer.

A range of 'smalls' with commemorative Four Flags of the Allies was produced.
Value   from £5.00

Buildings — White
Laxey Wheel.   40.00

Animals
Pig, standing. 70mm long.   8.25

Home/Nostalgic
Grandfather Clock. 100mm.   9.00
Horn Lantern. 85mm.   5.50

Sport
Trophy Cup. 70mm.   10.00

Fairyware

For additional mark see *Crested China*, p. 129.

Trademark used by Schmidt and Co., Carlsbad (Bohemia). (Usual trademark Gemma). These marks appear in blue, red, green or black.

Ancient Artefacts
Loving Cup, 3 handled. 39mm.   3.00
Puzzle Jug. 65mm.   5.50

Historical/Folklore
Coronation Chair. 100mm.   4.50

Seaside Souvenirs
Lighthouse on rocks. 105mm.   4.75

Animals
Cow cream jug. 103mm long.
  (Probably a reproduction in
  miniature of an early
  Staffordshire 'creamer'.)   22.00
Dog, pug, lying, paws forward.   22.50
Tortoise dish with lid.
  80mm long.   7.50

Home/Nostalgic
Bucket with rope handle. 83mm.   3.00
Grandfather Clock, with arabic
  numerals. 105mm.   7.50
Grandmother Clock, with arabic
  numerals. 85mm.   4.75
Pipe, brown, on dish. 72mm long.   10.50
Kettle, very ornate. 71mm.   7.50
Watering Can. 65mm.   5.50

Miscellaneous
Winged Sphinx Jug. 85mm.   18.00

Hats
Top Hat. 43mm.   5.50

Footwear
Sabot. 90mm long.   4.00

Miniature Domestic
Cheese Dish and cover. 55mm.   4.75
Cup and Saucer. 45mm.   4.50
Milk Jug. 40mm.   3.00
Teapot with lid, oval, ribbed
  sides. 48mm.   7.50
Teapot with lid. 60mm.   7.50
Teapot with lid. 85mm.   7.50

Famous Henley China

For mark see *Crested China*, p. 130.

Trademark used by the retailer Hawkins,
Henley-on-Thames, manufactured by
Hewitt and Leadbeater, Willow Potteries
Ltd, Longton. (Usual trademark Willow
Art).

Seaside Souvenirs
Eddystone Lighthouse, not
  named. No. 135. 110mm.   4.75

Animals
Pig, standing.
  2 sizes: 80mm.   10.00
          94mm long.   12.50
Elephant, walking. 52mm.   13.00

Great War
Standing Soldier with rifle,
  inscribed: *Our Brave Defender.*
  130mm.   40.00

Home/Nostalgic
Watering Can. No. 126. 75mm.   5.50

Alcohol
Barrel. No. 100. 35mm long.   3.00

Miniature Domestic
Cheese Dish and cover. 50mm.   6.50

Fenton China

For mark see *Crested China*, p. 130.

Trademark used by E. Hughes and Co., Opal Works, Fenton.

Ancient Artefacts
Leather Bottle. 55mm.   3.00
Loving Cup. 39mm.   3.00

Home/Nostalgic
Iron Trivet. 70mm.   4.00

Miniature Domestic
Cheese Dish and cover. 55mm.   6.50
Cup and Saucer. 35mm.   5.50
Inkwell, square, with lid.
    50mm wide.   10.50

A range of useful domestic items such as egg cups and sealing wax holders was produced.
Value   £2.00-£7.50.

Filey China

Trademark used on wares made for a Filey retailer by Taylor and Kent (Ltd), Florence Works, Longton. (Usual trademark Florentine).

Ancient Artefacts
Loving Cup, 3 handled. 39mm.   3.00

F.L.

F. L.

Trademark used for a retailer on wares made by Arkinstall & Son Ltd, Arcadian Works, Stoke-on-Trent. (Usual mark Arcadian).

Great War
Tommy on Sentry Duty, model of.
110mm.   75.00

Florentine China

For mark see *Crested China*, p. 131.

Trademark used by Taylor and Kent (Ltd), Florence Works, Longton.

Ancient Artefacts
Aberdeen Bronze Pot, not named.
58mm.   2.25
Chester Roman Vase, not named.
62mm.   2.25
Irish Bronze Pot, not named.
52mm.   2.25
Loving Cup, not named. 39mm.   3.00
Puzzle Jug. 67mm.   5.50
Roman Lamp.
2 sizes: 62mm.   3.00
          100mm.   4.00
Salisbury Kettle, not named.
100mm.   2.25
Southwold Jar, not named.
100mm.   2.25
Windsor Urn, not named. 50mm.   2.25

Buildings — White
Blackpool Tower. 117mm.   10.00
London Bridge. 88mm long.   20.00
Marble Arch, not named. 50mm.   10.50
Old Pete's Cottage, near Ramsey.
75mm long.   25.00
St. Paul's Cathedral.
2 sizes: 93mm.   15.50
          130mm.   21.50
Tower Bridge. 115mm long.   25.00
Westminster Abbey, West Front.
85mm.   15.00

Monuments (including Crosses)
Caister-on-Sea, Lifeboat Memorial,
impressed: *1903.* 150mm.   19.50
Glastonbury Tor. 90mm. (rare).   40.00
Great Rock of Ages, Model of.
135mm.   10.50
Iona Cross. 108mm.   6.00
Nelson's Column. 121mm.   45.00

Historical/Folklore
Brussels Boy, 120mm.
Impressed: Mannekin pis.   75.00

Man in Pillory. 105mm.	17.00
Mother Shipton. 72mm.	13.00

Traditional/National Souvenirs

Lancashire Clog. 88mm long.	4.75
Laxey Wheel, Isle of Man, not named. 85mm.	40.00
Legs of Man in Lifebelt. 95mm.	16.00
Lincoln Imp on pedestal. 106mm.	10.00
Thistle Jug. 63mm.	3.00
Welsh Bardic Chair. 88mm.	19.50
Welsh Dragon Water Jug, with lid. 120mm.	13.00
Welsh Harp. 100mm.	5.50
Welsh Hat. 57mm.	4.75
with place name.	7.50

Seaside Souvenirs

Child sitting on Rock, hand to mouth. 110mm.	16.00
Basket Beach Chair.	
2 sizes: 80mm.	7.50
100mm.	10.50
Bathing Machine. 76mm.	7.50
Bathing Machine with figure on steps. 75mm.	14.50
Houseboat. 57mm.	5.00
Yacht, in full sail. 127mm long.	10.50
Fisherman, bust. 84mm.	19.50
Lighthouse, not named. 90mm.	4.50
Whelk Shell. 100mm long.	3.00
Portmanteau. 77mm long.	4.00

Animals

Camel, kneeling. 95mm long.	13.00
Cat, Manx. 61mm.	16.00
Cat, sitting.	
2 sizes: 62mm.	10.00
112mm.	12.50
Cat, sitting, detailed fur. 90mm.	10.00
Cat, with long neck, sitting. 115mm.	8.25
Cheshire cat, The, inscribed: *Always smiling.* 115mm.	7.50
Cat with bandaged face. 88mm.	21.50
Dog, with bandaged face. 90mm.	21.50
Dog, bulldog looking out of kennel. If with black face add £4.00. 73mm.	8.00
Dog, bulldog, sitting. 56mm.	12.00
Dog, King Charles Spaniel, sitting. 68mm and 88mm.	10.00
Dog, King Charles Spaniel, sitting, begging on cushion.	
70mm.	8.25
85mm.	13.00

Dog, lying in cradle. 90mm long.	10.50
Dog, puppy, sitting. 92mm.	10.00
Dogs, two King Charles Spaniels in a Top Hat. 65mm.	16.00
Dolphin Vase. 102mm.	5.50
Elephant, kneeling. 82mm long.	15.00
Fish, inscribed: *Caught at. . . .* 120mm long.	5.50
Fish, open mouthed. 115mm long.	3.00
Fish vase. 115mm.	5.00
Frog cream jug. 45mm.	5.50
Pig, lying down, alert ears. 80mm long.	8.25
Pig, standing.	
2 sizes: 80mm.	9.50
95mm long.	10.00
Larger size found inscribed: *The pig that won't go.*	
Piglet, kneeling. 70mm long.	8.25
Polar Bear. 95mm long.	30.00
Pony, small. 105mm long.	16.00
Rabbit. 98mm long.	8.50
Seal, with ball. 72mm.	16.00
Shetland Pony. 66mm.	22.00
Toad, flat. 74mm long.	10.50
Tortoise. 74mm long.	6.50

Birds

Baby Bird cream jug. 65mm.	5.50
Canary on Rock. 95mm.	10.50
Chicken, hatching from egg. 63mm long.	5.50
Hen roosting.	
2 sizes: 60mm long.	5.50
90mm long.	6.50
Kingfisher cream jug. 60mm.	5.50
Kingfisher with long beak. 80mm.	20.50
Owl. 75mm.	10.50
Parakeet. 75mm.	8.00
Parrot. 94mm.	10.50
Pelican cream jug. 83mm long.	5.50
Sparrow. 63mm.	17.50
Swan.	
2 sizes: 65mm.	6.50
80mm.	6.50
Swan posy holder. 88mm long.	4.75

Great War

Monoplane with 4 bladed prop. 170mm long.	75.00
Battleship. 175mm long.	40.00
Red Cross Van. 88mm long.	23.00

Tank with trailing wheels.
127mm long.   17.50
Tank. 125mm long. (wide variety).   21.00
Shell. 75mm.   3.00
Telescope, folded. 70mm.   13.00
Cenotaph, inscribed: *The blood of heroes is the seed of freedom.* 140mm.   5.50
Gravesend War Memorial. 140mm.   95.00
Great Yarmouth War Memorial, with inscription on all four sides.
2 sizes: 145mm.   22.00
         175mm.   22.00

Home/Nostalgic

Baby in Bootee. 95mm long.   11.00
Baby in Hip Bath. 100mm long.   11.00
Bellows. 107mm long.   5.50
Case, Attaché. 60mm long.   5.50
Chamber Pot. 40mm.   2.50
Coal Bucket. 60mm.   3.50
Cradle on rockers.   6.50
Dolly Tub with two pegs and clothes protruding. 82mm.   26.00
Flat Iron. 76mm.   8.00
Garden Roller. 85mm.   7.50
Grandfather Clock. 135mm.   10.50
Keys on Ring. 46mm.   22.50
Lantern. 65mm.   5.50
Milk Churn and lid. 72mm.   4.50
Oil Lamp. 60mm.   4.75
Old Armchair, The. 85mm.   7.50
Oriental Lamp (Aladdin's Lamp).
2 sizes: 100mm.   4.75
         198mm long.   4.75
Pillar Box, inscribed: *I can't get a letter from you so send you the box.* 76mm.   8.00
Shaving Mug. 55mm.   5.50
Sofa. 82mm long.   10.50
Travel bag, with moulded decoration. 145mm long.   7.50
Watering Can. 68mm.   5.50

Comic/Novelty

Boy's head on container base, two side holes could be used for flowers, candles? 75mm long.   7.50
Boy on Scooter. 106mm.   16.00
Jack in the Box. 90mm.   16.00
Negro Minstrel, bust. 100mm.   19.50

Pierrot, hands and face flesh coloured, black pompoms on hat and costume. 125mm.   30.00
Pixie sitting on Flower Pot. 180mm.   22.00
Pixie sitting on Thimble. 115mm.   22.00
Screw, inscribed: *You could do with a big fat screw.* (Wage rise). 75mm.   21.50

Cartoon/Comedy Characters
Ally Sloper, bust. Not named. 83mm.   19.50

Alcohol
Bottle of Champagne in Ice Bucket, inscribed: *Something good a bottle of the boy.* 85mm.   7.50
Carboy. 76mm.   3.00
Toby Jug. 65mm.   6.50

Sport
Boxing Glove. 65mm long.   30.00
Cricket Bag. 110mm long.   9.00
Golf Ball vase on brown base. 55mm.   12.50
Also found as a scent bottle.   12.00
Football. 70mm.   6.50

Musical Instruments
Grand Piano. 85mm long.   14.50
Tambourine. 70mm.   4.50

Transport
Charabanc with driver. 115mm long.   33.00
Motor Horn, inscribed. *Pip Pip.* 88mm.   22.50
Saloon Car. 88mm long.   30.00

Modern Equipment
Gramophone, hexagonal, with horn. 90mm.   30.00
Gramophone, square, without horn. 53mm.   15.25
Radio Horn. 102mm.   18.00

Footwear
Oriental Shoe with pointed turned up toe. 95mm long.   4.00
Shoe, ladies, 18th century. 95mm long.   7.50
Slipper, open with bow (Babies shoe) 100mm long.   20.00

Miscellaneous

Hair Brush pin box and lid.
134mm long.   14.00

Trowel pin box and lid.
140mm long.   14.00

Miniature Domestic

Cheese Dish, 1 piece. 45mm.	5.50
Cheese Dish and cover, 2 pieces. 45mm.	5.50
Coffee Pot and lid. 63mm.	7.50
Cup and Saucer. 40mm.	4.50
Jug and Bowl, ornate, tulip pattern in relief. 55mm.	5.50
Scent Bottle (contained 'Wallflowers' scent) with metal top which unscrews. 93mm.	12.50
Kettle and lid. 85mm.	7.50
Tea Pot with lid. 3 sizes: 50mm, 60mm and 70mm. All sizes.	7.50
Tea Pot with lid, squat and wide. 88mm long.	7.50
Tea Pot with lid, ribbed sides. 80mm.	7.50

The Foley China

For mark see *Crested China*, p. 135.

Trademark used by Wileman and Co., Foley Potteries, and Foley China Works, Fenton, Longton, subsequently renamed Shelleys Ltd.

All models will be found under Shelley entry.

Fords China

For mark see *Crested China*, p. 135.

Alternative factory mark. In 1874, Charles Ford took over T & C Ford and produced Swan China at Cannon Street, Hanley. Ford also owned Ford & Pointon who produced Fords China at the Norfolk Works, Hanley. Both firms subsequently became branches of J.A. Robinson & Sons. (Usual trademark Arcadian).

Alcohol
Soda Syphon. 100mm.   10.00

Miniature Domestic
Cup and Saucer, ornate. 60mm.   5.50

A range of domestic ware,
  trinket boxes, ashtrays,
  jugs etc.   2.00-6.50

FP & S

For mark see *Crested China*, p. 137.

Trademark used by Ford and Pointon Ltd, Norfolk Works, Hanley, subsequently a branch of J.A. Robinson and Sons, Ltd, and later Cauldon Ltd. (Usual trademark Coronet).

Ancient Artefacts
Loving Cup, 3 handles. No. 19.
  38mm.   3.00

Historical/Folklore
Miner's Lamp. 70mm.   16.00

Home/Nostalgic
Baby's Cradle. 63mm long.   6.50

Footwear
Boot. 35mm.   4.75
Oriental Shoe, with pointed toe.
  90mm long.   6.50

Miniature Domestic
Beaker. 39mm.   2.25
Cheese Dish and cover. 50mm.   5.50
Circular Trinket box and lid.
  60mm.   4.00

Furstenberg

The Garnion Ware

For mark see *Crested China*, p. 137.

Trademark used by a German manufacturer for German Souvenir China.

This mark has only been found on a small 60mm vase with the crest Köln Rh. (Cologne).

THE
GARNION
WARE

Mark used by an unknown manufacturer, thought to be foreign.

Only one small vase with a Guernsey crest has been recorded.   4.00

Gemma

For mark see *Crested China*, p. 137.

Trademark used by Schmidt and Co., Carlsbad (Bohemia). Almost all models can be found with a lustre finish.

Ancient Artefacts

Chester Roman Vase. 65mm.	2.25
Loving Cup, 3 handled.	
3 sizes: 39mm.	3.00
50mm.	
(can be found with	
silver rim).	8.00
68mm.	3.00
Puzzle Beaker. 64mm.	10.50
Puzzle Coffee Pot with inscription: *Try your skill, this pot to fill and not to spill don't use the spout except to pour out.* 64mm.	16.00
Puzzle Cup, actually a beaker without a handle, with verse: *Try how to drink and not to spill and prove the utmost of thy skill.* 35mm.	11.00
Puzzle Ewer. 70mm.	10.50
Puzzle Jug, with verse.	
2 sizes: 70mm.	5.50
80mm.	5.50
Puzzle Jug, no inscription but impressed with a shell pattern, lustre. 52mm.	10.50
Puzzle Milk Jug with verse. 42mm and 72mm.	10.50
Puzzle Loving Cup, 1 or 3 handled with verse. 46mm.	13.00
Puzzle Mug. 51mm.	10.50
Puzzle Tea Pot with verse. 45mm and 62mm.	16.00
Puzzle Teapot. 94mm long.	20.00
Puzzle Tankard. 50mm and 68mm.	10.50
Puzzle Watering Can. 48mm.	16.00

Quite a number of 'smalls' have been recorded, often in Victorian/Gothic style and very ornate, which may or may not be ancient artefacts — but are probably just ornamental!   2.25-4.00

Buildings — White

First and Last Refreshment House, not named. Also found in yellow/orange lustre. 72mm long.	9.50
Cottage. 72mm long.	6.50

Historical/Folklore

Coronation Chair. Can also be found in yellow/orange lustre. 98mm.	4.50
Miners Lamp. 58mm.	16.00

Traditional/National Souvenirs

Kelly from the Isle of Man posy holder, with cat. Inscribed: *A present from the Isle of Man.* 115mm.	40.00
Lancashire Clog. 125mm long.	5.00
Manx Legs inside lifebelt. 85mm.	9.00
Manx Man, three legged with Manx cat on triangular base. 115mm.	47.50
Welsh Candlestick, Welsh lady handle. Black hat. 80mm dia.	20.00
Welsh Hat, often found with 'Welsh' transfer print, add £4.00. 75mm dia.	4.00
Welsh milk jug, Welsh Lady handle, some colouring. 54mm.	24.50
Welsh Ladies' head cream jug. 72mm.	22.00
Welsh Lady, coloured, as handle of cream jug.	
2 sizes: 60mm.	24.50
90mm.	26.50
Welsh Lady, coloured, as handle of Cheese Dish and cover. 74mm long.	26.50
Welsh Lady, coloured, as handle of Watering Can. 65mm.	22.50

Seaside Souvenirs

Bathing Machine money box. 83mm.	14.00
Yacht. 102mm long.	9.00
Lighthouse. 95mm.	5.50
Lighthouse on Rock. 120mm.	5.50
Lobster Ashtray, red lobster forming handle. 63mm long.	10.00
Horn shaped lustre Shell on shell base. 80mm.	7.50

Open Bag on four feet.	6.50
Trunk with separate lid.	
60mm long.	5.50

Animals

Cat, sleeping, lying on side. Can be found inscribed: *Stop Yer Tickling Jock*, add £8.00. 83mm long.	24.50
Cat wearing boots (Puss in Boots). Cat has pink face and ears. 84mm.	30.00
Cat in Bowler Hat. Cat can be found coloured, add £10.00. 63mm.	20.00
Cat, Cavalier style with bows on boots, ruffles on trousers. 83mm.	30.00
Comical Cat, standing hands on hips.	20.00
Cat, sitting in Top Hat. 70mm.	20.00
Cat, in saucepan with black handle. 70mm long.	22.00
Cat, peeping out of frilled rim bowl. Cat's face coloured. 60mm.	25.00
Cat, peeping out of plain rimmed bowl. 58mm.	25.00
Cat, crouching, can have blue bead eyes. 50mm.	16.00
Cat, lying down. Comical. 90mm long.	30.00
Cat, sitting in ladies shoe, with shoe tongue flopping out. 80mm.	23.00
Cat, sitting, paw on rat. 80mm.	40.00
Manx Cat, sitting. 74mm.	25.00
Manx Cat, standing stretched. 94mm long.	30.00
Manx Cat handle on coffee pot or jug. Cat coloured. 80mm.	30.00
Manx Cat as handle on a cup. Cat coloured. 48mm.	30.00
Manx Cat handle, coloured, on miniature Cheese Dish and cover. 74mm long.	30.00
Manx Cats, as two handles on a vase. 73mm.	30.00
Cat's head bowl. 57mm.	14.00
Cow cream jug, some colouring. 127mm long.	22.00
Dog, cross-eyed, with fly on his nose. Can be found with some	

colouring. 76mm.	22.50
Dog, curled up on its side. 98mm long.	24.50
Dog, King Charles Spaniel, sitting. 83mm.	10.50
Dog, pug lying down. 92mm long.	22.50
Dog, pug sitting. 100mm long. Some colouring to face.	20.00
Dolphin Vase. 100mm.	11.00
Fish with open mouth. 140mm long.	3.00
Fish pin cushion holder. 106mm long.	4.50
Fish, pepper pot, black features. 110mm long.	3.00
Fish vase. 110mm long.	4.00
Frog Prince (Frog with crown on head) with colouring. 90mm.	35.00 / 45.00
Pig in Top Hat. Pig has pink muzzle and ears. 60mm.	22.50
Pig as above but with Chef's Hat. 93mm.	50.00
Pig in saucepan with black handle. Pig coloured pink as above. 57mm.	30.00
Pig, standing, hands on hips, pink muzzle and ears. Can also be found in yellow/orange lustre. 100mm long.	30.00
Pig, sitting, can have pink muzzle and ears. 100mm long.	12.50
Pig, curled/lying, pink ears and muzzle. 82mm long.	30.00
Pig, pink, lying on edge of horseshoe ashtray. 65mm long.	19.00
Court Room Pigs	
All coloured pink as follows:	
Policeman, with black helmet with yellow badge. 80mm.	82.50
Barrister, with monocle. 80mm.	55.00
Prisoner, trotters padlocked. 80mm.	75.00
Witnesses, female with balmoral bonnet, male with bowler. 80mm.	80.00
Judge, robed. 80mm.	75.00
Jury Box of six Piglets. 120mm long.	130.00
Shetland Pony. 108mm long.	22.00
Tortoise trinket box and lid. 80mm long.	7.50

Birds

Cockatoo on branch, some colouring. 102mm.	21.00
Hen Egg Basket, 2 pieces, red comb. 85mm long.	7.50
Swan. 80mm.	5.50
Swan posy holder. 90mm long.	4.75

Great War

Despatch Rider's Cap with Goggles. 65mm dia.	25.00
With colouring.	30.00

Home/Nostalgic

Armchair, straight backed. 50mm.	5.50
Basket. 60mm and 90mm.	3.00
Basket, star-shaped. 65mm dia.	3.00
Bucket with looped handle. 80mm.	4.00
Bucket with rope handle. 51mm.	3.00
Candlestick. 80mm.	3.00
Clock, bracket. 76mm.	10.50
Coal Bucket and lid, ornate. 55mm.	6.50
Coal Scuttle, cylinder shaped. 65mm.	5.50
Coal Scuttle, box shaped. 50mm.	3.00
Coal Scuttle, helmet shaped. 70mm.	5.50
Cradle on rockers. 60mm long.	6.50
Dressing Stool. 4 legged. 62mm long.	5.50
Fireplace, inscribed: *There's no place like home.* Some colouring. 68mm.	8.50
Flat Iron.	8.50
Garden Trog. 80mm long.	3.50
Grandmother Clock. Can be found in yellow/orange lustre. 88mm.	5.00
Home Bank, you don't miss what goes in — what comes out will surprise you. 58mm.	10.50
Ink Stand and pen holder with lid.	10.00
Jardiniere. 80mm.	3.00
Jardiniere pot and stand. 121mm.	3.00
Mantel Clock, ornate. 85mm.	10.50
Milk Churn with lid. 72mm.	3.00
Pillar Box, oval. Can be found inscribed: *Letters*, add £3.00. 90mm.	9.50

Policeman's Lamp. 45mm.	4.50
Rocking Chair. 60mm.	12.50
Saucepan with silver lid and black handle. 70mm long.	7.50
Shaving Mug. 60mm.	5.00
Shaving Mug, with raised shell pattern. 55mm.	6.00
Sofa, very ornate. 60mm.	8.50
Stool, circular with 3 legs. 55mm.	4.00
Table. 45mm.	5.50
Tobacco Jar with brown pipe on lid. 70mm.	9.50
Wash Bowl and Jug set. 58mm.	5.50
Watering Can, also yellow/orange lustre. 70mm.	5.50
Wheelbarrow, also in yellow/orange lustre. 3 sizes: 45mm.	5.50
63mm long.	6.50
95mm long.	6.50

Comic/Novelty

Briar Pipe, brown. 76mm long.	10.50
Briar Pipe, brown on leaf tray. 72mm long.	10.50

Alcohol

Beer Mug. 47mm.	4.00

Sport

FA Cup, not named. 68mm.	13.00
FA Cup and lid. 110mm.	6.50
Trophy, 2 handled with separate lid. 150mm.	16.00

Musical Instruments

Tambourine ashtray with gilded discs. 68mm long.	4.50

Modern Equipment

Cash Register. 35mm.	16.00

Shoes

Boot.	
2 sizes: 88mm.	4.75
135mm long. (pierced eyelets)	7.50
Dinant Wooden Shoe. 80mm long.	7.50
Dutch Sabot. 88mm long.	4.00
Ladies Shoe with high heel and fluted tongue. Two different moulds. 75mm long & 80mm long.	7.50

Ladies Shoe with pronounced
   heel & instep. 58mm.   10.00
Clog with buckle. 125mm long.   6.50
Shoe with lace holes. 90mm long.   6.50

Hats
Bowler Hat. 83mm long.   24.50
Fireman's Helmet. 74mm.   30.00
Peaked Cap, very large.
   118mm long. Unglazed.   10.50
Straw Boater. 75mm dia.   7.50
Top Hat, can be match striker.
   45mm.   5.50

Miniature Domestic
Complete tea sets can be found
   on round or square trays. These
   usually consist of teapot, sugar
   bowl, milk jug and two cups and
   saucers. Usually, except saucers,
   each piece is crested but on
   really small sets only the tray
   carries a crest.   15.00-25.00
Cake Dish. Can also be found in
   yellow/orange lustre.
   70mm dia.   3.00
Candlestick. 78mm dia.   3.00
Candleholder shaped match holder
   with striking surface. 60mm.   4.75
Stilton Cheese Dish and cover,
   round. 45mm dia.   7.50
Cheese Dish and cover.
   2 sizes: 63mm.   4.75
       76mm long.   4.75
These can be found coloured, lustre,
   beige and with transfers as well
   as crested in the usual manner.
Cheese Dish with large handle to
   cover. 77mm long.   14.00
Coffee Pot with lid, ribbed sides.
   63mm.   7.50
Coffee Pot with lid with ornate
   handle. 78mm.   5.50
Cup and Saucer. 40mm.   4.50
   Found yellow.   add £4.00
Cylinder Box and lid, moulded
   hinge, for cigarettes. Match
   striker base. No. 2065½.
   63mm.   3.50
   Also found with fixed lid and
   money box slot.   4.00
Dressing Table Set, miniature.
These usually comprise 1 tray,
   2 candlesticks, 1 ring tree and 3

powder bowls with lids.   25.00
Kettle with lid. 75mm.   7.50
Meat Dish and lid, oval.
   76mm long.   6.50
Moustache Cup. 47mm.   6.50
Mug. 50mm.   2.25
Photograph Frame, glazed, with
   cardboard backing. 94mm.   13.00
   No backing.   7.00
Ribbon Plate, hexagonal.
   78mm long.   4.75
Tea Pot, also found in
   yellow/orange lustre.
   3 sizes: 50mm.   7.50
       60mm.   7.50
       70mm.   7.50
Tea Pot, square with lid. 64mm.   12.00
Tea Pot and lid, diamond shaped.
   64mm.   14.00
Toastrack.
   2 sizes: 39mm.   7.50
       70mm.   9.50

W.H. Goss

Gladstone China

For marks see *Crested China*, p. 141.

The prices and a full listing of every Goss piece known to the author will be found in the companion volume to this guide, *The Concise Encyclopaedia and Price Guide to Goss China* by Nicholas Pine.

Values of the thousands of crests and decorations to be found on Goss china appear in *Goss China, Arms, Decorations and Their Values* by the same author. Full details of marks, including 36 illustrations, will be found in chapter 2. of *The Price Guide to Goss China*.

It has been realized during research for *Crested China* that many pieces appear bearing either Arcadian, Willow Art, W.H. Goss or W.H. Goss England marks as the later period of crested china (1925—37) saw much merging of companies and liberal use of marks.

Any piece with the W.H. Goss or W.H. Goss England mark is worth a premium over a similar piece not so marked and a priced list of Goss England, or Third Period items will be found in *The Price Guide to Goss China* previously referred to. New pieces are constantly coming to light however, and that list is by no means exhaustive.

The values of Arcadian and Willow Art models have increased rapidly over the past few years and the differential between these and examples marketed by the Goss factory has narrowed considerably.

Trademark used by Taylor and Kent (Ltd.), Florence Works, Longton (usual trademark Florentine).

Miniature Domestic

Cheese Dish and cover. 50mm.	5.50
Mug, one handle. 35mm.	2.25
Hexagonal Vase. 77mm.	2.25
Ewer. 83mm.	2.25

Gothic China

BRITISH
MANUFACTURE

Trademark used by James Reeves, Victoria Works, Fenton (usual trademark Victoria).

National Souvenirs
Welsh Hat, blue cord and gold tassels, longest place name round brim. 51mm.   7.50

Grafton China

Alternative factory mark, used after 1915 mainly on later domestic ware, in green or black.

For additional marks see *Crested China*, p. 155.

Trademark used by Alfred B. Jones and Sons Ltd., Grafton China Works, Longton, Staffs.

NB. Although the Grafton stock numbering system is very reliable, several items have been found with the wrong numbers. The most usual number is given here. It is not unusual to find two models consistently given the same number.

Parian/Unglazed
Bust of John Peel, inscribed: *D'ye ken John Peel with his coat so grey.* 120mm.   30.00
Bust of Albert I of Belgium, inscribed: *Albert I.* 125mm   60.00
Bust of *Allenby*, impressed, square glazed base. 145mm.   65.00
Bust of George V, inscribed: *George V.* 125mm.   45.00
Bust of David Lloyd George. No.415. 135mm.   45.00
Bust of *Foch*, impressed. Square glazed base. 135mm.   50.00
Bust of Field Marshal, Sir John French. 135mm.   45.00
Bust of Admiral Sir John Jellicoe. 135mm.   47.50

Bust of General Joffre. 155mm.	47.50
Bust of Lord Kitchener, with inscription and impressed on back: *Kitchener. No. 395* 102mm and 125mm.	40.00
Bust of General Pershing on square glazed base. 148mm	82.50
Bust of Lord Roberts, impressed on back: *Roberts.* 135mm.	47.50
Bust of *Sir Walter Scott*, impressed: *Scott*, on circular glazed base. 120mm.	16.00
Bust of President Wilson. 140mm.	75.00

Ancient Artefacts

These models are often found not named and are quite often decorated with a coloured transfer view rather than a crest.

Ancient Kettle with 2 spouts, not found named. No.325. 52mm.	2.25
Aberdeen Bronze Pot. No. 217. 65mm.	2.25
Ale Pot. No.176. 60mm.	3.00
Brading Vase. No.195. 35mm dia.	3.00

Brading Roman Vase. 5 vases of different shape:

No. 135. 60mm.	3.00
No. 136. 62mm.	3.00
No. 137. 62mm.	3.00
No. 139. 55mm.	3.00
No. 195. 30mm.	4.50
Burial Urn, inscribed: *Ancient British Burial Urn excavated in Cornwall.* 64mm	3.00
British Vase. No. 17. 40mm.	3.00
Butter Pot. No. 185. 40mm.	3.00
Canterbury Pilgrim Bottle. Rd No. 470749. No. 317. 52mm.	3.00
Chester Roman Vase. No. 165. 60mm.	3.00

This has been found inscribed wrongly:*Roman Lamp Pompeii 1st century AD.*

Chinese Pilgrim Bottle. No. 269. 88m.	3.00

Chinese Teapot and lid. 2 different models:

No. 70. 54mm.	4.50
No. 77. 54mm.	4.50

Chinese Vase. 3 vases of different shapes:

No. 276. 86mm.	3.00
No. 278. 85mm.	3.00
No. 282. 75mm.	3.00
Collingbourne Ducis, Medieval Pilgrim Bottle found at. No. 181. 53mm.	3.00
Cyprus Vase. No. 120. 70mm.	
Elizabethan Bushel, not named.	4.00

Ely Drinking Mug. 2 shapes:

No. 186. 40mm.	3.00
No.187. 39mm and 46mm.	3.00

English Wine Glass. 4 glasses of different shape:

No. 309. 75mm. (Ale glass)	4.75
No. 310. 75mm. (Goblet)	4.75
No. 311. 70mm. (Tumbler)	4.75
No. 312. 70mm. (Ovoid bowl)	4.75

Egyptian Pottery — these specimens were discovered by Doctor Flinders Petra (sic) *in Egypt, manufactured about 4,000 BC.*

No. 155. 60mm.	3.00
No. 156. 50mm.	3.00
No. 157. 60mm.	3.00
No. 158. 51mm.	3.00

The following two models have this inscription and further inscriptions.

Egyptian Bottle. No. 159. 57mm.	3.00
Egyptian Tear Bottle. No. 151. 42mm.	3.00
Egyptian Vase. No. 323. 45mm.	3.00
Hereford Kettle. This model has a separate lid. No. 179. 80mm. (Can be found wrongly numbered 174.)	5.50
Hythe Crowellian Mortar. 40mm.	3.00

London Vessels. 6 different models:

No. 202. No size details	3.00
No. 204. 44mm.	3.00
No. 205. 48mm.	3.00
No. 206. 45mm.	3.00
No. 207. 84mm.	3.00
No. 208. 70mm.	3.00
Norman Pot, inscribed: *Norman pot from original in Burley Hill Museum.* No. 182. 45mm.	3.00
Pompeian Vase. No. 110. 35mm.	3.00

Pompeian 1st Century Lamp.

No. 118. 75mm.	4.75

Portland Vases, not named. 50mm.

No. 150 and No. 530.	3.00

Loving Cup, not found named.
No. 145. 40mm. 3.00
Reading Roman Vase. 50mm. 3.00
Roman Lamp. No. 119. 60mm. 3.00
Roman Vase. No. 160. 48mm. 3.00
Romsey Bushel, Model of Ancient.
No. 149. 53mm. 6.00
Salisbury Kettle.
No. 173. 97mm. 3.00
No. 174 105mm. 3.00
(Can be found wrongly
numbered No. 179.)
Shakespeare's Jug. No. 124.
76mm. 3.00
Shrewsbury Roman Ewer,
inscribed:*Roman Ewer found at*
Uriconium original now in
Shrewsbury Museum. No. 175.
76mm. 3.00
Southwold Jar. 3.00
Swiss Urn, inscribed: *Urn from*
Swiss Tacustrine Habitation.
No. 184. 40mm. 3.00
Swiss Urn. No. 185. 44mm. 3.00
Yaverland Roman Vase, 50mm. 3.00

Buildings — Coloured

Bell Hotel, Tewkesbury.
88mm long. 50.00
Captain Cook's house Great Ayton
re-erected in Melbourne.
95mm long (rare) 125.00
Couch's House, Polperro, on roof,
with arms of Polperro. 90.00
House on the Props, Polperro.
100mm long. 85.00
Old Chapel, Lantern Hill,
Ilfracombe. 72mm long. 65.00
Old Toll Bar, Gretna Green.
125mm long. 195.00

Buildings — White

Bath Abbey. 112mm. 26.00
Bath Abbey, West front. 105mm. 19.50
Bargate, Southampton. 90mm. 20.00
The Tower, Blackpool. No. 521
2 sizes: 116mm. 12.50
135mm. 13.50
Carnarvon Castle. 90mm. 57.50
Citadel Gateway, Plymouth.
105mm. 28.00
Cottage, not found named.
No. 501. 68mm long. 10.00
First and Last Refreshment House in

England, Land's End, found
numbered 469 and 627.
75mm long. 16.00
Gynn Inn, Blackpool, inscribed:
Model of Blackpools famous
landmark, the old Gynn Inn
demolished 1921. No. 520.
125mm long. 55.00
Houses of Parliament. No. 424.
115mm. 30.00
Irish Round Tower (not named),
often has green shamrocks
on base. No. 417. 137mm. 10.50
with shamrocks 14.50
Lincoln Cathedral, West Front.
115mm. 20.00
Old Cornish Cottages. 125mm long. 47.50
Old Chapel, Lantern Hill,
Ilfracombe. 75mm long. 21.50
Old Toll-Gate House, including
path with gate, inscribed:
Ye olde toll-gate house. No. 498.
130mm long. 40.00
Old Toll-Gate House, as above
but not on base with path and
gate, and not named. No. 502
and No. 501. 63mm long. 22.00
Oldest Chemists Shop in England
established 1790, also can be
found inscribed: *Model of the*
oldest pharmacy in England,
Knaresborough, Yorkshire.
Established in the reign of George
1st 1790, some colouring.
97mm long. 60.00
Plas Mawr, Conway. 93mm (rare). 56.50
St. Pauls Cathedral, London.
2 sizes: No. 423. 137mm. 19.50
No. 633. 115mm. 16.00
Scarborough Castle Ruins, not
named. 104mm. 40.00
Skegness Clock Tower, not
named. 127mm. 12.00
Smallest House in Great Britain,
Conway. No. 560. 92mm. 24.50
Tonbridge Castle. 88mm long. 30.00
Westminster Abbey, front.
No. 422. 121mm. 30.00

Monuments (including Crosses)

Banbury Cross. 141mm. 17.00
Irish Cross, not named, green
shamrocks on base.
No. 419. 138mm. 12.50

Lady Warrior in duck boat,
holding shield & sword. 125mm. 110.00
Lloyd George Statue, Carnarvon.
150mm. 65.00
Ramsgate Lifeboat Memorial
(Statue of Lifeboatman), not
named but often found with the
inscription: *Souvenir from the
Imperial Bazaar Albion Hill,
Ramsgate, which was twice
wrecked by Zeppelin bombs on May
17th 1915 and June 17th 1917* on
base. 140mm. 30.00
Rufus Stone. 96mm. 5.50
(John) Ruskin Memorial Stone,
inscribed: *John Ruskin
MDCCCXIX-MDCCC* and
religious verse.
No. 515. 120mm. 12.50
St. Anne's Lifeboat Memorial.
No. 495. 161mm. 14.50
Sandbach Crosses. 130mm. 75.00
Southport Lifeboat Memorial.
121mm. 14.50

Historical/Folklore
Antique Hornwork Box, Model of,
plus lid. No. 308. 70mm long. 16.00
Antique Bureau. 64mm. 11.00
Ark, rectangular. 73mm long. 14.00
Burn's Chair. No. 667. 88mm. 7.50
Charles I bottle with removable
head lid, not named and
thought by some collectors to be
Guy Fawkes. No. 209. 96mm. 40.00
Coaching Hat, not named.
No. 213. 60mm long. 7.50
*President Wilson's Grandfather's
Chair.* No. 491 and 492. 75mm. 14.50
Ride a cock horse to Banbury Cross
(lady on horse). No. 569.
106mm long. 40.00
Robin Hood. 135mm. 75.00
St. Thomas A Becket. 130mm. 40.00
Saint Wilfred of Ripon. 136mm. 40.00
Ye Old Chertsey Bell. 57mm. 10.50

Traditional/National Souvenirs
Blackpool Big Wheel, not named.
2 sizes: 78mm. 10.50
100mm. 14.50
Cornish Pasty. No. 340.
95mm and 110mm long. 7.50

A Cornish Pasty. No. 578.
90mm long. 7.50
John Peel, Bust. 72mm. 22.00
Lancashire Clog, sometimes
found inscribed: *Model of
Lancashire Clog.* No. 407.
90mm long. 5.50
with inscription 6.50
Leaking Boot, Cleethorpes, statue of
boy, boot joined to hand by
string. 156mm. 50.00
Lincoln Imp on pedestal. 108mm. 8.50
Prime Cheddar Cheese. 38mm. 6.50
Cheddar Cheese with floral decoration and verse. Never found
factory marked. 60mm dia. 7.50
Ripon Horn Blower, often found not
named, inscribed: *The horn is
blown every night at 9. Formerly it
denoted that the watch was set for
the night.* 136mm. 12.50
Toby Jug, coloured. Irish. 80mm. 30.00
Toby Jug, coloured. Scots. 80mm. 30.00
Toby Jug, coloured. Welsh Lady.
76mm. 30.00
Welsh Harp. No. 418. 80mm. 10.00
Welsh Hat, with blue band and
bow, found with longest Welsh
place name printed round
brim. No. 183. 50mm. 7.50
Welsh Milk Can. No. 479.
103mm. 4.75
Yarmouth Bloater. 115mm. 5.50

Seaside Souvenirs
Bathing Machine. No. 256.
2 sizes. 55mm long. 7.50
65mm long. 8.50
Boat with billowing sail,
inscribed: *Polly.* No. 448.
115mm long. 30.00
Boat, flat bottomed with bird's
head as figurehead. No. 442.
80mm long. 5.50
Lifeboat. No. 332. 110mm long. 9.50
Fisherman, bust on round,
waisted plinth. No. 254. 116mm. 16.00
Punt with two girls aboard.
115mm long with wooden pole. 40.00
Rowing Boat, can be found
inscribed: *Sant Cybi* (patron
saint of Holyhead) on models
with a Holyhead crest, *Robin
Hoods Bay and Whitby.* No. 169.
130mm long. 7.50
inscribed 12.00

Fisherman's Creel with lid.
No. 292. 72mm long. 4.00
Beachy Head Lighthouse, with black
band. No. 3. 135mm. 11.50
Eddystone Lighthouse. No. 315.
102mm. 7.50
Lighthouse, with steps on base and
gilded windows. No. 47. 145mm. 7.50
Lighthouse, miniature. 71mm. 6.50
Lighthouse pepper pot.
108mm. 5.00
Shell dish. No. 533. 63mm long. 3.00
Shell with handle. No. 536. 54mm. 4.00
Oyster Shell, on coral legs.
No. 496. 51mm. 5.50
Oyster Shell, on stand. No. 496.
83mm dia. 3.00
Shell dish with handle. No. 537.
80mm. 3.00
Shell Jug. No. 524 on 3 small
whelk shell feet. 76mm. 12.50
Whelk Shell,
5 sizes: No. 57. 80mm long. 4.00
No. 65. 45mm long. 4.00
No. 65. 85mm long. 4.00
No. 428. 70mm long. 4.00
No. 528. 115mm long. 6.50
Bathing Beauty, reclining,
wearing swimsuit and
mob-cap, holding parasol.
135mm (uncommon). 60.00
Boy holding model yacht, on
beach base, coloured hair and
yacht. No. 563. 85mm. 75.00
Boy swimming on a rectangular
'sea' base. Hair and eyes
coloured. No. 565.
120mm long. 75.00
Girl kneeling on 'beach' base
with red bucket and spade,
brown hair and red hat brim.
No. 564. 75mm (563-565 are all
quite rare). 75.00
Toddler on Donkey. 85mm and
109mm. 75.00

Countryside.
Axe in Tree Stump. No. 61. 80mm. 10.50

Animals
Some Grafton animals were given
tiny glass bead eyes, more often
than not these are missing, leaving
small holes. Even without these
beads the models remain very
attractive, but obviously a complete

model is more desirable and £8.00
should be added for models
having glass eyes. The range of
large comical cats with these
coloured bead eyes and coloured
bows are particularly appealing
but are hard to find.
Bear, dressed as boy, standing on
shell tray. 85mm. 40.00
Bear and Ragged Staff.
2 sizes: 85mm. 19.50
100mm. 23.00
The larger version is No. 224
and has bead eyes.
Water Buffalo, lying with head
turned, curved horns.
110mm. (very rare). 90.00
Calf, not named, but mostly
found with cartoon transfer
of farmer and wife behind gate
with calf on the other side (add
£7.00). No. 287. 100mm long. 20.00
Camel, 2 humps. No. 242. 30.00
Cat, Cheshire, inscribed: *The
Cheshire Cat* and *Always smiling.*
1 yellow glass eye. No. 288.
86mm. 11.00
Cat, Cheshire, with red mouth
and nose, one bead eye (green
or red) and one eye closed,
inscribed: *The Cheshire Cat.*
Found with and without separate shield carrying crest.
No. 171.
2 sizes: 86mm. 7.50
100mm. 12.00
Cat, crouching and angry.
No. 211. 55mm. 26.00
Cat, crouching, fat and angry
with tail in the air. Found with
bead eyes. No. 303. 88mm long. 30.00
Cat in Jar, inscribed: *From Chicago
Perishable.* No. 277. 80mm. 57.50
Cat singing, red mouth and
green bow. 75mm. 33.00
Cat Scent Bottle, sitting with removable head. 93mm. 40.00
Cat, sitting and comical, green
bow and tail at front with bead
eyes (blue or green). No. 319.
2 sizes: 88mm. 24.50
103mm. 28.50
Cat, sitting and winking. No. 612.
2 sizes: 80mm red or orange
bow. 24.50
105mm yellow bow. 26.50

Cat, sitting and comical, yellow bow. Found with verse: *As I was going to St.Ives.* No. 351. 94mm.	26.50
Cat, sitting and comical, green bow and tail at front, with bead eyes. No. 339. 154mm.	30.00
Cat, sitting and comical, yellow bow and tail at back, with bead eyes. No. 344 or No. 420 (no colouring £20.00). 146mm.	30.00
Cat, sitting, winking with both thumbs in *Thumbs Up* position, Orange bow, thumbs painted black. 83mm.	40.00
Cat, sitting, tail at back, yellow bow. No. 320. 104mm.	30.00
Cat, standing, arched back and tail in the air with green bow. No. 303. 100mm.	30.00
Cat, standing, arched back, small tail, green bow. No. 527. 78mm.	25.00
Cat, standing and comical, blue bow and green eyes. 88mm long.	28.50
(Cat) Kitten. No. 211. 50mm.	26.00
Lady Cat, upright, wearing coat and bonnet and carrying hand-bag, bow to neck. 90mm.	80.00
Cat salt pot, red open mouth and green bow tied at back. No. 729. 92mm.	16.00
The Jersey Cow, often found not named. No. 545. 60mm.	16.00
Bulldog, British, inscribed: *Slow to start but what a hold*. 83mm.	19.50
Bulldog, standing with feet wide apart. No. 391. 51mm.	13.00
Bulldog, sitting, can have bead eyes (yellow or green). No. 250. 2 sizes: 88mm.	40.00
102mm.	45.00
Bull-terrier pepper pot. 80mm.	13.00
Dog in boater and clothes. 88mm.	80.00
Dog, scent bottle with head lid. No. 232. 100mm.	40.00
Dog, Greyhound, standing with front legs on small oval base. No. 709. 102mm long.	47.50
Dog, with 2 heads, one head is smiling and the other is sad. Two varieties. Sometimes found with a paper tag around neck inscribed: *Two heads are better than one.* No. 645. 38mm.	40.00

No. 646. 63mm.	40.00
Dog, King Charles Spaniel, sitting. No. 390. 53mm.	11.50
Dog, kneeling, wearing a green cap. No. 488. Can be found coloured with match holder. 85mm.	45.00
Dog, Labrador Pup, sitting with bead eyes (yellow or green). Can be found painted yellow.	19.00
No. 355. 85mm. painted	30.00
Dog, Puppy, sitting, one ear raised and scratching with back leg. (Often found coloured with no crest.) No. 410. 85mm.	14.00
Coloured	20.00
Dog, running, with fly or bee on tail, some colouring. 95mm long.	47.50
A stylised version of this was made as a menu holder, coloured yellow and white. (late) 80mm long.	40.00
Dog, Scottie, standing. No. 432. Can be found with bead eyes. 94mm long.	26.00
Three varieties of dog, all with some colouring and marked *Swains Studdy Series* are as follows:	
Dog, yawning, on ashtray base. 105mm long.	25.00
Dog, with ball in mouth, on ashtray base. 105mm.	25.00
Dog, yawning. 46mm.	30.00
Dog, with ball in mouth. 46mm.	30.00
Elephant, circus, standing on forelegs on stool. 105mm.	82.50
Elephant, sitting and comical. No. 438. 127mm.	40.00
Found coloured purple.	65.00
Elephant, sitting with trunk raised, comical. 75mm.	40.00
Elephant, walking. No. 426. 100mm.	30.00
Elephant, walking. No. 470. 2 sizes: 50mm.	25.00
80mm.	30.00
Can be found painted red or purple.	45.00
Elephant, walking. No. 490.	24.50
Can be found coloured purple.	45.00
Elephant, with sandwich boards, crest one side and inscribed: *Turn me round* on the other. 102mm.	100.00
Fish, curved vase. No. 196. 57mm.	5.50

Fish, curved tail and open
mouth. No. 392. 105mm long.   5.50
Fish, curved with bead eyes.
No. 196. 125mm long.   5.50
Fish, curved body and open
mouth. No. 393. 80mm long.   8.25
Fish. No. 244. 110mm long.   4.50
Fish, straight and fat. No. 247.
2 sizes: 88mm long.   4.50
         110mm long. (bead eyes)   5.50
Fish, straight and fat with open
mouth. No. 341. 102mm long.   4.00
Fish, straight with open mouth.
No. 97. 100mm long.   3.50
Fish, straight and thin. No. 302.
2 sizes: 76mm long.   3.50
         112mm long.   5.50
Large size can be found with
bead eyes.
Fox with bead eyes (yellow). No. 462.
2 sizes: 80mm long.   50.00
         140mm long.   56.50
Fox, without bead eyes (i.e.
model designed without them).
135mm long.   50.00
Can be found painted red.
Fox with pheasant on stand.
No. 434. Can be found painted
red. 139mm long (late).   60.00
Fox crouching. No. 467.
76mm long.   55.00
Frog, with closed mouth, can be
found with bead eyes. No. 204.
72mm.   20.50
Jersey Cow. 60mm.   26.00
Lion, standing. 105mm long.   16.00
Monkey with bead eyes.
No. 242. 87mm.   13.00
No. 245. 70mm.   13.00
No. 286. 70mm.   13.00
Can be found painted yellow,
red, green or blue.   30.00
Monkey, sitting, wearing coat.
No. 245. 62mm.   13.00
Can be found painted yellow
or blue.   30.00
Mouse, sitting up. No. 210.
42mm.   16.00
Mouse, sitting up, holding nut,
yellow bead eyes. No. 243.
43mm.   27.00
Mouse. No. 222. 68mm.
(Candlesnuffer).   16.00
Mouse on cheese, can be found
purple or blue with pink ears.
No. 459. 55mm (late).   37.50

Pig, fat, lying asleep, inscribed:
Wunt be druv. No. 421. 83mm.   22.00
Pig, running, red bead eyes.
No. 416. 87mm.   30.00
Pig, sitting, long pointed nose
and long ears tilted forward.
No. 263. 90mm long.   30.00
Pig, sitting with raised ears.
No. 203. 70mm.   24.50
Pig, sitting and laughing,
inscribed: *Wunt be druv.*
No. 338. 65mm.   47.50
Pig, sitting, is much fatter than
the above, inscribed: *Wunt be
druv.* No. 341. 95mm long.   25.00
Pig, sitting up on hind legs,
found inscribed: *Wunt be druv,*
or *I won't be drove.*
No. 417. 70mm.   28.50
No. 420. 80mm.   28.50
Pig, standing, fat and inscribed:
Wunt be druv.
No. 342. 98mm long.   30.00
Pig, standing, can be found with
no inscription but normally
found inscribed: *Wunt be druv* or
I won't be drove. No. 343.
70mm long.   10.00
Pig, standing, inscribed: *Wunt
be druv.* 88mm long.   15.00
Polar Bear. No. 102. 105mm long.   47.50
Polar Bear, standing on rocky
base. 117mm long.   56.50
Pony, not named. No. 493.
2 sizes: 70mm.   20.00
         105mm long.   23.50
Very rarely largest size found
inscribed: *New Forest Ponies.*   30.00
Rabbit, with bead eyes (yellow).
No. 240. 112mm long.   13.00
Rabbit trinket dish, pink eyes.
No. 734. 120mm long.   15.00
Rat, sitting up. Candle snuffer.
No.210. 65mm.   30.00
Seal. No. 402. 70mm long.
(This is a very delicate model).   17.50
Snail. No. 328. 80mm long.   13.00
Squirrel holding nut, can be
found with bead eyes. No. 327.
75mm.   17.00
Terrapin. No. 253. 92mm long.   10.50

Birds
Bird/fledgling, some colouring.
No. 435. 65mm. (very plump
and pretty).   21.50

Grotesque Chick posy holder with orange legs. No. 737. 68mm. — 29.00

Birds, two with long beaks and spread wings in the form of a tall taper vase. 145mm. — 13.00

Chicken hatching from Egg, can be found with bead eyes. No. 326. 73mm long. — 9.50

Chick. 60mm. — 11.50

Cock on circular base. No. 454. 100mm (pair with hen). — 17.50

Duck, swimming, occasionally found inscribed: *Aylesbury duck*. No. 377. 96mm long. — 19.50
inscribed. — 27.50

Duck posy holder. No. 442. 80mm. — 7.50

Duck posy or cigarette holder, some colouring. No. 732 115mm. — 30.00

Duck match holder, striker and ashtray. Some colouring. No. 735. 80mm. — 30.00

Hen, on circular base. No. 453. 100mm (pair with cock). — 17.50

Hen, roosting on basket base. 82mm. — 10.50

Kingfisher on base. No. 670. 62mm. — 40.00

Owl on rocky base. No. 687. 132mm. — 16.00
(very impressive model).

Penguin. No. 329. 88mm. — 14.50

Swan, head under wing. No. 409. 85mm long. — 15.00

Great War

American Soldier (Doughboy), squatting. — 100.00
One Model found fully coloured. — 350.00
Also appears painted black except for cigar. No. 85. 80mm. — 200.00

British Territorial Bulldog, seated figure of Tommy with bulldog face, red and blue bands on hat. No. 262. 88mm. — 120.00

Kitchener bust (glazed) on circular base, inscribed: *Lord Kitchener of Khartoum creator of British Army 1914/1918. Born June 24th 1850. Died serving his country June 5th 1916 by the sinking of HMS Hampshire off the Orkneys.* No. 395.

2 sizes: 100mm. — 35.00
130mm. — 40.00

Kitchener match holder, caricature of Kitchener's head inside with life-belt, some colouring. No. 214. 95mm dia.
plain — 30.00
coloured — 56.50
Or could it possibly be the Kaiser?

Sailor, seated and holding a model submarine, hat band impressed: *Victory*. Is often found inscribed: *Weve got 'U' well in hand*. — 60.00
Can also be found fully coloured. No. 452. 80mm. (very rare). — 135.00

Soldier leaving Trench, inscribed: *Over the top*. No. 483. 118mm. — 125.00

Soldier throwing Hand Grenade, inscribed: *The Bomb Thrower*. No. 425. 140mm. — 125.00

Soldier throwing Hand Grenade, without the ammunition box which must have been added for stability. A forerunner of above. One example known. 140mm (very rare). — 250.00

Biplane, fixed prop. No. 450 145mm long. (rare) — 115.00

Monoplane, fixed prop. No. 414. 135mm long. — 55.00

HMS Dreadnought, ship with high prow. No. 408. 142mm long.
Same ship with same stock number found inscribed: *HMS Gosport* or *HMS Victory*. — 65.00
No name. — 40.00

HMS Iron Duke. No. 431. 155mm long. — 85.00

Submarine, inscribed:*E9*. No. 406. 145mm long. — 35.00

Motor Ambulance with curtains, inscribed: *Motor ambulance car given by Staffordshire china operatives. British Red Cross Society: St John Ambulance Association. Load not to exceed 1 driver, 1 attendant and patients.* No. 397. 98mm long. — 40.00

Motor Tractor, inscribed: *Model of motor tractor used on western front*. No. 456. 80mm long. — 170.00

Renault Tank. 100mm long. — 65.00

Tank with steering wheels,
inscribed: *H.M. Landship Creme
de Menthe.* No. 413.
118mm long.   22.50

Tank, no steering wheels,
inscribed: *H.M. Landship Creme
de Menthe.* No. 413. 98mm long.   24.50

Also found inscribed: *Model of
Whippet Tank.* Rare. 98mm long.   70.00

Whippet Tank, inscribed: *Model
of Whippet Tank.* No. 449.
115mm long.   115.00

Alpine Gun with moving wheels,
inscribed: *Model of Alpine gun.*
No. 394. Very rare. 105mm long.   350.00

Desert Gun. No. 430.
155mm long.   52.50

Field Gun on Sledge, inscribed:
French 75. No. 412. 160mm long.   47.50

German Gun captured by British.
No. 403. 153mm long.   30.00

Trench Howitzer (found with
Ramsgate Imperial Bazaar
inscription. See Monuments.
Ramsgate Lifeboat Memorial)
No. 404. 75mm long.   10.50

Cannon Shell. No. 400. 76mm.   5.25

Cannon Shell, inscribed:*Jack
Johnson.* No. 339. 90mm.   10.50

German Incendiary Bomb. No. 405.
80mm.   11.00

Mills Hand Grenade with removable
metal pin, often found without
inscription. No. 411. 83mm.   22.00

Bandsman's Drum. No. 235.
45mm.   5.50

Bell Tent with open flaps, with or
without base. No. 239. 65mm.   10.50

Boot with Puttee. No. 389. 75mm.   22.00

Anzac Hat with blue band.
110mm long.   25.00

Colonial Soldier's Hat. No. 238.
89mm long.   12.50

Water Bottle. No. 234. 80mm.   13.00

Cenotaph, inscribed: *MCMXIV—
MCMXIX — The Glorious Dead*
and 3 coloured flags on reverse.
2 sizes: 135mm.   12.00
    (Flags add £12.00).
155mm.   16.00
    (Flags add £12.00).

Glandford Brigg War Memorial.
114mm.   115.00

Home/Nostalgic

Anvil on heavy base. No. 552.

70mm.   6.50

Baby crawling naked, brown hair,
blue eyes. No. 544.
100mm long.   95.00

Baby sitting up. No. 481. 63mm.   16.00

Baby's Rocking Cradle. No. 294.
62mm long.   7.50

Basket with handle. No. 29.
52mm.   3.00

Cabin Trunk. 56mm long. No. 351.   7.50

Flat Iron. No. 162. 65mm long.   8.50

Grandfather Clock. No. 396.
110mm.   16.00

Horn Lantern, inscribed. No. 306.
76mm.   7.50

Laundry Basket. No. 534.
75mm long.   6.50

Milk Can and Lid. No. 417.
106mm.   5.50

Milk Can and Lid. No. 478.
72mm.   4.75

Rocking Horse. 125mm long.   40.00

Shaving Mug. 40mm.   5.50

Village Water Pump. No. 331.
80mm.   6.50

Watering Can.   6.50

Wing Chair. No. 389. 73mm.   15.25

Comic/Novelty

Billiken. No. 291. 44mm.   5.00

Boy, grotesque, sitting
cross-legged, top of head on
egg-cup. 62mm.   30.00

Boy Scout holding bugle. 133mm.   85.00

Chinese Man Pepper Pot, some
colouring. No. 726. 70mm.
(There must be a matching Salt
Pot).   17.50

Deep Sea Diver. No. 261.
105mm.   125.00

Dutchman, sitting cross legged,
and holding cheese. No. 230.
85mm.   17.00

Fu Hing God of Happiness, Chinese
Priest sitting upright, holding
baby, some colouring. 115mm.   40.00

Gladiators Head, Candlesnuffer.
No. 228.   23.50

Head on a rock, comic, could be
Kitchener wearing a pharaoh's
headress. 67mm.   30.00

Head, comic salt pot, miserable
face and droopy bow tie.
No. 225. 85mm (matches below).   12.50

Head, comic pepper pot,
   happy face and perky bow tie.
   No. 258. 85mm. (matches above). 12.50
Lemon with lid, stalk handle.
   No. 62. 60mm. 7.50
Pierrot, sitting cross-legged on
   box playing banjo, some
   colouring. Found with
   inscription: *As I was going to
   St. Ives*. No. 566. 103mm. 30.00
Teapot Man, face on lid, spout
   and handle form arms, some
   colouring. 48mm. 45.00
Watch Stand, Father Time head
   with beard forming legs.
   No. 154. 110mm. 40.00

Cartoon Characters
Bonzo Dog, pepper pot. 80mm. 25.75
Sunny Jim with red bow tie and
   black topper. 86mm. 45.00

Alcohol
Bottle with cork. No. 715.
   68mm. 5.50
Champagne Bottle. No. 221.
   102mm. 7.50
Champagne Bottle pepper pot.
   No. 225. 102mm. 7.50
Man in Barrel, head and feet
   protruding, inscribed: *No beer.*
   No. 429. 115mm. 34.50
Tankard. 80mm. 3.00

Sport
Footballer with ball on small base.
   130mm. 80.00
Golfer holding bag of golf clubs,
   comic figure, inscribed: *The
   Colonel*. No. 352. Cigarette is
   often broken off. 90mm. 30.00
   Can be found fully coloured. 52.50
Golf Ball salt pot. 52mm. 6.50
Golf Ball pepper pot. No. 293.
   52mm. 6.50
Tennis player, lady holding
   racquet (reputedly Suzanne
   Lenglen). 133mm. 85.00

Transport
Charabanc, with 5 rows of seats,
   inscribed: *Dreadnought*.
   No. 568. 100mm long. 45.00
   if inscribed 55.00

Mons Bleriot, bust, inscribed: *First
   man to fly across the channel in an
   aeroplane July 25th 1900*. 85mm. 75.00

Modern Equipment
Horn Gramophone, square base.
   No. 641. 92mm. 22.00

Hats
Bowler Hat. No. 710. 93mm long. 30.00
Top Hat. No. 189. 37mm. 7.50
Fireman's Helmet. No. 66. 65mm. 22.00

Footwear
Boot. No. 237. 80mm long. 7.50
Sabot. No. 212. 80mm long. 4.75
   Also appears with manufactured
   hole for wall hanging. Same price.
Oriental Shoe, pointed. No. 170.
   80mm and 95mm long. 6.50
Shoe, lady's 18th century. No. 50.
   83mm long. 8.50
Slipper Wall Pocket. 100mm long. 7.50

Miscellaneous
Bell, miniature. No. 250. 55mm. 5.50
Handbell, no clapper.
   2 sizes: No. 15. 82mm. 7.50
                No. 265. 51mm. 4.50
Bell. No. 153. 86mm. 6.50
Horse's Hoof. No. 236.
   72mm long. 5.50
Dice, Trump Indicator, heart,
   diamond, club and spade and
   no trump on five sides. 35mm. 23.00

Miniature Domestic
Beaker. No. 73. 52mm. 2.25
Candleholder, circular. No. 80. 3.00
Cheese Dish and cover (2 pieces)
   No. 78. 65mm long. 7.50
Cup and Saucer, fancy. No. 107.
   48mm. 5.50
Cup and Saucer, No. 108.
   110mm dia. 5.50
Cup and Saucer. No. 122.
   67mm dia. 5.50
Cup. No. 147. 39mm. 2.25
Milk Jug. No. 72. 40mm. 2.25
Mug with handle. No. 36. 48mm. 2.25
Mug with handle. No. 143. 41mm. 2.25

Numbered Domestic and Ornamental Wares

No. 2. Vase. Ivy covered. 60mm.	3.50
No. 3. Jug, elongated spout. 80mm.	2.25
No. 4. Dish, crinkle edged. 69mm. or Jug. 75mm.	2.25
No. 5. Vase. Bagware. 45mm.	3.00
No. 8. Vase. 61mm.	2.25
No. 9. Vase, shaped edge. 62mm.	2.50
No. 10. Vase, shaped. 70mm.	2.25
No. 11. Vase. 66mm.	2.25
No. 12. Jug. 77mm.	2.25
No. 13. Jug. 67mm.	2.25
No. 16. Vase. 37mm	2.25
No. 19. Vase, shaped. 65mm.	2.25
No. 20. Crinkle top vase. 70mm.	2.25
No. 22. Vase, bulbous. 50mm.	2.25
No. 23. Vase, with moulding. 60mm.	2.25
No. 25. Vase, 2 handles. 60mm.	2.25
No. 27. Vase, bulbous. 60mm.	2.25
No. 29. Churn. 52mm.	3.00
No. 30. Vase. 50mm.	2.25
No. 31. Beaker. 62mm.	2.50
No. 36. Tankard Mug. 66mm.	2.25
No. 44. Jug. 60mm.	2.25
No. 45. Jug, Bagware. 40mm.	3.00
No. 52. Ewer. 80mm.	2.25
No. 53. Ewer. 76mm.	2.25
No. 55. Pot and lid, ribbed. 60mm.	4.00
No. 57. Jug, fluted base. 68mm.	3.00
No. 60. Vase, 2 handled. 38mm.	2.25
No. 65. Posy Bowl. 68mm long.	2.25
No. 67. Tray, diamond shaped. 121mm long.	3.00
No. 68. Tray, heart shaped. 100mm long.	3.00
No. 71. Tray, club shaped. 100mm long.	3.00
or Vase, 2 handles. 40mm.	2.25
No. 72. Jug. 40mm.	2.25
No. 73. Beaker. 52mm.	2.50
No. 74. Pot with 3 blunt feet. 47mm.	2.25
No. 75. Jug. 39mm.	2.25
No. 80. Miniature circular Candle-holder.	3.00
No. 82. Diamond pin box and lid. 90mm long.	5.50
No. 83. Heart shaped pin box and lid. 63mm dia.	5.50
No. 84. Spade or Heart shaped pin box and lid. 68mm.	5.50

No. 85. Club shaped pin box and lid. 68mm.	5.50
No. 86. Bowl. 48mm dia.	2.25
No. 87. Vase, fluted and one handled. 30mm.	2.25
No. 88. Vase. 40mm.	2.25
No. 91. Vase. 39mm.	2.25
No. 92. Tray, hexagonal. 69mm dia.	3.00
No. 94. Vase. 44mm.	2.25
No. 95. Vase, Globe with crinkle top. 43mm.	2.25
No. 96. Vase, Taper. 45mm.	2.25
No. 99. Dish, Trefoil. 80mm wide.	3.00
No. 100. Tray, spade shaped. 78mm long.	3.00
No. 102. Ewer (But Polar Bear found with same No.)	2.25
No. 104. Vase. 65mm.	2.25
No. 105. Pitcher with high looped handle. 64mm.	2.25
No. 106. Jar. 60mm.	2.25
No. 125. Vase, 2 handles. 70mm.	2.25
No. 127. Pot, round. 52mm.	2.25
No. 127. Vase, long necked. 62mm.	2.25
No. 128. Vase. 70mm.	2.25
No. 130. Bowl with handle.	2.25
No. 131. Basket. 123mm long.	3.00
No. 140. (or 146) *Hair Tidy* and lid. 90mm.	5.00
No. 141. *Hair Pins,* oval box & lid. 120mm long.	6.50
No. 143. 1-handled Mug. 40mm.	4.00
No. 149. Tobacco Jar with lid, inscribed: *Tobacco* on lid. 120mm.	7.50
No. 152. Vase with ornate handle. 145mm.	3.00
No. 155. Cylinder vase. 60mm.	2.25
No. 157. Ribbed Jug. 70mm.	2.75
No. 161. Fluted Jug. 62mm.	7.50
No. 177. Vase, bulbous. 40mm.	2.25
No. 191. Vase. 70mm.	2.25
No. 200. Aberdeen Bronze Pot. 55mm.	3.00
No. 205. Jug. 45mm.	2.50
No. 242. Stamp Box and lid. 47mm long.	5.50
No. 260. Vase, 2 handles. 37mm.	4.00
No. 263. Salve Pot and lid. 45mm dia.	4.00
No. 267. Round Pot and lid. 45mm dia.	4.00
No. 278. Shaped Vase. 80mm.	3.00

No. 296. Circular Box and lid.
43mm dia. 4.00
No. 297. Pill Box and lid, oval.
45mm long. 4.00
No. 298. Pill Box and lid,
rectangular. 45mm long. 4.00
No. 299. Pill Box and lid, 5 sided.
28mm. 4.00
No. 300. Stamp Box and lid,
5 sided. 50mm dia. 5.50
No. 301. Vase, bulbous. 50mm. 2.25
No. 302. Vase. 48mm. 2.25
No. 311. Vase. 50mm. 2.50
No. 314. Vase. 39mm. 2.50
No. 318. Pill Box and lid, decorated
with angel's heads. 63mm. 8.50
No. 323. Tall narrow Vase. 45mm. 2.25
No. 325. Urn with spout, handle
and lid. 48mm. 4.50
No. 348. Jug. 63mm. 2.25
No. 349. Jug, slim. 66mm. 2.25
No. 358. Sauce Boat. 105mm long. 5.00
No. 360. Pin Tray, triangular.
85mm long. 3.00
No. 367. Pin Box, oval.
90mm long. 3.00
No. 372. Jug, slim neck. 76mm. 2.25
No. 373. Jug, long necked. 75mm. 2.25
No. 374. Jug, fluted base. 73mm. 2.25
No. 375. Vase, double mouthed.
63mm. 2.25
No. 378. Sauce Boat. 120mm long. 4.00
No. 386. Ashtray, triangular on 3
feet. 75mm dia. 2.25
No. 387. Candlestick. 160mm. 3.00
No. 500. Casket with lid.
84mm long, lions head handles. 11.25
No. 502. Mustard Pot with lid and
spoon. 70mm. 5.50
No. 504. Vase, octagonal. 60mm. 2.25
No. 505. Vase. 56mm. 2.25
No. 506. Vase, eight sided. 54mm. 2.25
No. 507. Taper Vase, octagonal.
60mm. 2.25
No. 526. Bowl, 2 handled.
118mm wide. 9.50
No. 526. (Also). Decagon Jug
(10 sided). 55mm high,
110mm long. 7.50
No. 529. Vase, with moulding.
45mm. 2.25
No. 530. Vase. 50mm. 2.25
No. 531. Vase, curious wedge
shaped. 50mm. 2.25

No. 532. Vase, ribbed. 53mm. 2.25
No. 533. Grain Scoop. 60mm long. 7.50
No. 535. Vase, shaped. 52mm. 2.25
No. 589. Vase. 112mm. 5.50
No. 590. Tray. 150mm long. 3.00
No. 616. Cylinder lip salve pot
and lid. 30mm. 4.00
No. 634. Vase, wide top. 34mm. 2.25
No. 649. Vase, hexagonal wide
top. 51mm. 2.25
No. 650. Vase, hexagonal wide
top. 55mm. 2.25
No. 651. Vase, octagonal. 58mm. 2.25
No. 652. Vae, hexagonal shaped
top. 57mm. 2.25
No. 653. Vase, pentagonal
tapered. 57mm. 2.25
No. 654. Vase, hexagonal wide
top. 51mm. 2.25
No. 657. Vase, bulbous hexagonal
base. 44mm. 2.25
No. 658. Vase, octagonal. 50mm. 2.25
No. 660. Vase. 52mm. 2.25
No. 676. Cream Jug. 60mm. 2.25
No. 682. Pepper Pot,
egg-shaped. 45mm. 4.00
No. 712. Vase, shaped. 68mm. 2.25
No. 713. Vase. 70mm. 2.25
No. 714. Vase. 69mm. 2.25
Not numbered. Pill Box, ivy leaf
shaped. 57mm long. 3.50

Granic China

Grays Sports China

Trademark used by an unknown manufacturer but possibly Sampson Hancock (and Sons), Bridge Works, Stoke and later at the Garden Works, Hanley (usual trademark Corona).

Only one piece known with
Liverpool crest. Crinkle edged
vase. No. 262. 55mm.   4.00

For mark see *Crested China*, p. 174.

Trademark used by A.E. Gray & Co., Glebe Works, Mayer Street, Hanley.
The firm does not appear to have made crested china but the mark is included here because the 'Sports China' series very much appeals to collectors of pre-Great War souvenir china. Vases, jugs and beakers are found with transfer prints of footballers in the colours of League teams.
from £30.00 each

The Griffin China

For mark see *Crested China*, p. 174.

Trademark used by the London whole-salers, Sanderson & Young, 21 Red Lion Square. Manufactured by several potteries, probably branches of J.A. Robinson & Sons (Coronet Ware), and Taylor and Kent (Florentine).

Ancient Artefacts

Fountains Abbey, Abbot's Cup, not named. 49mm.	2.25
Lichfield Jug. No. 60. 62mm.	3.00
Loving Cup, 3 handles. 39mm.	3.00
Irish Bronze Pot. 50mm.	2.25
Newbury Leather Bottle, inscribed: *Leather bottle found at Newbury 1644 on Battlefield now in Museum.* No. 83. 65mm.	3.00
Scarborough Jug, inscribed: *Jug about 600 years old found in the Ancient Moat of Scarborough.* 50mm.	3.00

Buildings — Coloured

Cottage. 95mm.	17.50

Monuments

Iona Cross. 110mm.	6.00
Sailor's Stone, Hindhead. 94mm.	10.50

National Souvenirs

Welsh Hat, blue cord. 55mm.	4.75

Seaside Souvenirs

Suitcase, closed. 80mm long.	4.00

Animals

Cat, *The Cheshire Cat Always Smiling.* 88mm.	7.50
Cat, Manx. 83mm long.	16.00
Camel, one hump. 88mm.	13.00
Dog in wicker cradle. 90mm long.	14.50
Pig, standing. 90mm long.	8.25

Birds

Hen, roosting. 54mm.	5.00
Parrot. 78mm.	8.50

Baby Bird cream jug. 66mm.	5.50

Home/Nostalgic

Coal Scuttle. 75mm.	3.50
Coal Scuttle, helmet shaped. 60mm.	4.50
Lantern. 70mm.	5.50
Pillar Box. 75mm.	8.00
Watering Can.	5.50

Sport

Cricket Bag. 115mm long.	8.00

Musical Instruments

Drum. 57mm dia.	5.00
Tambourine. 68mm dia.	4.50

Footwear

Lady's 18th Century Shoe. 90mm long.	7.50
Oriental Slipper. 95mm long.	4.00

Miniature Domestic

Candle Holder. 77mm dia.	3.00
Napkin ring.	4.00
Teapot and lid. 52mm.	9.50

Grimwades

Grimwades also produced a range
of Victory & Peace commemoratives.

Trademark used by Grimwades Ltd,
Winton, Upper Hanley and Elgin
Potteries, Stoke.
Earthenware firm more noted for hotel and
domestic ware. Obviously made this one
late piece for export.

Jug.No. 1823. 69mm. Crest
Dominion of Canada   4.50

Grimwades also produced a range of beige
Great War miniature domestic pieces of
some interest.
*The War Time Butter Dish (for a
family of ten),* inscribed: *Made by
the girls of Staffordshire during the
winter of 1917/18. When the boys
were in the trenches, fighting for
Liberty and Civilisation.
Special message from Rt. Hon. D.
Lloyd George, Prime Minister:
'I have no hesitation in saying that
economy in the consumption and
use of food in this country is a
matter of the greatest possible
importance to the Empire at the
present time'.* 110mm dia.
*The War Time Bread and Butter
plate,* similar inscription.
200mm dia.
*The Patriotic Sugar basin for a
family of ten* with a message from
Lloyd George. 40mm.
Approximate value of pieces in
this range.   15.00-25.00

Grosvenor Series

Trademark used by Arkinstall & Son Ltd., Arcadian Works, Stoke on Trent. (Usual trademark Arcadian).

Home/Nostalgic
Open Umbrella. 35mm.   14.50

Grosvenor Ware

For mark see *Crested China,* p. 175.

Trademark used by Sampson Hancock (& Sons), Bridge Works, Stoke and later at the Garden Works, Hanley (renamed Corona Pottery. Usual trademark Corona).

Ancient Artefacts
Jersey Milk Can and lid. 53mm.   4.75
Leather Jack. 58mm.   2.25

Buildings — White
Blackpool Tower, on heavy
  detailed base. 127mm.   9.00

National Souvenirs
Laxey Wheel. 80mm.   40.00
Welsh Harp. 90mm.   7.50

Animals
Cat, sitting, large ruff of fur.
  100mm.   16.00
Cow Creamer. No. 376.
  130mm long.   19.50
Fish. 88mm long.   3.50
Lion, lying down. No. 369.
  140mm long.   19.00
Pig, standing. No. 158.
  84mm long.   8.25
Tortoise. 70mm long.   6.50

Great War
Submarine, inscribed:*E4.*
  110mm long.   16.00
Renault Tank. 100mm long.   65.00
Torpedo, Model of. 150mm long.   47.50
Ghurka Knife. 140mm long.   20.00
Newnham War Memorial. No
  details of size (rare).   90.00

Home/Nostalgic
Grandfather Clock. 123mm.   9.50
Watering can. 72mm.   5.50
Post Box. 62mm. Inscribed *I can't
  get a letter. . .*   8.00

Novelty
Cigarette Case. 70mm long.   13.00
Desk Top. 35mm.   7.50
Tobacco Pouch. 75mm long.   9.50

Sport
Tennis Racquet. 136mm long.   13.00

Musical Instruments
Piano with open lid. 60mm.   12.50

Modern Equipment
Gas Cooker with match striker
   top. 70mm.   8.50

Miscellaneous
Horseshoe on slope. 70mm long.   3.00
Knight Chess Piece. 72mm.   8.25

Footwear
Ladies 18th Century Shoe.
   90mm long.   7.50

Miniature Domestic
Column Candlestick. 100mm.   3.00

Gwalia Ware

GWALIA
PORCELAIN
Oldbury, Knighton,
& Llandrindod Wells.

Trademark used for a Llandrindod Wells
retailer by an unknown manufacturer.
Only 2 pieces recorded, bearing
Llandrindod Wells crests.

Ancient Artefacts
Chester Roman Kettle, not
   named.   4.00
Loving Cup, one handled. 40mm.   4.00

H & L

For mark see *Crested China*, p. 175.

Impressed mark used by Hewitt & Leadbeater, Willow Potteries, Longton. Usual trademark Willow Art, these impressed initials are often found on models that also carry the Willow Art mark.

Parian/Unglazed
Bust of *Bourne*. 154mm.	55.00
Bust of *Clowes*. 150mm.	55.00
Bust of Field Marshall Lord Kitchener. Impressed '*C.S. Chadwick copyright Sep 11th 1914*. 170mm.	47.50
Bust of Lord Roberts on square glazed base. 166mm.	47.50
Bust of *Shakespeare* on square base.	
2 sizes: 105mm.	17.50
112mm.	17.50

Buildings — Coloured
Ann Hathaway's Cottage	
3 sizes: 60mm long.	16.00
105mm long.	30.00
125mm long.	
Mason Croft, Residence of Miss Marie Corelli. 73mm.	110.00

Historical/Folklore
Font in which Shakespeare was baptized, Model of. 95mm dia.	15.25
Lincoln Imp, not named. 130mm.	8.50

Cartoon/Comedy Characters
Dr Beetle and Sunny Jim, sitting on striped armchair with rose and brown colouring. 95mm.	65.00

H & S

For mark see *Crested China*, p. 176.

Trademark used for a Plymouth retailer by Hewitt & Leadbeater, Willow Potteries, Longton (usual trademark Willow Art).

Unglazed
Bust of Field Marshall Lord Kitchener on square base. 170mm.	47.50

Buildings — White
Derry's Clock, Plymouth. 150mm.	16.00
Hastings Castle Ruins. 100mm.	22.00

Monuments
Burns, statue on square base. 170mm.	16.00
Drake, statue, Plymouth. 160mm.	13.00

Animals
Pig, sitting with inscription: *You may push. . .* 75mm.	12.50

Great War
Battleship, impressed:	
HMS *Lion*. 140mm long.	22.50
Submarine. 120mm long.	16.00
Tank. 125mm long.	14.50

Home/Nostalgic
Coal Scuttle. 53mm.	4.50
Church Bell, inscribed: *Curfew must not ring tonight*. 70mm.	7.50
Garden Trug. 70mm.	3.50

Hamilton China

For mark see *Crested China*, p. 176.

Trademark used for H. Hamilton, Milton &
Amber, Saltburn, for products of J.A.
Robinson & Sons Ltd. (Coronet Ware).

Seaside Souvenirs
Two curling waves on an
octagonal base, inscribed: *The*
glad sea waves. 50mm.   14.00

Birds
Kingfisher. 77mm.   21.50

Comic/Novelty
Jack-in-the-Box. 90mm.   16.00

Heathcote China

Trademark used by H.M. Williamson &
Sons, Bridge Pottery, Longton.

Domestic manufacturer not known
to have made crested souvenirs,
only domestic wares found:

Cup and saucer with Burgh of
Stirling crest with early mark.   3.00
Cup and saucer with Troon crest
with late mark.   3.00

Herald China

For mark see *Crested China*, p. 176.

Trademark used for a wholesaler or retailer probably by Alfred B. Jones & Sons Ltd, Grafton China Works, Longton, Staffs. (Usual trademark Grafton).

Ancient Artefacts
Aberdeen Bronze Pot, not named.
  60mm. 2.25

Animals
Pig, sitting. Inscribed:
  Wunt be druv. 90mm long. 30.00
Squirrel. 70mm. 17.00

Novelty
Dutchman, sitting cross legged
  holding cheese. 85mm. 17.00

Miscellaneous
Diamond pintray. 120mm long. 3.00

Heraldic China

For mark see *Crested China*, p. 177.

Trademark used by Sampson Hancock (and Sons), Bridge Works, Stoke. (Usual trademark Corona).

Ancient Artefacts
Exeter Vase. No. 129. 70mm. 2.25

Animals
Bulldog in Kennel. 66mm. 8.50

Birds
Baby Bird cream jug. 70mm. 5.50

Home/Nostalgic
Oil Lamp. 34mm. 4.75

Alcohol
Barrel on legs. 4.00
Tankard. 70mm. 3.00

Miscellaneous
Queen, chess piece. 90mm. 24.50
King, chess piece. 108mm. 19.50
Ladies 18th Century Shoe.
  105mm long. 7.50

Heraldic China

Trademark used by an unknown manufacturer.

Only 42mm jug has been found with a Whitehead crest.   4.00

Herald Series

For mark see *Crested China,* p. 177.

Trademark used for William Holmes & Co, fancy goods importers, Glasgow, on china manufactured by Alfred B. Jones & Sons Ltd, Grafton China Works, Longton, Staffs. (Usual trademark Grafton).

Ancient Artefacts
Chester Roman Vase. 60mm.   2.25

Seaside Souvenirs
Whelk Shell. 83mm long.   4.00

Animals
Cheshire Cat, The. Always Smiling.
   One green glass eye. 86mm.   7.50
Bulldog, sitting. No. 250. 88mm.   40.00
Dog, King Charles Spaniel,
   sitting. No. 390. 55mm.   11.50
Dog, Puppy, sitting with one ear
   up, scratching with back leg.
   No. 410. 85mm.   14.00
Monkey sitting wearing coat.
   70mm.   13.00
Pig, sitting. No. 341. 90mm long.   25.00
Shetland Pony, not named. 105mm
   long. (This model can be found
   with a crest of Shetland.)   23.50

Birds
Duck, sitting. No. 47. 90mm long.   19.50

Great War
Tank, no steering wheels, inscribed:
   HM Landship Creme-de-Menthe.
   No. 413. Rd. No. 659588.
   98mm long.   24.50
Hand Grenade with removable
   pin. 83mm.   21.50
Cannon Shell, inscribed: *Jack
   Johnson.* No. 399. 90mm.   10.50
Bell Tent with open flaps.
   No. 239. 65mm.   10.50
Killin War Memorial, with extended
   base and railings. 160mm.   130.00

Alcohol
Champagne Bottle. 100mm.   7.50

Miscellaneous
Horses Hoof vase. 45mm.   4.50

E. Hughes and Co. China

For mark see *Crested China*, p. 177.

Trademark used by E. Hughes & Co., Opal Works, Fenton. (Usual trademarks Fenton & Royal).

Seaside Souvenirs
Oyster Shell dish. 130mm long.   3.00

Miniature Domestic
Cheese Dish and cover.
  70mm long.   6.50

Some Domestic ware found too. 2.50-10.00

Iceni Crest China

For mark see *Crested China*, p. 178.

Trademark used for wholesalers by J.A. Robinson & Sons, subsequently Cauldon Ltd. (Usual trademark Arcadian).

Ancient Artefacts
Cadogan Tea Pot.   10.50
Goodwin Sands Carafe. 82mm.   2.25

Buildings — White
Cottage. 62mm long.   6.50

Monuments
Caister on Sea Lifeboat Memorial.
  150mm.   19.00

Seaside Souvenirs
Lighthouse. 150mm.   9.00

Animals
Cat, sitting and smiling
  grotesque, rather similar to
  Cheshire Cat). 75mm.   7.50
Black Cats, 3 on sledge.
  118mm long.   95.00
Frog, open mouthed. 58mm.   6.50
Sussex Pig, Model of, sitting
  inscribed: *You can push or you
  can shuv but I'm hanged if I'll be
  druv.* No. 148. 88mm long.   12.50
Sussex Pig. Model of, standing.
  Inscribed as above. No. 148.
  88mm long.   12.50

Birds/Eggs
Chick, breaking out of egg.
  63mm long.   5.50
Hen, red comb. 80mm.   10.50
Owl. 67mm.   10.50

Great War
Monoplane, movable prop.
  149mm long.   55.00
Tank. 100mm long.   60.00
German Incendiary Bomb. 80mm.   30.00
Clip of bullets, Model of. 87mm.   13.00
Colonial Hat, Model of. 88mm.   10.50

Home/Nostalgic
Candlestick, square. 35mm.   3.00
Chair, highbacked. 90mm.   5.50
Coal Bucket. 55mm.   4.75

Footwear
Ankle Boot. 74mm long.   4.75

Sport
Football. 46mm.   6.50

Imperial

For additional mark see *Crested China*, p. 178.

Trademark used by Wedgwood and Co (Ltd), Unicorn and Pinnox Works, Tunstall, on cheaply produced souvenir wares.

Ancient Artefacts
Lincoln Jack, not named. 54mm.   2.25

Seaside Souvenirs
Suitcase. 79mm long.   4.00

Animals
Dog, sitting. 70mm.   10.00
Elephant, walking. 52mm.   13.00

Birds
Pelican jug.   5.50

Sport
Football. 65mm.   6.50

Home/Nostalgic
Coal Scuttle. 35mm.   4.00

Hats
Top Hat. 40mm.   5.50

Footwear
Dutch Sabot. 83mm long.   4.00

Impero

Ionic Heraldic

For mark see *Crested China*, p. 178.

For mark see *Crested China*, p. 179.

Trademark used by the German manufacturer Kutzscher & Co, Schwarzenberg, Saxony (now in East Germany) on crested china for export to Britain.

Trademark used for the Glasgow wholesaler CR & Co. by an unknown manufacturer, but probably Taylor & Kent. (Usual trademark Florentine).

Buildings — White

Boston Stump Church. 125mm.	21.50
Grimsby, The Tower. 170mm.	21.50
York, *Bootham Bar.* 135mm.	15.25

Monuments

Captain Scott, figure on square base.	
2 sizes: 135mm.	22.50
150mm.	22.50
Clock Tower, Skegness. 124mm.	7.50
Hall Cross, Doncaster. 158mm.	22.50
Hull Fisherman's Memorial with inscription. 125mm.	10.50
Hull Soldiers' War Memorial, with inscription: *Erected to the memory of the men of Hull who fell in the late South African War.* 120mm.	22.50
Laceby Monument. 145mm.	23.00
Lincoln Stonebow. 105mm long.	23.50

Traditional/National Souvenirs

Devil looking over Lincoln. 95mm.	14.50
The Lincoln Imp. 112mm.	7.50
The Fiddler, York. 120mm (rare).	47.50

Seaside Souvenirs

The Lighthouse, Flamborough. 125mm.	17.00
Withernsea Lighthouse. 135mm.	17.00

Animals

Two Elephants on Sledge. Comic. 70mm.	30.00
A Native of Shetland, Shetland Pony. 80mm.	16.00

Birds

Swan posy bowl. 74mm.	4.75

Animals

Pig, fat. 70mm long.	10.00

Home

Bucket with rope handle. 75mm.	3.50

Ivora Ware

Trademark used by William Richie and Sons Ltd., on a range of domestic ware. (Usual trademark Porcelle).

Ancient Artefacts
Three-handled loving cup. 38mm.   3.00

Historical/Folklore
Miner's Lamp. 70mm.   21.50

Footwear
Boot. 65mm long.   5.25

Miscellaneous
Coal Bucket. 70mm.   3.50

Miniature Domestic
Cheese Dish and cover. 50mm.   5.50
1-handled mug. 36mm.   2.25

NB: Badly printed marks which appear to by *Ivyknot?* **are** *Wyknot?* **(See Wy not?).**

JBC

For mark see *Crested China,* p. 180.

Trademark used for a Manchester wholesaler by Hewitt & Leadbeater, Willow Potteries, Longton. (Usual trademark Willow Art).

Traditional/National Souvenirs
Model of James' the Fifth Chair at Stirling Castle. 100mm.   7.50
Welsh hat, blue band.   4.75
Can be found with the longest place name round brim. No. 75. 57mm.   7.50

Animals
Pig, fat and standing. Tail forms a circle and rejoins the body. 80mm long.   12.50

Alcohol
Bottle inscribed: *One Special Scotch.* 90mm.   7.50

Miscellaneous
Hand holding Tulip vase. 80mm.   4.00

JBM

JP

For mark see *Crested China*, p. 180.

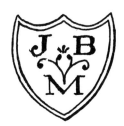

Trademark used by a French manufacturer
for the French souvenir market.

One Vase, 70mm high, has been
recorded with this mark with
the crest Boulogne Sur Mer.   4.00

Trademark used for the Manchester
wholesaler JB & Co by Sampson Hancock
(& Sons), Bridge Works, Stoke. (Usual
trademark Corona).

Footwear
Ladies Button Boot. No. 149. 65mm. 8.00

JW

For mark see *Crested China*, p. 180.

Trademark used for a retailer by J.A. Robinson Ltd. (Usual trademark Arcadian).

Great War
Tommy and his machine gun, Model of. 130mm.   30.00
Red Cross Van. 80mm long.   23.00

Footwear
Dutch Clog. 102mm long.   4.50

Kangaroo Art China

Trademark used for the retailer Valentine & Sons, Melbourne by an English manufacturer, most probably Hewitt & Leadbeater. (Usual mark Willow/Willow Art).

Animals
Kangaroo. 113mm.   75.00

Great War
Nurse, inscribed:
A Friend in Need. 130mm.   40.00

Kangaroo Brand

Keltic

China manufactured by Wiltshaw & Robinson Ltd. Under the usual Carlton mark the following trademark can be found:
Made in England for G.F. Lucas
S.F. Cal
Kangaroo Brand.

The one model found has a crest of the Panama California Exposition. The model was found in California and was obviously made for the U.S. market.

Animals
Polar Bear, walking. 125mm long.   50.00

BRITISH MAKE

KELTIC

Trademark used by Taylor and Kent (Ltd), Florence Works, Longton, (usual trademark Florentine), for Irish and Scottish retailers.

Ancient Artefacts
Puzzle Jug. 68mm.   5.50

Historical/Folklore
Miners Lamp. 69mm.   14.00

Seaside Souvenirs
The Glad Sea Waves on base. 50mm.   17.00

Animals
Camel, kneeling. 95mm long.   13.00
Pig, standing. 95mm long.   9.50

Home/Nostalgic
Shaving Mug. 55mm.   5.50

Comic Novelty
Policeman's lamp. 70mm.   4.75

Footwear
Shoe, Ladies' 18th Century.
     95mm long.   7.50

Kensington China

No details of mark available.

Trademark used by Royal Crown Pottery Co., Burslem, a branch of J.A. Robinson Ltd. (Usual trademark Arcadian and Willow Art).

Historical/Folklore
English Folksong Bride beside
  chest. No. 036. 93mm.   40.00

Traditional/National Souvenirs
Welsh Hat. No. 75. 57mm.   4.75

Seaside Souvenirs
Lighthouse, octagonal. 112mm.   5.50

Animals
Cat, Cheshire, inscribed:
  Still smiling. No. 159.
  95mm.   7.50
Cat, haunched. 70mm.   10.50
Elephant, walking.
  No. 113. 52mm.   13.00
Open mouthed Fish. 128mm long.   3.00
Teddy Bear, sitting. 90mm.   8.50
Shetland Pony. 108mm long.   22.00

Great War
Sailor, standing. Inscribed:
  Our Brave Defender. 127mm.   40.00
Nurse, inscribed: *A friend in need.*
  130mm.   40.00
Battleship, impressed: *HMS Lion.*
  140mm long.   22.50
Model of New Submarine.   16.00
British Tank. 90mm long.   13.00
Red Cross Van. 58mm.   23.00
Field Gun, with screen.
  115mm long.   18.50
Fireplace with cooking pot,
  inscribed: *Keep the home fires
  burning.* 77mm.   9.00

Home/Nostalgic
Coal scuttle. 52mm.   4.00
Grandfather Clock, inscribed:

*Make use of time let not advantage
slip. Shakespeare.*
No. 149. 128mm.   10.50

Novelty
Pixie, crouching on a rectangular
  base. 78mm. (Could well be
  Billiken the god of luck).   8.75

Alcohol
Barrel on stand. 58mm.   3.00

Sport
Tennis Racquet, with tennis ball.
  138mm long.   15.50

Transport
Open Tourer. 115mm long.   40.00

Footwear
Clog. 70mm long.   4.50

Miscellaneous
Hand holding Tulip.
  No. 74. 80mm.   4.00

King China

For mark see *Crested China*, p. 181.

Trademark used for a retailer or wholesaler by Alfred B. Jones and Sons Ltd., Grafton China Works, Longton, Staffs.

One 64mm fluted vase with a Swansea crest found with this mark.   4.50

Kingsway Art or Crest China

For mark see *Crested China*, p. 183.

Trademark used for W.H. Smith by Hewitt and Leadbeater, Willow Potteries, Longton. (Usual trademark Willow Art). The standard of quality is very high.

Ancient Artefacts
Pilgrims Bottle.   3.00
Salt Maller, Model of.   3.00

Buildings — White
St. Botolph's Church, Boston.
  112mm.   45.00

Monuments
Princetown Lifeboatmans
  Monument. 130mm.   40.00
Maiwand Memorial. 98mm.   15.00

Historical/Folklore
Bunyan's Chair. 92mm.   10.50
Burn's Chair, Dumfries. 85mm.   7.50
English Folksong Bride beside
  chest. 93mm.   40.00
James V Chair, Stirling Castle.
  100mm.   7.50
Mary Queen of Scots Chair,
  Edinburgh Castle, Model of. 75mm.   6.50
Man in the Moon. 50mm.   19.50

Traditional/National Souvenirs
Lancashire Clog. 78mm long.   4.75
Bagpipes with turquoise ribbon.
  118mm long.   15.00
Burns and Highland Mary, sitting
  on a rock. 112mm.   30.00
Welsh Lady, bust, with black hat.
  110mm.   20.00
Welsh Leek. 55mm.   3.50

Seaside Souvenirs
Yacht in full sail. 122mm.   10.50
Lifeboat on rocks. 110mm long.   12.50
Lifeboat, blue and yellow ropes.
  116mm long.   8.25

Lighthouse. No. 027. 140mm. 4.75

Lighthouse on base, not named.
110mm. 4.75

Lighthouse, octagonal. No. 174.
192mm. 5.50

Eddystone Lighthouse, Model of.
86mm. 6.50

Crab. 83mm long. 10.50

Whelk Shell, inscribed:
Listen to the Sea. 93mm long. 3.00

Countryside

Acorn. 56mm. 5.50

Pine Cone. 87mm. 4.00

Animals

Cat, Cheshire, inscribed: *Still
smiling.* 95mm. 7.50

Cat, sitting.
2 sizes: 57mm. 10.00
67mm. 13.00

Cat, standing, with blue bow.
70mm. 10.50

Dog, Bulldog sitting. 54mm. 13.00

Dog, black Bulldog emerging from
kennel. No. 30. Inscribed: *The
Black Watch.* 73mm long. 15.25

Dog, Dachshund. No. 021.
75mm long. 40.00

Dog, Scottie, wearing a
Glengarry. Some colouring.
2 sizes: 58mm. 10.50
87mm. 12.50

Dog, Scottish Terrier, standing.
90mm long. 12.50

Elephant, sitting with trunk in
air. 97mm. 22.00

Elephant, walking.98mm. 13.00

Elephant Jug. No. 78. 70mm. 7.50

Hare. 77mm long. 9.00

Monkey, holding a Coconut.
No. 429. 80mm. 17.50

Three Wise Monkeys, with usual
verse. 77mm. 13.00

Pig, sitting. Inscribed:
You may. . . 75mm. 12.50

Pig, sitting on haunches,
inscribed. 80mm. 9.00

Pig, standing, double chin.
No. 014. 96mm. 12.50

Rabbit, sitting. 70mm long. 6.50

Ram with curly horns.
90mm long. 40.00

Teddy Bear. 75mm. 10.50

Birds

Chick, fluffy, large feet. 70mm. 14.00

Goose. 95mm. 22.50

Owl. 115mm. 10.50

Swan. No. 012. 65mm. 6.50

Great War

Standing soldier inscribed: *Our
brave defender.* 130mm. 40.00

Submarine. *E4.* 125mm long. 16.00

Red Cross Van. 87mm. 23.00

Field Gun with screen.
115mm long. 18.50

Bugle. 70mm. 12.50

Drum. No. 030. 60mm dia. 5.00

*Edith Cavell, Nurse. Patriot and
Martyr, Memorial Statue,
Norwich.* 115mm. (Found
impressed 296). 23.00

*Florence Nightingale Statue,
Model of.* 160mm. 16.50

Home/Nostalgic

Anvil. 70mm long. 5.50

Basket. No. 244. 80mm long. 3.00

Bell, inscribed: *Curfew must not
ring tonight.* No. 107. 65mm. 7.50

Book. No. 76. 60mm. 5.00

Desk, writing slope. 80mm long. 7.50

Flat Iron. No. 018. 65mm. 8.50

Milk Can and lid. 4.75

Pillar Box, inscribed: *GVR* and *If
you haven't time to post a line,
here's the pillar box.*
No. 18. 80mm. 9.50

Pillar Box, impressed: G.R.
No. 203 and 024. 90mm. 17.00

Sundial, circular, with round
base, and inscription: *I Mark
not the hours.* 118mm. 10.50

Sundial, circular base. No. 205
and 024. 93mm. 7.50

Thimble, large. 10.50

Comic/Novelty

Baby with outstretched arms,
inscribed: *Cheerio.*
No. 024. 128mm. 30.00

Dutch Boy. 80mm. 12.00

Dutch Girl. 80mm. 12.00

Hammer Head match holder.
Inscribed: *My speciality is
striking.* 82mm long. 11.00

Sack of Meal with mouse,
inscribed: *May the mouse ne'er
leave yer meal wi' a tear-drop'n
its e'e*. 63mm.   13.00

Alcohol
Beer Barrel. 60mm.   3.00
Foaming Tankard, inscribed: *The
more we are together the merrier
we will be*. 58mm.   6.50
Whisky Bottle, inscribed: *A
Special Scotch*. 100mm.   7.50

Sport
Football. 48mm.   6.50
Golf Ball. 45mm.   5.50

Footwear
Sabot/Clog. No. 152. 90mm long.   4.75
Shoe with blue painted bow.
115mm long.   13.00

Miscellaneous
Club pintray. No. 009.
58mm long.   3.00
Diamond, trump indicator.
No. 009. 65mm.   4.75
Diamond pintray. No. 009.
58mm long.   3.00
Spade, trump indicator. 70mm.   4.75
Handbell. 82mm.   6.00
Hand holding Beaker. 50mm.   5.50
Two models reported from
Shelley range:
Cycle Lamp (No. 342). 83mm.   50.00
Roll Topped Desk (No. 380),
here No. 030. 86mm.   16.00

Kyle Series

For mark see *Crested China*, p. 184.

Trademark used by Charles Waine (& Co.),
Derby Works, Longton. (Usual trademark Venetia).

Great War
Biplane with fixed prop.
150mm long.   75.00

Transport
Tram. 50mm.   135.00

LAB

Mark used for a retailer by an unknown English manufacturer.

One 62mm Vase, with Arms of
Seaford, found.   4.00

Lawrence Sheriffe Ware

For mark see *Crested China*, p. 184.

Trademark used by an unidentified manufacturer. (Only crest known — Rugby, with retailers name, Hands & Son, Rugby).

Ancient Artefacts
Loving Cup, 3 handles. 37mm.   4.00

Leadbeater Art China

For mark see *Crested China*, p. 184.

Trademark used by Edwin Leadbeater, Drewery Place, Commerce Street, Longton. Same quality and 'feel' as Panorama China and H & L.

Parian/Unglazed

Bust of *Pope Pius XI*. 190mm.	80.00
Bust of *Scott* on column base. 172mm.	23.00

Buildings — Coloured

Christchurch Priory.	125.00
Gate House, Stokesay Castle. 102mm long.	130.00
Irish Cottage. 105mm long.	110.00
Isaac Walton's Cottage, Shallowford. 114mm long.	110.00
Old Market Hall, Church Stretton 1617-1839. 2 sizes: 95mm and 105mm long.	110.00
The Tan House, Little Stretton. 109mm long.	125.00

Buildings — White

Ann Hathaway's Cottage, not named. 2 sizes: 58mm.	16.00
144mm long.	18.00
Burns Cottage, with inscription. 70mm long.	15.00
Margate Clock Tower, Margate. 150mm.	12.00
Old Church, Bonchurch. 110mm long.	70.00

Monuments

Limerick Monument, inscribed: *The treaty of Limerick signed AD 1696.* 120mm.	65.00
Margate Lifeboat Memorial. 160mm.	21.50
Sir Walter Scott. Statue. 178mm.	16.00

Historical

Bunyan's Chair. 95mm.	10.50
James Vth Chair, Stirling Castle, Model of. 102mm.	7.50
Mary Queen of Scots Chair. 85mm.	6.50

Traditional/National Souvenirs

Welsh Hat. No. 57. 60mm.	4.75

Seaside Souvenirs

Lifeboat. 100mm long.	8.25
Lighthouse. 110mm.	4.75

Animals

Cheshire Cat, inscribed: *Still smiling.* 2 sizes: 85mm.	7.50
115mm.	8.50
Dog, sitting, with bow. No. 77. 75mm.	10.50
Dog, labrador, sitting. 76mm.	10.50
Dog, with long neck, possibly Staffordshire Bull Terrier. 115mm.	10.50
Lion, walking. 114mm long.	8.75
Pig, fat. 102mm long.	14.50

Birds

Chick posy holder. 60mm long.	4.75
Duck posy holder. 45mm.	6.50

Great War

Red Cross Van. No. 105. 88mm long.	23.00
Cumberland and Westmorland War Memorial. 148mm.	110.00
Derby War Memorial. 150mm.	100.00
Harrogate War Memorial, on unglazed obelisk on base with spiral steps. 153mm.	95.00
Nottingham War Memorial. 150mm.	90.00
Nurse Cavell, Memorial. 200mm.	65.00
Plymouth Armada War Memorial, with inscription: *He blew with his winds and they were scattered.* No. 107. 168mm.	30.00
Crich Stand, Notts and Derby War Memorial. 150mm.	100.00
Ulster War Memorial, Thiepvel, with inscription: *They died that we might live.* 140mm.	200.00

Home/Nostalgic

Anvil. No. 78. 58mm.	5.50
Grandfather Clock, inscribed: *Make use of time, let not advantage slip.* 143mm.	10.50

Comic/Novelty

Jester, double faced bust,
    happy/sad. 85mm.   7.50
Monk, standing. 91mm.   10.50

Sport

Footballer with ball on plinth.
    Inscribed: *Play up.* Fully
    coloured figure with brown
    football. 158mm.   100.00

Footwear

Sabot. 80mm long.   4.75

Hats

School Boy's Cap. 67mm long.   19.50

Lion China

For mark see *Crested China*, p. 186.

Trademark used by Wiltshaw & Robinson,
    Ltd., Carlton Works, Stoke-on-Trent.
    (Usual trademark Carlton).

Monuments

Rock of Ages, with inscriptions.
    82mm.   7.50

Animals

Dog (Puppy) sitting on a silvered
    hand mirror, inscribed: *Me
    twice.* 105mm long.   33.50
Pug Dog with coloured features.
    115mm.   17.00

Limoges

Liverpool Rd Pottery

For mark see *Crested China,* p. 186.

LIMOGES

FRANCE

Trademark used by Liverpool Rd. Pottery
Ltd., Stoke-on-Trent.

Seaside Souvenirs
Scallop Shell standing upright.
110mm long. (This carries a
map as well as a crest of
Norfolk).   16.00

Transport
Open Motor Car. 90mm long.   30.00

A range of domestic ware was made
by this famous manufacturer
with the exception of the
following:

Novelty
Boy's Cap Money Box.
80mm long.   21.00
Match striker pot with lid (striker
is on inside of lid).
102mm long.   5.00

Transport
Open Motor Car. 90mm long.   30.00

Lochinvar

or with Nicholson and Carter in place of N & C.

Trademark used for the retailers Nicholson & Carter by Hewitt and Leadbeater, Willow Potteries, Longton. (Usual trademark Willow Art).

National Souvenirs
Welsh Hat. No. 75. 54mm.   4.75

Great War
Field Gun with screen. 115mm.   18.50
Bell Tent with open flaps. 85mm.   10.50

Alcohol
Whiskey Quaich or bowl.
  No. 110. 100mm long.   4.75

Locke and Co

For mark see *Crested China*, p. 186.

Trademark used by Locke and Co (Ltd) Shrub Hill Works, Worcester.
The firm was established in 1896. The first manager being Edward Locke who had been Manager of the Potting Dept at Royal China Works, Worcester. After liquidation in 1902 they were prevented by the Worcester factory from describing their wares as Locke Worcester. Production eventually ceased in 1915.

All of the following models can be found in bisque — a biscuit coloured ground, as well as white.

Ancient Artefacts
Bath Roman Ewer, not named.
  No. 46. 70mm.   7.50
Chester Roman Vase, not named.
  No. 78. 55mm.   7.50
Hastings Kettle, not named.
  2 sizes: 48mm.   7.50
  No. 67. 64mm.   7.50
Irish Bronze Pot, not named.
  No. 99 or 66! 40mm.   7.50
Leather Jack, not named.
  No. 36. 72mm.   7.50
Newbury Leather Bottle, not
  named. No. 84. 70mm.   7.50
Roman Lamp. 100mm long.   7.50

National Souvenirs
Welsh Hat. No. 61. 56mm.   10.50

Home/Nostalgic
Thimble. 35mm.   13.00
Top Hat, matchstriker. No. 52.
  45mm.   7.00

Alcohol
Tankard, very ornate. 70mm.   7.50

Sport
Trophy. 65mm.   13.00

Footwear
Dutch Sabot. No. 19.
   3 sizes: 60mm long.   9.00
         80mm long.   9.50
         90mm long.   10.00

Miniature Domestic
Beaker. No. 51. 51mm.   7.50
Cream Jug with rope handle.
   No. 80. 54mm.   7.50
Cup and Saucer. 78mm dia.   9.50

Numbered Ornamental and Domestic Wares
Some of the following may well be Ancient Artefacts, not named:
No. 3. Vase. 38mm.   7.50
No. 9. Vase. 78mm.   7.50
No. 10. Bowl. 33mm.   7.50
No. 13. Vase, circular, could have
   a lid. 40mm.   7.50
No. 14. Vase. 53mm.   7.50
No. 16. Large Pot. 65mm.   7.50
No. 18. Vase. 53mm.   7.50
No. 20. Vase. 83mm.   7.50
No. 21. Vase. 110mm.   7.50
No. 26. Ewer/Jug. 70mm.   7.50
No. 27. Vase. 74mm.   7.50
No. 28. Vase. 50mm.   7.50
No. 29. Vase. 62mm.   7.50
No. 31. Vase. 60mm.   7.50
No. 36. Vase. 41mm.   7.50
No. 37. Ewer. 70mm.   7.50
No. 39. Vase. 60mm.   7.50
No. 40. Diamond mouth Vase.
   67mm.   7.50
No. 41. Cream Jug. 63mm.   7.50
No. 42. Cone Vase. 64mm.   7.50
No. 43. Vase. 43mm.   7.50
No. 47. Jug. 55mm.   7.50
No. 51. Beaker. 51mm.   7.50
No. 53. Vase. 54mm.   7.50
No. 54. Vase. 70mm.   7.50
No. 55. Ewer. 78mm.   7.50
No. 58. Vase, Bagware. 53mm. 7.50
No. 60. Vase. 60mm.   7.50
No. 62. Vase. 62mm.   7.50
No. 69. Vase, 2 handles. 60mm. 7.50
No. 74. Ewer. 59mm.   7.50
No. 79. Ewer. 62mm.   7.50
No. 80. Ewer, small twisted handle.
   53mm.   7.50
No. 85. Narrow necked Vase.
   90mm.   7.50

No. 87. Vase. 85mm.   7.50
No. 89. Ewer, 1 handle. 82mm. 7.50
No. 90. Vase. 78mm.   7.50
(This appears to be the same model
   as No. 9).
No. 95. Vase, with 2 handles.
   63mm.   7.50
No. 101. Vase. 2 handles. 68mm. 7.50
No. 102. Vase. 50mm.   7.50
No. 112. Vase, narrow neck. 97mm. 7.50
No. 118. Beaker with shallow fluted
   top. 60mm.   7.50
No. 120. Vase. 74mm.   7.50
No. 121. Vase. 83mm.   7.50
No. 178. Crinkle-top Ball Vase.
   58mm.   7.50
No. 754. Vase. 105mm.   7.50
No. 857. Base of Pepper or Salt Pot.
   63mm.   7.50

Non numbered ornamental and Domestic Wares
Ball Vase, swirled, crinkle top.
   67mm.   7.50
Creamer. 60mm.   7.50
Fairy Beaker. 32mm.   7.50
Wall Pocket. 85mm.   7.50

Lynton China   M

For mark see *Crested China*, p. 187.

LYNTON CHINA
MADE IN ENGLAND

Trademark used by an unknown English manufacturer.

Mark found only on 2 small pieces — no details of crest.   4.00

Trademark used by an unknown English manufacturer.

This very obscure and unusual mark has only been found on one Great War Commermorative.

The colour transfer print of five flags and a field gun is found on a mug with a large handle. 59mm high. Inscribed: *Allies United 1914.*   15.00

Macintyre

C McDMann
& Co Ltd

For mark see *Crested China*, p. 187.

Trademark used by James Macintyre & Co.
Ltd, Washington Works, Burslem.
(Usual trademark Argonauta Porcelain).

Domestic/Novelty/Eggs

Eggcup fixed to small saucer with
two depressions inscribed: *salt*
and *pepper*. Saucer also holds
two eggs (salt and pepper pots)
one white and one speckled
brown. 66mm.   7.50
Inkwell, stippled.   8.25
Tea Pot. 130mm.   7.50

Small vases have also been found
with this mark and china was
also produced for manufacturers
to add silver mounts. These
seem to be very early/pre
1905.   3.00-10.00

Retailer's mark used by Arkinstall & Son,
Arcadian Works, Stoke-on-Trent. (Usual
trademark Acradian)

Only two small Arcadian shapes found:
Ewer with The Forts, Boxhill crest.
52mm.   4.00
Vase with scroll handles, also with
The Forts, Boxhill crest, in blue
as is the retailer's mark
underneath   4.00

Marine Art China

For mark see *Crested China*, p. 187.

Trademark used by Hewitt & Leadbeater, Drewery Place, Commerce St., Longton. (Usual marks Willow and Leadbeater).

Birds
Chick posy holder. 60mm long.　　6.50

Maxim China

For mark see *Crested China*, p. 189.

Trademark used by Max Emanuel & Co., Mitterteich, (Bavaria). (Usual trademark Mosanic).

Seaside
Beachy Head Lighthouse, black
　band. 145mm.　　5.50

Footwear
Sabot, pointed toe. 93mm long.　　4.50

A range of 'smalls' and a
　trinket box.　　1.50-3.50

Mayfair Ware

For additional mark see *Crested China*, p. 187.

This mark has now been traced to Sampson Hancock (& Sons), Bridge Works, Stoke and later at the Garden Works, Hanley (usual trademark Corona).

Animals
Bulldog, standing. 125mm long.   15.00

Great War
Tank with inset wheels.
  100mm long.   17.50

Meir Arms China

For mark see *Crested China*, p. 189.

Trademark used by Barker Bros. Ltd., Meir Works, Barker Street, Longton.

Ancient Artefacts
Puzzle Jug with verse. 70mm.   5.50

Historical/Folklore
Mary Queen of Scots Chair.
  75mm.   6.50
Mons Meg, Edinburgh Castle,
  Model of. 57mm.   11.00

Traditional/National Souvenirs
Lancashire Clog. No. 33.
  2 sizes: 70mm long.   4.75
           115mm long.   5.50

Seaside Souvenirs
Eddystone Lighthouse. 109mm.   5.50

Animals
Cat in Boot. 88mm long.   14.50
Cheshire Cat, inscribed:
  Still Smiling. 90mm.   7.50
Pig, standing. 88mm long.   10.00

Great War
Red Cross Van. 85mm long.   23.00
Tank.   13.00

Alcohol
Barrel. 52mm.   3.00

Miscellaneous
Hand holding a Tulip. 83mm.   4.00

Footwear
Sabot. 92mm long.   4.00

Melba Bone China

Melba China

GUARANTEED
MADE IN
ENGLAND

ENGLAND

Trademark used by Mayer & Sherratt, Clifton Works, Longton.

This mark is only found on late crested domestic ware.   from 3.00

Original china made by Mayer & Sherratt, Clifton Works, Longton. Over printed mark used by Sampson Hancock (& Sons), Bridge Works, Stoke. (Usual trademark Corona).

Only one piece of domestic ware has been found with this mark. It seems likely that Mayer and Sherratt produced china which was later decorated with crests by S. Hancock perhaps to fill an urgent order!

This Melba china mark is earlier than the Melba mark above left which was used from about 1925.

Domestic Wares
Cream Jug. 60mm with a Chesham Crest.   4.00

Mermaid

For additional mark see *Crested China,* p. 189.

Trademark used by William Ritchie and Sons Ltd, 24, 26 and 28 Elder Street, Edinburgh. (Usual trademark Porcelle).

Mark mostly found on crested
domestic ware.   2.00-5.00

Great War
Tank, sometimes inscribed: *HMS
Donner Blitzen,* with details of
Ancre. 130mm long.   30.00

Sport
Cricket Bag. 110mm long.   9.00

Footwear
Ladies 18th Century Shoe.
80mm long.   7.50

The Milton China

For alternative mark see *Crested China,* p. 189.

Alternative mark found on domestic ware with transfer prints.

Trademark used by Hewitt Bros., Willow Potteries, Longton, on china for a London wholesaler (G.G. & Co.).

Ancient Artefacts
Aberdeen Bronze Pot, not named.
52mm.   2.25
Ancient Tyg, 2 handled.   2.25
Loving Cup, 3 handled. 55mm.   3.00

Monuments
Drake Statue, Plymouth. 160mm.   13.00
Hull Fisherman's Memorial.   16.00

Historical/Folklore
Crown. 60mm.   21.50
Model of Mons Meg, Edinburgh
Castle. 130mm long.   11.00

Traditional/National Souvenirs
Bagpipes with turquoise ribbon.
115mm long.   15.00
Welsh Hat. 62mm.   4.75

Seaside Souvenirs
Bathing Machine. Can be inscribed:
A Morning Dip. 70mm long.   7.50
Lighthouse, octagonal. 114mm.   5.50
Shell on coral base. 93mm.   4.75

Animals

Bear, Polar, standing upright.
95mm. — 40.00
Cheshire Cat, inscribed:
Still Smiling. 90mm. — 7.50
Dog, Scottie, wearing a
glengarry. 60mm. — 10.50
Donkey with saddle. No. 904.
2 sizes. 105mm long. — 24.75
120mm long. — 24.75
Elephant, with trunk in the air.
80mm long. — 22.00
Elephant, (trunk down).
75mm long. — 13.00
Elephant Jug. 70mm. (Trunk is
handle). — 7.50
Frog, with open mouth. 60mm. — 5.50
Lion, poised to pounce, red
roaring mouth. 83mm long. — 19.50
Lion, standing. 115mm long. — 12.50
Lion standing on ashtray,
inscribed: *Ash Tray* and *Who
burned the tablecloth.*
110mm long. — 20.00
Lion, roaring at mouse, sitting on
apple. Inscribed: *Much Ado
About Nothing.* Some colouring. — 55.00
Pig, standing. 95mm long. — 12.50
Rabbit, sitting with ears flat on
back. 54mm long. — 6.50
Ram, with curly horns.
90mm long. — 40.00

Birds

Chicken, very fluffy. No. 325.
65mm. — 14.00
Swan. 69mm. — 6.50

Great War

Nurse, inscribed: *A friend in need.*
130mm. — 40.00
Aeroplane Propeller. Rarely
factory marked. 150mm long. — 21.75
Airship (Observation Balloon) not
named. 80mm long. — 30.00
Submarine, impressed: *E4.*
116mm long. — 16.00
British Tank, Model of. 98mm long. — 13.00
Red Cross Van. 90mm long. — 23.00
Field Gun. 116mm long. — 17.00
Incendiary Bomb, rope handle.
82mm. — 11.00
Bandsman's Drum with cording.
60mm. — 5.00

Bugle. 70mm. — 12.50
Kit Bag with verse: *Pack up your
troubles.* 74mm. — 15.00
Telescope. 70mm. — 13.00
Kitchen Range, pot on fire.
Inscribed: *Keep the home fires
burning.* Some colouring. No. 6.
80mm long. — 9.00

Home/Nostalgic

Anvil. 60mm. — 5.50
Book. 60mm. — 5.00
Coal Scuttle. 65mm. — 4.50
Shaving Mug. 55mm. — 5.50
Watering Can. No. 126. 74mm. — 5.50
Wheelbarrow. 105mm long. — 10.50

Comic/Novelty

Dutch Girl, standing. 76mm. — 12.50
A truck of coal from. . . Wagon of
black coal. 90mm long. — 16.00

Cartoon/Comedy Characters

Baby, saluting, inscribed: *One of
the b'hoys.* Some colouring.
160mm. — 30.00
(Great war cartoon character
could be 'Pooksie').
Dr. Beetle, impressed: Charlie
Tolkard's character in Daily
Mail. 142mm. — 56.50

Sport

Racehorse. 102mm. — 75.00

Musical Instruments

Guitar. 163mm long. — 10.50

Miscellaneous

Dagger, in decorative scabbard.
No. 374. 135mm long (rare). — 21.50

Footwear

Ladies' 18th century shoe.
90mm long. — 7.50
Slipper wall pocket, blue blow.
No. 259. 150mm long. — 12.50

Miniature Domestic

Mug, one handled. 38mm. — 2.25
Jug, bagware, no colour.
No. 161 or 191. 55mm. — 2.25
Tea Pot with lid. 53mm. — 7.50

Domestic Wares
Hair Pins oval fluted box and lid.
  105mm long.   6.00

Moore Bros

MOORE BROS.
STAFF
Rᴅ Nᵒ
442279

Mark used from 1891-1905.

Trademark used by Moore (Bros).), St Mary's Works, Longton.

A range of 'smalls' with a Christmas crest and a sprig of holly recorded.   12.00

The earlier Moore England mark can be found on very Victorian/ornate looking smalls.

Mosanic

For mark see *Crested China*, p. 190.

Trademark used by the German firm, Max Emanuel & Co., The Mosanic Pottery, Mitterteich, Bavaria. They exported a range of brown/stone unglazed buildings to Britain. Model numbers are four figure and begin with 0. The Registration numbers are six figure and begin with 5 or 6.

All models unglazed and brown/stone coloured.

Buildings

Abbots of Buckfast Town House, inscribed: *Ye olde town house of ye Abbots of Buckfast ye close Exeter.* No. 0372. Rd. No. 567827. 100mm long. — 30.00

Aberdeen, Old Machor Cathedral. No. 1313. Rd. No. 55628(?). 75mm long. — 37.00

Aberystwyth, The College. No. 0350. Rd. No. 561630. 110mm long. — 40.00

Bank of Ireland. No. 0365. Rd. No. 587364. 129mm long. — 30.00

Birmingham Town Hall. 72mm long. — 26.00

Town Hall, Bradford. No. 554743. — 37.50

Bridlington Priory Church. No. 7533. 65mm. — 35.00

Burns Cottage. 113mm long. — 30.00

Canterbury Cathedral. No. 0326. Rd. No. 558188. 112mm long. — 30.00

Carlisle Cathedral. No. 0361 Rd. No. 576552. 97mm long. — 30.00

Chester Cathedral. No. 0340 Rd. No. 559941. 100mm long. — 30.00
Two varieties with east and west transepts transposed.

Christchurch Priory. Rd. No. 562002 2 sizes: No. 0345I. 98mm long. — 30.00
No. 0345II. 133mm long. — 32.50

Crosthwaite Church, Keswick Rd. No. 0382. No. 579266.

127mm long. — 32.50

Crystal Palace. No. 0386 Rd. No. 58157(?). 170mm long. — 40.00

Dartmouth, The Old Butterwalk No. 0375. Rd. No. 576629. 105mm long. — 30.00

Douglas, Tower of Refuge. 75mm long. — 35.00

Durham Cathedral. No. 0353. No. 570731. — 35.00

Edinburgh Castle. No. 0337. Rd. No. 559939. 113mm long. — 37.50

Exeter Cathedral. No. 0348. Rd. No. 564035. 150mm long. — 30.00

Exeter Guildhall, inscribed: *Ye olde Guilde Hall of ye Ancient and Loyal Cittie of Exeter.* 65mm. — 30.00

Exeter, St Mary's Steps & Stepcote Hill. No. 0304. Rd. No. 598554. 93mm long. — 30.00

Fairmaids House, Perth. No. 0318. Rd. No. 558196. 72mm. — 35.00

Gloucester Cathedral. No. 0347 Rd. No. 579265. 120mm long. — 30.00

Guy's Cliff, The Mill. No. 0309 Rd. No. 554739. 93mm long. — 40.00

Halifax, Parish Church. No. 0323 Rd. No. 558194. 90mm long. — 30.00

Harrogate, Royal Pump Room, Old Sulphur Well. No. 1301. Rd. No. 554744. 60mm. — 30.00

Hathaways Cottage, Stratford No. 0378. Rd. No. 576880. 120mm long. — 25.00

Hereford Cathedral. No. 0325. No. 558195. 92mm long. — 30.00

Hexham, The Abbey. No. 0371. Rd. No. 581571. 109mm long. — 30.00

Hawarden Castle. No. 0335 Rd. No. 559936. 110mm long. — 32.50

Hawarden Church. No. 0333 Rd. No. 559934. 85mm long. — 30.00

Hawarden, Gladstone Memorial Public Library. No. 0330. No. 559937. 115mm long. — 30.00

Hawthorns Hotel, Centenary Fetes, Bournemouth 1910. — 45.00

Houses of Parliament. No. 0398 Rd. No. 599955. 70mm. — 30.00

Iffley Church. No. 0360. Rd. No. 587402. 113mm long. — 30.00

Kirk Braddon Church. Rd. No. 557800. 80mm long. — 30.00

Lancaster Castle. No. 0363.
No. 578553. 130mm long.   30.00
Lichfield Cathedral. No. 0352
Rd. No. 580372.   30.00
Lincoln Castle. No. 0315.
Rd. No. 556282. 110mm long.   30.00
Londonderry Cathedral. No. 0391.
No. 587036.   35.00
Lowther Castle. No. 0317.
Rd. No. 566283. 105mm long.   30.00
Madame Tussauds. No. 0388.
No. 582363.   45.00
Malvern Priory. No. 0322.
Rd. No. 558186. 95mm long.   30.00
Manchester Cathedral.
No. 0356. Rd. No. 100mm long.   30.00
Marble Arch (white). No. 0422
90mm.   12.00
Molls Coffee House, Exeter.
No. 6936. 70mm long.   30.00
Newark Castle. No. 0307
Rd. No. 554738. 108mm long.   30.00
Medieval Bridge, Newcastle on
Tyne. No. 0392 No. 591208.   30.00
Newcastle Cathedral. No. 0343
Rd. No. 560727. 95mm long.   30.00
Newcastle-on-Tyne, Black Gate.
No. 0389. No. 585808.
80mm long.   30.00
Newcastle-on-Tyne, The Castle.
No. 0307, 0419 or 0390.
Rd. No. 554738 or 585809. (it is
possible that there is more than
one model). 95mm.   30.00
Plas Newydd, Llangollen, No. 0319.
No. 521568.86mm long.   40.00
Ripon Cathedral. No. 0385
Rd. No. 580773. 109mm long.   30.00
*Robinson Brewers Ltd, Ho'ton
(Ales & Stout).* No. 0379.
112mm long.   30.00
Rowton Tower, inscribed: *King
Charles stood on this tower
Sep 2nd 1645 and saw his army
defeated on Rowton Moor.*
No. 0327. No. 558197. 85mm.   30.00
St Andrews's Home, Folkestone.
No. 0331. No. 559935. 54mm.   40.00
St Johns Church, Perth. No. 0357
Rd. No. 568187. 85mm.   36.00
St Mary's Church, Scarborough.
No.0303. 97mm long.   30.00
St. Mary's Church, Taunton.
No. 0403. No. 604413.   30.00

St Patrick's Cathedral.
No. 587037. 103mm.   30.00
St Pauls Cathedral, not named.
Two numbers recorded, No. 0387
and No. 7332. Rd. No. 564098.
88mm long.   28.50
St Tudno's Church, Llandudno.
No. 0303. Rd. No. 564142.
84mm.   30.00
Salisbury Cathedral. No. 0351.
Rd. No. 567854. 105mm long.   35.00
Scarborough, The Castle.
No. 0398. 78mm.   32.50
*Shakespeares House,
Stratford-on-Avon.* No. 0380.
Rd. No. 576829. 110mm long.   25.00
Tintern Abbey. No. 0328.
No. 558187.   36.00
Upleatham Church. No. 0381
Rd. No. 582362. 97mm long.   30.00
Wells Cathedral. No. 583280.
105mm long.   30.00
Westminster Abbey. No. 0341.
Rd. No. 560726. 110mm long.   30.00
Winchester Cathedral. No. 0430
Rd. No. 632519. 144mm long.   30.00
Worcester Cathedral. No. 0334.
No. 564564.   30.00
York Minster. Rd. No. 556287.
2 sizes: No. 0312. 82mm long.   30.00
No. 0312II. 138mm long.   30.00

Monuments
The Cross, Banbury. No. 0316.
No. 536284 and No. 556281.
110mm.   27.50

Historical/Folklore
Christchurch, Rogers Tomb,
Trinket box and lid. No. 0429.
No. 632133. 113mm long.   26.00
*Old Norman Font, St Mary's Church
Steps, Exeter.* No. 0376.
Rd. No. 579668.   26.00
Scott Memorial, Edinburgh.
No. 0332. No. 559938.   25.00
Westminster Abbey Coronation Chair.
116mm.   13.00

Seaside Souvenirs
*Corbierre Lighthouse, Jersey, Model
of.* No. 0419. Rd. No. 558636.
84mm.   20.00
Flamborohead Lighthouse. 67mm.   22.00

Moschendorf

For mark see *Crested China*, p. 191.

Trademark used by the German firm Hof-Moschendorf (Bayern).

This mark has only been found on a crested tea plate.
150mm wide.   3.00

Mother Shipton China

For mark see *Crested China*, p. 191.

Trademark used for the retailer J.W. Simpson, Dropping Well, Knaresboro' by Wiltshaw and Robinson Ltd, Carlton Works, Stoke-on-Trent. (Usual trademark Carlton).

Historical/Folklore
Knaresborough Dropping Well,
  with colouring and inscription.
  103mm. (White £19.00).   27.50
Mother Shipton, with some
  colouring.
  3 sizes: 92mm.   24.50
         110mm.   30.00
         190mm.   40.00
Mother Shipton with some
  colouring, standing on lustre
  oval base. 90mm.   30.00
Mother Shipton, some colouring,
  standing on ashtray base, with
  inscription.   30.00

Seaside Souvenirs
Suitcase. 36mm. With inscription:
  *Near to the Knaresboro' Dropping
  Well*   8.50

Animals
Cat, sitting wearing black top hat
  and bow tie. 85mm.   13.00
Stag, with antlers. 217mm.   75.00

Great War
Munitions Worker, inscribed:
  *Doing her bit. Shells and more
  shells.* Some colouring. 140mm.   80.00
French 75mm Field Gun.
  125mm long.   17.00
Edith Cavell, statue, inscribed:
  *Brussels dawn October 12th
  1915. Sacrifice, Humanity.*
  163mm.   14.50

Home/Nostalgic
Frying Pan. 110mm long.   6.50
Warming Pan. No. 392.
  127mm long.   8.75

Comic/Novelty
I'm forever blowing bubbles. Pears
advert Blue Boy blowing
bubbles. Clothes blue, bubble
and bowl lustre. 110mm.   75.00

Alcohol
Toby Jug, with inscription.
70mm.   7.50

Musical Instruments
Upright Piano open keyboard.
64mm.   18.50

Nautilus Porcelain

For mark see *Crested China*, p. 193.

Trademark used by the Nautilus Porcelain
Co., Possil Pottery, Glasgow.

Crosses
Iona Cross. 162mm.   16.00

Ancient Artefacts
Aberdeen Bronze Pot. 65mm.   7.50
Hastings Kettle. 52mm.   7.50
Loving Cup, three handled.
2 sizes: 39mm.   7.50
        50mm.   7.50
Puzzle Jug. 70mm.   9.50

Traditional/National Souvenirs
Irish Wooden Noggin. 57mm.   9.00
Balmoral Bonnet, not named.
75mm dia.   27.00
Highland Whisky Bowl. Can
have 2 or 3 handles. 60mm dia.   10.50
Thistle Jug. 64mm.   8.00

Animals
Pig, fat and standing. 70mm long. 15.25

Home/Nostalgic
Coal scuttle, cylindrical on bow
feet. 70mm long.   8.50
Dust Pan. 50mm long.   12.00
Garden Urn. 63mm.   6.50
Milk Churn. 76mm.   8.50
Miner's Lamp. 63mm.   22.00
Watering Can, flat top. 50mm.   10.00

Alcohol
Carboy. 70mm.   6.50

Footwear
Dutch Sabot. 90mm long.   10.50
Old Boot. 63mm long.   10.50
Oriental Slipper. 92mm long.   10.50

Hats
Top Hat, match striker. 46mm.   8.25

Miscellaneous
Leaf Pin Tray with twig handle.
   120mm long.   6.50

Miniature Domestic
Beaker. 39mm.   5.50
Candlestick. 52mm.   5.50
Cheese Dish and cover.
   70mm long.   10.50
Cup. 39mm.   5.50
Milk Jug, tall and ornate.
   95mm.   5.50
Tea pot with lid. 48mm.   11.00

Nelson China

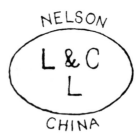

Trademark used for a Liverpool retailer by an unknown English manufacturer but probably a branch of J.A. Robinson & Sons.

Seaside Souvenirs
Bathing Machine.   7.50

Great War
Model of a pair of Field Glasses.
   60mm long.   13.00

Ness

Niagara Art China

"NESS CHINA"

NIAGARA
ART
CHINA

Trademark used for an Inverness firm by Schmidt and Co., Carlsbad (Bohemia). (Usual trademark Gemma).

Great War
French Infantry Helmet.
60mm long.   40.00

Trademark used by Birks, Rawlins and Co (Ltd), Vine Pottery, Stoke. (Usual trademark Savoy).

Great War
Tommy's Steel Helmet.
76mm long.   24.50

Footwear
Lace-up Riding Shoe. 115mm long.   10.00

Norfolk Crest China

For mark see *Crested China,* p. 193.
Mark has also been found with CHEST
rather than crest, obviously a misprint.

Trademark used for W.H. Smith & Sons by
Hewitt & Leadbeater, Willow Potteries,
Longton — subsequently Hewitt Bros.
(Usual trademark Willow Art).

Parian/Unglazed
Bust of Burns on column base.
170mm.   24.00

Buildings — White
Shakespeare's House.
59mm long.   10.00

Monuments
Sir Robert Peel statue. 168mm.   30.00

Historical/Folklore
James V Chair. 101mm.   7.50

Traditional/National Souvenirs
Lancashire Clog. 88mm long.   4.75
Welsh Hat, with blue band.
No. 75. 57mm.   4.75

Seaside Souvenirs
Lifeboat. 95mm long.   8.75
Lighthouse, not named. 105mm.   4.75

Animals
Cat, on cushion, playing fiddle,
holding bow. 110mm.
inscribed: *Cat and Fiddle, Buxton.*   40.00
Dog, Bull Terrier, standing.
60mm.   13.00
Dog, sitting, bow at neck.
Brown eyes. No. 22. 76mm.   10.50
Dog, sitting, head to one side.
No. 23. 70mm.   13.00
Dog, wearing medallion.   13.00
Elephant, walking. 52mm.   13.00
Elephant, walking, trunk over
head. No. 113. 53mm.   21.50
Pig, standing. 85mm long.   10.00

Pony inscribed 'A Native of
Shetland'. 105mm long.   22.00

Birds
Duck posy holder, yellow beak.
80mm long.   7.50
Hen egg cup. 76mm long.   8.25

Great War
Battleship, impressed:
HMS Lion. 140mm long.   22.50
British Tank. 102mm long.   13.00
Tank with trailing wheels.
123mm long.   14.50
Red Cross Van. No. 712.
88mm long.   23.00
Military Cap. 80mm dia.   13.00
Kitbag with verse. 74mm.   15.00
Nurse Cavell, War Memorial statue.
194mm.   82.50
Matlock Bath War Memorial.
182mm.   40.00
Florence Nightingale statue.
160mm.   16.50

Home/Nostalgic
Grandfather clock, inscribed:
*Make use of time let not advantage
slip. Shakespeare.* 128mm.   10.50
Hatpins Holder. 124mm.   10.50

Comic/Novelty
Jester, double faced bust.
Some colouring.
3 sizes: 65mm.   8.25
80mm.   9.00
90mm.   12.50
Monk, jovial and plump.
No glass. 90mm.   12.50

Alcohol
Monk, jovial and holding glass.
70mm.   13.00

Sport
Cricket Cap. 67mm long.   22.00

Miscellaneous
Thistle vase. 58mm.   3.00

Noritaké

Noritaké

Made in Japan.

One small found; a 110mm vase with a transfer print of St Annes with a crest in foreground. There is very little Japanese souvenir ware around and certainly the British Potteries did not see the Japanese as much of a threat as they did the Germans.

Nornesford China

For mark see *Crested China*, p. 194.

Trademark used by a Longton firm, probably R.H. and S.L. Plant (Ltd), Tuscan Works, Longton. (Usual trademark Tuscan).

Animals

Cheshire Cat, with brown bead right eye. 90mm.	11.00
Fish with open mouth and bead eyes. 120mm long.	8.25

Birds

Chick hatching from egg. 70mm long.	7.50

Home/Nostalgic

Bellows. 105mm.	5.50
Loaf of Bread. 55mm.	15.25
Pillar Box. No. 181. 73mm.	8.00
Shaving Mug. 53mm.	5.50
Wee Willie Winkie Candle Snuffer. 90mm.	21.75

Hats

Top Hat. No. 173. 45mm.	5.50

One and All

For mark see *Crested China*, p. 194.

Trademark used by J.A. Robinson & Sons, Stoke-on-Trent. (Usual trademark Arcadian).

Ancient Artefacts
Salisbury Jack, not named.
50mm.   2.25

Buildings — White
Anne Hathaway's Cottage.
105mm long.   13.00

Animals
Black Cat on jug. 85mm.   45.00
Bulldog, sitting. 50mm.   21.50
Dog, Collie lying down.
78mm long.   12.50
Teddy Bear. No. 27. 65mm.   8.50
Squirrel, eating nut. 60mm.   15.00

Birds
Goose. 95mm.   19.50

Home/Nostalgic
Cauldron with handle. 82mm.   3.00
Fire Bucket. 53mm.   3.00
Grandmother Clock. 110mm.   10.50

Comic/Novelty
Black Boy and Girl on log,
coloured. 75mm long.   75.00
Jester, sitting on heart shaped
ashtray. 65mm.   70.00

Transport
Petrol Can, impressed:
Motor Spirit. 55mm.   13.00

Miscellaneous
Domed Jam Pot and cover. 80mm.   5.00

Footwear
Ladies Ankle Boot. 72mm long.   6.50

Oxford Art China

For additional mark see *Crested China*, p. 195.

Trademark used for an Oxfordshire retailer by Hewitt & Leadbeater, Willow Potteries, Longton. (Usual trademark Willow Art).

Historical/Folklore
Sir Walter Scott's Chair, Abbotsford.
80mm.   7.50

Traditional/National Souvenirs
Lancashire Clog.   4.75

P

Palantine China

For mark see *Crested China*, p. 195.

For mark see *Crested China*, p. 195.

Trademark used by Hutschenreuther, Probstzella, Thüringia (not the more famous Bavarian firm of the same name).

Trademark used for Pearsons, of Blackpool by J.A. Robinson Ltd. (Usual trademark Arcadian).

Ancient Artefacts

Aberdeen Bronze Pot. 68mm.	2.25
Ancient Tyg, 2 handled.	2.25
Loving Cup, 3 handled & 2 handled. 38mm.	3.00
Puzzle Jug. 67mm.	5.50

Seaside Souvenirs

Suitcase. 90mm.	4.00

Home/Nostalgic

Cauldron.	3.00
Shaving Mug. 55mm.	5.50

Miniature Domestic

Candlestick and snuffer. 85mm dia.	5.50
Cheese Dish and cover, 2 pieces. 55mm.	4.75
Tea Pot with lid. 65mm.	7.50
Tea Urn with lid, tapered. 65mm.	8.50

Animals

Dog, sitting with a tear on cheek. 80mm.	30.00

Great War

Armoured Car, Model of. 120mm long.	30.00
Red Cross Van, inscribed: *EH139.* 88mm long.	23.00
Tank, Model of. 115mm.	15.00

Palmer

Trademark used by Hewitt and Leadbeater, Willow Potteries, Longton. (Usual trademark Willow Art.) This piece was obviously ordered by their Buckingham agent and it bears the arms of the town.

Comic/Novelty
Billiken sitting. 78mm.   4.00

P.A.L.T.

For mark see *Crested China,* p. 195.

Trademark used by a German firm on domestic wares, after the Great War.

Domestic ware only.   from £3.00

Panorama

For mark see *Crested China*, p. 197.

Trademark used by Wagstaff and Brunt on
china manufactured by Edwin Leadbeater, Commerce Street, Longton.
Similar to Leadbeater Art China.

Many of these wares are found
with a transfer print view
rather than a crest.

Unglazed/Parian
Burns and Highland Mary.
  125mm.   30.00
Bust of Dickens, on circular
  glazed base. 170mm.   35.00

Ancient Artefacts
*Model of Bowl found in lake village
Glastonbury.* 65mm dia.   3.00

Monuments
Sir Robert Peel statue on large
  plinth. 165mm.   55.00

Historical
Bunyans Chair, Model of. 95mm.   10.50
*Model of Mons Meg Edinburgh
  Castle.* 130mm long.   11.00
*Sir Walter Scott's Chair at
  Abbotsford.* No. 85. 80mm.   7.50

Traditional/National Souvenirs
Welsh Hat. No. 57. 60mm.   4.75

Animals
Cat sitting, left ear raised, one
  green eye. 105mm.   9.50
Pug Dog, sitting. 67mm.   10.50
Labrador sitting, red eyes.   12.50

Birds
Chick. 33mm.   4.00

Great War
Red Cross Van. No. 103.
  88mm long.   23.00

Home/Nostalgic
Anvil. No. 78. 58mm.   5.50

Comic/Novelty
Monk. 88mm.   10.50

Alcohol
Toby Jug. 74mm.   6.50

Sport
Cricket Cap. 67mm long.   19.50
Footballer, coloured holding
  brown ball on white plinth.
  Inscribed: *Play Up* 166mm.   100.00

Paragon China

PARAGON
CHINA
ENGLAND

Trademarks used by Star China Co., Atlas Works (and other addresses), Longton. Subsequently Paragon China (Co) Ltd.

The star mark was used on domestic wares with Great War, Commemorative, Four Flags of the Allies with inscription: *For right and freedom.* from £5.50

The crown mark is found on smalls with ordinary crests. 2.25

Park, For the People, China

PARK, FOR THE PEOPLE CHINA

Mark used by unknown English manufacturer for a charity, (possibly) in Newtown, Mid-Wales.

This mark has been found on several 'smalls' all with a Newtown crest, could they have been sold at a charity or fund raising bazaar? 4.00

Patriotic China

Pearl Arms China

For mark see *Crested China*, p. 197.

For mark see *Crested China*, p. 197.

Trademark used during the Great War by Birks, Rawlins and Co (Ltd), Vine Pottery, Stoke. (Usual trademark Savoy).

Trademark used for a wholesaler by Hewitt Bros, Willow Potteries Ltd, Longton. (Usual trademark Willow Art).

Range of wares all with military crests and Great War inscriptions. £8.00 upwards

Ancient Artefacts
Carlisle Salt Pot, not named.
46mm. 2.25

Parian/Unglazed
Bust of Admiral Sir David Beatty.
Union Jack and laurel wreath.
Inscribed: *To Victory*. Verse
at rear *Be Briton still to Briton
true*. 150mm. 65.00

Historical/Folklore
James V Chair, Stirling Castle.
100mm. 7.50
*Mary, Queen of Scots Chair,
Edinburgh Castle*, Model of.
75mm. 6.50
Royal Crown. 55mm. 21.50

Animals
Bulldog standing.
Identical Union Jack and Laurel
Wreath. Inscribed: *To Victory*
and verse as on the bust.
135mm long. 65.00
Lion, walking with Burns verse:
Be Briton still to Briton true.
135mm long. 22.00

Traditional/National Souvenirs
Blackpool Big Wheel. 100mm. 12.00
Lancashire Clog. 88mm long. 4.75
Welsh Hat with longest Welsh
place name around brim.
No. 75. 55mm. 7.50

Seaside Souvenirs
Lighthouse. 105mm. 4.75

Miniature Domestic
Beaker. 80mm. 2.25
Tea Pot with lid. 65mm. 7.50

Animals
Cat, angry, tail in the air. Bow
not coloured. 80mm long. 12.50
Cat, sitting. 70mm. 10.00
Cat sitting in boot, blue bow.
88mm long. 14.50
Cat, standing, blue bow. 80mm. 10.00
Cat, standing, chubby. 70mm. 12.50
Bulldog, black, emerging from
kennel, inscribed: *The Black
Watch*. 70mm long. 15.25
Dog, Collie, standing. 52mm. 12.50
Dog, Scottie with tam-o'-shanter.
95mm. 10.50
Elephant, walking. 52mm. 13.00
Elephant, cream jug. 72mm. 7.50
Fish. 128mm long. 3.00
Hampshire Hog with inscription.
100mm long. 14.00
Mouse. 62mm. 16.00
Pig standing. 95mm long. 12.50

Pig, sitting, inscribed: *You may push me* etc. 73mm.   11.00
Pig, standing. 85mm long.   12.50
Rabbit, right ear erect. 66mm long.   6.50

Birds

Canary on rock. 98mm.   13.00
Swan, with head on breast. 58mm.   4.75

Great War

Sailor, inscribed: *Our brave defender.* 130mm.   40.00
Monoplane, with movable prop. 150mm long.   55.00
Monoplane, with fixed prop. 146mm long.   55.00
Battleship, 4 funnels. 127mm long.   19.00
Battleship, 3 funnels. Impressed *HMS Lion.* 140mm long.   22.50
British Tank, Model of, with trailing wheels. 130mm long.   14.50
British Tank, Model of. 92mm long.   13.00
Bugle. No. 370. 70mm.   12.50
Kit Bag with verse: *Pack up your troubles in your old kit bag.* 74mm.   15.00
Officer's Peaked Cap. 70mm dia.   10.00
Pickelhaube. (German spiked helmet). 50mm.   17.50
Fireplace inscribed: *Keep the home fires burning.* Some colouring. 100mm long.   13.00

Home/Nostalgic

Anvil. 60mm.   5.50
Basket, oblong with handle. 76mm long.   3.50
Book, leather bound. 60mm.   5.00
Bucket. 65mm.   3.50
Coal scuttle, helmet shaped. No. 101. 53mm.   4.50
Grandfather Clock, inscribed: *Make use of time let not advantage slip. Shakespeare.* 128mm.   10.50
Pillar Box, outpressed: *G.R.* 90mm.   17.00
Sundial, circular on square base, with inscription: *I mark not the hours.* 98mm.   7.50
Watering Can. 72mm.   5.50

Comic/Novelty

Billiken, the God of Luck, often found unnamed. 73mm.   4.00
Billiken, the God of Luck, sitting on high-backed chair. 100mm.   5.50

Alcohol

Whiskey Bottle with cork, inscribed: *One special scotch.* 88mm.   7.50

Transport

Open Tourer, 4 seater. 114mm long.   30.00

Miscellaneous

Hand holding a tulip. 80mm.   4.00

Hats

Policeman's Helmet.   17.50

Miniature Domestic

Cheese Dish and cover. 45mm.   4.75
Cup and Saucer. 35mm.   5.50
Coffee Pot with lid. 69mm.   4.75

Phoenix China

For additional mark see *Crested China*, p. 198.

Trademark used by Thomas Forester & Sons (Ltd.), Phoenix Works, Longton.

A range of crested domestic ware was produced.

Miniature Domestic

Wash Bowl. 50mm.	2.50
Wash Jug. 80mm.	2.50

Miscellaneous

Teaplate. 180mm dia.	2.00

Podmore China

For mark see *Crested China*, p. 199.

Trademark used by Podmore China Co., Elm Street, Hanley.

Unglazed/Parian

Bust of *Bunyan*, square unglazed base. 135mm.	20.00
Bust of Burns, on square unglazed base with crest. 150mm.	14.50

Buildings — Coloured.
Bell Hotel, Abel Fletcher's house in John Halifax Gentleman.

2 sizes: 67mm.	30.00
85mm.	40.00

Buildings — White

Bell Hotel, Abel Fletcher's house in John Halifax Gentleman. 67mm.	26.00
Big Ben. 101mm.	10.00
Blackpool Tower. 130mm.	11.50
Clifton Suspension Bridge. 190mm long.	40.00
God's Providence House, Chester. AD1652.	
2 sizes: 70mm.	14.50
90mm.	16.00
Hastings Clock Tower. 167mm.	10.50
Leicester Clock Tower. 184mm.	19.00
Lincoln Cathedral, West front. 106mm.	19.50
Margate Clock Tower. 143mm.	10.50
Matlock Bath, The Tower. 120mm.	17.00
Rowton Tower (King Charles Tower, Chester) 88mm.	30.00
St. Albans, Clock Tower. 125mm.	16.00
St. Pauls Cathedral. 105mm.	15.50
Westminster Abbey. 127mm.	40.00

Monuments

Banbury, The Cross. 158mm.	21.50
Black Watch Memorial. 130mm.	65.00
Bunyan's Statue, Model of.	
2 sizes: 173mm.	17.00
206mm.	19.00

Nelsons Column. 140mm.	40.00
St Albans Statue. 160mm.	40.00

Historical/Folklore

Armour, breast plate. 75mm.	35.00
Bunyan's Chair. 99mm.	10.50
Burns Chair, Model of. 93mm.	7.50
Mary Queen of Scots Chair in Edinburgh Castle, Model of. 80mm.	6.50
Mother Shipton, standing figure. 75mm.	21.75
Tewkesbury Cross Stocks and Whipping Post. 105mm (rare).	50.00

Traditional/National Souvenirs

Blackpool Big Wheel. 95mm.	8.50
Chester Imp, recumbent. 100mm long.	30.00
Chester Imp on base, some colouring. 83mm long.	30.00
Lancashire Clog. 73mm long.	4.75
Lincoln Imp sitting on pedestal. 105mm.	6.50

Seaside Souvenirs

Lifeboat with deep blue cord. 115mm long.	8.25
Yacht. 111mm.	13.00
Lifeboatman on plinth. 142mm.	16.00
Beachy Head Lighthouse, with black band. 120mm.	7.50
Needles Rocks and Lighthouse, Isle of Wight. 125mm long.	26.00
North Foreland Lighthouse, Broadstairs. 128mm.	19.50
Oyster Shell on coral base. 80mm.	3.50
Whelk Shell, inscribed: *Listen to the sea.* 100mm long.	3.00
Child, sitting with knees under chin, wearing a bathing suit. Impressed: *Splash me.* Some colouring. 140mm (rare).	40.00
Child, standing on rock draped in towel. Some colouring. 115mm. and 140mm.	19.00

Animals

Cat, standing with arched back and tail up. Coloured eyes and mouth. 110mm.	12.50
Cat, grotesque with almost human face and wearing a black cap. Inscribed: *Puss Puss.* 105mm.	40.00
Cat, grotesque with long neck, named in orange *Luck.* 136mm.	8.25
Cat with long neck. 120mm.	6.50
Cat on round pouffe. Inscribed: *Luck.* 80mm.	9.50
Dog, Scottie, looking out of kennel.	7.00
Inscribed: *Black Watch.*	9.00
Dog, black with green bow. 70mm.	16.00
Dog, Scottie, wearing a tam-o'shanter. 75mm.	10.50
Dog, sitting. 68mm.	8.75
Dog, sitting next to a bright red pillar box on ashtray.	30.00
Elephant. 64mm long.	13.00
Pig, standing. 100mm long.	10.00
Shetland Pony. 100mm long.	22.00

Birds

Cock, standing, red comb. 65mm.	8.00
Cock with red comb, on green base. 45mm.	13.00
Hen on green base. 70mm long.	13.00
Hen, with red comb. 66mm.	8.00
Kingfisher, coloured, on pearl lustre trinket tray. 82mm long.	30.00
Penguin. 88mm.	11.50

Great War

HRH, Prince of Wales, in uniform, standing on square base. 155mm.	80.00
Monoplane with revolving prop.	55.00
Grandfather Clock, same mould as usual Grandfather clock but clockface at 3.25, inscribed: *World War 1914-1919, Peace signed 3.25pm June 28th 1919.* 137mm.	56.50
Cenotaph, inscribed: *The Glorious Dead. MCMXIV-MCMXIX.* Green wreaths.	
3 sizes: 84mm.	4.00
130mm.	5.50
165mm.	5.50
Edith Cavell Memorial, London. Inscribed: *Edith Cavell Brussels dawn October 12th 1915. Humanity Sacrifice.*	
2 sizes: 142mm.	14.50
170mm.	16.00
Edith Cavell Statue, Norwich. 165mm.	22.50

Leek War Memorial. *Model of War Memorial Leek, presented by Sir Arthur & Lady Nicholson.* 158mm.   82.50

Matlock Bath War Memorial. Often found unnamed. 190mm.   21.50

Ad Astra, R.A.F. Memorial. Unveiled by HRH Prince of Wales July 16th 1923. 152mm.   85.00

Rushden War Memorial. *Their names liveth for ever, To keep in mind those from this town who gave their lives in the Great War. 1914-1918.* 155mm.   56.50

Blackpool War Memorial, inscribed: *1914 in memory of our glorious dead 1918.* 145mm.   55.00

Home/Nostalgic

Baby's Bootee. 52mm.   12.50
Baby's Cradle. 65mm long.   6.50
Basket. 72mm long.   4.00
Grandfather Clock, with inscription: *Make use of time*
120mm.   10.50
140mm.   10.50
Fireplace with clock on mantelpiece, inscribed: *Home sweet home. East or west home is best.* Some colouring. 98mm.   16.00

Comic/Novelty

Billiken, sitting on high backed chair, inscribed: *The God of things as they ought to be.*
102mm.   5.00
Inscribed   6.00
The Bridegroom, God Help Him.
145mm.   35.00
Child, some colouring, standing on ashtray base. 95mm.   22.00
Sack of Coal, some colouring.
2 sizes: 60mm.   12.50
95mm.   12.50
Can be found inscribed: *If you can't afford a truck — buy a sack.*   16.00
Schoolboy, comic coloured face.
100mm.   35.00

Cartoon/Comedy Characters

Mr Pussy Foot. All water we don't think. Standing by a pump, some colouring. 96mm.   30.00
Wilfred Wilfred, coloured.   35.00

Alcohol

Beer Barrel on stand, fixed.
60mm.   4.50

Sport

Golf Ball, inscribed: *The ancient game of golf was first played in 1448.* 40mm.   6.50
The Sprinter, gangly athlete with comic face, kneeling, on oval base. 98mm.   45.00

Musical Instruments

Double Bass. 140mm long.   33.00

Transport

Charabanc. 127mm long.   30.00

Modern Equipment

Horn Gramophone. 93mm.   19.00

Miscellaneous

Hand holding a tulip. 95mm.   3.00
Horseshoe Pintray. 80mm long.   3.00

Miniature Domestic

Cheese Dish, 1 piece. 50mm.   5.50
Cheese Dish and cover.
71mm long.   5.50

Poppyland

**POPPYLAND
CHINA
ENGLISH
B.A.WATTS
SHERINGHAM**

Trademark used by Taylor and Kent Ltd, Florence Works, Longton. (Usual trademark Florentine.)

The only piece recorded is a 60mm 2 handled vase decorated with red poppies for the Norfolk Broads market.   12.00

Porcelle

For mark see *Crested China*, p. 201.

Trademark used by William Ritchie & Son Ltd., 24, 26, 28 Elder Street, Edinburgh. Many, if not all, these models are from Savoy moulds and this firm was a retailer of heraldic china, obtaining supplies from Birks, Rawlins and Co. (Usual trademark Savoy). William Ritchie was an Edinburgh wholesale stationer who also issued heraldic postcards.

Unglazed/Parian

Bust of Robbie Burns on glazed plinth. 135mm.	17.50
Bust of Sir John Jellicoe, impressed: *W.C. Lawton sculp. copyright. 23rd Sept 1914.* 170mm.	47.50

Ancient Artefacts

Newbury Leather Bottle. 65mm.	2.25
Puzzle Jug. 70mm.	5.50
Whiskey Quaich. 30mm.	4.00

Buildings — White

Burns Cottage, Model of.	
2 sizes: 70mm long.	16.00
115mm long.	19.50
Cottage. 75mm long.	6.50
Windmill, with revolving sails. 108mm.	20.00

Historical/Folklore

Mary Queen of Scots Chair, Edinburgh Castle, Model of. 70mm.	6.50

Traditional/National Souvenirs

Irish Harp with moulded shamrocks. 105mm.	10.50
Bagpipes. 115mm long.	15.00
Thistle vase. 48mm.	3.00

Seaside Souvenirs

Bathing Machine, inscribed: *Morning dip.* 87mm.	7.50
Lighthouse on rocky base. 104mm.	4.75

Fisherman, with Tub, inscribed:
Waiting for the smacks. 67mm. 30.00
Shell ashtray. 81mm long. 3.00
Scallop Shell. 70mm long. 3.00
Whelk Shell. No. 451. 100mm long. 3.50
Holdall. 95mm long. 17.00

Animals
Cat, sitting, long neck and tail
joined to shoulders. 105mm. 16.00
Cat, sitting. 51mm. 10.50
Cat, squatting, wide grin.
105mm. 30.00
Dog, puppy begging. 68mm. 12.50
Labrador Puppy sitting, all legs
forward. 80mm. 13.00
Dog, sitting with short turned
down ears. 67mm. 13.00
Dog, Terrier, looking out of
kennel, inscribed: *Black Watch,*
dog black. 55mm. 10.50
Hare, sitting up. 106mm. 35.00
Pig, kneeling. 65mm long. 8.25
Pig, lying down. 80mm long. 9.50
Pig, standing. 70mm long. 10.00
Rabbit, crouching with flat ears.
30mm. 6.50
Rabbit, sitting. 80mm. 21.50
Seal. 50mm. 11.00
Grotesque animal/bird. 105mm. 10.00
Animal jug, tail is handle. 70mm. 5.50

Birds
Duck, swimming. 70mm long. 8.00
Hen, sitting. 93mm long. 7.50
Cockerel Pepper Pot, egg shaped.
85mm. 10.00
Swan. 50mm. 6.50

Great War
Sailor, standing with hands on
hips. 130mm. 175.00
Bust of Sailor. Inscribed:
HMS Queen Elizabeth. 90mm. 30.00
British Airship on stand.
130mm long. 20.00
Battleship, inscribed:
HMS Lion, with 3 funnels,
168mm long. 56.50
Battleship, inscribed
HMS King George V, with
2 funnels. 168mm long. 56.50
HMS Queen Elizabeth Battleship.
165mm long. 50.00
Torpedo Boat Destroyer, Model of.
2 sizes: 110mm long. 87.50

140mm long. 87.50
Submarine, inscribed: *E1.*
150mm long. 40.00
Submarine, inscribed: *E4.*
95mm. 16.00
Armoured Car with 2 guns.
127mm long. 80.00
British Motor Searchlight, Model of
90mm long. 145.00
Red Cross Van. 110mm long. 30.00
Tank with 2 inset steering wheels,
inscribed: *HMS Donner Blitzen*
and *Model of British tank first
used by British troops at the Battle
of Ancre Sept. 1916.*
2 sizes: 130mm long. 30.00
160mm long. 40.00
Field Gun. 170mm long. 17.00
Howitzer.
2 sizes: 140mm. 27.50
168mm long. 27.50
Machine gun, Model of, on tripod
(2 pieces). 80mm. 120.00
Trench Mortar Gun. 98mm long. 47.50
Land Mine. Similar to curling
stone but with rectangular
firing mechanism. No. 429.
52mm. 75.00
Mills Hand Grenade. 80mm. 13.00
Shell inscribed: *Iron rations for
Fritz.* 78mm. 7.50
Glengarry.
2 sizes: 70mm. 16.00
100mm long. 16.00
Larger model has coloured
heather in band.
Anzacs Cap, Model of, with maple
leaf, impressed: *CANADA.*
90mm long. 25.00
Colonial Soldiers Hat.
90mm long. 10.50
Peaked Cap. No. 516.
70mm long. 10.00
Pith Helmet. 80mm. 15.50
Poilu, French Trench Helmet.
84mm long. 40.00
Sailors Cap. 70mm dia. 57.50
Tommy's Steel Helmet.
82mm long. 24.50
Fireplace, inscribed: *Keep the
home fires burning.* 70mm. 14.50

Home/Nostalgic
Baby's Cradle. 55mm. 7.50
Grandfather Clock. 132mm. 10.50
Iron and stand. 70mm long. 10.50

Jelly Mould. 55mm. 17.00
Lady in bonnet and muff, candle-
snuffer. 80mm. 16.00
Milk Churn with fixed top.
60mm. 3.00
Watering Can, miniature. 50mm. 10.50
Wheelbarrow. 114mm long. 10.50
Wooden Tub. 39mm. 3.00

Comic/Novelty
Felix the Cat on oval base. 75.00
Hindu God on circular base
wearing beads. No. 35. 88mm. 8.50
Policeman, hands behind back.
No. 327. 113mm. 24.50

Alcohol
Beer Bottle. 92mm. 6.50

Cartoon/Comedy Characters
Winkie the Gladeye Bird cruet
set, salt, pepper and mustard.
68mm. each 14.50
Can be found coloured. each 35.00

Sport
Curling Stone. 52mm. 13.00
Golf Club Head. 65mm. 10.50

Musical Instruments
Banjo. 137mm long. 12.50

Transport
Open Motor Car. 30.00

Modern Equipment
Square Gramophone. 55mm. 18.50

Hats
Top Hat. 45mm. 5.50

Footwear
Ankle Boot. 72mm long. 4.75
Boot. 58mm long. 4.75
Dutch Sabot. 75mm long. 4.75
Ladies 18th century Shoe. 7.50
Oriental Shoe with turned up
toe. 88mm long. 4.75

Miscellaneous
Toby Jug. 60mm. 8.25

Miniature Domestic
Cup and Saucer. 40mm. 4.50
Mug. 47mm. 2.25
Thistle Shaped Jug. 65mm. 3.00

Premier

For mark see *Crested China*, p. 202.

Trademark used by a wholesaler on china
manufactured by Taylor & Kent (Ltd),
Florence Works, Longton. (Usual trademark Florentine).

Ancient Artefacts
Fountains Abbey Cup. 48mm. 2.25

Monuments
Iona Cross. 108mm. 6.00

Traditional/National Souvenirs
Welsh Hat. 57mm. 4.75

Seaside Souvenirs
Lighthouse, open base. 105mm. 5.00
Portmanteau. 77mm. 4.00

Animals
Cheshire Cat always smiling. 87mm. 7.50
Manx Cat. 61mm. 16.00
Elephant, kneeling. 88mm long. 15.00
Fish. 120mm long. 3.00
Pig, standing, inscribed: *The pig
that won't go.* 95mm long. 10.00
Toad. 72mm long. 10.50

Birds
Baby Bird Jug. 65mm. 5.50

Home/Nostalgic
Bellows. 107mm long. 5.50
Coal Bucket. 64mm. 3.00
Coal Scuttle, helmet shaped.
65mm. 4.00
Oriental Lamp. (Aladdin's
Lamp). 100mm long. 4.75
Shaving Mug. 60mm. 5.50

Musical Instruments
Tambourine. 70mm dia. 4.50

Footwear
Shoe, Ladies, 18th Century.
95mm long. 7.50

Miniature Domestic
Coffee Pot with lid. 55mm. 7.50

Princess China

Queen China

For mark see *Crested China*, p. 203.

Trademark used for a Blackpool retailer probably by Wilhelm Kutzscher & Co., Schwarzenberg Porzellanfabrik, Schwarzenberg, Saxony. (Now in East Germany). (This firm used several trademarks and produced a large number of German models just labelled; Germany, Saxony or foreign).

Buildings — White
Blackpool Tower, with buildings.
155mm.   7.50

Traditional/National Souvenirs
Blackpool, Big Wheel. 89mm.   9.00

Birds
Bird standing on rock. 80mm.   8.25

Unknown German manufacturer's mark, possibly the product of a German prison where the inmates specialised in exporting souvenir ware to the English market to avoid competition with their own German potteries at home. The mark is very like those used by several German potters, especially Hof-Moschendorf (Bayern). Two models known:

Domestic Wares
Napkin ring with a crest of
Ripon. 50mm dia.   4.00
Small square dish, crest of
Swanage.   2.00

Queens China or Ware

For mark see *Crested China*, p. 203.

Trademark used by Birks, Rawlins & Co (Ltd), Vine Pottery, Stoke. (Usual trademark Savoy). Pieces marked Queens are usually seconds and have firing flaws, only pristine wares carrying the Savoy mark. Prices are the same as Savoy however unless flaws are particularly notable.

Ancient Artefacts

Chester Roman Vase. 60mm.	2.25
Glastonbury Bowl. 40mm.	2.25
Phoenician Vase. 85mm.	2.50
Puzzle Jug. 68mm.	5.50
Shakespeare's Jug. 63mm.	3.00

Historical/Folklore

Burns Chair. 76mm.	7.50
Execution Block. 98mm long.	8.50
Rufus Stone. 100mm.	4.75

Traditional/National Souvenirs

Cornish Pasty. 104mm long.	7.50
Welsh Hat. 50mm.	5.50

Seaside Souvenirs

Bathing Machine. No. 425 and No. 428. 60mm.	7.50
Lighthouse on rocky base. 134mm.	5.50
Rowing Boat. 127mm long.	10.50
Oyster Shell dish. 80mm long.	3.50
Shell on base. 80mm long.	4.00
Closed Suitcase. 96mm long.	17.00

Countryside

Beehive. 70mm.	7.50

Animals

Bear dancing, with muzzle. 102mm.	35.00
Cat, detailed fur. 80mm.	11.50
Manx Cat. 80mm.	16.00
Dog, angry and barking. 100mm long.	29.00
Fish. 102mm long.	3.00
Puffer Fish vase. 90mm.	10.00
Frog, realistic, giant-size. 73mm.	30.00
Grotesque Animal Jug. 72mm.	7.50
Grotesque Animal. 100mm.	10.00
Hare. 74mm.	20.00
Lion, sitting on base. (This was originally designed by Alfred Stevens for the British Museum). 104mm.	24.50
Pig, lying down. 80mm long.	10.00
Pig, sitting, large. 100mm long.	12.50
Pig, standing. 65mm long.	12.50
Seal. 55mm long.	14.00

Birds

Baby Bird jug. 70mm.	5.50
Birds on tree trunk.	23.00
Duck, swimming. 40mm long.	9.00
Duck's head feeding bottle. 130mm long.	13.00
Penguin. 76mm.	16.00

Great War

Submarine. *E1*. 149mm long.	40.00
Tank. 152mm long.	45.00
Ambulance, Red Cross Van. 108mm long.	30.00
Ambulance, with Rolls Royce front. 115mm long.	40.00
Armoured Car. 125mm long.	65.00
Motor Searchlight. 100mm long.	145.00
Field Gun, with fish tail. 140mm long. (scarce).	85.00
Machine Gun on tripod, two-piece. 80mm.	117.50
British Trench Mortar Gun. 110mm long.	47.50
Howitzer. 145mm long.	27.50
Hand Grenade. 88mm.	13.00
Shell. 70mm. No. 556.	4.00
Balmoral Bonnet. 70mm long.	20.00
R.F.C. Cap. 72mm long.	40.00
Colonial Hat. 92mm long.	10.50
French Trench Helmet. 72mm long. (Not named £30.00).	40.00
Glengarry. 70mm long.	16.00
Officer's Peaked Cap. 72mm long.	10.00
New Zealand Hat. 83mm long.	16.00
Sailors Cap. No. 533. 70mm.	56.50
Bandsman's Drum. 55mm dia.	6.00

Home/Nostalgic

Dog Kennel. 55mm. 6.50

Grandfather Clock, narrow design.
149mm. 22.00

Post Box. 60mm. 12.00

Comic/Novelty

Humpty Dumpty salt and
pepper pots. 80mm. pair 60.00

Man, shirt off, leaning into barrel.
68mm long. 30.00

Policeman holding truncheon.
105mm. 24.50

Cartoon/Comedy Characters

Bonzo, not named. 118mm. 30.00

Sport

Golf Caddie with bag of clubs on
heart shaped pin tray/ashtray.
80mm. 40.00

Golf Club Head. 80mm. 12.00

Curling Stone, not named.
53mm. 13.00

Musical Instruments

Banjo. 136mm long. 12.50

Miscellaneous

Clog. 75mm long. 5.00

Queens Crest China

For mark see *Crested China*, p. 205.

Trademark used for S.P. & Co Ltd, of 57
King St, Manchester, by Arkinstall & Son
Ltd, Arcadian Works, Stoke-on-Trent.
(Usual trademark Arcadian).

Parian/Unglazed

Bust Albert, King of the Belgians.
153mm. 65.00

Ancient Artefacts

Colchester Vase. No. 504. 50mm. 2.25

Dorchester Jug, inscribed: *Model
of old jug found in North Square,
Dorchester.* No. 1774. 52mm. 3.00

Fountains Abbey Cup.
No. 23821. 50mm. 2.25

Glastonbury Bowl, inscribed:
*Bowl from the Ancient British
Lake Village near Glastonbury.*
No. 1724. 40mm. 3.00

Irish Bronze Pot.
No. 1834. 45mm. 2.25

Jersey Milk Can and lid.
No. 3424. 60mm. 4.75

*Lincoln Jack from original in
museum.* No. 1564. 65mm. 3.00

Newbury Bottle, inscribed:
*Leather bottle found at Newbury
1644 on Battlefield now in
museum.* No. 2294. 65mm. 3.00

Animals

Manx Cat, crouching. 65mm. 16.00

Elephant, Indian. 77mm long. 13.00

Tortoise. 72mm long. 6.50

Numbered Ornamental Wares

Some of these could be unnamed
ancient artefacts. Value £2.25
each.

No. 594. Fluted jug. 54mm.

No. 1724. Small pot on three feet.
This is also the number of a
Glastonbury bowl — see above.
43mm. 2.25

No. 1824. Ewer. 60mm. 2.25

No. 3164. Pot. 50mm. 2.25

No. 3594. Vase. 50mm.   2.25
No. 3884. Vase. 54mm.   2.25
No. 7061. Vase. 65mm.   2.25
No. 14715. Vase, with narrow
  neck. 100mm.   2.25

Queeny China

No details of mark available.

Mark used by an unknown manufacturer
for an agent in Hastings.

Buildings
Cottage. 70mm long. Bears
  the arms of Hastings.   6.50

Raleigh China

R & M

For mark see *Crested China*, p. 206.

For mark see *Crested China*, p. 206.

Trademark used for a retailer by Sampson Hancock (and Sons), Bridge Works, Stoke and later at the Garden Works, Hanley. (renamed Corona Pottery). (Usual trademark Corona).

Trademark used by Roper & Meredith, Garfield Pottery, Longton.

Birds
Bird, with open wings.
75mm long.   12.50

Historical/Folklore
Ark. 92mm long.   4.75

Great War
March War Memorial. 174mm.   90.00
St. Ives War Memorial Cross.
135mm.   90.00

Traditional/National Souvenirs
Lancashire Clog. 102mm long.   6.50
Welsh Hat. No. 198. 45mm.   4.75

Comic/Novelty
Truck of Coal, inscribed: *Black Diamonds*. Black coal.
79mm long.   16.00

Great War
Submarine, inscribed: *E4*.   16.00
Tank, with inset wheels.
  2 sizes: 103mm.   17.50
         160mm long.   21.50
Field Gun. 125mm long.   13.00
Bell Tent, open flap. 80mm.   10.50

Sport
Rugby Player, holding rugby ball, on oval ashtray. Inscribed: *Play up*. Fully coloured. 126mm.   75.00

Home/Nostalgic
Gas Stove. 70mm.   8.50

Miniature Domestic
Candlestick. 128mm.   3.00

Musical Instruments
Upright Piano. 60mm.   12.50

Miniature Domestic
Candlestick. 105mm.   3.00
Cheese Dish. 45mm.   5.50

Raphael China

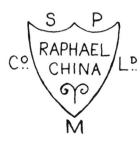

Trademark used for S.P. & Co. Ltd, of 57 King St, Manchester, by Arkinstall & Son Ltd, Arcadian Works, Stoke-on-Trent. (Usual trademark Arcadian).

The only other items known are smalls with either printed decorations or the crests of Canada, Sweden, Switzerland or Austria. (Spelt that way so not for export).

Ancient Artefacts
Kendal Jug. 76mm.   3.00

Alcohol
Highland Whisky Bowl, Model of.
  No. 4158. 90mm dia.   4.75

Regency Ware

For mark see *Crested China,* p. 207.

Trademark used for a retailer by Sampson Hancock (& Sons), Bridge Works, Stoke. (Usual trademark Corona).

Buildings
Model of Clifton Suspension Bridge.
  120mm long.   40.00

Seaside Souvenirs
Bathing Machine. 75mm.   8.25
Lighthouse on Rocky Base.
  125mm.   5.50

Animals
Cat, sitting with ruff of fur round
  neck. 100mm.   16.00
Cat, standing. 60mm.   12.00
Cat, Manx standing. 60mm.   16.00
Pig, standing. 85mm long.   10.00

Great War
Zeppelin. 153mm long.   20.00
Flash Lamp. 85mm.   10.50
Gurkha Knife. 140mm long.   20.00

Home/Nostalgic
Cigarette Case. 70mm.   13.00
Tobacco Pouch. 72mm long.   9.50

Musical Instruments
Banjo. 140mm long.   8.50

Modern Equipment
Gas Cooker. 68mm.   8.50
Gramophone, square cabinet, no
  horn. 85mm.   15.25

Miscellaneous
Pawn, chess piece. 90mm.   19.00

Regis

For mark see *Crested China*, p. 207.

Trademark used by Hewitt Bros, Willow Potteries, Longton. (Usual trademark Willow Art), for wholesaler/agents based in Weymouth & Glasgow.

Parian/Unglazed

Bust of Lord Beatty. 165mm.	55.00
Bust of *Burns*. 157mm.	24.00
Bust of *Scott*. 140mm.	17.50

Buildings — White

Weymouth Jubilee Clock Tower. 126mm.	23.00

Monuments

Black Watch Memorial. 152mm.	65.00
Highland Mary statue. 155mm.	21.75

Historical/Folklore

Dutch Girl. 78mm.	12.50
Mary Bull holding black cat in basket. Standing figure. (Mary Bull was a witch!) 105mm.	40.00
Mary Queen of Scots Chair, Edinburgh Castle, Model of. No. 163. 75mm.	6.50
Souter Johnny sitting on chair on square base. 133mm.	30.00

Traditional/National Souvenirs

Bagpipes. 120mm long.	15.00
Welsh Hat. 58mm.	4.75

Seaside Souvenirs

Lifeboat, coloured ropes. 118mm long.	8.25
Lighthouse, not named. 100mm.	4.75
Corbiere Lighthouse, with coloured rock base. 96mm.	26.00

Animals

Cat with bow, standing. 85mm.	12.50
Cat, chubby & standing. 70mm.	10.00
Dog, Collie, standing. 85mm.	12.50
Dog, Scottie, wearing a glengarry, some colouring on hat. 85mm.	10.50
Elephant with hunter and two Indian riders on back. 90mm.	30.00

Great War

Airship, *Beta*. 80mm long.	30.00
British Tank. 92mm long.	13.00
British Tank with trailing wheels. 127mm long.	14.50
Cannon Shell salt pot. 83mm.	4.00
Kit Bag with verse: *Pack up your troubles in your old kit bag.* 74mm.	15.00
Forage Cap. 83mm long.	16.00
Officers Peaked Cap. 75mm long.	10.00
Cenotaph. 145mm.	5.50
Florence Nightingale Statue, inscribed: *Florence Nightingale 1820-1910.* 160mm.	16.50
Weymouth War Memorial. 152mm.	85.00

Home/Nostalgic

Anvil. 76mm.	5.50
Bucket, rope handle. 65mm.	4.00
Coal Scuttle. 55mm.	4.50
Shaving Mug. 55mm.	5.50

Comic/Novelty

Billiken. 73mm.	4.00
Billiken, the God of Luck, sitting on high backed chair. 100mm.	8.50

Cartoon/Comedy Characters

Baby, standing to attention, some colouring. Inscribed: *One of the B'hoys.* 160mm.	30.00
Baby, standing with arms outstretched. Some colouring to face. 110mm.	30.00

Alcohol

Toby Jug. 83mm.	6.50

Miscellaneous

Hand holding tulip. 80mm.	4.00

Registry Ware

Trademark used by an unknown manufacturer.

This mark has been found with Scarborough crests on a curve sided lip salve pot and a small vase.   each 4.00

C.L. Reis and Co

For mark see *Crested China*, p. 113.

C.L. Reis is probably a retailer, trademark being used on porcelain with Irish crests. (It seems likely that the china was manufactured by Alfred B. Jones & Sons Ltd. — usual trademark Grafton). The porcelain is much greyer than Grafton although typical Grafton shapes.

Ancient Artefacts
Butter Pot, not named. 40mm.   3.00

Seaside Souvenirs
Whelk Shell. 82mm long.   3.00

Animals
Pig, standing, inscribed: *Wunt be druv.* 70mm long.   13.00

Birds
Penguin. 95mm.   14.50

Miscellaneous
Basket. No. 240.   3.00

Rex China

Rialto China

For mark see *Crested China,* p. 209.

For mark see *Crested China,* p. 209.

The trademark of Moschendorf, Hof, Bavaria.

Trademark used by British Art Pottery Co. (Fenton) Ltd, Rialto Works, High Street, Fenton. Resembles Carlton China.

Traditional/National Souvenirs
Tam-o'shanter. 72mm dia.   21.50

Ancient Artefacts
Salisbury Kettle. 88mm.   2.25

Animals
Pig, ears pointing forward.
    68mm long.   11.00

Seaside Souvenirs
Dolphin supporting sea shell.
    85mm.   20.00

Home/Nostalgic
Milk Churn and lid. 75mm.   4.75

Animals
Bulldog in kennel, inscribed: *The
    Black Watch.* 79mm.   11.00
Bulldog can be found coloured
    black.   15.00

Miniature Domestic
Cheese Dish, with gilded rope
    handle. 70mm.   4.75

Great War
Battleship with inscription: *Great
    War 1914-1918. The German
    Fleet surrendered 74 warships Nov
    21st 1918.* 153mm long.   30.00

Home/Nostalgic
Watchman's Lamp.   4.75
Ornate carved wooden Chair.
    110mm.   12.50

Ribblesdale China

Eugene Rimmel

"RIBBLESDALE' CHINA
ENGLISH MANUFACTURE
GIBSON & HOWORTH
13 FISHERGATE
PRESTON

Trademark used by an unknown English manufacturer for the Pennines market.

The only piece recorded is a one-handled mug. 39mm.   4.00

Trademark used by Wiltshaw and Robinson Ltd., Carlton Works, Stoke-on-Trent.

Only one small scent bottle known with a Brighton crest and metal screw top. Rimmel was a perfumier in the mid 19th century.   15.00

Rita China Series

For mark see *Crested China*, p. 210.

Trademark used for the retailer L & L of
Weston-Super-Mare by unknown manu-
facturers, one of whom seems to be
Hewitt & Leadbeater. (Usual mark
Willow Art).

Unglazed/Parian

Bunyan Statue. 125mm.	19.50
Burns, bust, on circular unglazed base. 176mm.	24.00
Rt. Hon. D. Lloyd George, on square unglazed base. 192mm.	35.00
Scott, bust, on circular unglazed base. 176mm.	17.50

Ancient Artefacts

Loving cup, 2 handled.	3.00

Buildings — White

Ann Hathaway's Cottage. 55mm long.	9.50
The Folly, Pontypool. 80mm.	50.00
Glastonbury Tor. 83mm.	40.00
Llangynwyd Church. 107mm long.	40.00

Monuments

Drake Statue. 160mm.	13.00
Great Rock of Ages, Burrington Coombe, Near Cheddar, Somerset, with verses of hymn. 125mm.	11.00
King Alfred's Statue. 160mm.	47.50
Robert Blake, Statue. 170mm.	30.00

Historical/Folklore

Burns Chair, Model of. 88mm.	7.50
James V Chair, Stirling Castle.	7.50
Mary Queen of Scots Chair, Edinburgh Castle, Model of. 85mm.	6.50

Animals

Dog, sitting with bow. 75mm.	10.50
Cat, long neck, features coloured. 110mm.	7.50
Fish. 115mm long.	3.00

Birds

Bird posy holder, tiny. 57mm long.	6.50
Duck posy holder, yellow beak. 74mm long.	7.50

Great War

Florence Nightingale Statue. 180mm.	16.50

Home/Nostalgic

Grandfather Clock, inscribed: *Make use of time, let not advantage slip. Shakespeare.* 145mm.	10.50

Comic/Novelty

Clown, bust.	8.25
Jester, double faced bust, inscribed: *Awake Asleep.*	8.25
Monk, jovial & plump. No glass. No. 95. 90mm.	16.00

Modern Equipment

Horn Gramophone. 90mm.	19.50

Footwear

Dutch Sabot. 85mm long.	4.75

Hats

Schoolboy's Cap. 65mm long.	21.50
Straw Boater. 85mm long.	8.75

Robinson & Leadbeater

For additional mark see *Crested China*, p. 205.

Also found with a printed mark.

Trademark used by Robinson & Leadbeater, Wolfe Street, Stoke-on-Trent and subsequently a branch of J.A. Robinson Ltd.

Parian
Bust of John Wesley.   25.00

Ancient Artefacts
Chester Roman Vase. 2 sizes:
  63mm and 76mm.   2.25
Loving Cup, 2 handled. 45mm.   3.00
Loving Cup, 3 handled. 39mm.   3.00

Buildings — Coloured
Mason Croft, the house of Miss
  Marie Corelli. 2 sizes:
  75mm long.   85.00
  90mm long.   95.00
Shakespeare's Cottage.
  40mm long.   30.00

Seaside Souvenirs
Scallop Shell. 73mm dia.
  110mm dia.   3.00
Scallop Shell on 3 tiny feet.
  120mm long.   4.00

Birds/Eggs
Egg flower holder. 80mm long.   3.00

Swan with yellow beak and feet.
  70mm.   6.50

Home/Nostalgic
Bellows. 105mm long.   5.50
Thimble salt pot. 37mm.   10.50

Miniature Domestic
Cheese Dish and cover.
  80mm long.   4.75
Tea pot with lid, thistle knob
  on lid. 100mm.   8.75
Bagware Tea pot. 98mm.   11.50
Trinket box and lid with floral
  decoration in relief. 115mm.   8.75

NB: Robinson and Leadbeater specialized in producing parian ware, especially busts. These were produced in great numbers and some are very fine indeed. Although they are much collected they are not 'crested china' as they were not made to carry crests.

Roman Bath China

Trademark used for a retailer by Hewitt & Leadbeater, Willow Potteries Ltd, Longton. (Usual trademark Willow Art).

One small found with this mark
and Chester crest.   4.00

Rosina Queens China

For alternative mark see *Crested China*, p. 210.

Trademark used by George Warrilow & Sons (Ltd), Queens Pottery, Longton.

A small quantity of crested domestic ware has been found.

Rowena China

For alternative mark see *Crested China*, p. 210.

Trademark used by R.H. & S.L. Plant (Ltd), Tuscan Works, Longton. (Usual trademark Tuscan).

Ancient Artefacts

Gastrica Cyprian Bottle. 71mm.	3.00

Animals

Fish posy vase. 130mm long.	5.00
Giant open-mouthed fish.	
130mm long.	5.50
Dog kennel.	4.75

Comic/Novelty

Two seater Car ashtray, inscribed: *Petrol consumption nil.*
135mm long.   110.00
The car ashtray is identical to the Tuscan example called 'Dennis Two Seater'
Tomato, green leaves. 57mm dia.   16.00

Cartoon Characters

These fine coloured models form a series from The Daily Sketch Cartoon. Some white, glazed, examples have been seen.
Don, little boy in short trousers and blue cardigan. 130mm.   85.00
Dr. Dromedary, camel, in black top hat and suit. 130mm.   85.00

Lord Lion, lion in pale blue jacket. 130mm.   85.00
Oo Jah, Flip Flap, Elephant, in pink striped pyjamas. 130mm.   85.00
Pa Piggins, Pig, in Edwardian Sporting clothes. 130mm.   85.00
Snooker, or the kitten cat, yellow with crown on head. 130mm.   85.00

Royal Albert Crown China

Royal Arms China

For additional mark see *Crested China,* p. 211

Trademark used by Thomas C. Wild, Crown China Works, High St, Longton.

A small range of domestic ware and 'smalls' found with this mark. One vase bears a cartoon featuring children and insects.   18.00

Trademark used for a Birmingham retailer by an unknown manufacturer.

Three pieces recorded.

Buildings — White
Thatched cottage. 48mm.   10.50

Animals
Frog. 70mm long.   10.50
Toad. 73mm long.   10.50

Royal China

For mark see *Crested China*, p. 211.

Trademark used by E. Hughes and Co.,
Opal Works, Fenton. (Also used marks,
Fenton & E. Hughes & Co.).

Miniature Domestic

Cheese Dish and cover. 50mm.	6.50

Royal China Works, Worcester

For mark see *Crested China*, p. 211.

Trademark used by Grainger, Worcester,
when taken over by the Worcester
Porcelain Co. Ltd.

Miniature Domestic

Two handled Loving Cup. 45mm.	15.00
Mug, with one handle. 40mm.	12.00
Vase, swirl pattern. 65mm.	15.00

Royal Coburg

Royal Doulton

For mark see *Crested China*, p. 212.

For mark see *Crested China*, p. 212.

Trademark used by an unknown manufacturer.

Trademark used by Doulton & Co. (Ltd),
Nile St, Burslem.

Home/Nostalgic
Chair with 2 gold tassels.   10.00

Range of smalls with foreign and
English crests.

Miniature Domestic
Cheese Dish and cover. 50mm.   4.75

Ancient Artefacts
Loving Cup, 3 handled. 49mm.   10.00

Royal Ivory Porcelain

For mark see *Crested China*, p. 212.

Trademark used by Robinson & Leadbeater Ltd and for the London wholesalers E.B. & Co. (Usual trademark R&L).

Ancient Artefacts

Chester Roman Vase. 63mm.	2.25
Kendal Jug. 70mm.	2.25
Loving Cup, 2 & 3 handled. 45mm.	3.00

Birds

Swan posy holder. Some colouring. 70mm.	4.75

Home/Nostalgic

Bellows. 115mm long.	5.50

Alcohol

Highland Whisky Bowl, Model of.	4.50

Hats

Bishop's Mitre.	6.50
Slipper wall pocket. 100mm long.	7.50

Miniature Domestic

Cheese Dish and cover. 74mm long.	4.75
Tea Pot with lid. 55mm.	7.50

Royal Stafford China

For mark see *Crested China*, p. 213.

Trademark used by Thomas Poole, Cobden Works, Longton. Products identical to Willow Art.

Animals

Elephant, walking. 52mm.	13.00
Elephant cream jug. 65mm.	7.50

Great War

Submarine, inscribed: *E4*. 115mm long.	16.00
Brick Kiln, inscribed: *Keep the home fires burning*. 78mm.	9.50
Bell Tent, open flap. 70mm.	10.50
Bugle. 72mm.	12.50

Miscellaneous

Spade, playing card suit. 68mm.	4.00

Royal 'Vale' China

For mark see *Crested China,* p. 213.

Trademark used by H.J. Colcough, Vale Works, Goddard Street, Longton for goods supplied by Taylor and Kent (Ltd), Florence Works, Longton (usual trademark Florentine).

Ancient Artefacts
Hastings Kettle, not named. 55mm.   2.25

Seaside Souvenirs
Lighthouse. 105mm.   4.50
Lighthouse on circular base.
  115mm.   5.50

Animals
Pig, fat, lying forward, pricked
  ears. 100mm long.   75.00
Pig, fat, sitting. 63mm.   12.50

Great War
Water Bottle. 70mm.   13.00
Cenotaph. 146mm.   5.50

Footwear
Ladies 18th Century Shoe.
  95mm long.   7.50

Royal Worcester

For mark see *Crested China,* p. 213.

Trademark used by Worcester Royal Porcelain Company Ltd. (Royal Worcester).

Ancient Artefacts
Chester Roman Vase. 60mm.   10.00
Loving Cup. 2 & 3 handled.
  40mm.   10.00

Miniature Domestic
Mug, one handled. 45mm.   10.00

Ryecroft China Series

Trademark used by Robinson & Leadbeater, Wolfe Street, Stoke-on-Trent.

Busts
Bust of *Burns* on circular
    base. 176mm.   24.00

Buildings — White
Roche Abbey, ruins, unglazed.
    85mm.   46.50
Town Hall, Stockton-on-Tees,
    glazed. 94mm.   55.00

Monuments
Woodhouse Eaves Cross.   37.50

Seaside Souvenirs
Lifeboat. 101mm long.   8.25

Birds
Duck posy bowl, yellow beak.
    50mm.   7.50

Sport
Cricket Cap. 65mm long.   21.50

S

For mark see *Crested China*, p. 215.

Trademark used by P. Donath, Tiefenfurt.
    (Silesia).

Very little crested china of this
    manufacture has been found
    and all known pieces are small
    domestic items of only nominal
    value. One of the firms main
    areas of specialization was pink
    souvenir ware and white souvenir
    ware bearing transfer printed views.

St. George China

Trademark used by Wilhelm Kutzscher & Co., Schwarzenberger Porzellanfabric, Schwarzenberg, Saxony. (Now in East Germany). (Usual trademark Saxony)

This manufacturer made many unmarked pieces for the English market.

Ancient Artefacts
Puzzle Jug, with verse. 60mm.   4.50

Seaside Souvenirs
Lighthouse. 121mm.   4.00

Animals
Two Puppies and a Kitten in a
  basket. 62mm.   22.50
Cat, with drumstick, sitting on a
  drum. 90mm.   22.50
Dog, coal hod with handle.
  80mm.   15.25
Elephants, two on a sledge on
  slope. 70mm.   30.00
Grotesque Animal with winged
  legs, sitting. 80mm.   9.00

Birds
Hen and Cock on circular base,
  one pecking and one standing.
  80mm.   14.00

Home/Nostalgic
Jardiniere on stand, fixed. 95mm.   4.00
Pail with wire handle. 45mm.   4.00

Sport
Tennis Racquet with ball.
  140mm long.   14.00

Footwear
Ladies heeled shoe. 84mm.   7.50
Ladies heeled shoe with eyelets.
  85mm long.   12.50

St. Pauls

Trademark used for export to Canada by Hewitt & Leadbeater, Willow Pottery, Longton. (Usual trademark Willow Art).

National Souvenirs

Welsh Hat. No. 75. 54mm.
(the only model recorded has a
Yukon crest).   8.75

Sandifords Ceramic China

Trademark used by an unknown manufacturer for the retailer Sandifords.

Only a pin tray and two 'smalls' recorded all with Chorley crest.   each 4.00

San Juan

For mark see *Crested China*, p. 216.

Mark used by an unknown manufacturer.

Only model known carries a
Madrid crest.

Ancient Artefacts
Portland Vase. 51mm.   4.00

Savoy China

CHINA
MADE IN ENGLAND

Mark found on a Carlton mould fisherman
and on a black cat on pouffé — obviously
after firms merged.

For additional mark see *Crested China* p.
216.

Trademark used by Birks, Rawlins and Co
(Ltd), Vine Pottery, Stoke. Merged in
1932 with Wiltshaw & Robinson Ltd.
(Makers of Carlton).

Parian/Unglazed
Bust of Edward VII as the Prince
of Wales with inscription.
135mm.   65.00
Bust of Albert King of the
Belgians. 150mm.   65.00
Bust of Admiral Sir David Beatty,
found with inscription: *British
Naval Victory, German Cruiser
Blucher sunk January 24th 1915.
England declared War on Germany
August 4th 1914.* 150mm.   65.00
Bust of David Lloyd George with
inscription on reverse. 186mm.   40.00
Bust of Lord Kitchener, found
with inscription: *Lord Kitchener
of Khartoum Field Marshall KG KP
Secretary for War. Born 1851. June
15th, drowned at sea off the
Orkneys 1916.*
2 sizes: 107mm.   40.00
        120mm.   40.00
Bust of Sailor, can be inscribed:
HMS Iron Duke, HMS Tiger, or
HMS Warspite. 108mm.   35.00

Bust of Sailor, inscribed: *HMS Iron Duke, HMS Lion* and *HMS Ocean* (rare), on round glazed base. No. 532. 135mm. — 95.00

Bust of John Travers Cornwell, inscription: *John Travers Cornwell, age 16. Faithful unto death. Hero Battle of Jutland* 108mm. — 350.00

Ancient Artefacts

Ancient Jug. No. 87. 74mm. — 3.00

Ancient Jug, Model of. Dug out of the Foundations of Lichfield Museum. 62mm. — 3.00

Barrel Mug, Model of. No. 7 45mm. — 3.00

British Urn. 50mm. — 3.00

Carlisle Elizabeth Measure, no details. — 5.50

Carlisle Jug, *14th Century Jug found in an old tank at Carlisle gaol, by permission of Com Tullie House.* No. 179. 70mm. — 3.00

Carlisle Vase. No. 177. 70mm. — 2.25

Chester Roman Vase, inscribed: *Roman Vase, original now in Chester Museum.* No. 134. 70mm. — 3.00

China Tot, Model of. No. 33. — 3.00

Chinese Vase. No. 67. 70mm. — 3.00

Chinese Vase in South Kensington Museum. No. 219. 70mm. — 3.00

Chinese Jade Vase, inscribed: *Model of Vase of Chinese Jade.* No. 152. 68mm. — 3.00

Colchester Vase. *Ancient Vase original in Colchester Museum.* No. 349. 50mm. — 3.00

Colchester Roman Vase, inscribed: *Roman Vase found in Cloaca, now in Colchester Castle.* No. 196. 30mm. — 3.00

Exeter Vase from original in Museum.

Globe Vase. No. 62. 42mm. — 3.00

Greek Vase. No. 77. 69mm. — 3.00

Hastings Kettle. No. 140. 60mm. — 3.00

Italian Vase. No. 30. — 3.00

Itford Urn. 44mm. — 3.00

Launceston Bottle. No. 193. 65mm. — 3.00

Lewes Vase, not named. No. 197. 35mm. — 3.00

Maltese Fire Grate. No. 39 and No. 721. 45mm. — 7.50

Newbury Leather Bottle. No. 14. 63mm. — 3.00

Pear Bottle. No. 17. 70mm. — 3.00

Penrith Salt Pot. No. 182. 60mm. — 3.00

Persian Bottle. No. 68. 95mm. — 3.00

Pilgrims Bottle Nevers ware. No. 172. 75mm. — 3.00

Pompeian Vase. No. 161. 124mm. — 3.00

Pompeian Vessel. No. 264. — 3.00

Portland Vase. No. 16. 51mm. — 3.00

Puzzle Jug. No. 378. 68mm. — 5.50

Salt Maller, Model of. No. 106. 60mm. — 3.00

Scarborough Jug. No. 454 or No. 10. 48mm. — 3.00

Silchester Roman Urn. No. 74. 51mm. — 3.00

Shakespeare's Jug, *the jug of William Shakespeare,* with his signature. 60mm. — 4.50

Southwold Jar. No. 175. 90mm. — 3.00

Staffordshire salt glaze tea pot, Model of, with separate lid. No. 202. 75mm. — 11.00

Tear Bottle. 70mm. — 4.25

Teapot, copy of early 18th century stoneware (shaped as as camel). 100mm long.(rare). — 30.00

Windsor Roman Urn. *Roman urn dug up at old Windsor from original now in British Museum.* No. 138. 45mm. — 3.00

York Roman Ewer. *Roman Ewer from the original in Hospitium found at York.* No. 20. — 3.00

Buildings — Coloured

Exeter Cathedral, brown coloured. 150mm long. — 127.50

Tumbledown Cottage, not named, highly coloured and glazed. Impressed 1800. 105mm long. — 90.00

Buildings — White

Aberystwyth, The University. No. 68. 146mm long. — 125.00

Burns Cottage. 70mm long. — 16.00

Citadel Gateway, Plymouth. No. 209. 114mm. — 27.50

Clifton Suspension Bridge. 132mm long. — 40.00

Cottage, not named, inscribed:
I wouldn't leave my little wooden
hut for you. 63mm long. 19.50
First and Last Refreshment House
in England. No. 301. 72mm. 10.50
Monnow Gate, Monmouth.
112mm. 40.00
Portsmouth Town Hall.
No. 7. 80mm. 47.50
Tumbledown Cottage.
105mm long. 30.00

Monuments
Derry's Clock, Plymouth.
No. 17. 152mm. 16.00
Hastings Clock Tower. No. 274.
156mm. 16.00
Margate Clock Tower. 160mm. 16.00
Model of Lewes Martyr's Memorial.
Erected in 1901 to the memory
of the 16 Protestants burnt to
death in front of the Star Hotel
1555-1557. 140mm. No. 45. 70.00
Rufus Stone, with usual
inscriptions. 100mm. 5.50

Historical/Folklore
Burns Chair, Dumfries. 85mm. 7.50
Gargoyle or Devils Head, open
mouth, inscribed: My word if
you're not off. No. 230.
90mm long. 10.50
Mary Queen of Scots Chair, Edinburgh Castle. 77mm. 6.50

Traditional/National Souvenirs
A Cornish Pasty. 100mm long. 7.50
Ripon Horn Blower. No. 497.
100mm. 13.00
Bagpipes. 110mm long. 15.00
Monmouth Cap. 50mm. 21.50
Thistle Vase. 47mm. 3.00
Welsh Hat with longest place
name round brim. No. 6.
2 sizes: 35mm. 6.50
55mm. 7.50
Welsh Lady carrying a basket.
110mm. 30.00

Seaside Souvenirs
Bathing Machine, inscribed:
Morning Dip. 62mm. 7.50
Boat. No. 434. 128mm long. 10.50
Lifeboat. If inscribed: Zetland, add
£7.00. 13.50

Rowing Boat. No. 118.
130mm long. 10.50
Yacht. 115mm long. 12.50
Beachy Head Lighthouse.
No. 371. 130mm. 7.50
Eddystone Lighthouse. No. 136. 5.50
Also found inscribed:
St. Catherines Lighthouse. 92mm. 17.00
Lizard Lighthouse. 17.00
Lighthouse salt pot, inscribed:
salt. 105mm. 4.75
Lighthouse pepper pot, inscribed:
pepper. No. 768. 4.75
Crab ashtray or dish. 52mm. long. 7.50
Lobster pintray with lid.
97mm long. 16.00
Child draped in towel, standing
on a rock. 133mm. 18.00
Suitcase with straps. No. 745.
58mm. 17.00

Countryside
Acorn, Model of. No. 110. 56mm. 5.50
Can also be found as a pepper
pot marked 'P'. 6.00

Animals
Cat, Cheshire. No. 17. 80mm. 7.50
Cat sitting, miniature, with long
neck. 68mm. 10.00
Cat, angry with arched back,
inscribed: Me backs up. No. 195.
100mm long. 15.50
Cat with long neck. No. 217.
105mm. 16.00
Cat, sitting, detailed fur.
2 sizes: 56mm. 10.50
90mm. 11.50
Cat, standing with huge grin,
erect bushy tail, comic.
105mm long. 30.00
Cat, on oval lustre base. Inscribed:
Good Luck. Cat coloured black.
90mm. (Carlton Mould). 21.50
Dog cream jug. No. 106. 60mm. 13.00
Dog (no particular breed) sitting.
55mm. 40.00
Dog (curly tail) standing. 65mm. 13.00
Dog, Basset/Dachshund. No. 296.
132mm long. 30.00
Bulldog, lying, inscribed: Another
Dreadnought. 118mm long. 40.00
Bulldog, standing, with verse.
Be Briton Still to Britain True.
No. 364. 130mm long. 23.00

Dog, crouched and barking.
No. 253. 100mm long. 29.00
Dog, Scottie, wearing glengarry.
No.477. 86mm. 15.00
Dog, Scottie, wearing a
tam-o'shanter.
2 sizes: 63mm. 10.50
80mm. 14.50
Dog, Scottie, looking out of
kennel. Can be found with
inscription: *The Black Watch*.
No. 154. 80mm long. 10.50
Dog, Spaniel, begging. 65mm. 12.50
Donkey, standing. 120mm long. 25.25
Elephant, sitting with trunk in
the air. No. 218. 63mm. 17.50
Elephant, standing. No. 250.
65mm. 15.00
Elephant, standing, trunk raised.
No. 253. 100mm long. 22.00
Elephant with howdah. 66mm. 30.00
Fish. 104mm long. 3.00
Fish Vase. No. 33. 88mm. 5.00
Frog, sitting, well detailed. 70mm. 21.50
Hare, crouching, No. 235.
80mm long. 20.00
Hare, sitting, ears raised.
No. 245. 70mm. 20.00
Hare, looking left, 2 upright ears.
No. 253. 80mm. 40.00
Hippo, with pointed teeth.
113mm long. 60.00
Lion, sitting on square base. This
was originally designed by
Alfred Stevens for the British
Museum. 108mm. 24.50
Lion, walking. Inscribed:
Be Briton. . . No. 123. 21.00
Mouse. 65mm long. 14.50
Pig, lying down. No. 544.
80mm long. 10.00
Pig, standing and fat. No. 109.
2 sizes: 70mm and 100mm long. 12.50
Large size can be found
inscribed: *Model of Irish Pig*. 20.00
Pig, standing, open mouthed.
122mm long. 100.00
Pig, inscribed: *Model of Sussex
Pig*. No. 198 and No. 281.
78mm long. 10.50
Pig, standing, alert ears. No. 199.
100mm long. 10.50
Pig, sitting, long nose. 110mm. 35.00
Piglet with long ears. No. 33.
65mm long. 13.50
Polar Bear. No. 236. 145mm long. 75.00

Rabbit. 66mm long. 6.50
Rabbit, crouching. 88mm long. 8.50
Rabbit, sitting, one ear up.
No. 548. 70mm long. 40.00
Rabbit, sitting on hind legs,
upright. No. 242. 104mm. 30.00
Rhino, grotesque. No. 284.
130mm long. 47.50
Seal.
2 sizes: 63mm long. 11.00
80mm long. 15.00
Snail. No. 252. 84mm long. 13.00
Teddy Bear. 90mm. 12.50
Tiger, sabre toothed, or Wild Cat
with inscription: *My word if
you're not off.* 128mm long. 100.00
Toad. No. 331. 75mm. 20.00
Warthog or Wild Pig, open mouth.
Grotesque. 122mm long. 100.00

Birds
Clara Cluck candlesnuffer.
No. 324. 87mm. 19.00
Duck, swimming. No. 562.
65mm long. 7.00
Duck, standing. 150mm. 30.00
Duck, standing on green base. 22.00
Can be found coloured. 170mm. 40.00
Duckling, standing on tree trunk,
colouring on trunk and beak.
186mm. 35.00
Duckling, comic, with a wasp
on its beak. 30.00
Also found partly coloured.
165mm. 40.00
Duck, lying down, could be
dead. No. 237. 105mm long. 30.00
Grotesque Bird jug. No. 127. 10.50
Goose in full length cloak.
72mm. 30.00
Hen, sitting, red comb. No. 23.
55mm. 9.00
Owl, comic. No. 33 or No. 329.
60mm. 15.00
Penguin. No. 549. 76mm. 16.00
Penguin. No. 332. 80mm. 18.00
Penguin on heart shaped
ashtray. 85mm. 16.00
Swan, detailed plumage. No. 579.
50mm. 7.50

Great War
Highland Infantryman, with pack,
rifle and bayonet. Either glazed or
parian, both on round glazed
plinth. No. 530. 165mm. 110.00

Sailor, standing, arms folded, unglazed on round glazed base. (rare) No. 538. 160mm. 120.00

British Lion, wearing puttees, inscribed: *Another Dreadnought*. No. 288. 130mm long. 75.00

Nurse, with red cross on chest, holding bandage. Can be found inscribed: *Nurse Cavell*. No. 531. 165mm. 75.00

Biplane, with prop., 2 different models exist:
(a) One has open struts between the wings. (see page 60 of *Take Me Back To Dear Old Blighty* by Robert Southall. 185.00
(b) The other model is identical but has the struts filled in solid between the wings. 140mm long. Both models have coloured roundels and tail. 175.00

Monoplane, pointed wings and fixed prop. No. 523. 130mm long. 60.00

Monoplane, pointed wings and revolving prop. No. 521. 130mm long. 60.00

Zeppelin with revolving 2-bladed propeller, can be found with inscripton: *Zeppelin destroyed by Lt. Robinson V.C. at Cuffley Essex Sept. 3rd 1916*. No. 567. 175mm long. 160.00

Battleship, 3 funnels, inscribed: *HMS Lion*. 168mm long. 56.50

Battleship, 2 funnels, inscribed: *HMS Iron Duke, HMS Queen Elizabeth* (£50.00), *HMS Barham, HMS Tiger* or *HMS Warspite*. 168mm long. 56.50

British Minesweeper, Model of. No. 641. 150mm long. (very rare). 250.00

Torpedo Boat Destroyer, model of. Rare. 140mm long. 95.00

Submarine, inscribed: *E1*. Usually found with inscription: *Commander Noel Lawrence. Large German Transport Sunk July 30th 1915. German Cruiser Moltke torpedoed August 19th 1915*. No. 575. 150mm long. 40.00

Ambulance, with 3 red crosses — one on cab top. No. 520. 110mm long. 30.00

Ambulance with 'Rolls Royce' front. No. 520. 115mm long. 40.00

Armoured Car (reputedly a 'Talbot' but not named). 125mm long. 80.00

British Motor Searchlight. No.123. 103mm long. (Rare). 145.00

Model of British Tank first used by British Troops at the Battle of Ancre, Sept. 1916 with inset steering wheels and inscribed *HMS Donner Blitzen, 515*. Long or short rear facing guns.
2 sizes: No. 597. 138mm long. 30.00
No. 586. 160mm long. 40.00

Tank with no trailing wheels, inscribed exactly as above. Short forward and rear facing guns protruding from side gun turrets. Also a short gun protruding from front of upper turret.
2 sizes: No. 151. 135mm long. 30.00
No. 643. 155mm long. 45.00

Tank with no trailing wheels inscribed: *HMS Donner Blitzen* and *515* on side only. Has a curved exhaust pipe on roof. and one small gun protruding from front of side turrets. It differs from the other tanks and is rather flat in appearance. No. 675. 108mm long. (rare) 85.00

Field Gun, Model of, with fish tail. No. 616. 140mm long. 85.00

Howitzer. No. 926. 140mm long. 27.50

Howitzer. 170mm long. 27.50

Machine Gun, 2 pieces, swivels on tripod. No. 402. 153mm long. 120.00

British Trench Mortar Gun. No. 613. 98mm long. 47.50

Shell, inscribed: *Iron rations for Fritz*. No. 5.
2 sizes: No. 556. 70mm. 7.50
No. 558. 110mm. 8.25
(Shell 'salt' and 'pepper' pots also found. 80mm). 5.25

Model of Stokes Bomb. No. 575. 24mm dia. at base (very rare). 105mm long. 250.00

Trench Mortar Bomb. Often found not named. No. 574. 86mm. 56.50

Hand Grenade. No. 556.75mm. 13.00

Anzacs Hat, Model of. No. 111. 90mm long. 22.00

Balmoral Bonnet, Model of. 74mm long. 20.00

Colonial Hat. No. 48. 92mm long. 10.50

French Trench Helmet, worn by the Dauntless French Poilu. No. 69. 82mm long. (Not named £30.00). 40.00

Glengarry. No. 508. 78mm long. 16.00

New Zealand Hat, Model of. No. 613. 80mm long. 20.00

Officer's Peaked Cap. No. 516. 72mm long. 10.00

Rumanian Soldier's Steel Helmet, Model of, found with Bucharest Crest and Rumanian War declaration inscription. 82mm long. 60.00

R.F.C. Cap, Model of. Cap badge clearly moulded. No. 577. 80mm long. 40.00

Sailor's Hat, inscribed on band: *HMS Lion, HMS Queen Elizabeth* or *HMS Tiger.* Blue bow. No. 533. 71mm dia. 57.50

Tommy's Steel Helmet. 82mm long. 24.50

Bandsman's Drum. 55mm dia. 6.00

Bell Tent. No. 118. 65mm. 12.00

Water Bottle. No. 219. 57mm. 13.00

Tommy in Dug Out, not named. No. 669. 85mm. Very rare. 170.00

Fireplace, inscribed: *Keep the home fires burning till the boys come home.* No. 68. 94mm. 16.50

Cenotaph, inscribed: *The Glorious Dead.* 130mm. 7.50

Edith Cavell Memorial, Norwich, inscribed: *Nurse Cavell.* Red Cross on apron. No. 110. 168mm. 22.00

Home/Nostalgic

Babies Cradle on rockers. 74mm long. 14.00

Bellows. 140mm long. 6.50

Flat Iron. 65mm. 8.50

Kennel, inscribed: *Beware of the dog.* No. 397. 53mm. 6.50

Trivet for flat iron. No. 544. 70mm long. 4.75

Grandfather Clock, inscribed: *Nae man can tether time nor tide.* No. 622. 150mm. 22.00

Jardiniere on stand. No. 86. 77mm. 4.00

Lantern. 82mm. 8.25

Milk Can, inscribed: *Ye olde Devonshire Milk Can.* 78mm. 9.00

Pillar Box, miniature. 56mm. 12.00

Sundial. 93mm. 8.75

Watering Can. No. 455. 76mm. 10.50

Wheelbarrow. 120mm long. 10.50

Comic/Novelty

Billiken. 75mm. 4.00

Candlesnuffer in form of young boy in nightwear, yawning and stretching. 85mm. 15.50

Caterpillar with human face. No. 543. 74mm. 16.00

Also found coloured 30.00

Choirboy. No. 542. 85mm. 13.00

Choirboy, coloured. 104mm. 30.00

Dutch Boy, standing coloured, salt pot. 128mm. 40.00

Edwardian Girl candlesnuffer wearing bonnet, coat and muff. 77mm and 86mm. No. 175. 17.00

Hindu god sitting on rock, blue beads. No. 28 or No. 554. 90mm. (Blue beads add £3.00). 8.50

Huntley and Palmer's Biscuit hat pin holder. 26.00

Policeman, short and fat. 103mm. 70.00

Tea pot in shape of man's head, spout coming out of mouth. No. 332. 60mm. 22.00

Winkie the Glad Eyed Bird, not named, as pepper pot. Fully coloured. 70mm. 40.00

Cartoon/Comedy Characters

Bonzo, dog (1920s cartoon character). No. 927. 80mm. 30.00

Tweedledum and Tweedledee, fully coloured, pair of separate sitting figures. 70mm each. 30.00

Winkie the Gladeye Bird. white. 14.50

or coloured. 80mm long. 35.00

Winkie can also be found as salt, pepper and mustard set, in colour. 35.00

Alcohol

Beer Barrel. No. 406. 55mm. 3.50

Beer Barrel with separate base. 57mm. 7.50

Old Beer Jug, Model of. No. 84. 80mm. 4.50

Bottle. No. 408. 90mm. 7.50

Carboy. No. 92. 80mm. 4.00

Soda Syphon. 8.50

Sport

Cricket Bag. No. 745. 95mm long. 9.00

Golf Ball, Model of. No. 111. 40mm.   6.50
Golf Club head. No. 442. 70mm.   12.00

Saxony

Musical Instruments
Banjo. 137mm long.   12.50
Double Bass. 145mm long.   33.00
Upright Piano. No. 887.
83mm long.   12.50
Violin. 136mm long.   40.00

Transport
Charabanc, (24 seater). No. 811.
134mm long.   40.00

Modern Equipment
Gramophone, square with large
horn. 102mm.   22.00

Miscellaneous
Bell, *Model of,* porcelain clapper.
No. 5. 85mm.   7.50
Inkwell, square, with lid & pen
rest. No. 433. 45mm.   11.00

Footwear
Clog, gilded studs. 83mm long.   6.50
Dutch Clog. No. 424. 70mm long.   5.00
Oriental Slipper. No. 312.
85mm long.   12.50

Hats
Top Hat. 44mm.   5.50

Miniature Domestic
Barrel shaped Mug. 50mm.   3.00
Basket weave Mug. 60mm.   3.00
Cheese Dish, one piece. 40mm.   9.00
Cheese Stand, Model of, with lid.
No. 200.or No. 45. 55mm long.   10.00
Extinguisher, Model of.
(Candlesnuffer). No. 42.
51mm and 64mm.   4.75
Jug, ribbed. No. 116. 60mm.   2.25
Teapot with lid, diamond shaped.
No. 202. 80mm.   10.50
Teaset on Tray. No. 401.
Tray. 106mm long.   20.00
Trinket Set on Tray. No. 436.   20.00
Vase. No. 317. 35mm.   2.25

For mark see *Crested China,* p. 304.

Country of origin mark used by Wilhelm
Kutzscher & Co, Schwarzenberger Porzellanfabrik, Schwarzenberg, Saxony.

Ancient Artefacts
Carlisle Salt Pot, not named.   2.25
Old Roman Salt Pot, 14th Century,
found near Carlisle by Permission
of Tullie House Committee.
63mm.   3.00
Puzzle Jug with verse. 66mm.   4.50

Buildings — White
Hall Cross, Doncaster. 158mm.   26.00
Holy Trinity Church, Margate.
100mm. An impressive model.   56.50
Iona Cathedral. 50mm.   30.00
Llandudno Church.   40.00
Ross-on-Wye, *Town Hall.* 85mm.   35.00
St Tudno's Church. 60mm long.   40.00
Skegness Clock Tower. 123mm.   7.50
Wallingford, Town Hall. 90mm.   35.00
Weymouth Clock Tower. 124mm.   13.00

Monuments
Captain Scott Memorial. 148mm.   21.75
Largs Memorial.   14.50
Fishermen's Memorial.   16.00

Traditional/National Souvenirs
John Bull standing with Bulldog.
102mm.   19.50
Gretna Priest, standing figure.   30.00
Welsh Hat, with longest place
name round brim. 44mm.   6.50
Welsh Lady, seated. 102mm.   24.50

Seaside Souvenirs
Beach Chair, wicker. 70mm.   12.50
Fisherwoman with bundle.
117mm.   25.75
Lifeboat. 135mm long.   6.50
Lightboatman. 114mm.   17.00
Beachy Head Lighthouse   6.50
If with black band.   9.00
Lighthouse with open windows.
115mm.   6.50

Needles Lighthouse. 125mm.	19.50
Sea Waves.	7.50
Mermaids, two on an oval base holding up a large shell. 105mm.	20.00

Countryside

Four bar Gate and stile with milestone. 100mm long.	6.50

Animals

Cat singing, holding sheet Music. 66mm.	22.50
Cat, holding book. 74mm.	22.50
Cat in Bandages. 90mm.	19.00
Cat with Mandolin. 74mm.	22.50
Cat in Gladstone Bag, right paw raised. Can be found inscribed: *Good Morning*. 55mm long.	22.50
Cat in Gladstone Bag, left paw raised. 55mm long. (pair).	22.50
Frog under Tulip, candleholder. 100mm.	14.00
Hare, sitting. 95mm long.	8.50
Spaniel sitting. 60mm.	12.50
Three Puppies in a Basket. 65mm.	22.50
Two Puppies and a Kitten in a basket. 65mm.	22.50
Polar Bear on ashtray. 85mm.	22.50
Tortoise dish with shell lid. 75mm long.	7.50

Birds

Duck, airing wings, some colouring. 88mm.	12.00
Duck on round base, brown beak and feet. 98mm.	11.00
Eagle on Perch.	17.00
Seagull on rock, black edging on wings. 109mm.	12.50
Seagull on rock, huge spead wings. 130mm.	16.00
Seagull posy holder. 114mm.	6.00
Egg, imprisoning a rabbit (he looks through a barred window). A large hare in tail coat standing beside it. 67mm.	40.00
Swan, open wings. 80mm.	4.75
Wagtail on tree trunk, black edging to wings. 110mm.	12.00

Great War

Monoplane, fixed prop and pilot. 100mm long.	30.00
Clacton War Memorial, with inscription. 140mm.	14.50
Folkestone War Memorial. 160mm.	25.00
Great Yarmouth War Memorial. 130mm.	22.50
Matlock Bath War Memorial. 150mm.	15.00

Home/Nostalgic

Pillar Box, inscribed: *I cant get a letter from you. . .* 72mm.	8.50
Watering Can. 67mm.	5.50
Shaving Mug. 54mm.	5.50
Mantle Clock with twisted side pillars. 92mm.	10.00
Grandmother Clock. 85mm.	5.50

Musical Instruments

Harp with wide base. 90mm.	6.50

Transport

Steam Locomotive, inscribed: R.H. and D.R. (Romney Hythe and Dymchurch Railway). 115mm long.	70.00

Modern Equipment

Gramophone, with horn. 85mm.	19.50

Miscellaneous

Mans Head spill vase or pin cushion. 85mm.	7.50
Rectangular Basket. 75mm long.	3.00

Footwear

Ladies Shoe. 115mm long.	8.75

Scotch Porcelain

For mark see *Crested China*, p. 226.

Trademark used for a Scottish retailer by an unknown manufacturer.

Parian/Unglazed
Bust of Scott, on circular glazed
base. 108mm.   17.50

Alcohol
Tankard. 62mm.   4.00

Shamrock China

For mark see *Crested China*, p. 226.

Trademark used by Belleek Pottery. (David McBirney and Co), Belleek, Co. Fermanagh, N. Ireland.

Ancient Artefacts
Canterbury Roman Ewer. 64mm.   3.00
Puzzle Jug. 68mm.   6.50

National Souvenirs
Shamrock. 90mm wide.   16.00

Animals
Pig, standing. Inscribed: *Wun't
be druv*. 70mm long.
No. 148. 60mm.   30.00

Birds
Cockerel, with orange face and
yellow beak. 100mm.   17.00

Miniature Domestic
Cheese Dish and cover.
76mm long.   12.50

Shamrock Crest China

For alternative mark see *Crested China*, p. 227.

Trademark used for a Belfast wholesaler by R.H. & S.L. Plant (Ltd), Tuscan Works, Longton. (Usual trademark Tuscan).

Seaside Souvenirs
Shell. No. 56. 82mm long.   7.00

Alcohol
Carboy. 68mm.   6.00

J. Shaw

For mark see *Crested China*, p. 227.

Trademark used by J. Shaw & Sons, Longton, subsequently John Shaw & Sons (Longton) Ltd, Willow Pottery, Longton.

Buildings
Shakespeare's Cottage.
130mm long.   16.00

Home/Nostalgic
Milk Churn and lid. 72mm.   4.75

Novelty
Biscuit impressed: *Huntley and Palmer.* Biscuit coloured on white shaped base.
68mm long. (Has been recorded with a Dolgelly crest).   30.00

Shell China

Shelley China

For marks see *Crested China*, p. 228.

Trademark used by Wileman & Co, Foley Potteries and Foley China Works, Fenton, Longton and subsequently renamed Shelleys Ltd.

NB: These lists include pieces marked Shelley, Foley and Shelley late Foley.

See *Crested China*, p. 227.

Trademark used by an unknown Staffordshire Pottery but resembles Arcadian.

Traditional/National Souvenirs
Welsh Hat. 55mm.   4.00

Miniature Domestic
Cheese Dish and cover. 45mm.   6.50

Unglazed/Parian
Bust of *Albert*, King of the
Belgians. 1915. 118mm.   47.50
Bust of *Burns* on square glazed
base. 140mm.   24.50
Bust of *The Right Hon. Winston
Churchill First Lord of the
Admiralty.* 125mm.   110.00
Bust of HM King George V.
130mm.   45.00
Bust of French, with inscription:
*Field Marshall Sir John French,
Commander in Chief of the
Expeditionary Force.* 118mm.   40.00
Bust of Jellicoe, with inscription:
*Admiral Sir John Jellicoe. In
Supreme Command of the North
Sea Fleet.* 118mm.   43.50
Bust of Joffre, with inscription:
*General Joffre, Commander in
Chief of the French Army 1915.*
130mm.   47.50
Bust of Kitchener, with inscription:
*Field Marshall Earl
Kitchener, Secretary of State for
War.* 118mm.   34.50
Bust of *The Rt Hon David Lloyd
George.* 2 sizes:
118mm & 130mm.   40.00
Sailor standing with hands on
hips, square base. Inscribed:
Ready! Aye! Ready! and
impressed: *HMS Lion.*
Coloured. 170mm.   125.00

Ancient Artefacts

Early Models (marked Foley) are sometimes found with no printed number or inscription. Models can be found with coloured transfer views, etc., instead of crests. All inscriptions begin: *Model of* so this will not be repeated throughout the list.

Ancient Cyprian Water Bottle. No. 140. 45mm.	4.00
Antique Tea Caddy — Queen Anne. No. 153. 70mm.	7.50
Aqua Mivel for pouring water over the hands of the priest. No. 137. 74mm wide.	7.75
Arabian Wine Vessel. No. 203. 75mm.	6.50
Caerswys Roman Vessel. No. 204 55mm.	5.25
Celtic Jar (an ancient). No. 200. 65mm.	4.00
Celtic Water Bottle. No. 205. 63mm.	4.50
Chester Roman Urn, inscribed: *A very rare Roman urn found near Chester now in possession of J.W. Salt Esq.* No. 118. 54mm.	4.75
Chinese Jar 12th Century. No. 304. 121mm.	11.00
Chinese Vase of great antiquity and beauty date about 5000 BC. Belongs to the nation. No. 115. 62mm.	4.75
Chinese Vase, about 500 AD. No. 213. 60mm.	4.75
Cinerary Urn of rare form. from Northants. No. 134. 40mm.	7.00
Cleopatra's Vase, inscribed: *An Egyptian vase taken from the tomb of Cleopatra.* No. 114. 50mm.	7.50
Colchester Famous Vase, inscribed: *Famous Colchester Vase in the museum.* No. 110. 48mm.	4.00
Cyprian Vase about 5000 BC. No. 206.	4.00
Cyprian Water Bottle. No. 192. 76mm.	4.00
Derby Roman Vase, inscribed: *Roman Vase found at Little Chester, Derby.* No. 83.	7.50
Dorset Cinerary Urn, inscribed: *Cinerary Urn with handles found at Dorset.* No. 132. 56mm.	6.50

Dover Cinerary Urn, inscribed: *Cinerary Urn found in Dover.* No. 141. 63mm.	6.50 7.50
Eastern Olive Jar. No. 208. 53mm dia.	4.00
Egyptian Vase, inscribed: *Ancient Egyptian Vase about 250 BC.* No. 84. 43mm.	4.00
Ely Saxon Vase, inscribed: *Ancient Saxon Vase, found in Ely.* No. 310. 88mm.	7.50
Exeter Vase. Unnamed Foley model. No. 117. 55mm.	4.00
Flemish Jug 14th century. No. 312. 70mm.	6.50
Gastrica Vase, inscribed: *Vase or bottle found in Gastrica. Ancient Cyprian pottery 900 BC.* No. 138. 51mm.	4.75
Glastonbury Bowl, inscribed: *Bowl from the ancient British lake village near Glastonbury.* No. 101. 50mm.	4.00
Glastonbury Vase, inscribed: *Vase from the Ancient British Lake Village near Glastonbury.* No. 104. 50mm.	4.00
Hanley Chinese Vase, inscribed: *Chinese Vase, originally in Hanley Museum.* No. 80. 63mm.	4.75
Hanley Egyptian Vase, inscribed: *Ancient Egyptian vase now in Hanley Museum.* No. 88. 63mm.	10.50
Herpes Jug, inscribed: *Jug from cemetary at Herpes, Charente.* No. 133. 45mm.	6.50
Horsham Jug, unnamed Foley model. No. 20. 65mm.	4.00
Indian Wine Vessel from Temple, Delhi. No. 303. 152mm.	8.75
Irish Bronze Pot. No. 109. 35mm.	3.50
Italian Vase. 16th Century. No. 301. 100mm.	7.50
Italian Vase. 16th Century. No. 309. 100mm.	6.50
(The) Kai Ping Vase, date about 2500 BC. No. 119. 63mm.	5.50
Kang Hi Tea Caddy. No. 144. 63mm.	8.75
Kang Hi Vase, presented to George V. No. 305. 120mm.	8.25
Kent Roman Urn, inscribed: *Roman urn from warriors grave, Kent.* No. 211. 52mm.	4.00

Lesser Pyramid Vase, inscribed:
Vase taken from a tomb under the
Lesser Pyramid about 3500 BC.
No. 117. 57mm. 5.50
Letchworth Celtic Urn, inscribed:
Celtic Urn found in Letchworth.
No. 199. 80mm. 6.50
Lord Byron's Vase, inscribed: *Fine*
model of a Greek vase presented to
the nation by Lord Byron. Now in
South Kensington Museum.
No. 116. 57mm. 7.50
Loving Cup, 3 handled. Not
found numbered. 40mm. 4.00
Malta Chatty. No. 89. 44mm. 6.75
Mayer Jug 1870, Model of. No. 326.
71mm. 14.50
Newbury Leather Bottle,
inscribed: *Leather Bottle found on*
battlefield of Newbury. 1644. Now
in Museum. No. 103. 60mm. 4.00
Notre Dame Candlestick,
inscribed: *Altar Candlestick in*
church of Notre Dame. No. 306.
115mm. 9.50
Penmaenmawr Urn, inscribed:
Ancient Urn found on
Penmaenmawr. No. 108. 48mm. 4.00
Persian Cafeterre (fine), 15th
Century. No. 302. 118mm. 10.50
Persian Scent Bottle 700 AD.
No. 212. 55mm. 5.50
Persian Wallace Vase. No. 82. 8.00
Persian Wine Server. 13th Century.
No. 308. 105mm. 8.00
Phoenician Vase, original in Stoke-
on-Trent Museum. No. 86.
57mm. 4.00
Phoenician Water Jar 1000 BC.
No. 207. 65mm. 6.00
Pompeian Vessel in Burslem
Museum. No. 87. 60mm. 4.75
Pompeian Wine Bottle, inscribed:
Wine Bottle taken from ruins
Pompeii. No. 135. 54mm. 15.00
Potters Vessel, found in Temple to
Bhudda. No. 150. 54mm. 5.50
Puzzle Jug, with verse. No. 180.
65mm. 8.25
Roman Money Box, found at Lincoln
AD 307. No. 131. 53mm. 7.50
Roman Tear Vase, 200 BC. No. 201.
63mm. 5.00

Roman Wine Vessel, 500 BC.
No. 142. 51mm. 6.00
Sacred Vessel found in Bethlehem.
No. 146. 68mm. 15.50
Salamis Lampshade, inscribed:
Ancient Cyprian pottery. No. 130.
60mm. 7.00
Salonika Vase, inscribed: *Ancient*
Greek vase found at Salonika by the
British troops when entrenching
Jan 1916. No. 170. 70mm. 17.50
Scandinavian Water Bottle. No. 143.
83mm. 5.50
Sevres Vase, 18th Century. No. 300.
88mm. 7.00
Sherborne Vase, inscribed: *Model*
of Roman Vase found in Sherborne.
A rather detailed, battered
shape. Reg. No. 456392. 95mm. 30.00
Silchester Urn, inscribed: *Roman*
Urn, from Silchester in Reading
Museum. No. 107. 50mm. 4.00
Silchester Vase, inscribed: *Vase*
from Silchester in Reading
Museum. No. 102. 51mm. 4.00
Silver Rose Bowl. No. 147. 63mm. 8.00
Sofia Cup, inscribed: *Very quaint*
cup found with silver belt, Sofia,
Bulgaria. No. 139. 42mm. 7.50
Swindon Vase, inscribed: *Vase*
dug up near Swindon. No. 105.
58mm. 4.00
Tara Vase, now in the Vatican, Rome.
No. 113. 50mm. 6.00
Tibet Sacred Vase, inscribed:
Sacred Vase from Temple in Tibet.
No. 209. 60mm. 4.00
Turkish Scent Jar. S.K. No. 202.
66mm. 6.00
Vatican Urn, inscribed: *Golden Urn*
in the Vatican. No. 145. 78mm. 10.00
Vestal Lamp, inscribed: *Roman*
vestal lamp. 500 BC. No. 149.
78mm. 7.50
Has been found with a black
boy's head popping out of
lamp. 55.00
Water Bottle, inscribed: *Ancient*
water Bottle of rare form. No. 136.
80mm long. 5.50
Water Bottle from tomb of Rameses II.
No. 210. 10.00

Weymouth Vase, inscribed:
Roman Vase found at Jordan Hill,
Weymouth now in Dorset
Museum. No. 85.   8.00
York Roman Ewer, inscribed:
Roman Ewer from original in
Hospitium, found in York. No. 81.
63mm.   4.00

Buildings — White
The Tower, Blackpool, Model of.
No. 322. 135mm.   14.50
Blackpool Tower with buildings.
No. 412. 160mm.   14.50
Burns Cottage, Model of. No. 189.
68mm long.   19.50
Forth Bridge. 130mm long.   40.00
Manx Cottage, Model of (as Burns
cottage above. No. 198 — with
different inscription.
68mm long.   25.00
Ross, Town Hall, with Clock
Tower (not found numbered).
123mm.   50.00
Skegness, Clock Tower, can also be
found inscribed: *Monmouth*
clock tower. No. 371. 155mm.   33.50
Windsor Round Tower. No. 372.
88mm.   16.00

Monuments
Douglas Isle of Man. Queen
Victoria Jubilee Clock Tower.
1887.   55.00
King Alfred, Statue (not found
numbered). 165mm.   30.00
Peel Monument. Inscribed: *Peel*
Monument Halcombe Hill Rams-
bottom. Built 1851 in Commemor-
ation of the Repeal of the Corn
Laws. No. 385. 123mm.
This is a square tower on a
square building, detailed
brickwork.   115.00
Southport Lifeboat Memorial.
No. 318. 140mm.   19.00
Rock of Ages, with verse (not
found numbered). 125mm.   10.50
Rufus Stone, with lengthy
inscriptions (not found
numbered). 95mm.   5.50

Historical/Folklore
Bunyan's Chair (also found
inscribed: *The old armchair).*
No. 347. 90mm.   13.00

Burn's Chair. No. 336. 86mm.   9.00
Burn's Clock, Model of old
Grandfather clock in Burns
Cottage, Ayr. No. 307. 130mm.   19.50
Ducking Stool, Leominster.
120mm long.   85.00
Mother Shipton with black hat and
cat. With verse: *Near to the*
Knaresboro Dropping Well. I first
drew breath as records tell.
No. 409. 110mm.   30.00
Sir Walter Scott's chair at
Abbotsford, Model of. No. 325.
68mm.   12.50

Traditional/National Souvenirs
Highland Mary Statue. No. 411.   28.50
Burns and Highland Mary on oval
base (not found numbered).
118mm.   35.00
Blackpool Ferris Wheel.
No. 373. 117mm.   17.50
Lancashire Clog. No. 162.
98mm long.   14.00
Legs of Man, model of.
No. 351. 90mm.   19.50
Lincoln Imp, model of the, on
pedestal. No. 160. 122mm.   18.00
Ripon Horn Blower, model of
the, with inscription: *The old*
time custom of sounding the horn
at 9pm each day is still observed.
No. 158. 110mm.   14.50
Manx Loving Cup, 3 handles as
legs of Man. 80mm. (Foley mark
only).   23.00
Kathleen Mavourneen, standing
figure of Irish lady. Some
colouring. No. 405. 98mm.   60.00
Pat's Hat and Dudeen, model of.
(Irish Topper with pipe moulded
on top). No. 159. 53mm.   17.00
Thistle Vase, can be found
inscribed: *Just a wee deoch-an*
Doris. No. 181.
2 sizes: 50mm.   4.75
65mm.   6.25
Welsh Lady, seated, inscribed:
Cymru-Am-Byth.
No. 404. 95mm (rare).   57.50
Welsh Hat, model of the. Can be
found with longest Welsh
place name round brim. (Very
occasionally the hat can be
found painted black with a red
hat band). No. 154. 35mm.

Plain	7.50
Welsh name	12.50
Coloured	20.00
Swiss Cattle Bell. No. 314. 95mm.	17.00
Swiss Cattle Bell, not found numbered, with 'Late Foley' mark. 63mm.	15.00

Seaside Souvenirs

Bathing Machine. No. 320. 75mm long.	14.00
Lifebelt. No. 47. 100mm dia.	13.50
Lifeboatman, standing by Capstan, inscribed: *A Life Saver*. Some colouring. No. 410. 112mm.	40.00
Lifeboat, with gold anchor. No. 323. Can be found inscribed: *Maud Pickup*, add £7.00. 115mm long.	12.50
Boat, almost canoe shaped on two supports, with hole at top possibly for candle. 160mm long. (Foley mark only).	15.00
Motor Boat with driver. No. 353. 112mm long.	19.50
Paddle Steamer, model of. No. 362. 160mm long.	75.00
Yacht in full sail. No. 401. 112mm.	14.00
Fisherman's Basket, inscribed: *A good catch*. No. 186. 88mm long.	7.50
Beachy Head Lighthouse. No. 178. 100mm.	9.00
Pharos Lighthouse. No. 73. 98mm.	9.00
Lighthouse on rock. 90mm.	5.50
Scallop Shell. No. 166. 78mm wide.	6.00
Whelk Shell, inscribed: *What are the wild waves saying*. No. 168. 70mm long. Can also be found inscribed. *Sheringham Whelk*. Add £6.00.	10.00
Whelk Shell. No. 169. 70mm long.	8.00
Cabin Trunk. No. 167. 65mm long.	11.00
Valise, half open. No. 58. 73mm long.	7.50

Countryside

Pine Cone, closed, on its side. 90mm long.	4.00

Animals

Bear, walking. No. 67. 80mm long.	35.00

Camel, kneeling (1 hump). No. 64. 102mm long.	19.50
Cat, angry, inscribed: *Me backs up*. 2 sizes: No. 195. 90mm.	25.75
No. 198. 76mm.	33.00
Latter with no tail—Manx.	
Cat, comical, and sitting with red bow. No. 333. 132mm.	24.00
Cat, sitting. No. 68. 64mm long.	27.00
Cat, sitting, head slightly to one side, tail curled around, ruffled fur. No. 268. 96mm.	26.00
Cat, standing, with long body. No. 381.	35.00
Cheshire Cat, model of the Real, impressed: *Tim*. No. 148. 82mm.	19.50
Cow, *Staffordshire Cow cream jug*. No. 317.	21.50
Bulldog, seated, inscribed: *Another Dreadnought*. No. 233. 63mm.	25.00
Bulldog, black, in kennel, inscribed: *Blackwatch*.	15.25
(Also found with bulldog not painted and no inscription £12.00). No. 316. 95mm.	14.00
Bulldog, seated. No. 324.	22.00
Pup, standing on hand mirror, inscribed: *Some pup!* No. 382.	30.00
(This number 382 is also found on a large comical Pup, inscribed: *Some pup!* It has black ears and spots. 116mm).	60.00
Dog, alert terrier. No. 377. 80mm.	34.50
Dog, Scottie, sitting. No. 505. 76mm.	22.00
Dog, Scottie, wearing black tam-o'shanter. No. 506.	40.00
Dog, Scottie, wearing glengarry. No. 507. 75mm.	40.00
Dogs, 2 Scotties sitting, one wearing tam-o'shanter and other wearing glengarry. Both hats beautifully coloured. Can be found inscribed: *Scots Guards*. No. 386. 88mm.	65.00
Donkey. No. 376. 115mm.	30.00
Elephant, lying down. No. 70. 80mm long.	20.00
Elephant, standing. No. 363.	20.00
Fish Jug (tail forms handle). No. 350. 105mm.	21.00
Fox, sitting. No. 62. 78mm.	50.00
Hare, looking round. 82mm long.	16.00
Lion. No. 369.	45.00

Monkey, sitting, can be found
inscribed: *Who hung the monkey?*
No. 61. 64mm.   17.00
Mouse, sitting with paws raised.
No. 65. 70mm.   32.50
Pig, standing with inscription:
*You can push, you can shuv but
I'm hanged if I'll be druv.*   25.00
or *Putney on a Pig.* No. 74.
90mm long.   45.00
Pig, sitting, with folded arms,
found inscribed: *Very umble*   45.00
or *Sussex Pig, won't be druv.*   29.50
or *Putney on a pig.* No. 60.
Rd. No. 447312. 80mm.   45.00
Piglet, standing. No. 90.   15.00
Rabbit, sitting..
No. 66. 90mm long.   12.50
Toad. No. 71. 47mm.   12.50
Terrapin. No. 69. 85mm.   9.00

Birds
Duck, sitting. *A real prize
Aylesbury Duck.*
Reg. No. 582115. 85mm.   40.00
Goose, plump. No. 63. 93mm.   19.50
Penguin, with black beak, and
holding newspaper. No. 384.
100mm.   85.00
Swan, open wings, with
coloured beak. No. 321.
85mm long.   18.50

Great War
Scottish Soldier, standing figure,
inscribed: *Scotland for ever.*
No. 402. 114mm.   115.00
Britannia, standing figure
inscribed: *Rule Britannia.* Some
colouring. No. 403.
108mm (rare).   95.00
Marianne, inscribed: *Vive la
France.* Some colouring.
No. 406. 108mm (rare).   105.00
Soldier, playing concertina
outside tent, inscribed: *Blighty
is the place for Me-e-e.* No. 341.
108mm long.   75.00
Biplane, usually found with a
fixed prop, but can be found
with a movable one. No. 344.
150mm long.   75.00
Bleriot Warplane, model of.

Monoplane with fixed prop.
No. 311. 150mm long.   65.00
Zeppelin, model of.
No. 332. 154mm long.   65.00
Battleship, not found named.
No. 319. 125mm long.   19.50
Submarine, inscribed: *E9.*
No. 328. 150mm long.   40.00
Armoured Car, model of.
No. 329. 120mm long.   40.00
British Tank, model of, with
trailing steering wheels.
No. 400. 115mm long.   18.00
Model of British Tank without
trailing wheels.
No. 400A. 140mm long.   85.00
Tank Bank, as above but as
money box. No. 413. 140mm.
Also found numbered 511.   45.00
Red Cross Van, model of.
No. 330. 95mm long.   26.50
Howitzer. No. 340. 148mm long.   35.00
Field Gun. No. 331. 132mm long.   23.00
Trench Mortar, model of.
Inscribed: *For freedom.* No. 179
or No. 327. 63mm.   11.50
9.2mm Shell, model of.
No. 175. 90mm.   11.00
Not named.   7.00
With Lydd crest.   14.00
German Zeppelin Bomb, model
of. No. 177. 85mm.   11.50
Mills Hand Grenade, model of.
No. 334. 78mm.   17.00
*Model of German Mine washed up on
the East Coast.*   55.00
Can be found wrongly in-
scribed: *Head of German torpedo
(Model of).* No. 188. 68mm
(rare).   65.00
Head of German Torpedo, Model of.
No. 187. 70mm (scarce).   110.00
Bandsman's Drum.
No. 57. 32mm.   5.00
Bugle. No. 354. 112mm.   30.00
Field Glasses. No. 343. 83mm.   17.00
Peaked Cap. No. 54. 53mm dia.   9.50
Glengarry. No. 176. 86mm long.   17.00
*Anti Zeppelin Candlestick as used
during the Great War — souvenir.*
No. 348. 83mm.   45.00
Fireplace, inscribed: *Keep the home
fires burning.* No. 338. 70mm.   20.50

Cenotaph, flags in relief. No. 368.

2 sizes: 130mm.	15.00
152mm.	24.00

Florence Nightingale, sitting
figure. No. 408. 102mm (rare). 110.00
Matlock Bath War Memorial, not
found numbered. 180mm. 32.50

Home/Nostalgic

Anvil, inscribed: *Every morning
sees some task to be done.*
No. 183. 83mm long. 7.50
Armchair, inscribed: *The old
armchair.*
(Also found inscribed: *Bunyan's
Chair*). No. 347. 90mm. 17.00
Baby's Cradle. (Often found not
numbered when marked *Foley*).
Found No. 50 and No. 503
(Shelley). 80mm long. 10.50
Bellows. No. 55. 95mm long. 10.50
Book. No. 56. 63mm. 5.50
Clock, long case, inscribed: *Model
of 14th Century clock in Wallace
collection.* Usually inscribed:
Wake up and get to business,
or more rarely: *The moving
finger writes and having writ moves
on* (add £10.00), or *Burns Clock*
(add £4.00). No. 307. 130mm. 16.00
Desk, roll-topped. No. 380.
80mm long. 16.00
Lace Iron. No. 504. 70mm. 10.00
Garden Roller. No. 358.
104mm long. 12.50
Handbag. No. 184. 85mm. 12.50
Kennel. No. 49. 55mm. 7.50
Lantern, inscribed: *Model of ye olde
lanterne and Ancient lights.*
No. 346. 105mm. 12.50
Milk Can and lid. No. 34. 64mm. 6.00
Milk Churn. No. 46. 71mm. 7.00
Can be found inscribed: *Straight
from the Coo.* 10.00
Pocket Watch and Matchbox
Holder. No. 379. 100mm. 40.00
Shaving Mug. No. 164. 54mm. 7.50
Sundial, octagonal with transfer
of dial face. No. 359. 120mm. 16.00
Swing Mirror on stand. No. 376.
88mm. 17.00
Victorian Pillar Box, model of.
No. 157. 90mm. 19.00
Watering Can. No. 163. 63mm. 10.50

Water Pump. No. 51. 83mm. 10.00
Wheelbarrow.
No. 355. 110mm long. 12.50

Comic/Novelty

Black Boy in bath, inscribed: *How
ink is made.* Fully coloured.
No. 374. 108mm long. 82.50
Box of Matches, open to reveal
contents. Some colouring.
No. 190. 74mm long. 17.00
Cigarette Case holding 6
gold-tipped cigarettes.
No. 349. 14.50
Coal Hod, inscribed: *Coal rations,
Yours to a cinder* or *Your rations
to a cinder.* No. 185. 10.50
Japanese Lady, inscribed: *Yum,
Yum,* some colouring.
No. 407. 123mm. 55.00
Tobacco Pouch, 2 crossed pipes
in relief on front.
No. 501. 98mm long. 19.00
Truck of black coal, inscribed:
Black diamonds from. . .
No. 389. 62mm long. 14.50

Alcohol

Beer Barrel. No. 48. 63mm. 5.50
Beer Barrel on stand.
No. 161. 65mm. 9.00
Bottle with cork, inscribed: *All
Scotch.* No. 214. 90mm. 8.50
No inscription. 5.50
Soda Syphon. No. 502. 11.50
Toby Jug, with verse: *No tongue
can tell* etc. No. 335. 95mm. 16.00

Sport

Boxer, inscribed: *England's hope.*
Brown boxing gloves. No. 375.
100mm. 125.00
Golf Bag and Clubs. No. 197.
108mm. 60.00
Golf Ball. No. 210. 50mm. 8.50
Golf Ball on Tee. No. 215.
52mm. 7.50
Tennis Racquet with 3 Balls.
No. 194. 116mm long. 14.00

Musical Instruments

Banjo. No. 72. 127mm long. 10.50
Piano, upright. No. 345. 76mm. 21.50

Transport

Charabanc, inscribed: *The Monarch*. No. 352. 125mm long.   47.50

Cycle Lamp, very rarely found inscribed: *Model of cycle oil head Lamp*. No. 342. 83mm.   50.00

Locomotive. No. 365. 150mm long.   95.00

Motor Coupé. No. 360. 135mm long.   265.00

Open Motor Car. No. 361. 135mm long.   145.00

Single Decker closed Motorbus 'K' type. No. 370. 120mm long.   135.00

Double Decker Omnibus. No. 370.   275.00

Steamroller. No. 364. 130mm long.   400.00

Modern Equipment

Flash Lamp, model of. No. 191. 70mm.   13.00

Horn Gramophone. No. 337. 95mm.   30.00

Hats

Bishop's Mitre. No. 58. 70mm.   10.50

Top Hat, found numbered 11 and 35. 60mm wide.   6.50

Trilby Hat, with black band. No. 500.   20.00

Footwear

Dutch Sabot. No. 36. 84mm long.   7.50

Leather Highboot. No. 47. 69mm.   16.00

Miscellaneous

Ewer with shamrock shape top. 38mm.   5.00

Horseshoe. No. 182.   23.00

Horse's Hoof. No. 52. (often found not numbered). 45mm.   5.50

Ink well and pen rest. No. 165. 60mm long.   13.00

Shield on stand, not found numbered. 52mm.   9.00

Miniature Domestic

Candleholder. No. 339.   10.50

Cheese Dish and lid. No. 196. 50mm.   14.00

Cup and Saucer. 38mm.   5.00

Tea Pot, inscribed: *Take a cup of tea*. No. 38. 50mm.   16.00

Numbered Ornamental Wares

No. 1. Pin Tray.   5.00

No. 2. Vase.   3.00

No. 3. Dish with ribbed sides. 120mm dia.   8.00

No. 4. 2 handled Loving Cup. 40mm.   4.00

No. 5. Fluted Trinket Tray. 70mm dia.   4.00

No. 6. Bell shaped vase.   5.00

No. 7. Vase, 2 handled with crinkle top. 56mm.   5.00

No. 16. Jug, with high looped handle. 63mm.   11.00

No. 18. Small Jug.   3.00

No. 20. Jug. 65mm.   4.50

No. 21. Vase. 70mm.   8.25

No. 22. Vase, shaped. 38mm.   6.00

No. 24. Pot, with lid. 50mm dia.   8.75

No. 25. Vase, 2 handles, with bulbous base. 60mm.   5.00

No. 26. Vase, 2 handles. 40mm.   5.00

No. 27. Vase, 2 handles, with crinkle top. 85mm.   4.75

No. 28. Jug, square. 35mm.   4.00

No. 29. Two-handled Vase. 64mm.   10.00

No. 30. Jug. 72mm.   5.00

No. 31. Cauldron. 2 handled. 35mm.   4.00

No. 32. Jug, small. 38mm.   5.00

No. 33. Vase, 2 handles. 54mm.   10.50

No. 40. Cream Jug. 55mm.   4.00

No. 41. Jug. 63mm.   4.00

No. 42. Jug. 65mm.   5.00

No. 43. Vase, 2 handles. 54mm.   4.00

No. 44. Jug, 2 handles. 50mm.   6.00

No. 45. Vase, crinkle top. 52mm.   3.00

No. 106. Vase. 65mm.   4.00

No. 111. Urn. 58mm.   3.00

No. 112. Taper Vase. 60mm.   6.50

No. 120. Box, heart-shaped.   7.00

No. 121. Pin Box and lid.   6.50

No. 123. Pin Box and lid, square.   6.50

No. 124. Pin Box, crinkle edge.   6.50

No. 146. Jug. 66m.   6.50

No. 151. Bulbous Vase with 2 handles and spout.   4.00

No. 171. Salt Pot.   10.00

No. 173. Salt Pot, circular.
  100mm.   11.00
No. 174. Pepper Pot, circular.
  100mm.   11.00

Signal Series or
Signal China

For additional mark see *Crested China,*
p. 244.

Trademark used by Hewitt and Leadbeater,
  Willow Potteries, Longton (Usual
  trademark Willow Art) for their Dublin
  agent.

'Smalls' only found with this
  mark, except for the following:

Home/Nostalgic
Anvil. 65mm long.   5.50

Miniature Domestic
Cheese Dish and cover.   6.50

Skarab China

Trademark used for J. Baker & Son, Bristol, by an unknown manufacturer.

Only one small and two animals found with this mark.

Animals

Pig, kneeling. 70mm long.   10.00
Squirrel eating nut. 60mm.   15.00

Snowdon China

For mark see *Crested China*, p. 244.

Trademark used for the Snowdon Mountain Tramroad and Hotels Co. Ltd, on china manufactured by Arkinstall & Sons Ltd, Arcadian Works, Stoke-on-Trent. (Usual trademark Arcadian).

Traditional/National Souvenirs

Welsh Harp. 80mm.   8.25
Welsh Hat, model of, with longest Welsh place name round brim. 52mm.   8.25

Animals

Black Cat sitting on a pouffe inscribed: *Good Luck.*   19.50

Home/Nostalgic

Umbrella, open. 50mm dia.   14.50

Comic/Novelty

Bookmaker with greyhound and hare on ashtray. Some colouring. 90mm long.   46.50

Modern Equipment

Camera folding. 60mm.   30.00

Souvenir Series

S P Co Ltd

For mark see *Crested China,* p. 244.

Trademark used by an unknown manufacturer for a London wholesaler or
retailer.

Traditional/National Souvenirs
Lancashire Clog. 85mm long.   4.75

Seaside Souvenirs
Whelk Shell. 90mm long.   3.00

Animals
Pig. Inscribed: *The Pig*
that wont go. 95mm long.   12.50

Trademark used for a wholesaler or retailer
in Manchester by an unknown
manufacturer.

Ancient Artefacts
Swindon Vase (not named).   2.25
Pin Tray 75mm long Rectangular
Stamp Box and lid. 63mm long.   5.50

Spencer Art China

Sphinx

For mark see *Crested China*, p. 245.

Trademark used for a retailer by a Fenton manufacturer.

Buildings — White
Osborne House. 150mm long.   82.50
The Old Village, Shanklin, IoW.
100mm long.   75.00

Monuments
Arch Rock, Freshwater Bay.
82mm.   28.00

Trademark used by a foreign (French or German) manufacturer for the Belgian souvenir market.

Traditional/National Souvenirs
Cheshire Cat, inscribed:
Still Smiling. 82mm.   7.50

The only model found has crest of Bruxelles.

Historical
Mons Meg, Edinburgh Castle, model of. 130mm long.   11.00

Historical/Folklore
Coach and Horses with 3 figures, coloured, on base. 100mm long.   40.00

Sporting Series

SR

SPORTING SERIES
G. V. & Cº
REG. APPLIED FOR

Trademark used by Arkinstall & Son Ltd., Arcadian Works, Stoke-on-Trent, usual trademark Arcadian.

Only one piece has been recorded with this mark, a spade shaped club with colour transfer of pheasants. It would appear that the Sporting Series was not a commercial success.

For mark see *Crested China*, p. 215.

Trademark used by Samuel Radford (Ltd), High St, Fenton.

Ancient Artefacts
Loving Cup, 3 handled. 35mm.   30.00

Home/Nostalgic
Milk Churn and lid. 70mm.   4.75

Miniature Domestic
Cheese Dish and cover.
  64mm long.   4.75

Stanley China

Star Bazaar Art China

For mark see *Crested China*, p. 245.

$$\mathcal{S}^{\mathcal{A}^{NLEY}}C_{H_{I_{N_A}}}$$
$$\underset{L}{C.A}$$

See *Crested China*, p. 245.

Trademark used by Charles Amison (& Co. Ltd), Stanley China Works, Wedgwood St, Longton.

Ancient Artefacts
Puzzle Jug. 66mm.   3.50

Traditional/National Souvenirs
Lancashire Clog. 135mm long.   6.50

Animals
Dog, bulldog sitting. Some
    colouring. 68mm.   10.00

Birds
Parakeet, some colouring.
    110mm.   21.75

Great War
Battleship. 119mm long.   16.00

Home/Nostalgic
Grandfather Clock. 105mm.   8.75
Pillar Box. 76mm.   7.50

Footwear
Boot. 70mm.   7.00
Sabot. 80mm long.   4.75

Miniature Domestic
Cheese Dish and cover. 50mm.   4.75
Pin Box and Lid, rectangular.
    56mm long.   4.00

Trademark used for the Star Bazaar, Douglas, Isle of Man, on china thought to have been manufactured by Hewitt & Leadbeater, Willow Potteries, Longton. (Usual trademark Willow Art).

Traditional/National Souvenirs
Manx Man, John Bull mould with
    extra leg at back. 126mm.   50.00

Animals
Manx cat with collar, not named.
    63mm.   16.00

Home/Nostalgic
Anvil. 50mm.   5.50

Strand China

Success (Art) China

For mark see *Crested China*, p. 247.

For mark see *Crested China*, p. 247.

Trademark used for a London retailer by Podmore China Co, Elm Street, Hanley. (Usual trademark Podmore). This retailer obviously supplied towns all over the country as crests other than London are found.

Trademark used by an unknown manu-facturer/s.

Parian/Unglazed
Bust of *John Peel* with details of
verse. 136mm.   21.75

Monuments
Nelson's Column. 144mm.   45.00

Ancient Artefacts
Salisbury Leather Kettle. 61mm.   2.25

Animals
Angry Cat, with arched back and
tail. 100mm.   12.50
Dog in kennel, inscribed: *Black
Watch*. 67mm.   9.00
Elephant, standing. 75mm.   13.00

National Souvenirs
Thistle vase with inscription:
A wee Deoch-&-Doris. 50mm.   4.00

Seaside Souvenirs
Lighthouse, black band. 105mm.   5.50

Birds
Penguin. 84mm.   11.50
Woodpecker.   21.50

Great War
Torpedo. 145mm long.   47.50

Home/Nostalgic
Anvil. 58mm.   5.50
Grandfather Clock. 121mm.   8.75

Great War
Cenotaph, inscribed.
3 sizes: 80mm.   4.00
            130mm.   5.50
            167mm.   5.50
Edith Cavell Memorial, London
  Inscribed: *Edith Cavell Brussels
  dawn October 12th 1915.
  Humanity sacrifice*. 142mm.   14.50

Home/Nostalgic
Thimble. 43mm.   10.50

Sussex China

For mark see *Crested China*, p. 247.

Trademark used for an Eastbourne retailer by Sampson Hancock (& Sons), Bridge Works, Stoke. Pieces were sold with Sussex coats of arms. (Usual trademark Corona).

Buildings — White
Bridge. Rarely found inscribed
  Weymouth Bridge Add £15.00
  130mm long.   19.50

Historical/Folklore
Ark. 90mm long.   4.75

Traditional/National Souvenirs
Lancashire Clog. 105mm long.   6.50
Laxey Wheel. 80mm.   40.00
Harp. 90mm.   5.50
Mother Shipton. 73mm.   13.00

Seaside Souvenirs
Lighthouse. 104mm.   5.50
Beachy Head Lighthouse, black band.
  3 sizes: 102mm.   6.50
           118mm.   7.50
           150mm.   7.50

Animals
Staffordshire Bull Terrier. 79mm.   10.50
Teddy Bear, sitting. 85mm.   8.50

Great War
British Airship on base.
  128mm long.   20.00
Lusitania. 163mm long.   75.00
Submarine, inscribed: *E4*.
  102mm long.   16.00
Submarine, inscribed: *E5*.
  125mm long.   16.00
Torpedo. 150mm long.   47.50

Home/Nostalgic
Cigarette Case. 70mm long.   13.00
Hip Bath. 95mm long.   7.00

Miscellaneous
King, chess piece. 110mm.   19.50
Pawn, chess piece. 60mm.   19.00

Miniature Domestic
Candlestick, column. 89mm.   3.00

Sussex China S.P. Co.

For mark see *Crested China*, p. 248.

Trademark used for a Sussex wholesaler by Arkinstall & Son Ltd, Arcadian Works, Stoke-on-Trent. (Usual trademark Arcadian).

Ancient Artefacts
Newbury Leather Bottle. 65mm.   2.25

Buildings — White
Cottage. 55mm.   6.50
Hastings Clock Tower. 157mm.   10.50

Traditional/National Souvenirs
Lancashire Clog. 100mm.   4.75
Welsh Hat. 35mm.   4.75

Seaside Souvenirs
Houseboat. 58mm.   4.75
Lifeboat, inscribed: *Charles Arkcoll*
  115mm long.   15.25
Whelk Shell. 100mm long.   3.00

Countryside
Hay Stack, circular. 57mm.   4.75

Animals
Dog, Staffordshire bull terrier,
  sitting. 72mm.   10.50
Pig, sitting. 63mm long.   8.25
Rabbit, lying, ears along back.
  70mm long.   6.50
Tortoise. 70mm long.   6.50

Birds
Swan. 62mm long.   6.50

Great War
British Airship found wrongly
  named *Model of Super Zeppelin*.
  128mm long.   20.00
Battleship, 3 funnels and tiny
  gun fore and aft. 120mm long.   15.50
Red Cross Van. 85mm long.   23.00
Howitzer. 140mm long.   17.50
Mills Hand Grenade, model of.
  62mm.   13.00

Colonial Hat. 88mm long.   10.50
Bell Tent. 64mm dia.   10.50
Gurkha Knife, model of.
  110mm long.   20.00
Sandbag, model of. 73mm long.   13.00
Trench Dagger, model of.
  102mm long.   40.00

Home/Nostalgic
Old Armchair, not named.
  90mm.   6.00
Lantern. 90mm.   5.50
Milk Churn and lid. 60mm.   4.75

Comic/Novelty
Bean Pod, curved and split to
  reveal peas. 133mm long.   16.00
Policeman, no inscription.
  140mm.   24.75

Musical Instruments
Banjo. 140mm long.   8.50
Double Bass. 151mm.   30.00
Piano, upright. 70mm long.   12.50

Miscellaneous
King, chess piece. 110mm.   19.50
Knight, chess piece. 63mm.   8.25
Pin Box and lid — circular.
  64mm dia.   4.00

Sussex Ware

No details of mark available.

Trademark used for Cheesman & Co, Brighton by Hewitt & Leadbeater, Willow Potteries, Longton. (Usual mark Willow Art).

A model of 'Ye Olde Sussex Pig' was reputedly made but so far has not been seen.   15.00

Swan China

For additional mark see *Crested China*, p.249.

Trademark used by Charles Ford, Cannon St, Hanley, subsequently a branch of J.A. Robinson & Sons Ltd. (Usual trademark Arcadian).

Unglazed/Parian
These busts can be found with crests on their glazed bases, add £10.00 if the bust carries the correct Royal coat of arms.
Bust of King Edward VII on
circular glazed base. 140mm.   35.00
Bust of Queen Alexandra, on
circular glazed base. 140mm.   35.00
Bust of King George V, on circular
glazed base. 135mm.   35.00
Bust of Queen Mary, can be found
inscribed: *Queen Mary, born May
26th 1867.* 135mm.   35.00
Bust of Sir John Jellicoe on square
glazed base. 175mm.   65.00
Bust of General Joffre, on square
glazed base. 155mm.   47.50
Bust of Lloyd George, on circular
glazed base. 135mm.   40.00
Bust of Burns. 80mm.   17.50
Bust of Wordsworth on glazed
base. 118mm.   17.50

Ancient Artefacts
British Bronze Pot. No. 160.
70mm.   2.25

Butter Pot, old, of 17th Century.
45mm. — 3.00
Canterbury Roman Ewer,
inscribed: *Roman Ewer found*
near Canterbury original in
Canterbury Museum.
No. 294. 64mm. — 3.00
Canterbury Roman Vase. 65mm.
No. 282. — 3.00
Chinese Vase original in Hanley
Museum. 58mm. — 3.00
Devon Oak Pitcher. 60mm.
No. 192. — 3.00
Eddystone Jug, inscribed: *old*
Spanish jug dredged up near
Eddystone now in Atheneum,
Plymouth. No. 585. 58mm. — 3.00
Egyptian Vase, inscribed: *Ancient*
Egyptian Vase 230BC.
No. 155. 42mm. — 3.00
Egyptian Water Bottle.
No. 156. 58mm long. — 3.00
Fountains Abbey Cup. No. 709. — 2.25
Glastonbury Vase. No. 642.
50mm. — 2.25
Highland Whisky Bowl.
134mm wide. — 4.75
Irish Bronze Pot. No. 110.
35mm. — 2.25
Kendal Jug. 75mm. No. 210. — 2.25
Lincoln Jack from Original in
Museum. 62mm. No. 50. — 2.25
Loving Cup originated by Henry
of Navarre, King of France.
3 handled.
2 sizes: 40mm. — 3.00
52mm. — 3.00
Newbury Leather Bottle. 67mm. — 2.25
Phoenician Vase, originally in
Stoke-on-Trent Museum.
No. 217. 60mm. — 3.00
Puzzle Jug, original in South
Kensington Museum, with
verse: *Try how to drink and*
not to spill. No. 147 and
No. 303. 70mm. — 5.50
Salopian Roman Ewer inscribed:
Roman Salopian Ewer found at
Uriconium now in Shrewsbury
Museum. 70mm. — 3.00
Shakespeare's Jug. 54mm. — 3.00
Southwold Jar. — 3.00

Toby Jug.
2 sizes: 61mm. — 6.50
75mm. — 7.50
Upstones Jug, inscribed: *Ancient*
jug found near Upstones, Staffs.
No. 221. 62mm. — 3.00
(Also found inscribed Ipstones).
It seems Upstones was a spelling
mistake.
Winchelsea Vase. 82mm. — 3.00
Winchester Vase. — 3.00
York Roman Ewer. No. 57.
55mm. — 3.00
York Roman Urn. — 3.00

Buildings — Coloured
Shakespeare's House.
84mm long. — 20.00

Buildings — White
The Tower Blackpool. 104mm. — 13.00
Anne Hathaway's Cottage,
Shottery, near Stratford-on-
Avon. 83mm long. — 11.00
First and Last Refreshment House
in England. 73mm long. — 10.50
Highland Cottage, model of.
80mm. — 21.50
Irish Round Tower. 106mm. — 10.50
Marble Arch. 65mm. — 13.00
Southampton Bargate. 66mm. — 21.50
Tower Bridge. 92mm. — 29.00
Welsh Cottage, Model of. Same
model as Highland Cottage).
79mm long. — 21.50

Monuments (including Crosses)
Barrow's Monument, Ulverston.
145mm. — 52.50
Celtic Cross, not named. 125mm. — 12.00
Iona Cross, not named. 120mm. — 6.00

Historical/Folklore
Bishop's Mitre. 55mm. — 6.50
Ancient Coaching Hat, model of.
65mm long. — 7.50
Davey Safety Lamp '1836'. 85mm. — 16.50
Font, inscribed: *Model of ancient*
font in Tideswell church dates back
to the 14th century. 90mm. — 14.50
Jenny Geddes Stool. 45mm. — 10.50

Judge, bust, with inscription:
*Defend the children of the poor
and punish the wrong doer.
Copy of inscription of New
Bailey Court, London.* With
inscription add £10.00

2 sizes: 55mm.	8.50
70mm.	14.00

Robinson Crusoe, holding Rifle.

120mm.	110.00

Mother Shipton, with verse: *Near
to Knaresboro dropping well.*

2 sizes: 76mm.	13.00
115mm.	15.00
Man in Stocks. 88mm.	19.00
Suffragette Handbell. 70mm.	21.50

Traditional/National Souvenirs

John Bull, bust. 66mm.	14.50
Lancashire Clog. 92mm long.	4.75
Luton Boater. 78mm dia.	8.75

Monmouth Hat with verse.

54mm.	21.50

Melton Mowbray Pie, The. Pie with
moulded pastry adornments

and verse. 50mm.	14.50

Ripon Horn blower with

inscription. 130mm.	10.50
Irish Colleen. Bust. 85mm.	30.00

Thistle Vase, with verse: *Just a
wee deoch-&-doris* No. 14.

65mm.	3.00
Welsh Lady, bust. 65mm.	16.00

Welsh Leek, can be found with
inscription: *King Henry V. The
Welshmen did goot servace (at
Crecy) in a garden where leeks did
grow. Shakespeare.* 98mm.   5.25

Seaside Souvenirs

Bathing Machine with '32' above
the door.

2 sizes: 60mm.	7.50
85mm.	8.50
Bell Rock lighthouse. 141mm.	21.50

Lifeboat with blue band and

yellow rigging.	8.25

Sometimes found named
Elizabeth Simpson, John Birch
or *Nancy Lucy.*   15.25

Novel Collecting Box for the
Royal National Lifeboat
Institution Robin Hoods Bay,
model of fish standing on
square base inscribed: *My diet is
£.s.d.* 128mm.   40.00

Lifeboatman bust. 85mm.	19.50

Fishing Basket, found inscribed:

A good catch. 50mm.	5.50

Beachy Head Lighthouse,

2 sizes: 102mm.	7.50
140mm.	9.00

Eddystone Lighthouse.

2 sizes: 105mm.	7.50
140mm.	10.50

Pharos Lighthouse, Fleetwood,
model of.

2 sizes: 88mm.	5.50
130mm.	10.50

Lighthouse on circular base.

100mm.	4.00
Crab. 85mm long.	8.25
Scallop Shell. 70mm dia.	3.50

Scallop Shell Menu Holder.

62mm.	10.50

Shell ink well, one open shell
inverted on another inscribed:
*We are always glad to hear from
you.* 105mm.   10.50

Whelk Shell, inscribed: *Listen to
the sea.* 85mm long.   4.00

Punch, bust, not named, some
colouring. 83mm.   27.00

Countryside

Beehive on table. 78mm.	7.50
Hay Stack, circular. 58mm.	4.75
Hay Stack, rectangular. 50mm.	5.50
Pinecone. 90mm long.	4.00

Animals

Cat, angry, standing with arched
back and green eyes.

63mm long.	12.50
Cat, Cheshire. 100mm.	7.50

Cat, climbing in boot, chasing
mouse (peeping out of toe).

105mm long.	40.00

Cat, long necked and sitting.   8.75
Inscribed: *My word if you're not
off.* 108mm.   13.00

Cat, sitting, and smiling
(grotesque, rather similar to

Cheshire Cat). 75mm.	7.50

Cat, sitting, with bow round

neck. 56mm.	10.00

Black Cat, sitting in octagonal

dish. 100mm wide.	24.50

Three Black cats on Sledge.
118mm long. 95.00
Bulldog, ferocious. 129mm long. 12.50
Bill Sykes Bulldog, inscribed: *My
word if you're not off.* 100mm long. 13.00
Dog, standing. 95mm long. 12.50
Dog, Collie, lying down,
inscribed: *Shetland Collie.*
78mm long. 14.50
Dog, lying, with crossed paws.
108mm long. 16.00
Great Dane, sitting, wearing top
hat, 1 ear raised, gold band
around hat. 112mm. 45.00
Dog, King Charles Spaniel,
begging on cushion.
2 sizes: 68mm. 8.25
95mm. 12.50
Spaniel wearing black top hat,
coloured with glass on green
ashtray base. Reg. No. 67858.
70mm. 52.50
Dog, pup, with one ear raised.
68mm. 7.50
Dog, Pug, sitting. 78mm. 10.50
Dog, puppy, sitting, inscribed:
*Daddy wouldn't buy me a
bow-wow.* 75mm. 17.50
Dog, *Scottish Terrier.* 66mm long. 11.00
Donkey, inscribed: *Hee Haw.*
120mm. 34.00
Elephant, African (big ears).
58mm. 15.00
Elephant, trunk modelled free
from body, inscribed: *Baby
Jumbo.* 50mm. 17.50
If inscribed add £5.00.
Fish, open-mouthed.
108mm long. 4.50
Fish shaped dish. Inscribed:
A "Plaice" for everything. 7.50
Frog, open-mouthed and green
eyes. 80mm. 10.50
Hare. 73mm long. 9.00
Lion, walking. Found inscribed:
King of the Forest. 110mm. Add
£4.00. 14.50
Monkey, sitting, hand to mouth.
65mm. 13.00
Otter with fish in mouth.
125mm long. 47.50
Pig, lying down, alert ears.
78mm long. 8.25
Pig, lying down, inscribed: *I wunt
be druv.* 90mm long. 10.00
Pig, sitting and fat. No. 587, can

be found inscribed: *My word
if you're not off.* 90mm long. 14.50
Pig, standing, with drooping
ears. No. 300.
2 sizes: 90mm long. 8.25
105mm long. 8.25
Sussex Pig, model of, standing
thin pig, inscribed: *You can push
or you can shuv but I'm hanged if
I'll be druv.* No. 148. 78mm long. 12.50
Piglet, standing, with erect ears.
No. 277. 73mm long. 8.25
Polar Bear.
2 sizes: 100mm. 40.00
136mm long. 47.50
Rabbit, crouching. 70mm long. 5.50
Teddy Bear.
2 sizes: 68mm. 8.50
87mm. 10.50
Large size can be inscribed with
verse: *Come and be my Teddy
Bear.* Add £6.00
Tortoise. 72mm long. 6.50
Welsh Goat, model of, inscribed:
Yr Afr Cymreig. 100mm long. 47.50

Birds (including Eggs)
Chick breaking out of egg.
2 sizes: 63mm. 5.50
73mm long. 5.50
Egg, with flattened base. 44mm. 4.00
Cock, standing, legs modelled
separately, inscribed: *Cock o'th'
North.* Some colouring to head.
100mm. 14.50
Hen, roosting. 54mm. 5.00
Norwich Canary.
2 sizes: 90mm. 7.50
125mm. With whistle. 21.50
Owl, baby. 40mm. 12.50
Owl, long eared. 95mm. 10.50
Parrot inscribed: *Pretty Polly.*
75mm. 12.50
Swan. 70mm long. 4.75
Swan. No. 295. 55mm long. 5.50

Great War
British Soldier, model of, on oval
domed base. 135mm. 87.00
Despatch Rider, model of, on
motorbike. 120mm long. 43.50
Nurse and Wounded Tommy,
model of. 108mm long. 85.00
Nurse, inscribed: *Soldier's friend.*
Red Cross on chest. 132mm. 47.50
Russian Cossack, model of, on
horseback. 122mm. 145.00

Sailor, bust, found with hatband impressed: *HMS Dreadnought* or *HMS Queen Elizabeth*. Inscribed: *The handyman*. 92mm.   30.00

Sailor, bust, inscribed: *Sailor beware* and with verse: *Hearts of Oak*. (Add £5.00). 95mm.   30.00

Sailor, standing with hands on hips. 132mm.   75.00

Sailor, Winding Capstan, model of. 105mm.   82.50

Scots Soldier, model of, on domed oval base. 135mm.   135.00

Soldier, bust, inscribed: *Tommy Atkins* with verse: *Soldiers of the King* or *Territorial*.
Some colouring. 90mm.   30.00
with verse   40.00

Soldier with Respirator, bust inscribed: *Model of new gas mask* (rare). 95mm.   195.00

Tommy Driving a Steam Roller over the Kaiser, inscribed: *To Berlin*. 120mm long.
(Very Rare).   435.00

Tommy in Bayonet Attack, model of. 130mm.   130.00

Tommy and his Machine Gun. 100mm long.   30.00

Tommy on Sentry Duty, model of. 110mm.   75.00

Tommy Throwing Grenade, model of. 130mm.   130.00

New Aeroplane, model of. Biplane with fixed prop, and roundels in relief. 120mm long.   100.00

New Aeroplane, model of, with revolving prop. 135mm long.   55.00

British Airship on stand. 128mm long.   20.00

Observer or Sausage Balloon, model of. 84mm.   47.50

Super Zeppelin, model of. 127mm long.   20.00

Battleship, inscribed: *HMS Queen Elizabeth*. 115mm long.   30.00

Battleship, 3 funnels. 120mm long.   15.50

Torpedo Boat Destroyer, model of. 126mm long.   19.50

Submarine, inscribed: *E4*. 95mm long.   16.00

Submarine, inscribed: *E5*. 126mm long.   16.00

Armoured Car, model of. 95mm long.   30.00

Red Cross Van, red cross on each side and rear. 'EH 139' printed on radiator. 115mm long.   23.00

Tank, model of. 115mm long.   13.00

Tank, model of, with inset steering wheels. 115mm long.   15.00

Tank, model of, with one wheel. 145mm long.   350.00

Tank, model of, with trailing steering wheels. Can be found inscribed: *Original made in Lincoln* with Lincoln crest and £15.00 should be added for this. 144mm long.   17.50

Field Gun.
2 sizes: 112mm long.   15.00
140mm long.   17.00

Field Gun with screen. 100mm long.   18.50

German Howitzer. 140mm long.   19.50

Trench Mortar, model of. 70mm long.   10.50

Revolver, model of. 83mm long.   35.00

Anti Aircraft Shell, model of. 98mm.   17.50

Cannon Shell.
2 sizes: 70mm.   3.00
90mm.   3.50
The 90mm size is often inscribed: *Jack Johnson*.   *8.00*
or *Hartlepools Bombardment Dec 16th 1914*.   11.50

Clip of Bullets, model of. 57mm.   13.00

Bomb dropped on Bury St Edmunds. 75mm.   11.00

Bomb which killed a chicken at Southend, Model of. (Rare) 75mm.   45.00

Bomb dropped from Zeppelin, model of. 75mm.   11.00

British Aerial Bomb. 75mm.   30.00

Canister Bomb, model of. 60mm.   13.00

Plum Pudding Bomb, Model of. 72mm long. (rare)   80.00

German Aerial Torpedo. 88mm long.   30.00

Hair Brush Grenade. 105mm long.   130.00

Mills Hand Grenade, Model of. 62mm.   13.00

Bandsman's Drum. 53mm.   5.00

Bell Tent, open base and flap. 60mm.   10.50

Capstan. 56mm.   10.00

Gurkha Knife, model of. 110mm long.   20.00

Pair of Field Glasses, model of.	
78mm long.	13.00
Sandbag. 70mm long.	13.00
Tommy's Hut, model of.	
105mm long.	40.00
Trench Dagger. 102mm long.	40.00
Trench Lamp. 70mm.	10.50
Water Bottle, model of. 65mm.	13.00
Colonial Hat, model of.	
88mm wide.	10.50
Glengarry. 90mm long.	16.00
Officer's Peaked Cap, with	
coloured badge and hatband.	
65mm dia.	9.00
Pith Helmet. 85mm long.	16.00
Anti-Zeppelin Candle Holder.	
62mm.	14.00
Fireplace, inscribed: *We've kept the*	
home fires burning. 90mm.	12.50
Kitchen Range with pot.	
Inscribed: *Keep the home*	
fires burning. 78mm long.	9.00
Plymouth Armada War Memorial.	
180mm.	30.00

Home/Nostalgic

Anvil. 66mm.	5.50
Bellows. 95mm long.	6.50
Chair, highbacked. 90mm.	5.50
Firebucket. 55mm.	3.50
Frying pan. 110mm long.	6.50
Grandfather Clock, model of a	
usually found inscribed: *Make*	
use of time let not advantage slip.	
Shakespeare. Can be found	
inscribed: *The time of day.*	
110mm.	10.50
Kennel inscribed *Beware of the*	
Dog 54mm.	6.50
Milk Churn with lid. 63mm.	3.00
Pillar Box, inscribed: *GRV* and *If*	
you haven't time to post a line	
here's the pillar box. 63mm.	10.00
Saucepan and lid. No. 178.	
80mm long.	7.50
Stool, 3 legged. 40mm.	5.50
Table, square. 39mm.	5.50
Warming Pan, inscribed: *Model of*	
old Warming Pan and *Polly*	
warm the Bed 125mm long.	10.00
Water Pump. 90mm.	7.50
Watering Can. 78mm.	· 5.50
Wicker Basket, twisted handle,	3.50
inscribed: *Fruit Basket.* 63mm.	6.50

Comic/Novelty

Arry, Bust of a Pearly King.	
83mm.	55.00
Billiken. 65mm.	4.00
Clown, bust, inscribed: *Put me*	
amongst the girls, some	
colouring. 80mm.	17.00
Golliwog, fully coloured, verse	
to rear.	85.00
Japanese lady sitting with fan.	
62mm.	34.00
Jester, double faced, happy and	
sad, and eyes open and closed.	
Can be found inscribed: *Ye jester*	
awake, ye jester asleep.	
2 sizes: 65mm.	8.25
90mm.	9.00
Inscribed	12.50
Policeman on duty, with verse.	
148mm.	25.00
Potato. 77mm long.	30.00
Suffragette handbell, double-	
faced. Front, sour old lady,	
inscribed: *Votes for women.* Back	
pretty young girl, inscribed:	
This one shall have the vote. Some	
colouring. 98mm.	30.00
Suffragette double faced bust.	
Same face and inscriptions as	
the handbell above.98mm.	30.00

Cartoon/Comedy Characters

Ally Sloper, Bust with verse.	
100mm.	40.00
Harry Lauder, bust, not named.	
Inscribed: *Stop ye're tickling Jock.*	
83mm.	17.00
Mrs Gummidge, standing figure,	
with inscription: *A lone lorn*	
creetur and everything goes	
contrairy with her. 112mm.	40.00

Alcohol

Beer Barrel, on stand. 40mm.	4.00
Monk, jovial and holding glass,	
with verse: *A jovial Monk am I.*	
2 sizes: 70mm.	12.50
112mm.	16.00
Soda Syphon. 100mm.	10.00
Thimble, inscribed: *Take a*	
thimblefull. 40mm.	10.50
Toby Jug. 62mm.	6.50
Toby Jug with verse. 74mm.	8.50

Sport

Cricket Bag. 80mm long.	8.50

Football. 50mm dia. — 6.50

Golf Ball, inscribed: *The game of golf was first played in the year 1448.* 42mm. — 6.50

Golf Club head. 100mm long. — 10.50

Tennis Racquet. 90mm long. — 7.50

Trophy, 2 handled. 49mm. — 10.00

Musical Instruments

Banjo. 154mm long. — 9.50

Guitar. 153mm long. — 10.50

Harp. 105mm. — 5.50

Piano, upright. 70mm long. — 13.50

Tambourine. 70mm dia. — 7.50

Transport

Car, Saloon, inscribed: *EH 139.* 76mm long. — 30.00

Open Sports Car, inscribed: *EH 139.* 110mm long. — 40.00

Can of Petrol, impressed: *Motor Spirit.* 55mm. — 13.00

Modern Equipment

Gramophone with horn. 112mm. — 19.50

Hats

Fireman's Helmet. 82mm long. — 25.00

Mortar Board. 66mm long. — 16.00

Footwear

Oriental Shoe. No. 302. 102mm long. — 6.50

Ankle Boot. 83mm long. — 5.50

Leather Highboot. 75mm. — 10.00

Miscellaneous

Handbell, no clapper. 53mm. — 4.75

Horses Hoof Vase. 60mm long. — 4.00

Horses Hoof Inkwell, with inscription: *We're aye prood tae hear fra ye.* — 12.50

Knight chess piece. 62mm. — 9.00

Rook chess piece. 55mm. — 4.00

Miniature Domestic

Cheese Dish, one piece. 50mm. — 7.50

Cheese Dish and cover. 50mm. — 7.50

Cup and saucer. 37mm. — 5.50

Cup and saucer, fancy. 49mm. — 4.50

Tea Pot with lid. No. 145. 40mm. — 7.50

Tea Pot, Puzzle. 86mm long. — 10.00

Trinket box and lid, heart shaped. No. 321. 60mm. — 4.00

Sylvan China

For mark see *Crested China,* p. 254.

Trademark used by Dura Porcelain Co. Ltd, Empress Pottery, Hanley.

Ancient Artefacts

Puzzle Jug. 70mm. — 5.50

Historical/Folklore

Burns Chair, model of. — 7.50

Mary Queen of Scots Chair, Edinburgh Castle, Model of. 76mm. — 6.50

Traditional/National Souvenirs

Welsh Hat. 55mm. — 4.75

Animals

Cat sitting on circular pouffe, inscribed: *Luck* in orange. 80mm. — 10.50

Scottie Dog, black, looking out of Kennel. Inscribed: *Black Watch.* Green bow. 68mm. — 15.25

Scottie Dog, sitting wearing tam-o'-shanter. 76mm. — 10.50

Scottie Dog, standing. 90mm long. — 11.50

Pony, standing. 123mm long. — 21.50

Birds

Cockerel. 65mm. — 10.00

Great War

Lady of the Lamp, Florence Nightingale. 1820-1910. — 14.50

Home/Nostalgic

Fireplace, inscribed: *East or West home is best, Home Sweet Home.* Some colouring. 95mm long. — 13.00

Comic/Novelty

Billiken sitting on throne, inscribed: *the God of things as they ought to be.* 100mm. — 7.50

Cartoon/Comedy Characters
*Mr Pussyfoo!, all water!! We don't
think.* 97mm.   40.00

Alcohol
Toby Jug with verse. 88mm.   7.50

Sport
Golf Ball, inscribed: *The ancient
game of golf was first played in
1448.* 48mm.   6.50

Modern Equipment
Box Gramophone with Horn.
100mm.   19.50

Footwear
Clog. 76mm long.   4.50

Miscellaneous
Hand holding tulip. 90mm.   4.00

Miniature Domestic
Cheese Dish and cover. 45mm.   5.50

Syren China

For mark see *Crested China*, p. 255.

Trademark used by Wiltshaw & Robinson
Ltd, Carlton Works, Stoke-on-Trent.
(Usual trademark Carlton).

Birds
Comic Duck on green base.
108mm.   28.00

Sport
Sports Trophy. 132mm.   14.00

Talbot China

For mark see *Crested China*, p. 255.

Trademark used for a retailer by Sampson Hancock (and Sons), Bridge Works, Stoke. (Usual trademark Corona).

Seaside Souvenirs
Bathing Machine. 68mm.	7.50
Lighthouse. 105mm.	5.50

Animals
Fish vase. 60mm.	5.00
Pig, standing. 45mm.	10.00

Home/Nostalgic
Desk Top. 55mm long.	8.25

Musical Instruments
Harp. 95mm.	5.50

Modern Equipment
Gas Cooker. 70mm.	8.50

Miscellaneous
King chess piece. 115mm.	19.50
Queen chess piece. 112mm.	24.50

Taylor and Kent

TAYLOR&KENT
LONGTON
ENGLAND

Mark found on model exported to Australia.
For additional mark see *Crested China*, p.256.

Trademark used by Taylor and Kent (Ltd), Florence Works, Longton. (Usual trademark Florentine).

Buildings — Coloured
Ann Hathaway's Cottage.
4 sizes:	50mm long.	16.50
	70mm long.	16.50
	115mm long.	25.00
	135mm long.	30.00

Shakespeare's House.
2 sizes:	70mm long.	16.50
	115mm long.	25.00

Birds
Swan, posy holder. 81mm.	4.75

Home/Nostalgic
Baby in hip bath. 100mm long.	11.00

Miniature Domestic
Cheese Dish and cover. 70mm long.	5.50

Temple Porcelain

For mark see *Crested China*, p. 256.

Trademark used by an unknown manufacturer. It closely resembles products of the Nautilus Porcelain Co of Glasgow.

Ancient Artefacts
Loving Cup. Three handled.
39mm.	3.00
Puzzle Jug. 70mm.	5.50
Staffordshire Tyg, one handled, not named. 63mm.	2.25

Home/Nostalgic
Bellows.	6.50
Bucket with upright handle. 70mm.	3.50
Coal Scuttle, shell shaped, on two ball feet.	5.50
Cradle. 62mm long.	6.00
Lantern. 67mm.	5.50
Milk Churn and lid. 75mm.	4.75
Half-open Suitcase. 62mm long.	6.50

Alcohol
Carboy.	3.00

Sport
Curling Stone.	13.00

Miniature Domestic
Cheese Dish and cover. 50mm.	5.50

Footwear
Oriental Slipper. 98mm long.	6.50

Thistle China

For mark see *Crested China*, p. 236.

Trademark used for L.M. Mack, Ayr, by Hewitt & Leadbeater, Willow Potteries, Longton. (Usual trademark Willow Art).

Parian/Unglazed
Bust of *Burns*. 150mm (with
Ayr crest).	19.50

Buildings — Coloured
Model of Burns cottage, inscribed: *Robert Burns The Ayrshire Bard was born at Alloway, near Ayr on Jan 25th 1759. He died on 21st July 1796 at Dumfries where he was*
buried. 107mm long.	30.00

Monuments
Burns, statue.
2 sizes: 108mm.	16.50
177mm.	18.50

Great War
Monoplane with fixed prop.
146mm long.	55.00
New field gun with screen and sight groove. 109mm long.	18.50

Home/Nostalgic
Bucket. 76mm.	4.00
Carboy in Basket. 70mm.	3.00

T.M.W. and Co Ltd/ and S Ltd.

For mark see *Crested China*, p. 257.

Trademark used for a wholesaler by an unknown manufacturer.

Historical/Folklore
Mother Shipton. 105mm.   11.00

Traditional/National Souvenirs
Welsh Leek. 55mm.   4.00

Seaside
Yacht in full sail. 117mm.   16.50

Animals
Cat, sitting. 65mm.   10.50
Bulldog with black collar, sitting.
  55mm.   11.25
Scottie Dog, wearing blue, red
  and black glengarry. 60mm.   10.50

Birds
Chick. 65mm.   5.50

Alcohol
Barrel. 33mm.   3.00

Tourist Art China

For mark see *Crested China*, p. 257.

Trademark used for Frank Duncan Ltd, Auckland, New Zealand, by Hewitt & Leadbeater Ltd, Willow Potteries, Longton. (Usual trademark Willow Art).

NB: All models have New
  Zealand crests.

Seaside Souvenirs
Lighthouse. 110mm.   6.00

Birds
Kiwi. 66mm.   40.00

Home/Nostalgic
Wheelbarrow. 110mm long.   12.00

Alcohol
Barrel on stand. No. 35. 58mm.   7.00

Towy China

For mark see *Crested China*, p. 257.

Trademark used for a Welsh retailer by Hewitt and Leadbeater Ltd, Willow Potteries, Longton. (Usual trademark Willow Art).

Traditional/National Souvenirs
Welsh Hat. No. 75. 57mm.   4.75

Tre-Pol-Pen Series

Trademark used for an unknown English manufacturer.

Only one model recorded.

National Souvenirs
Cornish Pasty, inscribed: *Will ye ave a piece of my pasty.*
95mm long.   9.50

Triood

For mark see *Crested China*, p. 259.

Trademark used by Hoods Ltd, International Works, Fenton. Products are identical to the Corona factory.

Buildings — White

Bottle Oven, (Inside of). 81mm.	15.50
Micklegate Bar, York. 110mm.	19.50

Traditional/National Souvenirs

Lancashire Clog.	4.75
Welsh Hat. 49mm.	4.75

Seaside Souvenirs

Lighthouse. 108mm.	5.50

Animals

Collie Dog, sitting.	12.50
Elephant, standing trunk down. 75mm long.	13.00
Rabbit, ears raised. 62mm long.	6.50

Birds

Swan posy holder. 58mm.	4.75

Great War

Airship on base. 130mm long.	20.00
Monoplane with movable prop. 150mm long.	55.00
Battleship. 120mm long.	16.00
Submarine, impressed: *E4*. 104mm long.	16.00
Red Cross Van. 100mm long.	23.00
Tank, with inset steering wheels. 102mm long.	17.50
Field Gun. 130mm.	17.00
Bell Tent, with open flaps.	10.50
Pickelhaube. No. 58. 52mm.	16.00

Home/Nostalgic

Grandfather Clock. 125mm.	10.50
Iron Trivet. 74mm long.	4.00
Jardiniere on stand, fixed. 80mm.	3.00
Writing Slope. 50mm long.	7.50
Cigarette Case. 70mm.	13.00

Musical Instruments

Upright Piano. 62mm.	12.50

Modern Equipment

Gas Cooker. 70mm.	8.50

Footwear

Hob Nail Boot. 70mm long.	5.50
Ladies Shoe. 90mm long.	7.50

Miniature Domestic

Candlestick, round base. 85mm.	3.00
Cheese Dish, one piece. 58mm.	5.50
Cheese Dish and cover. 82mm long.	5.50
Club speciman vase. 72mm.	2.25
Coffee Pot with lid. No. 205. 70mm.	7.50

Tudor Arms China

Tuscan China

For mark see *Crested China*, p. 259.

For mark see *Crested China*, p. 259.

Trademark used by a wholesaler for ware by Hewitt & Leadbeater Ltd, Willow Potteries, Longton, (usual trademark Willow Art), and by Sampson Hancock of Hanley, (usual trademark Corona Pottery).

Trademark used by R.H. and S.L. Plant (Ltd), Tuscan Works, Longton.

Ancient Artefacts
Loving Cup, 3 handled. No. 82. 39mm.	3.00
Nose of Brasenose. 95mm long.	11.00
Roman Lamp. 84mm long.	3.00

Buildings — White
Bottle Oven. 85mm.	15.00
Lloyd George's Home. 102mm long.	40.00

Buildings — White
Newquay Look-Out-House, some colouring. 100mm.	40.00
Tower of Refuge, Isle of Man. 93mm.	30.00

Historical/Folklore
Model of Burns Chair. 88mm.	7.50
Corner seat version.	10.00
Gladiators Helmet. 80mm.	21.50
The Man in the Sun. 100mm.	47.50

Monuments
Peter Pan statue, not named. 140mm.	60.00

Traditional/National Souvenirs
Welsh Hat, with blue ribbon and longest place name around brim. No. 75. 57mm.	7.50

Historical/Folklore
Coronation Chair, ornate. 80mm.	7.50
The Chertsey Abbey or *Curfew Bell*, cast circa 1370. With clapper. on wooden base. 88mm.	26.00

Seaside Souvenirs
Bathing Machine. 65mm.	7.50

Animals
Cat in Boot. 88mm long.	14.50
Black Cat on Boot.	22.50
Bulldog, standing. 125mm long.	15.00
Dog, Alsatian, standing. 82mm.	21.75
Elephant, walking. 52mm.	13.00

National Souvenirs
Welsh Hat. 50mm.	4.75
Can be found with longest place name around brim.	7.50
Welsh Lady jug. 82mm.	20.00

Great War
Tank with trailing wheels. 125mm long.	14.50
Lusitania (as Corona model). 165mm long.	75.00
Submarine, E4. 97mm long.	16.00
Bell Tent with open flaps. 80mm.	10.50
Kit Bag with verse: *Pack up your troubles in your old kit bag*. 74mm.	15.00

Seaside Souvenirs
Lifeboat. 125mm long.	8.25
Lighthouse, not named. 90mm.	4.75
Withernsea Lighthouse, with details. 110mm.	11.00
Crab. 88mm long.	10.50
Seashell. 118mm long.	4.00
Seashell. No. 36. 84mm long.	4.00

Home/Nostalgic
Church Bell, inscribed: *Curfew must not ring tonight*. 70mm.	7.50
Coal Scuttle, helmet shaped. 53mm.	5.50

Countryside
Pine Cone. 75mm.	4.00

Footwear
Boot. 112mm long.	6.50

Animals
Camel with two humps, kneeling. 125mm long.	30.00

Cat, fat and angry with tail in air.
80mm. — 12.50

Cat, Cheshire with one bead eye.
91mm. — 11.00

Cow, said to be Indian, lying
down. 155mm long. — 18.50

Dog, Bulldog. 72mm long. — 10.00

Dog, Hound, running.
200mm long. — 35.00

Dog, Spaniel, sitting. 53mm. — 11.50

Donkey, lying down, yellow bead
eyes. 125mm long. — 30.00

Elephant, sitting and comical,
with yellow bead eyes. 80mm. — 32.00

Fish, curled. 105mm long. — 4.00

Fish, open mouthed with green
glass eyes. 120mm. — 8.25

Hippopotamus, inscribed: *My word
if I catch you bending.* 58mm. — 60.00

Mule. 130mm long. — 30.00

Pig, running, red bead eyes.
87mm. — 25.75

Polar Bear on tree trunk, bead
eyes. 110mm long. — 40.00

Rabbit. — 6.50

Snail. 85mm long. — 13.00

Terrapin. 95mm long. — 10.50

Tortoise/Turtle, standing with
bead eyes. 108mm long. — 30.00

Birds/Eggs

Egg, cracked open and lying on
side. 65mm long. — 5.00

Chicken, plump. 55mm. — 7.50

Swan. 60mm. — 4.75

Great War

E4, Submarine. 118mm long. — 16.00

Kit Bag, with no inscription.
63mm. — 15.00

Bandsman Drum. 33mm. — 5.00

Home/Nostalgic

Anvil. 60mm. — 6.50

Baby, naked, lying on tummy.
105mm long. — 40.00

Bellows. 106mm long. — 7.50

Feeding Bottle. 80mm long. — 8.50

Grandfather Clock, inscribed:
Time for tea 5 o'clock. 128mm. — 10.50

Loaf of Bread. 62mm. — 15.00

Milk Churn and lid. — 3.00

Shaving Mug. No. 180. 57mm. — 5.50

Comic/Novelty

Boy Scout, saluting. 140mm. — 85.00

Girl dressed as clown on square
base. 130mm. — 30.00

Lemon, open top. No. 35.
75mm long. — 6.50

Man in nightshirt and nightcap.
Could be Wee Willie Winkie.
2 sizes: 60mm. — 19.00
90mm. — 21.50
Can be described as a candlesnuffer.

Grotesque man, kneeling, red
bead eyes. No. 156. 55mm. — 30.00

Tomato with green leaves.
60mm dia. — 16.00

Cartoon/Comedy Characters

Snooker or the Kitten Cat, cat sitting
on square base putting on
crown. Can be found coloured
and unglazed. (Daily Sketch
Cartoon Character). 130mm. — 85.00

Alcohol

Carboy. No. 11. 70mm. — 3.00

Transport

Racing Car inscribed *Ash Tray,
Dennis Two Seater, Petrol Consumption Nil* 134mm long. — 125.00

Hats

Ladies decorative heeled shoe.
103mm long. — 7.50

Miscellaneous

Bamboo hat pin holder. 100mm. — 7.50

Bamboo Vase. 100mm. — 3.00

Top Hat matchstriker. 45mm. — 5.50

Miniature Domestic

Cheese Dish and cover. 2 pieces.
50mm. — 7.50

Numbered 'smalls'

No. 5. Vase. 65mm. — 2.25

No. 6. Vase. 60mm. — 2.25

No. 10. Ewer. 70mm. — 2.25

No. 21. Vase. — 2.25

No. 22. Vase. 30mm. — 2.25

No. 24. Jug. 45mm. — 2.25

No. 42. Crinkle top vase. 42mm. — 2.25

No. 57. Ewer. 58mm. — 2.25

No. 58. Ewer.   2.25
No. 59. Vase. 43mm.   2.25
No. 71. Vase. 63mm.   2.25
No. 72. Jug. 63mm.   2.25
No. 89. Vase. 55mm.   2.25
No. 97. Vase. 50mm.   2.25
No. 100. Urn. 65mm.   2.25
No. 101. Ewer.   2.25
No. 110. Jug. 51mm.   2.25

Tuskar Rock China

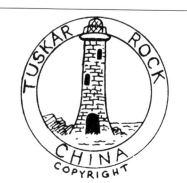

Trademark used for a Wexford retailer by
an unknown manufacturer.

Only one 'small' and the model
below found with a Wexford
crest.

Novelty
Girl with ostrich feathers on her
hat, inscribed: *Harriet*.
Reg No. 448566. 70mm.   95.00

Union Crest China

Trademark by an unknown manufacturer although it does resemble Carlton China.

Historical/Folklore
Model of Ancient Coaching Hat. No. 217.
No details of size.   7.00

Alcohol
Highland Whisky Bowl. 120mm dia. 7.50

Union K

For mark see *Crested China*, p. 261.

Trademark used by the German firm Klösterle (near Carlsbad), the former Gräflich Thun'sche Porzellanfabric.

Domestic ware only. £2.00 upwards.

Unity China

For mark see *Crested China*, p. 261.

Trademark used by the German firm of Max Emanuel and Co, Mitterteich. (Bavaria). (Usual trademark Mosanic).

Birds
Swan posy holder. Flags of Allies and bunting around rim. Central transfer print of *General Joffre* encircled by Flags of Allies and inscribed: *Unity*. 90mm.   22.00

Miniature Domestic
Cheese Dish. 50mm.   7.50

Universal Series

$$\bigcup N I V E R S A L$$
$$\stackrel{\cdot}{\underset{\cdot}{\stackrel{\mid}{\mathbin{\mathchoice{}{}{}{}}}}}$$
$$S E R I E S$$

For mark see *Crested China*, p. 261.

Trademark used by an unknown manufacturer but bears a remarkable resemblance to Porcelle China, which was made for William Ritchie and Son Ltd, 24/26/28 Elder Street, Edinburgh. The porcelain is more cream than white, and reasonbly fine. All pieces found bear Scottish crests.

Great War
Bandsman's Drum. 57mm dia.   6.00

Footwear
Oriental Slipper. 95mm long.   6.50

Vale China

Trademark used by an unknown manufacturer. No example of mark recorded. Only one small recorded with a Southport crest, and the following model with a Woking crest.

Footwear
High heeled ladies shoe.
97mm long.   7.50

Venetia China

For mark see *Crested China*, p. 263.

Trademark used by Charles Waine (and Co), Derby Works, Longton.

Ancient Artefacts
Loving Cup, 3 handles. 40mm.   3.00

Seaside Souvenirs
Lighthouse on rocky base.
114mm.   5.50

Birds
Swan posy bowl. 80mm.   4.75

Home/Nostalgic
Coal Scuttle. No. 35. 80mm.   4.00

Miniature Domestic
Cheese Dish and cover. 55mm.   5.50
Circular Cheese Dish and cover.
71mm dia.   7.50
Tea Pot with lid. 58mm.   7.50

Vectis/Victis Models

For mark see *Crested China*, p. 263.

Trademark used for Nigh, a fancy goods dealer in the Isle of Wight by J.A. Robinson and Sons, subsequently Cauldon Ltd. (Usual trademark Arcadian).

Parian/Unglazed
Osborne House, Isle of Wight.
  140mm long.   82.50
Sleep of Innocence. Osborne House,
  Cowes. I.O.W. Two babies lying
  on a couch. 96mm long.   60.00

Ancient Artefacts
Cadogan Teapot, not named.
  50mm.   11.00

Buildings — Coloured
The Old Village, Shanklin, I.o.W.
  100mm long.   100.00

Buildings — White
Carisbrooke Castle, Isle of Wight.
  80mm long.   87.00
Cottage on rectangular base, no
  inscription. 50mm.   7.50
Old Church, Bonchurch.
  105mm long.   75.00
The Old Village, Shanklin, I.o.W.
  100mm long.   75.00
Osborne House, Cowes, I.O.W.
  48mm.   85.00

Monuments
Arch Rock, Freshwater Bay,
  I.O.W. 80mm.   28.00
Maiwand Memorial Forbury Gardens,
  Reading. 98mm.   14.50

Traditional/National Souvenirs
Donkey in Wheel, donkey coloured,
  Carisbrooke Castle. 90mm.   40.00
Map of Isle of Wight. A coloured
  map standing upright on an
  oval ashtray. 106mm long.   30.00

Seaside Souvenirs
Needles Rock and Lighthouse.
  125mm long.   30.00

Animals
Calf. 100mm long.   14.50
Lion, walking. 145mm long.   19.50

Birds
Brooding Hen. 50mm.   5.00

Victoria Arms China

Trademark used on china produced by Hewitt & Leadbeater Ltd. (Usual trademark Willow Art).

Great War
Tank with trailing wheels,
  inscribed: *Model of British Tank.*
  130mm long. 14.50
Kit Bag, drawn string. 70mm. 15.00
Kitchen range, with pot on fire,
  inscribed: *Keep the home fires
  burning.* Some colouring.
  78mm long. 9.00

Victoria China

For additional marks see *Crested China*, p. 263-4.

Trademark was thought to have been used on crested wares by James Reeves, Victoria Works, Fenton. However, it is possible that J.R. & Co was a china wholesaler who purchased ranges from major firms. Wares look like the produce of J.A. Robinson (usual mark Arcadian). Taylor & Kent (usual mark Florentine) and Sampson Hancock (usual mark Corona).

Ancient Artefacts
Carlisle Salt Pot. 70mm. 2.25
Chester Roman Vase, named.
  58mm. 3.00
Fountains Abbey Cup. 50mm. 2.25
Puzzle Jug. 67mm. 5.50
Tyg. 1 handle. 70mm. 2.25

Buildings — White
Blackpool Tower, with buildings.
  142mm. 9.50
Bottle Oven. 82mm. 15.50

Old Pete's Cottage, I.o.M.
75mm long. 30.00

Monuments (including Crosses)
Iona Cross. 108mm. 5.50
Wallace Tower, Stirling.
120mm. 40.00

Historical/Folklore
Man in Pillory. 101mm. 17.00
Miner's Lamp. 84mm. 14.00
Mother Shipton. 70mm. 13.00
Suffragette handbell. 72mm. 21.50

Traditional/National Souvenirs
Blackpool Ferris Wheel. 108mm. 10.50
Laxey Wheel. Isle of Man. 95mm. 40.00
Legs of Man, inside life belt.
90mm. 16.00
Ripon Horn. 90mm. 12.00
Ripon Hornblower. 90mm. 12.00
Bust of Scotsman wearing tam-
o'shanter and plaid. 63mm. 22.50
Welsh Bardic Chair. 86mm.
(identical to Old Arm Chair.) 19.50
Welsh Harp. 90mm. 7.50
Welsh Hat with thin blue ribbon
band. 48mm and 58mm. 4.75
Welsh Hat, two different moulds
one with twisted cord band,
and the other with blue band
with gold tassels. Can be found
with Llanfair. . .etc. around
brim. 62mm. 4.75
Inscribed 7.50

Seaside Souvenirs
Baby seated on rock. 109mm. 16.00
Bathing Machine. 65mm long. 6.50
Yacht in full sail. 126mm. 10.50
Canoe. 102mm long. 5.50
Houseboat, rectangular.
90mm long. 9.00
Fisherman, bust. 87mm. 19.50
Fisherwoman, bust. 87mm. 19.50
Lighthouse. 97mm. 5.50
Lighthouse, unnamed
Flamborough. 110mm. 8.00
Whelk Shell, inscribed: Listen to
the sea. 95mm long. 3.00
Gladstone Bag. 45mm. 7.50
Portmanteau. 55mm. 4.00

Countryside
Acorn on plinth, pepper pot.
75mm. 6.00

Animals
Cat, with long neck. 115mm. 6.50
Cat, The Cheshire. Inscribed:
Always smiling. 80mm. 6.50
Cat, Manx. 80mm long. 16.00
Bulldog in kennel. 70mm long. 8.00
Dog, King Charles Spaniel in
cradle. 90mm long. 10.50
Dog, King Charles Spaniel,
begging on cushion. 70mm. 8.25
Dogs, two King Charles Spaniels
in Top Hat. 70mm. 16.00
Puppy sitting. 88mm. 9.50
Donkey, walking. 92mm long. 22.00
Elephant, kneeling. 80mm long. 15.00
Fish, inscribed: Caught at. . .
102mm long. 5.50
Frog cream jug. 75mm. 5.50
Hare, ears down. 77mm long. 9.50
Monkey, crouching, hands to
mouth. 88mm. 13.00
Pig, kneeling. 70mm long. 8.25
Pig, standing. 88mm long. 10.00
Rabbit with upright ears.
70mm long. 6.50
Rabbit, 98mm long. 12.50
Seal with ball. 73mm. 16.00
Teddy Bear, sitting. 98mm. 9.50
Toad. 39mm. 10.50

Birds
Canary on rock. 100mm. 9.50
Chick hatching from egg.
65mm long. 5.50
Hen, roosting. 92mm long. 5.50
Kingfisher cream jug. 58mm. 5.50
Kingfisher, with long beak.
80mm. 21.50
Owl.
2 sizes: 70mm. 10.50
100mm. 12.50
Parrot. 76mm. 10.50
Pelican jug. 63mm. 5.50
Swan.
2 sizes: 70mm. 6.50
90mm long. 6.50
Swan posy bowl. 80mm long. 4.75

Great War
Bust of Sailor. 90mm. 30.00
Airship on base. 128mm long. 20.00
Zeppelin. 132mm long. 20.00
Monoplane with roundels and
4-bladed movable prop.
170mm long. 75.00

Battleship. 120mm long.	16.00
Lusitania, 165mm long.	75.00
Torpedo Boat Destroyer. 110mm long.	19.50
Submarine, inscribed *E4*.	16.00
Submarine, inscribed *E9*. 147mm long.	16.00
Armoured Car (Arcadian). 94mm long.	30.00
Red Cross Van. 102mm long.	23.00
Red Cross Van, with painted not moulded crosses. 90mm long.	23.00
Renault Tank. 82mm long.	65.00
Tank, with inset steering wheels. 100mm long.	15.00
Tank, with large side turrets. 120mm long.	21.00
Field Gun. 127mm long.	17.00
Trench Mortar. 65mm.	10.50
Torpedo, fixed prop. 155mm long.	47.50
Mills Hand Grenade, not named. Rd No. 657211. 60mm.	13.00
Capstan. 55mm.	9.50
Colonial Soldier's Hat. 73mm long.	10.50
Drum. 38mm.	5.00
Field Glasses. 80mm long.	13.00
Ghurka Knife. 143mm long.	20.00
Grandfather Clock, usual model but with clock transfer at 3.25. With inscription: *World War 1914-1919. Peace signed 3.25pm June 28 1919.* 110mm.	56.50
Bell Tent, hexagonal, open flat. 89mm.	10.50
Kit Bag, open. 70mm.	13.00
Sandbag. 74mm long.	13.00
Water Bottle. 64mm.	13.00
Cenotaph. 135mm.	5.50
Florence Nightingale statue. 148mm.	16.00
Matlock Bath War Memorial. 178mm.	22.00
Ripon War Memorial. 118mm.	75.00

Home/Nostalgic

Baby in bath. 100mm long.	11.00
Broom Head. 105mm long.	15.25
Cradle. 80mm long.	6.00
Garden Roller. 85mm long.	7.50
Girl in Bonnet, salt pot. 93mm.	10.00
Lamp. 70mm.	4.75
Lantern. 86mm.	5.50
Milk Churn and lid. 70mm.	3.00
The Old Armchair, with inscription. 83mm.	7.50
Pillar Box, inscribed: *I cant get a letter from you, so send you the box.* 70mm.	10.00
Sundial on large square base, inscribed: *Tempus fugit.* 109mm.	10.50
Shaving Mug. 30mm.	5.50
Tobacco Pouch. 72mm long.	9.50
Watering Can. 70mm.	5.50

Comic/Novelty

Boy's face, smiling on cream jug. 73mm.	9.50
Boy on Scooter. 106mm.	16.00
Hair brush Trinket Box. 140mm long.	14.00
Jack in the Box. 95mm.	16.00
Pierrot playing banjo, some colouring. 120mm.	30.00
Screw, inscribed: *You could do with a big fat screw (wage rise).* 76mm.	20.00
Suffragette Handbell, two sided. One side ugly old lady, inscribed: *Votes for women.* Reverse, a pretty young girl, inscribed: *This one shall have a vote.* 108mm.	25.00

Cartoon/Comedy Characters

Ally Sloper bust, not named. 83mm.	19.50
Harry Lauder, bust. 63mm.	17.00

Alcohol

Champagne Bottle in ice bucket inscribed: *Something good — a bottle of the boy.* 83mm.	7.50
Whisky Bottle.	7.50

Sport

Cricket Bag. 115mm long.	9.00

Musical Instruments

Banjo. 137mm long.	8.50
Grand Piano, with closed lid. 80mm long.	14.50
Upright Piano. 63mm.	12.50
Tambourine. 68mm dia.	5.50

Transport

Charabanc, with driver. 115mm long.	33.00

Motor Horn, inscribed: *Pip Pip.*
90mm long. 22.50
Saloon Car. 80mm long. 30.00

Modern Equipment
Cash Register. 47mm. 16.00
Gramophone, square without
horn. 58mm. 15.25
Radio Horn. 95mm. 18.00

Footwear
Ladies 18th Century Shoe.
92mm long. 7.50
Oriental Shoe with pointed
turned-up toe. 95mm long. 4.00

Miscellaneous
Carboy. 72mm. 3.00
Chess Pawn. 60mm. 19.00
Lily Vase. 115mm. 5.00

Miniature Domestic
Cheese Dish and cover. 50mm. 5.50
Coffee Pot with lid. 69mm. 7.50
Cup and Saucer, diamond shaped.
50mm. 4.50
Tea Pot with lid. 60mm. 7.50
Tea Pot with lid, ball shaped.
75mm. 7.50

Victorian Porcelain

For mark see *Crested China*, p. 265.

Trademark used by Robinson and Leadbeater, Wolfe St, Stoke-on-Trent. (Usual
trademark Robinson & Leadbeater).

Ancient Artefacts
Loving Cup, 2 and 3 handled.
39mm. 3.00
Oxford Jug. 83mm. 3.00
Scarboro Jug, inscribed: *Jug about
600 years old found in ancient moat
Scarboro (sic).* No. 180. 42mm. 3.00

Birds
Swan posy holder, yellow beak &
feet. 75mm long. 5.50

Home/Nostalgic
Bellows. 110mm long. 6.50

Victoria (China)

For additional mark see *Crested China*,
p. 265.

Trademark used by two German manu-
facturers, Schmidt and Co, Carlsbad
(Bohemia), and Moschendorf, Hof,
Bavaria.

Seaside Souvenirs
Yacht, yellow/brown lustre.
No. 2276. 105mm long. 10.50

Birds
Hen, pepper pot, red comb &
beak. 70mm. 7.50
Swan posy bowl. 58mm. 4.75

Home/Nostalgic
Grandmother Clock, lustre.
88mm. 4.50

Footwear
Sabot. 84mm long. 4.75

Miniature Domestic
Cauldron. 58mm. 3.00
Cheese Dish and cover. 30mm. 4.75
Cup and Saucer with lithophane
of Blarney Castle. 60mm. 32.00
German Beer Mug. 50mm. 4.00

Vignaud

FRANCE
VIGNAUD
LIMOGES

Trademark used by a French china manufacturer, Vignaud, Limoges, France for the French souvenir market.

Only 60mm vase with a Paris crest recorded. 4.00.

W

For mark see *Crested China*, p. 267.

Trademark used by H.M. Williams and Sons, Bridge Pottery, Longton.

Ancient Artefacts
Loving Cup, 3 handles. 55mm.	3.00
Salisbury Kettle. 102mm.	3.00

Seaside Souvenirs
Portmanteau. 80mm long.	4.00

Animals
Cat, long necked. 112mm.	7.50
Cat, Manx. 60mm.	16.00
Frog cream jug. 60mm.	5.50
Pig, standing. 100mm long.	10.00
Rabbit, sitting. 86mm.	6.50
Seal.	13.00

Birds
Kingfisher cream jug. 58mm.	5.50
Swan posy bowl. 80mm long.	4.75

Home/Nostalgic
Oil Lamp. 58mm.	4.00
Policeman's Lamp. 71mm.	5.50
Shaving Mug. 55mm.	5.50
Watering Can. 55mm.	5.50

Sport
Cricket Bag. 110mm long.	8.50

Footwear
Ladies Shoe with high heel. 90mm long.	7.50

W & Sons

Warwick China

For mark see *Crested China*, p. 267.

W & Sons,
"MIKADO"
WARE
RᴰNo 438118

Trademark used for W.H. Smith and Sons by Arkinstall and Son Ltd, Arcadian Works, Stoke-on-Trent. (Usual trademark Arcadian).

Ancient Artefacts

Ancient Tyg, model of. 70mm.	3.00
Cambridge Roman Jug. 58mm.	3.00
Canterbury Roman Urn, inscribed: *Roman Urn found near Canterbury, original in Canterbury Museum.* 70mm.	3.00
Chester Roman Vase. 60mm.	3.00
Egyptian Vase, about 230BC. 41mm.	3.00
Lincoln Jack, from original in Museum. 62mm.	3.00
Newbury Leather Bottle. 65mm.	3.00
Winchelsea Roman Cup, inscribed: *Roman cup found near Winchelsea.* 51mm.	3.00

The only piece known is a ewer with pale green trim and handle displaying colour transfers of Japanese scenes. This is remarkably similar to a series of vases (unmarked) with a sprig of holly and crest of Carpe: Diem. The manufacturer is unknown, but a similar quality porcelain was produced by Albion China (Taylor and Kent Ltd), Florence Works, Longton, usual trademark Florentine. Albion also produced ware with green trim instead of gilding.

Buildings — White

Rowton Tower, with inscription: *King Charles I stood on this tower Sept 24th 1645 and saw his army defeated on Rowton Moor.* 105mm.	35.00

Historical/Folklore

Yorick's Skull, inscribed: *Alas poor Yorick.* 57mm.	10.50

Wade

Traditional/National Souvenirs

Prime Cheddar Cheese, with slice out. 60mm.	5.50

No details of mark available except that mark incorporates 'Wades'.

Seaside Souvenirs

Fishing Basket, inscribed: *A good catch.* 70mm long.	5.50
Lighthouse. 148mm.	7.50

Trademark used by Wade & Co, Union Pottery, Burslem, subsequently Wade, Heath & Co. (Ltd).

Animals

Dog, Collie. 95mm.	12.50
Otter, holding fish in mouth. 120mm long.	47.50

A small range of earthenware domestic wares was produced.
£2.00 upwards

Polar Bear. 96mm.	40.00
Pony, Shetland. 105mm long.	25.00
Teddy Bear, sitting. 90mm.	10.50

Birds

Chick breaking out of egg.	
63mm long.	5.50
Hen, roosting. 54mm.	5.00
Egg shaped salt pot, inscribed: *s*	
56mm.	4.00
Egg shaped pepper pot,	
inscribed: *p.* 56mm.	4.00

Great War

British Airship on stand.	
128mm long.	20.00
Red Cross Van, red cross on each	
side and rear. *'EH 139'* inscribed	
on radiator. 85mm long.	23.00
Field Glasses. 78mm long.	13.00
Bell Tent with open flap inscribed:	
Camping Out 65mm.	14.50

Home/Nostalgic

Grandfather Clock. 113mm.	10.50
Sundial on square base.	5.50
Three-legged stool. 42mm.	5.50

Alcohol

Highland Whisky Bowl. 90mm dia.	4.00

Sport

Cricket Bag. 80mm long.	8.50

Musical Instruments

Banjo. 155mm long.	9.50

Miscellaneous

Rook chess piece. 55mm.	4.00

Miniature Domestic

Cheese Dish and cover. 50mm.	5.50

Domestic Wares

Pair—salt and pepper pots, oct-	
agonal. Inscribed: *Salt* and	
Pepper. 88mm.	4.75

Waterfall Heraldic China

For mark see *Crested China,* p. 268.

Trademark used for a Northern wholesaler by Hewitt and Leadbeater, Willow Potteries, Longton. (Usual trademark Willow Art).

Ancient Artefacts

Lincoln Jack, not named. No. 44.	
60mm.	2.25
Portland Vase, not named. 53mm.	2.25

Buildings — White

Grimsby Hydraulic Tower. 165mm.	21.75

Monuments (including Crosses)

Hull Fishermans Memorial, with	
inscription.	
2 sizes: 135mm.	16.00
160mm.	19.00
Hull South African War	
Memorial, with inscription.	
165mm.	22.00
Kilnsea Cross, Hedon with	
inscription: *Erected at*	
Ravenspurne 1339 by King Henry	
IV. Re-erected at Hedon. 134mm.	56.50
Rufus Stone with inscription.	
110mm.	5.50
The Monument, Laceby, with	
inscriptions. 154mm.	24.75
Sir William de la Pole, Statue of,	
with long inscription. 160mm.	27.50
Charles Henry Wilson, First Baron	
Nunburnholme, statue, inscribed	
on front: *The largest private ship-*	
owner in the world. Born 1833.	
Died 1907. 32 years a member	
of parliament for Hull and a great	
benefactor to the city. Erected by	
public subscription, in the year	
AD 1912. 154mm.	55.00

Historical/Folklore

James V Chair, Stirling Castle,	
Model of. No. 200. 100mm.	7.50
Mary Queen of Scots Chair. 82mm.	6.50
Skull. 60mm long.	7.50

Traditional/National Souvenirs
Bagpipes, with turquoise ribbon.
   118mm long.   15.00
Welsh Hat. 53mm.   4.75

Seaside Souvenirs
Grimsby fisherman, bust. 83mm.   19.50
Lifeboatman, bust, inscribed:
   Hull Fisherman. 83mm.   19.50
Lighthouse, not named. 115mm.   4.75
Spurn Lighthouse, with
   inscription. 130mm.   19.50
Withernsea Lighthouse, with
   inscription. 105mm & 130mm.   13.00

Animals
Cat, Cheshire, inscribed: *Still smiling.*
   95mm.   7.50
Cat, sitting. No. 62. 75mm.   10.50
Cat with arched back. 65mm.   11.00
Black Cat on Boot. 90mm long.   19.50
Dog, Bull Terrier, standing.
   60mm.   10.00
Elephant, walking. 52mm.   13.00
Fish with open mouth.
   103mm long.   3.00
Lion, walking. 120mm long.   14.50
Teddy Bear, sitting. 76mm.   8.50

Great War
Monoplane, with revolving
   prop. 150mm long.   55.00
Battleship, impressed: *HMS
   Lion.* 140mm long.   22.50
Submarine impressed : *E4.*
   116mm long.   16.00
Submarine *E5.* 124mm long.   16.00
Red Cross Van. Red cross on
   side. 84mm long.   23.00
British Tank, Model of.
   92mm long.   13.00
British Tank, Model of with
   trailing wheels. 130mm long.   14.50
Field Gun. 120mm long.   17.00
Field Gun, with screen.
   115mm long.   18.50
Howitzer. 115mm long.   16.00
Glengarry, some colouring.
   83mm long.   16.00
Trench Lamp. 70mm.   10.50
Fireplace with cooking pot,
   inscribed: *Keep the Home Fires. . .*
   No. 199. 80mm long.   9.00

Home/Nostalgic
Grandfather Clock. 125mm.   10.50
Milk Can with lid. 60mm.   4.75
Watering Can. 75mm.   5.50

Comic/Novelty
Billiken, not named. 73mm.   4.00
Dutch Boy. 80mm.   12.50
Horses Hoof. 60mm long.   3.50

Alcohol
Beer Barrel on stand. 58mm.   5.50

Sport
Cricket Bat. 115mm long.   30.00

Footwear
Ladies Shoe with blue bow.
   114mm long.   13.00
Slipper Wall Pocket.
   152mm long.   7.50

Hats
Mortar Board. 65mm long.   20.00

Miniature Domestic
Cheese Dish and cover, circular.
   45mm.   7.50

Waterloo Ware

Trademark probably used by a retailer for items thought to be produced by Sampson, Hancock & Sons, Stoke. (Usual trademark Corona).

Buildings — White
Bottle Oven, inside of. 84mm.   15.50

Great War
Gurkha Knife. 135mm long.   20.00

Waverley China

For additional mark see *Crested China,* p. 269.

Trademark used for Wyman & Sons Ltd, by Arkinstall & Son, Ltd, Arcadian Works, Stoke-on-Trent. (Usual trademark Arcadian).

Alternative factory mark used for an agent in Glasgow

Ancient Artefacts
Dorothy Vase, Model of. bagware
   vase. No. 100. 48mm.   7.50
Glastonbury Bronze Bowl.
   2 models.
   No. 74. 40mm. No. 100. 41mm.   3.00
Hastings Kettle. No. 237. 62mm.   3.00
St. Davids Vase, inscribed: *Vase*
   found at St. Davids. 69mm.   3.00

WCG

Trademark used by an unknown manufacturer.

Domestic ware only.   2.00-5.00

Wedgwood

For mark see *Crested China*, p. 269.

Trademark used by Josiah Wedgwood (and Sons Ltd), Etruria.

The famous firm of Wedgwood made a few small vases with crests at the turn of the century.   10.00

There is also a series of small vases with gold ramshead handles with coloured transfers of soldiers. The regiments are named on the back of the vases. 60mm.   from 20.00

Wembley China

For mark see *Crested China*, p. 269.

Trademark used on china for sale at the British Empire Exhibition of 1924 and 1925 by the Cauldon Group of Companies. (Usual trademark Arcadian). All pieces therefore carry B.E.E. crests and are priced accordingly.

Parian/Unglazed
George V statue on glazed plinth inscribed: *A souvenir from Wembley*, with inscription: *King George V — Born June 3rd 1865 — Ascended the throne May 6th 1910.*
2 sizes: 125mm & 140mm.   45.00
Prince of Wales, (Edward VIII) bust on glazed plinth, with inscription: *HRH The Prince of Wales, Born June 23rd 1894.* 135mm.   65.00

Buildings — White
Cottage on base. 92mm long.   9.00

Historical/Folklore
Miner's Lamp. 70mm.   19.00
Mother Shipton. 115mm.   14.50
Man in Stocks. 88mm.   22.00

Traditional/National Souvenirs
Thistle Vase. 70mm.   5.50
Welsh Hat. 52mm.   7.50
Welsh Tea Party. 98mm.   43.50

Seaside Souvenirs
Bathing Machine. 65mm.   9.00
Yacht. 125mm.   16.00
Trawler with sails set on both masts. 125mm long.   21.50
Lighthouse, not named.
2 sizes: 110mm.   8.25
140mm.   8.25

Countryside
Beehive on table. 78mm.   10.00
Haystack, circular. 55m.   7.50

Animals
Cat with long neck, sitting. 108mm.   10.50

Black Cat, sitting on armchair.
55mm.   25.75
Fawn. 50mm.   34.50
Frog, with open mouth. 62mm.   8.25
Monkey sitting. 69mm.   17.00
Pig, sitting and smiling.
63mm long.   11.25

Birds
Cock, red comb and yellow
beak. 90mm.   16.50

Great War
Nurse and Wounded Tommy.
108mm long.   87.50
Sailor winding capstan, Model of.
105mm.   85.00
Soldier Bust, unnamed Tommy
Atkins. Some colouring. 90mm.   30.00
Biplane, in lustre. 120mm long.   82.50
Observer or Sausage Balloon.
82mm.   47.50
Armoured Car, model of.
95mm long.   32.00
Red Cross Van. 90mm long.   24.50
Tank, Model of. 115mm long.   17.00
Trench dagger. 105mm long.   43.00
Capstan. 56mm.   12.50
Pair of Field Glasses, Model of.
78mm long.   17.00
Colonial Hat. 86mm long.   12.50
Officer's Peaked Cap. 65mm dia.   11.50
Cavell Memorial, inscribed: *Nurse
Cavell.* 160mm.   25.00

Home/Nostalgic
Fireplace, no inscription but
much colouring. 90mm.   13.00
Grandfather Clock. 108mm.   13.00
Kennel. 50mm.   8.25
Lantern, horn. 85mm.   7.00

Comic/Novelty
Billiken. 60mm.   6.00
Hand holding Pig's trotter.
110mm long.   10.50
Policeman on duty. 145mm.   28.50

Sport
Curling Stone. 49mm.   18.00

Transport
Car, open tourer, (2 seater).
110mm long.   33.00

Hats
Boy Scout's Hat. 73mm dia.   19.50

Miscellaneous
Bishop chess piece. 72mm.   19.50

White Horse China

Trademark used for the Royal Mail Steam Packet Company by an unknown manufacturer, but closely resembling Carlton China.

Some pieces display transfer prints of ships.

Historical/Folklore
Coaching Hat, not named.
No. 124. 39mm.   12.50
*Carlisle Ancient Stone Roman
Altar, Model of.* 122mm.
(Bears the arms of Reading.)   30.00

The White House

For mark see *Crested China*, p. 270.

Trademark used for a Manchester retailer by an unknown manufacturer.

One small recorded. 4.00

Animals
Upright Cat playing flute. 70mm. 25.00

W.H.H. and S

For mark see *Crested China*, p. 270.

Trademark used by a German manufacturer, Wilhelm Kutzscher & Co. Schwarzenberger Porzellanfabrik, Schwarzenberg, Saxony (now in East Germany), for an outlet in south-west England.

Buildings — White
Clock Tower, not named. 125mm. 7.50

Monuments
Sir Frances Drake, statue.
Plymouth. 163mm. 13.00
Plymouth Armada Memorial.
175mm. 30.00

Animals
Dog, Spaniel, sitting. 60mm. 7.50
Elephants, two on a sledge on
slope. 76mm. 30.00

Birds
Duck posy bowl, yellow beak.
83mm long. 7.50

Great War
Plymouth War Memorial. 175mm. 30.00

Sport
Cricket Cap. 70mm long. 21.50

Miniature Domestic
Cheese Dish and cover.
76mm long. 5.50

Wilco Series

For mark see *Crested China*, p. 270.

Trademark used for a retailer probably by Hewitt and Leadbeater. Willow Potteries. Longton. (Usual trademark Willow Art).

Animals
Rabbit, crouching with alert ears.
No. 97. 60mm long.   6.50

Miniature Domestic
Cheese Dish and cover. 50mm.   6.50

Williamsons

For mark see *Crested China*, p. 293.

Trademark used by H.M. Williamson and Sons, Bridge Pottery, Longton.

A range of crested domestic ware.

Ancient Artefacts
Guernsey Milk Can, with lid.
105mm. (Found with a
Guernsey crest).   7.50

Willow Art and Willow China

For mark see *Crested China*, p. 271.

Trademark used by Hewitt and Leadbeater, Willow Potteries, Longton, subsequently, Hewitt Bros, and eventually Willow Potteries Ltd, a branch of Cauldon Ltd.

Models can be found marked Willow or Willow Art.

Parian/Unglazed
All the busts can be found impressed H. and L. (Hewitt and Leadbeater).

Busts

Bust of Albert King of the Belgians, not named, on square glazed base. 170mm.	65.00
Bust of French, not named, on square glazed base. 170mm.	47.50
Bust of Burns impressed: *Burns* and impressed on the reverse *H. Bros* on square unglazed base with a crest. 150mm.	24.00
Bust of Burns, not named, on circular glazed base. 140mm.	20.00
Bust of Sir Walter Scott, not named, on circular glazed base. 130mm.	17.50
Bust of Gladstone, not named, on circular glazed base. Can be found with crest of W.E. Gladstone on glazed base when £5 should be added. 160mm.	30.00
Bust of Shakespeare, on circular base. 120mm.	17.50
Bust of *Grace Darling*. 152mm.	28.00

Ancient Artefacts

Beccles Ringers Jug, with full inscription. 67mm.	15.00
Chester Roman vase, not named. 55mm.	2.25
Lincoln Jack, not named. 53mm.	2.25
Loving Cup. 2 and 3 handled.	3.00
Persian Wine Server, not named. 105mm.	3.00
Phoenician Water Jug, not named. 66mm.	3.00
Puzzle Jug with verse: *Try how to drink*. 70mm.	5.50

Buildings — Coloured
Coloured buildings can be found glazed or unglazed. Some of these models can also be found white.

Ann Hathaway's Cottage.	
3 sizes: 50mm long.	16.00
60mm long.	16.00
105mm long.	30.00
Battle Abbey Gateway.	
139mm long.	60.00
Bell Hotel, Abel Fletcher's House in John Halifax Gentlemen.	
3 sizes: 55mm.	40.00
84mm.	55.00
124mm.	65.00
John Bunyan's Cottage.	
75mm long.	65.00
Burns Cottage, Model of.	
105mm long.	30.00
Burns House, inscribed: *The poet occupied this house from 1793 until his death 21st July 1796.* 85mm.	40.00
Cat and Fiddle. 92mm.	125.00
Feathers Hotel, Ludlow.	110.00
Godalming Old Town Hall. 100mm.	110.00
Harlech Castle. 200mm long.	150.00
Knox's House, inscribed: *Model of the house in Edinburgh where John Knox the Scottish reformer died 24th Nov 1572.* 102mm.	110.00
Leycester Hospital. 157mm long.	160.00
Mason Croft, The House of Miss Marie Carelli. 90mm long.	110.00
Old Blacksmiths shop and marriage room, Gretna Green. 85mm long.	30.00
Old Chapel, Lantern Hill, Ilfracombe. 76mm long.	60.00
Old Curiosity Shop. No. 14, Portsmouth Street. 80mm long.	65.00
Old Maids Cottage, Lee near Ilfracombe. 59mm long.	47.50
Old Ostrich Inn, Colnbrook. 80mm.	115.00

Historical, Old Mint House,
Pevensey 1342 AD. 120mm long.   130.00
The Olde Trip to Jerusalem Inn,
1199 AD, inscribed: *Home*
Brewed Ales. 106mm long.   150.00
St. Bernards Monastery, Coalville.
102mm long.   110.00
St. Ann's Well, Gt. Malvern.
167mm long.   120.00
St. Nicholas Church, Great
Yarmouth. 140mm long. Also
found unglazed.   115.00
Shakespeare's House.
6 sizes: 52mm long.   16.00
         65mm long.   16.00
     110mm long.   30.00
     125mm long.   30.00
     135mm long.   30.00
     157mm long.   35.00
     210mm long.   40.00
Stokesay Castle Gate House.
100mm.   130.00
Tan House, Little Stretton.
120mm long.   125.00
Upleatham Church. 90mm.   95.00
Whittington Inn, with inscription.
100mm long.   100.00
Wilberforce Museum with
inscription. Coloured grey.
115mm long.   95.00

Buildings — White
Bath Abbey, West Front. 110mm.   25.00
Bell Hotel, Abel Fletchers House in
John Halifax Gentleman. 2 sizes:
84mm & 124mm long.   40.00
Bell Hotel, Abel Fletchers House in
John Halifax Gentleman, on
ashtray base. Some colouring.
75mm long.   36.50
Big Ben. 146mm.   17.00
Blackpool Tower. 125mm.   13.00
Blackpool Tower, with buildings.
150mm.   14.00
Blackpool Tower, with buildings,
impressed: *Variety, Dancing,*
Concert. 165mm.   20.50
Bourne Abbey, West Front. 108mm.   30.00
John Bunyan's Cottage, Model of.
75mm long.   22.00
Burns Cottage, Model of, with
inscription. 105mm long.   16.00
Burns Mausoleum, Dumfries.
95mm.   50.00

Bury St. Edmunds, Abbey Gate.
80mm.   57.50
Canterbury Cathedral, West Front.
125mm.   40.00
Canterbury, West Gate. 90mm.   26.00
Carillon Tower. 159mm.   60.00
Carnegie's Birthplace, inscribed:
The birthplace of Andrew
Carnegie. 85mm long.   40.00
Castle Hill Tower, Huddersfield.
115mm.   40.00
Chantry Front, Model of.
95mm long.   35.00
Chatham, Town Hall, Model of.
146mm.   65.00
Chesterfield Parish Church, Model
of, found with inscription.
125mm.   40.00
Citadel Gateway, Plymouth.
110mm.   28.00
Clifton Suspension Bridge, Model
of, with long inscription.
120mm long.   40.00
Conisborough Castle, The Keep.
95mm.   75.00
Cottage, inscribed: *Built in a day*
4th June 1819. 43mm long.   26.00
Crofter's Cottage. 55mm long.   30.00
Fair Maids House, Perth.
78mm long.   50.00
First and Last House in England.
83mm long. With green door.   16.00
First and Last House in England,
with annexe. 95mm long.   40.00
Gretna Green Marriage Room.
60mm long.   20.00
Grimsby Hydraulic Tower.
165mm.   23.00
Hampton Court Palace, flat frontage
on ashtray base. 108mm long.   30.00
Hamsfell Hospice, Grange over
Sands. (Often found not
named). 72mm.
An odd square building with
outside stairs and flat roof,
and with impressed Greek
inscription over door.   28.00
Hastings Castle Ruins. 100mm.   22.00
Hastings Clock Tower. 165mm.   16.00
Hay Castle. 94mm.   47.50
Hop Pole Inn, flat frontage on
ashtray base, with long
quotation referring to the inn
from Chapter 50 'The Pickwick

Papers' by Charles Dickens, on
ashtray. 60mm long.   50.00
King Charles Tower, Chester.
100mm.   35.00
Knox's House, with inscription
110mm.   40.00
Lancaster, Castle Gateway.
90mm.   32.00
Leicester Clock Tower. 175mm.   22.00
Lincoln Cathedral, West Front.
100mm and 118mm.   22.00
Lincoln, Stonebow. 104mm long.   22.50
Lloyd George's Home, inscribed.
102mm long.   47.50
Loch Leven Castle, Kinross. 75mm.   65.00
Old London Bridge on ashtray base,
small. 105mm long.   25.00
The Marble Arch. Unglazed.
98mm long.   16.00
Mickelgate Bar, York. 116mm.   24.00
Monnow Bridge, Monmouth.
92mm.   30.00
Monument, The. 160mm.   60.00
Morpeth Castle, Model of. 78mm.   56.50
Nottingham Castle, Model of.
92mm long.   37.50
Old Bridge House, Ambleside.
88mm.   56.50
*Old Nottingham Inn. Ye Olde Trip
to Jerusalem, 1199 AD, Model of.*
95mm.   50.00
Old Ostrich Inn, Colnbrook. 80mm.   47.50
Park Tower, Barnsley. 137mm.   45.00
Peterborough Cathedral, West Front.
80mm long.   30.00
Peveril Castle. 115mm long.   55.00
Pump Room, Harrogate. 75mm.   40.00
St. Albans Clock Tower. 120mm.   40.00
St. Ann's Well, Buxton. 120mm.   57.50
St. Ann's Well, Great Malvern.
102mm long.   50.00
St. Benet's Abbey, Norfolk Broads,
castle ruins on ashtray base.
70mm.   47.50
St. Botolph's Church, Boston.
112mm.   45.00
St. Denny's Church, Sleaford.
2 sizes: 95mm & 134mm.   58.50
St. Nicholas' Church,
Great Yarmouth. Unglazed.
143mm long.   50.00
St. Paul's Cathedral. 140mm.   22.50
Saville Fountain, Saville Gardens,
Windsor. No. 730. 140mm.   60.00
Saxon Church, Bradford on Avon.
74mm.   46.50

Shakespeare's House.
2 sizes: 120mm long.   14.00
160mm long.   16.00
Skegness, Clock Tower.
2 sizes: 125mm.   12.50
165mm.   16.00
Skegness, Pier Entrance.
85mm long.   57.00
Solomon's Temple, Grinlow Tower,
inscribed: *Erected on site of a
prehistoric barrow, Buxton.*
88mm.   35.00
Temple Bar, Waltham Cross.
100mm long.   56.50
Tennysons House, Mablethorpe.
85mm long.   70.00
*Tudor Gabled House, Taunton
AD 1800* also *AD 1578.* 100mm.   40.00
Upleatham Church. 88mm.   26.00
*Uttoxeter Market Place, Conduit,
Scene of Dr. Johnson's Penance.*
123mm.   40.00
Wainhouse Tower, Halifax.
130mm.   40.00
Wallingford, Town Hall. 84mm.   55.00
West Malling, Abbey Tower.
94mm.   42.50
Westminster Abbey, West Front.
114mm.   22.50
Whittington Inn, with inscription.
100mm long.   47.50
Wilberforce House, Hull. 86mm.   50.00
Windmill. 85mm.   30.00
Windsor Castle. 125mm long.   28.00
Windsor Castle, Round Tower.
76mm.   18.50
Worcester Cathedral. 144mm long.   40.00
Worksop, Priory Gate House.
88mm.   65.00

Monuments (including Crosses)
Ancient Runic Cross, Bakewell.
110mm.   30.00
*Arwenack Monument, erected by
Martin Killigrew. AD 1787,
Falmouth.* 132mm.   17.50
Ashington Boer War Memorial.
130mm.   40.00
Banbury Cross. 140mm.   30.00
Blackpool Big Wheel.   12.00
The Blackwatch Memorial.
Edinburgh. 127mm. This
monument is in the form of a
Scottish soldier on a square
base and is often not named.   65.00

Bovey Tracey, Old Cross. 140mm.	32.50
Bruce Statue, Stirling. 160mm.	60.00
Burns Statue, on square base. 170mm.	18.50
Burns and Highland Mary. 2 sizes: 117mm.	30.00
130mm.	30.00
Bunyan Statue. 165mm.	19.50
Burmah Cross, Taunton. inscribed: *Burmah 1885-6-7* and *Somerset Light Infantry.* 118mm.	75.00
Burton Statue, inscribed: *Michael Arthur, first Baron Burton.* 128mm.	20.50
Caister-on-Sea Lifeboat Memorial. Moulded in relief: *1903* and *Caister Lifeboat* on lifebelt. 162mm.	19.00
Andrew Carnegie, statue. 150mm.	30.00
Cleethorpes Fisherman's Memorial, with inscription: *Erected by Public Subscription to the memory of George Henry Smith (skipper) and William Richard Leggatt (Third Hand) etc. unveiled August 30th 1908.* 155mm.	24.00
Old Cornish Cross, Model of, 100mm.	17.50
Drake, Statue, Plymouth. 160mm.	13.00
Druids Well, Sutton Park, Sutton Coldfield. 45mm.	30.00
Flodden Cross, inscribed: *Flodden 1513, to the brave of both nations.* 136mm.	20.00
General Sir Redvers Buller's Cross at Crediton, model of. 100mm.	58.00
Gibbet Cross, Hindhead, inscribed: *Post Tenebras Lux In Luce Spes In Obrtu Pax Post Obitum Salus.* 136mm.	10.50
Gladstone Statue, Blackburn. 130mm.	40.00
Hector Macdonald Memorial, Dingwall. 112mm.	55.00
Highland Mary Statue, Dunoon, on plinth. 150mm.	23.50
Huddersfield, Market Cross. 150mm.	30.00
Tom Hughes Monument, Rugby School. 140mm.	30.00
Hull Fisherman's Memorial. 2 sizes: 135mm.	16.00
160mm.	18.00

Hull South African War Memorial, with inscription: *Erected to the memory of the men of Hull who fell in the late South African War.* 165mm.	22.00
Keppels Column 1778. 140mm.	40.00
King George Statue, Kingstown. 135mm.	60.00
Laceby, The Monument. 2 sizes: 120mm.	25.00
150mm.	27.00
Laceby Memorial. 160mm.	27.00
Lord Myton of Holderness. 155mm.	70.00
Lowestoft Fisherman's Memorial. 130mm.	26.00
Maiwand Memorial, Forbury Gardens, Reading. Lion sometimes coloured black or brown, add £5.00. 98mm.	14.50
Margate Lifeboat Memorial. 135mm.	21.50
Margate Surf Boat Monument, with usual lengthy inscription. 130mm.	22.00
Nelson's Column. 160mm.	45.00
Isaac Newton, statue. 165mm.	22.00
Peter Pan, statue. 140mm.	59.50
Queen Victoria's Statue, Blackburn.	35.00
Queen Victoria's Statue, Wakefield. 115mm.	40.00
Queen Victoria's Statue, Windsor. 2 sizes: 65mm.	30.00
160mm.	40.00
Richmond Market Cross. 137mm.	16.00
Rock of Ages, usual verse & inscription. 80mm.	7.50
C.S. Rolls Memorial, inscribed: *Memorial to the late Honourable C.S. Rolls.* 128mm.	30.00
Rufus Stone. 110mm.	5.50
Ruskin Memorial, Friars Crag. 180mm.	21.75
Sailor's Stone, Hindhead. 95mm.	10.50
St. Alban, Statue of. 146mm.	40.00
St. Anne's Lifeboat Memorial. 120mm.	16.00
Saville Fountain, Saville Gardens, Englefield Green. 140mm.	75.00
Saxon Soldier, statue on square base. 125mm.	40.00
Sir William de la Pole, Statue of, with long inscription of its presentation and the history of Sir William. 160mm.	19.50

Scone, The Cross. 142mm.	30.00
Toad Rock, Tunbridge Wells. 83mm.	14.50
Todmorden Memorial (obelisk on 4-sided base). 130mm.	57.50

Historical/Folklore

Archbishops Chair, Canterbury Cathedral. 100mm.	10.50
Inscribed.	12.50
Bangor Abbey Bell, inscribed: Model of the old bell, Bangor Abbey, Co. Down. 85mm.	24.50
Bill Sykes and his dog, standing figure on base. Coloured beige, no crest. Unglazed. 128mm.	40.00
Bishop's Jester, Wells Cathedral. Fully coloured. No crest.	
2 sizes: 110mm.	40.00
125mm.	45.00
Bunyan's Chair, Model of. 90mm.	10.50
Bunyan's Cushion, Model of. 105mm long.	16.00
Burns Chair, Dumfries. 85mm.	7.50
Can be found as corner seat.	10.00
Daniel Lambert, sitting on chair. With long inscription. 118mm.	47.50
Devil looking over Lincoln. 115mm.	19.50
The Ducking Stool, with inscription as Arcadian. 120mm.	85.00
Father Christmas carrying sack of toys. 110mm.	120.00
Font, not named. 2 sizes: 55mm & 87mm.	10.50
Gladiators Helmet. 80mm.	21.50
James V Chair, Stirling Castle. 100mm.	7.50
John Knox Chair, Edinburgh. brown no crest. 122mm.	17.00
Lady Godiva on horseback. 80mm.	26.00
Man in the Moon. 55mm.	19.50
Man in the Sun. 94mm.	47.50
Mary Queen of Scots Chair, Edinburgh Castle, Model of. 75mm.	6.50
Mermaid, seated on rock, combing hair. 105mm.	20.00
Mons Meg, Edinburgh Castle. 130mm long.	12.00
Mother Shipton. 2 sizes: 80mm.	12.00
105mm.	15.00
Peeping Tom, bust. 130mm.	20.00
Ripon Hornblower. 120mm.	12.00

A Rubbing Stone for Asses, a 17th century puzzle printed on a brick wall. 100mm long.	35.00
Shakespeare's Font, no plinth. Inscribed: Model of Font in which Shakespeare was Baptised. 85mm dia. 40mm.	15.25
Shakespeare's Font, on hexagonal plinth. Inscribed: Model of Font in which Shakespeare was Baptised. 128mm.	20.00
Sir Walter Scott's Chair, Abbotsford, Model of. 80mm.	7.50
Skull, can be inscribed: Alas poor Yorick. 60mm long.	7.50
Sundial, Tideswell Church, Model of. 110mm.	14.00
Trusty Servant, with verse on both sides, fully coloured. 132mm.	110.00

Traditional/National Souvenirs

John Bull, standing. 120mm.	30.00
Banbury Cake. 105mm wide.	28.50
Bolton Trotter. 135mm long.	7.50
Blackpool Big Wheel. 2 sizes: 88mm.	10.50
100mm.	12.00
Blackpool Big Wheel, rectangular base. 120mm.	16.00
Cheddar Cheese, slice out. 70mm dia.	5.50
Cornish Pasty. 100mm long.	7.50
Chester Imp, The. 80mm.	30.00
Englishman, bust, wearing black hat. No. 114. 76mm.	21.75
Lancashire Clog, yellow buckle. 88mm long.	4.75
Leaking Boot. Grimsby. Standing figure of young boy holding boot aloft (attached to his hand by string).	65.00
Lincoln Imp. 63mm.	6.50
Lincoln Imp, on pedestal. 102mm.	8.50
Manx Man, John Bull as above but with an extra leg added at rear. Same colouring. 120mm.	75.00
Melton Mowbray Pie with verse. 55mm.	17.00
Reading Biscuit, with verse: Than Reading biscuits there are no finer, Here's a good one reproduced in china. Coloured biscuit. 85mm long.	35.00
Can also be found on stand.	30.00

River Thames Pleasure Punt,
175mm long. 55.00
With coloured cushions add £20
Yarmouth Bloater. 121mm. 6.50
Irish Harp. 105mm. 7.50
Irishman, bust. No. 115. Wearing
Black hat. 78mm. 21.75
Bagpipes. 118mm long. 14.00
Blacksmiths Anvil, Gretna Green,
often found not named, with
inscription. 76mm. 6.50
Jimmy Strength, with inscription:
A well known Border character
whose name was James Stuart a
descendant of the Royal Family of
that name. He was famous for his
age and great strength and died in
his 123rd year. Figure on square
plinth. 114mm. 75.00
Scotsman, bust. No. 116. Wearing
coloured tam-o'shanter. 80mm. 21.75
Scotsman matches holder. Comic
fully coloured figure. Inscribed:
Matches. 90mm. 20.00
Souter Johnny, sitting figure, with
verse. 130mm. 30.00
Coloured. 47.50
Tam-o'shanter, sitting figure, with
verse. 135mm. 30.00
Coloured. 47.50
Thistle vase. 50mm. 3.00
Welsh Hat, Model of, with longest
place name. 52mm. (Arcadian
mould). 6.50
Welsh Hat, can have blue hat
band. Can be found with
longest Welsh place name
printed round brim.
57mm. 4.75
Inscribed: 6.50
Welsh Harp, very delicate.
90mm. 8.25
Welsh Lady, bust, with black hat.
No. 117. 110mm. 20.00
Welsh Leek. 55mm. 3.50
Welsh Tea Party, a figure group,
some colouring. 50mm. 35.00

Seaside Souvenirs
Bathing Machine, inscribed: *A*
morning dip.
2 sizes: 65mm. 7.50
80mm. 9.50

Lifeboat, coloured ropes, if found
inscribed: *A.E. Davies* add
£7.00. 118mm long. 8.25
Motorboat, with driver, at sea.
115mm long. 16.00
Paddlesteamer.
154mm long (rare). 82.50
Rowing Boat on rocks, can be
found insribed: *The City of*
Glasgow, add £8.00. 109mm long. 12.50
Yacht in full sail. 122mm. 10.50
Fisherman's Basket with handle
77mm long. 6.50
Fish Basket without handles.
80mm long. 5.50
A Yarmouth Fish Swill, basket.
40mm. 9.00
Lighthouse, not named. 105mm. 4.75
Lighthouse on rocks with brown
rowing boat. 133mm. 20.00
Beachy Head lighthouse, with black
band. 2 sizes: 100mm & 136mm. 7.50
Flamborough Lighthouse. 110mm. 30.00
North Foreland Lighthouse.
135mm. 25.75
Spurn Lighthouse, with details of
size and power. 125mm. 19.50
Withernsea Lighthouse, with
details of size and power.
110mm and 127mm. 13.00
Crab. 83mm long. 10.50
Oyster Shell posy holder. 89mm. 5.00
Shell menu holder on coral base.
No. 360. 90mm. 9.00
Scallop Shell hatpin holder on
rocky base. 92mm. 7.00
Whelk shell, inscribed: *Listen to*
the sea. 110mm. 3.50
Open bag with four feet. 4.50
Stick of Rock, pink stick with
resort printed (very realistic), so
far *Great Yarmouth* and *Southsea*
have been recorded. Has been
found as a salt and pepper pot.
75mm.
White 35.00
Pink 70.00
Truck of Sand, same model as
truck of coal but with coal
painted yellow, can be
inscribed: *Sand for the kiddies*
from. . . or *A truck of sand*
from. . . 90mm long. 65.00

Countryside

Pinecone. 90mm.	4.00
Treetrunk hat pin holder. 80mm.	10.50

Animals

Boar, standing on rocky base. 102mm long. Two varieties of base may be found.	47.50
Cat, angry, with tail in the air. Blue bow. 80mm long.	12.50
Cat, in boot, blue bow. 88mm long.	14.50
Cat, Cheshire, with coloured face. Inscribed: *Always smiling* or more rarely: *Cheshire Cat, 'still smiling'.* 95mm.	7.50
Cat's head on base. 60mm.	23.00
Cat, sitting, bow round neck. 80mm.	10.00
Cat, sitting, blue or red bow. 60mm.	10.00
Cat, sitting, large red bow, and red and green eyes. 70mm.	13.00
Cat, sitting, detailed thick coat, and tail around paws. Candle-snuffer. 57mm.	13.00
Cat, standing, chubby. 70mm.	10.50
Cat, standing (long back), green eyes and red tongue. 117mm long.	35.00

Black Cats

See *'Crested China'* page 281 for details of Willow Black Cats.	
Black Cat on Cushion. 100mm.	19.50
Black Cat on diamond ashtray, inscribed: *Ashtray and Good Luck.* 120mm long.	18.50
Black Cat on Pouffe, inscribed: *Good luck.* Can be found with red or blue bow. 85mm. Impressed. No. 539. 80mm, 90mm and 95mm.	19.50
Black Cat on pepper pot. 90mm.	19.50

Smaller Arcadian type Black Cats.

Black Cat, playing bagpipes. 60mm.	75.00
Black Cat with bottle. 70mm. (Arc. Mould).	40.00
Black Cat, wearing kilt and sitting on a curling stone.	75.00
Black Cat, playing bagpipes, and wearing kilt, standing on thistle ashtray. 88mm long.	75.00
Black Cat on golf ball. 70mm.	75.00

Black Cat, standing beside thistle vase. 57mm.	56.50
Black Cat, wearing a Welsh hat, standing beside a leek. 67mm.	75.00
Black Cat, climbing into cup, inscribed: *May your cup of Good Luck brim over.* 90mm.	56.50
Cow. 105mm long.	35.00
Deer, sitting.	
2 sizes: 64mm.	30.00
115mm long.	40.00
Dog, Bulldog, sitting, feet moulded separately. Black collar and red mouth. 55mm.	19.50
Dog, Bulldog, sitting, feet integrally moulded. 50mm.	13.00
Dog, Bulldog, black, emerging from kennel, inscribed: *The Black Watch.* 70mm long.	15.25
Dog, Bull Terrier, standing. 60mm.	10.00
Dog, Collie, sitting. 78mm.	12.50
Dog, Collie, standing. 85mm.	12.50
Dog, Dachshund, sitting, long ears and rather comic. 75mm long.	40.00
Dog, Foxhound. 69mm.	20.00
Dog, The Manx three legged, often found not named.	30.00
Inscribed: *Prince Toby Orry.* 70mm.	65.00
Dog, rather like St. Bernard. No. 116. 50mm.	12.00
Dog, Scottie, wearing a glengarry.	
2 sizes: 60mm.	10.50
100mm.	12.50
Dog, Scottie, wearing a tam-o' shanter. 60mm.	10.50
Dog, Scottish Terrier, standing. 90mm long.	12.50
Donkey in harness. No. 294. 110mm long.	24.75
Elephant, large. 104mm long.	18.00
Elephant, with trunk in the air. No. 336. 90mm long.	22.00
Elephant, walking. Can be inscribed: *Baby Jumbo.* No. 113. 52mm. (Coloured add £10).	13.00
Elephant Jug. 70mm.	7.50
Fish Ashtray, in shape of plaice. 78mm long.	6.50
Fish, curved. 75mm long.	4.00
Fish, straight. 130mm long.	3.00
Fish, straight, with open mouth. 115mm long.	3.00
Fox. 100mm.	40.00

Hare. 77mm long.	9.00
Highland Bull, inscribed: *King of the Herd*. 115mm long.	75.00
Kangaroo. 115mm.	75.00
Lion, crouching. Red open mouth. 82mm long.	19.50
Lion, crouching. Red open mouth, on base, roaring at a tiny mouse on a green apple, inscribed: *Much ado about nothing*. 110mm.	55.00
Lion, walking.	
3 sizes: 105mm long.	12.50
115mm long.	12.50
160mm long.	14.50
Lion with mane and 'furry' legs. 164mm long. (Pair with Arcadian Lioness).	16.00
Monkey, holding coconut. 85mm.	17.00
Three Monkeys on diamond shaped ashtray. Monkeys inscribed: *See not evil, speak not evil, hear not evil*. 130mm long.	13.00
Mouse. 62mm long.	16.00
Pig, sitting on haunches can be found inscribed: *You may push* etc. 60mm.	11.00
Pig, standing. Very fat, with double chin. 96mm long.	12.50
Pig, standing fat, ears pointing forward. 82mm long.	10.00
Polar Bear, on hind legs. 96mm.	40.00
Polar Bear, sitting. 83mm.	40.00
Pony, inscribed: *A Native of Shetland*. 108mm long.	23.00
Rabbit, lying down. 54mm long.	6.50
Rabbit, sitting, alert ears. 60mm long.	6.50
Ram, with curly horns. 90mm long.	40.00
Rhinoceros, standing. 87mm long.	56.50
Stag, lying down. 115mm long.	40.00
Teddy Bear, sitting. No. 112. 65mm and 75mm.	11.00
Toad, grotesque. 80mm long.	19.50
Tortoise. 88mm long.	6.50
Tortoise, standing wearing a blue hat/helmet. Rd. No. 70961. 62mm.	30.00
Isn't this Rabbit a Duck: On its base a rabbit, turned on its side, a duck. 75mm.	22.00

Birds (including eggs)

Bird (reputedly a tit). 77mm long.	12.00
Bird on plinth. 103mm.	10.50
Bird posy holder. 104mm long.	6.50
Canary on rock, can be found coloured yellow on green base, 98mm.	
White	13.00
Coloured	26.00
Chicken, very fluffy. No. 325. 65mm.	14.00
Chicken pepper pot. 70mm.	11.00
Chicken, yellow, emerging from egg, inscribed: *Every little helps mother will be pleased*. 50mm.	15.00
Cock. 46mm and 100mm.	14.00
Goose, comical, with long neck, some colouring. 155mm.	33.50
Pelican, with inscription: *A wonderful bird is the pelican, his beak will hold more than his belican*. 75mm.	30.00
Swan, with yellow beak. 60mm.	6.50
Swan, with head on breast. 58mm.	6.50
Swan posy holder.	
2 sizes: 65mm.	4.75
93mm long.	4.75
Turkey. 57mm.	13.00
Wise Owl with verse: *An aged owl sat in an oak* etc.	
2 sizes: 98mm & 115mm.	12.50

Great War

Airman, standing to attention. 140mm.	155.00
Air Force Officer, a hero holding medal. 140mm. Scarce.	220.00
Can rarely be found coloured.	300.00
Nurse, inscribed: *A friend in need*. 130mm.	40.00
Sailor, at attention, inscribed: *Our brave defender*. 130mm.	40.00
Solder, with rifle, inscribed: *Our brave defender*. Almost always found with gun broken off at top. It is still classed as perfect. 132mm.	40.00
Monoplane, with fixed prop. 164mm long.	55.00
Monoplane with revolving prop. no colourings. No. 67. 150mm long.	55.00
Monoplane with revolving prop., coloured roundels on wings, and stripes on tail. 150mm long.	75.00

Aeroplane Propeller.	
150mm long.	21.75
Can be found with RAF crest.	30.00
Airship (Observation Balloon),	
inscribed: *Beta*. 80mm long.	40.00
Battleship. 4 funnels.	
127mm long.	19.00
Battleship, impressed: *HMS*	
Lion. 140mm long.	22.50
A rare variety with black mast	
and red striped funnels has	
been seen.	70.00
Troop Carrier, Liner converted.	
No. 213. 140mm long.	90.00
Can rarely be found inscribed:	
HMS Lion.	115.00
Can also be found with 2	
forward facing guns mounted	
on forward deck (rare).	125.00
Submarine, impressed: *E5*.	
116mm long.	16.00
Submarine, inscribed: *E4*.	
95mm long.	16.00
Red Cross Van, red cross on side.	
84mm long.	23.00
British Tank, Model of. 92mm long.	13.00
Can be found either with side	
guns moulded flat against tank,	
or with side guns standing	
proud protruding from side	
turrets.	
British Tank, Model of. With	
trailing wheels. 130mm long.	14.50
Can be found with a Lincoln	
crest inscribed: *Model of 'British*	
Tank' original of which was made	
in Lincoln.	28.00
Field Gun. 120mm long.	17.00
Field Gun, with screen.	
115mm long.	18.50
Howitzer. 115mm long.	16.00
Cannon Shell. 70mm.	4.00
Bandsman's Drum, with cording.	
60mm.	5.00
Bugle. No. 379.	
2 sizes: 70mm.	12.50
115mm.	16.00
Field Glasses. 83mm.	15.00
Kit Bag with verse: *Pack up your*	
troubles in your old kit bag.	
No. 220. 74mm.	15.00
Forage Cap. 83mm long.	16.00
Glengarry. Some colouring.	
83mm long.	16.00

Officer's Peaked Cap. 70mm dia.	10.00
Officer's Peaked Cap, inscribed	
Souvenir of Canadian Forces 1915	40.00
Pickelhaube (German Spiked	
Helmet). 50mm.	17.50
Tommy's Steel Helmet. 76mm long.	21.00
Tent, cone shaped with open	
flaps on base. 70mm.	10.50
Tommy's Steel Helmet. 76mm long.	21.75
Trench Lamp. 70mm.	10.50
Fireplace, inscribed: *Keep the home*	
fires burning. Some colouring.	
100mm long.	13.00
Kitchen range, with pot on fire,	
inscribed: *Keep the home fires*	
burning. Some colouring.	
78mm long.	9.00
Edith Cavell. Statue, London,	
inscribed: *Brussels dawn Oct 12th*	
1915. Sacrifice, Humanity.	
2 sizes: 110mm.	12.00
150mm.	14.00
Edith Cavell, Nurse. Patriot and	
martyr, memorial Statue.	
Norwich.	
2 sizes: 155mm.	23.00
175mm.	25.00
Cenotaph, inscribed: *The Glorious*	
Dead MCMXIV—MCMXIX with	
green wreaths.	
3 sizes: 70mm.	4.00
145mm.	5.50
184mm.	7.00
Chatham *Naval War Memorial.*	
160mm.	65.00
Coalville War Memorial. 135mm.	95.00
Dumfries War Memorial,	
inscribed: *Black Watch.* 130mm.	65.00
Florence Nightingale Statue, Model	
of. Can be found inscribed:	
Florence Nightingale 1820-1910.	
2 sizes: 120mm.	15.50
160mm.	16.50
Great Yarmouth War Memorial.	
With inscription. 166mm.	21.00
Ilkeston War Memorial, with	
inscription.	125.00
Langholm War Memorial. 180mm.	130.00
Loughborough War Memorial.	
155mm.	90.00
Matlock Bath *War Memorial,*	
inscribed. 182mm.	40.00

Scarborough Lighthouse, with inscription: *This lighthouse was damaged in the bombardment by German warships on Wednesday December 16th 1914.* 132mm. 65.00

Scarborough Lighthouse, with rectangular buildings, depicting shell damage. 110mm. 65.00

Southsea. *Royal Naval War Memorial.* 160mm. (Chatham, Plymouth and Southsea War Memorials are identical in design and value). 40.00

Worthing War Memorial, inscribed: *Duty Nobly done 1914–1918.* 170mm. 56.50

Home/Nostalgic

Ali Baba Basket, very detailed. 75mm. 5.50

Anvil on base, can be found inscribed: *A Sussex Legend,* with verse, but more usually *Blacksmith's Anvil.* 35mm and 45mm. 12.00 / 5.50

Basket, oval with handle. 70mm long. 3.50

Bell, inscribed: *Curfew must not ring tonight.* No. 107. 65mm. 6.50

Book, Model of. No. 71. 57mm. 5.00

Chest and lid. 90mm long. 7.50

Child smiling, bust. 60mm. 16.00

Chinese Lantern. 80mm. 10.50

Coal Scuttle, helmet shaped. 53mm. 4.50

Desk, rolltop. 80mm long. 10.50

Dressing table mirror, with one drawer. 87mm. 12.00

Fireplace, inscribed: *There's no place like home.* 70mm. 13.00

Fireplace/Range with saucepan. Inscribed: *May yer fireside aye be cheers and yer kail-pat aye be fou. Copyright Allan Junior.* 75mm long. 16.00

Flat Iron. 64mm. 8.50

Flat Iron on stand. (2 pieces). 66mm. 10.00

Garden Roller. 51mm. 10.50

Garden Trug. 75mm long. 3.00

Grandfather Clock, found inscribed: *Make us of time let not advantage slip. Shakespeare,* or more rarely: *Nae man can tetha time or tide. Burns* (add £3.00). 2 sizes: 112mm and 128mm. 10.50

Hand mirror with reflective silvering. 150mm long. 20.00

Milk Can with lid. 60mm. 4.50

Old Armchair with verse. 88mm. 6.50

Pail, with moulded rope handle. 63mm. 3.00

Pillar box, impressed G.R., inscribed: *If you haven't got time to post a line here's the pillar box.* 78mm. 9.50

Pillar Box, outpressed G.R. open slit. 90mm. 17.00

Pipe. 2 sizes: 76mm & 93mm long. 16.00

Shaving Mug. No. 125. 2 sizes: 55mm. 5.50
70mm. 5.50

Sundial, circular with round base, with inscription: *I mark not the hours.* 118mm. 10.50

Sundial, circular on square base, No. 205, with inscription: *I mark not the hours.* 98mm. 7.50

Tobacco Jar with crossed coloured pipes on lid. Inscribed: *tobacco.* 115mm. 12.50

Umbrella. 50mm. 14.50

Watering Can. 75mm. 5.50

Wedding ring, gold, in open box. 60mm. 18.50

Wheelbarrow. 105mm long. 10.50

Comic/Novelty

Alarm Clock. Inscribed: *Many are called but few get up.* 65mm. 21.50

Basket of Milk, six bottles with brown tops. 64mm. 19.50

Billiken, The god of luck, often found unnamed. 73mm. 4.00

Billiken, The god of luck, sitting on high backed chair. 100mm. 7.50

Biscuit Lid trinket box on tray base. Impressed: *Oval High Tea.* Biscuit coloured. 75mm long. 30.00

Boy on Pig's back, boy fully coloured. 94mm long. 95.00

Broadbean pod splitting open, occasionally inscribed: *Good old bean.* 130mm long. 16.00

Dutch Boy. 80mm. Can be found fully coloured when £10.00 should be added. 12.00

Dutch Girl. 80mm. Can be found fully coloured when £10.00 should be added. (A pair to the Dutch Boy.) 12.00

Fan, open, hat pin holder. 90mm. 18.50

Fat Lady on weighing scales, scale registers 20 stone, inscribed: *Adding weight. Blue Bonnet.* 90mm. 24.50

Policeman, very jolly. 80mm. *Willow* version found fully coloured. 40.00

Regimental Sergeant-Major Pepper Pot. 84mm. 47.50

Sack of Meal with Mouse, inscribed: *May the mouse ne'er leave yer meal-poke wi' a teardrop'n its e'e.* 63mm. 13.00

With brown or grey mouse. 16.00

A truck of coal from. . . Wagon of black coal. 90mm long. 16.00

Also found with coal painted grey and inscribed: *A truck of iron ore from. . .* 30.00

Black Boys

All of these boys are fully coloured but sit on white boxes etc. All uncommon.

Black Boy, standing with hands in pockets. 94mm. 65.00

Black Boy, playing drum. 70mm. 75.00

Black Boy, in bath of ink, inscribed: *How ink is made.* 110mm long. 75.00

Black Boy, in bed with spider, inscribed: *A little study in black and fright.* Boy can have red or blue pyjamas. 70mm long. 56.50

Black Boy in bed, face coloured, inscribed: *Just a little Study in black and white.* 62mm long. 60.00

Black Boy, eating slice of melon, sitting on soap box. 80mm. 85.00

Black Boy with pumpkin. 80mm. 100.00

Black Boy, at table eating a boiled egg which has a chicken popping out. 70mm. 90.00

Two Black Boys, heads popping out of box, inscribed: *Box of chocolates.* Can be found with boys painted as white children, yellow hair and blue eyes and

is often found not coloured at all. 60mm.

Coloured 30.00

No colouring 22.00

Black Boy, holding container for matches. 100mm. 56.50

Little Birds

From Arcadian moulds. Head fully coloured, eggs white. Flapper's head hatching from egg, inscribed: *A little bird from . . .* 50mm long. 20.00

Black Boy's head hatching from egg, inscribed: *A blackbird from . . .* 50mm long. 30.00

Comic Ashtrays

Scotsman, really grotesque, sitting on white bench on white ashtray. 95mm. 32.50

Scotsman can be found coloured. 35.00

Bookie with coloured hare and greyhound on octagonal ashtray base. 70mm. 45.00

Cartoon/Comedy Characters

Baby, with arms outstretched, inscribed: *Cheerio.* Some colouring on face. 125mm. 30.00

Baby, saluting, inscribed: *One of the b'hoys.* Can be found with A.W.W.H. on chest. Some colouring on face. 2 sizes: 125mm & 150mm. 30.00

Harry Lauder, bust. Brown hat with thistle. 80mm. 17.00

Can be found named. 25.75

Dr. Beetle (impressed). 142mm. 56.50

Teddytail, impressed. 142mm. 56.50

Two Cartoon Characters sitting in Armchair. 90mm. (Thought to be Dr. Beetle and Sunny Jim!) 65.00

Winkie, not named, inscribed: *Glad Eyes* on beak. 60mm. 14.00

Alcohol

Barrel. 50mm. 3.00

Barrel on stand. No. 35. 58mm. 5.50

Barrel with opening on one side. 54mm long. 3.50

Beer Bottle with red hand. 98mm. 12.50

Beer Bottle and Tankard on
horseshoe ashtray, with
inscription: *The more we are
together the merrier we'll be.*
Silver Tankard. 85mm.   12.50
Beer Bottle and Tankard on
square ashtray. 78mm wide.
Verse as above.   12.50
Bottle. No. 104. Can be
inscribed: *One Special Scotch.*
90mm.   7.50
Drunk in Top Hat and Tails
draped drunkenly around a
white female statue (bust on
column). Inscribed: *How cold
you are tonight.* On blue
ashtray base. 96mm.   75.00
Drunks, two on ashtray,
inscribed: *Another little drink
wouldn't do us any harm.* 92mm.   47.50
Hand, holding beaker, inscribed:
Good health. 50mm.   6.50
Man, Mr Pickwick character (As
in Arcadian range) on rim of
beaker. 75mm.   34.50
Monk holding tankard. 155mm.   16.00
Stud, lapel with miniature bottle
attached, inscribed: *The More We
are together, the Merrier we will
be.*   31mm. Rare.   30.00
Tankard, foaming inscribed *The
more we are together. . .* 58mm.   6.50
Thimble, inscribed: *Just a
thimbleful.* 50mm.   12.50
Thistle vase, with verse: *A wee
Deoch an Doris.* 56mm.   4.00
Toby Jug. 78mm.   6.50
Whisky Bottle, inscribed: *One
special scotch.* 63mm.   6.50
Whisky Bottle, with cork,
inscribed: *One special scotch.*
88mm.   7.50
Whisky Bottle and Soda Syphon
on Tray, inscribed: *Scotch and
soda.* 88mm. dia.   14.00
Whisky Bottle, Soda Syphon and
Tumbler on horseshoe ashtray.
With inscription: *The more we
are together, the merrier we will
be* or *Scotch and Soda.* Some
colouring.
2 sizes: 87mm. long.   16.00
          115mm. long.   16.00

Sport
Golfer's Caddie holding golf bag,
figure coloured. 110mm.   65.00
Golf Clubs in Bag. 108mm.   75.00
Football. 50mm dia.   6.50
Jockey on Racehorse on oval
base found in different coloured
silks. Can be found coloured
but unglazed. 2 sizes:
104mm & 112mm.   65.00
Racehorse, impressed. 102mm.   75.00
Racehorse on circular base.
115mm.   65.00

Musical Instruments
Banjo. 160mm long.   8.50
Guitar. 163mm long.   10.50
Lute. 159mm long.   35.00

Transport
Car, open 4 seater. 2 sizes:
114mm & 140mm long.   30.00
Car, open 2 seater. 116mm long.   30.00
Car, open 2 seater, very detailed
model with spare wheel on side
running board. 108mm long.   40.00
Tram, double decker, open top.
Inscribed: *Life on the ocean wave.*
No. 333. 108mm long.   135.00
Tram, single decker.   135.00
Can of Petrol, impressed: *Motor
spirit.* 55mm.   13.00

Modern Equipment
Camera, folding. 60mm.   30.00
Horn Gramophone, square.
95mm.   19.50
Horn Gramophone on round
base. 60mm.   30.00
Radio Horn, inscribed: *Hello. . .
(name of town) calling.* 70mm.   25.00

Footwear
Boot. 112mm long.   11.00
Edwardian Shoe, blue bow.
110mm long.   10.50
Ladies' Riding Shoe, square toe
and blue tie. 115mm long.   13.00
Sabot. No. 334. 75mm long.   4.00
Slipper wall pocket, blue bow.
2 sizes: 152 & 178mm long.   12.50

Miscellaneous
Cauldron, 2 handles. 36mm.   3.00
Cauldron, on three feet. 60mm.   3.00
Bell. 60mm.   5.50

Hammer Head, Matchholder,
  inscribed: *My speciality is
  striking* or *Matches*. 80mm long. 11.00
Hand holding a tulip.
  No. 74. 80mm. 4.00
Horseshoe ashtray. 80mm. 3.00
Horseshoe ashtray with menu
  holder and rectangular slot
  possible for matches. Rd. No.
  708047. 110mm long. 12.50
Horseshoe Base menu holder.
  113mm. 10.00
Horsehoe pin box and lid.
  63mm long. 4.00
Tree Trunk vase. 80mm. 4.00

Miniature Domestic
Cheese Dish, one piece. 45mm. 6.50
Cheese Dish and cover. 45mm. 6.50
Coffee Pot with lid. 70mm. 7.50
Tea Pot with lid. 60mm. 7.50

Interesting Domestic Items with Crests.
Bagware Vase. No. 232. 73mm. 3.00
Basket Dish. 45mm. 6.00
Bridge Trump indicator.
  Coloured suit symbols on
  circular base, spinning cover
  allowing only one suit to be
  seen. Very ornate. Rd. No. 693774.
  No. 1015. 104mm dia. 50.00
Diamond, Trump indicator.
  65mm. 4.00
Hairpins, box and lid. 105mm. 6.00
Hat Pins, curved fluted holder.
  125mm. 10.50
Pin Box and lid, horseshoe shaped.
  62mm. 4.00
Pin Box, oval, with safety pin in
  relief on lid. 90mm long. 7.50
Playing cards, Box and lid.
  154mm long. 13.00
Preserves Jar and lid. 75mm. 5.25
Trinket Box, oval on eight collar
  stud feet with moulded
  cufflinks placed between each
  stud. Border of moulded
  cufflinks and tie pin in relief on
  lid. 90mm long. 12.00
Hexagonal Salt Pot. 100mm. 3.50
Pepper Pot. 75mm. 3.50
Bagware Teapot and lid. 108mm. 8.50

Willper Heraldic China

For mark see *Crested China*, p. 293.

Trademark used by Sampson Hancock &
  Sons, The Garden Works, Hanley.
  (Usual trademark Corona).

Only one small vase has been seen
  to date. 4.00

Wilton China

For mark see *Crested China*, p. 293.
N.B. The second mark given on that page
should be dated 1932-1934.

Trademark used by A.G. Harley Jones at
Wilton Pottery, Fenton. This firm
specialised in lustre ware.

Ancient Artefacts
Ancient Tyg, 1 handle. 70mm.	2.25
Bronze Pot, not named. 35mm.	2.25
Loving Cup, 3 handles. 39mm.	3.00

Buildings — Coloured
These can be found with crests
Anne Hathaway's Cottage, on ashtray base. 73mm long.	19.00
Feathers Hotel. 1600. Ludlow. 85mm long.	60.00
Shakespeare's House. 53mm long.	20.00

Buildings — White
Anne Hathaway's Cottage, in pearl lustre on oval base. 57mm long.	15.00
Anne Hathaway's Cottage, on ashtray base in lustre. 73mm long.	15.00
Ann Hathaway's night light in pearl lustre. 106mm long.	18.50
Blackpool Tower, found in lustre. 92mm.	13.00
Blackpool Tower and buildings. 175mm.	17.00
Christchurch Priory. 108mm.	40.00
Cottage, Thatched. (Probably unnamed Anne Hathaway's Cottage.) 56mm long.	15.00
Lichfield Cathedral, can be lustre. 85mm.	30.00
Peterborough Cathedral, West Front of. 90mm long.	22.00
Shakespeare's House. 53mm long.	10.50
Tamworth Castle. 130mm long.	40.00

Monuments
Liberty Statue. 175mm.	30.00
Toad Rock near Hathersage. 95mm long.	26.00

Historical/Folklore
Dick Whittington and cat on ashtray base, inscribed: *IV miles to London* on milestone and *Turn again Whittington* on ashtray. 110mm.	65.00

Traditional/National Souvenirs
Blackpool Big Wheel. 105mm.	12.50
Found with the Felix transfer and Pathe trademark, inscribed: *Felix the cat comes to Blackpool.*	30.00
Blackpool Tower and Wheel on ashtray base. 90mm.	21.00
Lancashire Clog with verse: *There's mony a factory lass wi clogs on her feet. . .* 120mm long.	6.50
Irish Harp, with green shamrocks. 105mm.	8.25
Welsh Hat.	
2 sizes: 35mm. (miniature)	8.50
70mm.	10.50

Seaside Souvenirs
Bathing Machine with girl in doorway. Can be found with some colouring, lustre or inscribed: *Morning Dip' 7a.m.!* 100mm.	14.50
Fisherman's Creel, fish on lid, inscribed: *A good catch.* 88mm long.	5.50
Sailing Yacht, inscribed: *Saucy Sue.* 125mm.	23.50
Can be found in lustre.	
Lighthouse, inscribed: *Sailor beware.* Found in lustre. 155mm.	9.00

Animals
Cat on pouffe, outpressed *Luck.* 62mm.	16.00
Cat, sitting, red bow. 60mm.	9.00
Cat, sitting, inscribed: *Luck.* Red tongue. 102mm.	15.00
Black cat on lid of fishing creel, inscribed: *I'm here just for luck.* 80mm.	26.00
Black cat on cheese, mouse at base. 80mm.	27.50

Bulldog, standing, inscribed:
What we have we hold.
130mm long. 16.00
Terrier Dog, sitting, can be
found in lustre. 85mm. 16.00
Dog, begging. 72mm. 11.25
Dog, Pug, 57mm. 13.50
Pig, inscribed: *You may push.* 12.50

Birds
Cock. 70mm long. 8.75
Cockerel Pepper Pot. 70mm. 7.50
Duck, sitting. Found in lustre.
50mm. 7.00
Turkey. 55mm. 11.00

Great War
Sailor, seated and holding
submarine. Blue cap band.
75mm coloured. 75.00
Battleship, tall top mast and no
forward guns. 115mm long. 26.00
Fieldglasses. 83mm. 13.00
Folkestone War Memorial,
inscribed: *Road of Remembrance.*
78mm. 30.00
Hay War Memorial. 150mm. 110.00
St. Anne's *War Memorial.* 152mm. 90.00
Thetford *War Memorial.* 150mm. 100.00
Walsall War Memorial. 115mm. 95.00

Home/Nostalgic
Book with clasp. 65mm. 5.00
Fireplace with clock and dogs
on mantlepiece, kettle & teapot
on hob. Inscribed: *Loves Old
Sweet Song.* 90mm long. 14.50
Grandfather Clock, inscribed:
*Make us of time let not advantage
slip.* 128mm. 10.50
Sundial, inscribed: *What o'clock*
and *Serene I stand among the
flowers and only count life's sunny
hours.* 146mm. 13.00
Garden Roller. 98mm long. 12.50

Comic/Novelty
Bookmaker, standing figure,
inscribed: *6 to 4 the field.* 80mm. 75.00
Broke to the wide, man standing
with head and shoulders
bowed. 82mm. 90.00
Open Razor ashtray, inscribed:
Got me through many a scrape,

found in lustre. 95mm long. 28.00
Tramp holding glass of beer,
sitting by milestone, inscribed:
*Its better to be alive with eighteen
pence than dead with a thousand
pounds.* 76mm. 85.00
Truck of Coal, inscribed: *Black
Diamonds.* Black coal,
sometimes found unpainted.
Found in lustre. 98mm long. 14.00

Cartoon/Comedy Characters
Bonzo Dog, Lustre. 48mm. 30.00
Can also be found sitting on a
lustre ashtray base.
110mm long. 35.00
Comedian, standing figure
wearing brown Oxford bags,
black jacket, blue tie, brown
trilby hat and black shoes.
96mm (rare). 65.00
Mutt and Jeff, on rectangular
base. 105mm long. 70.00

Alcohol
Barrel of Beer, on stand. 55mm. 5.50
Whiskey Bottle. 98mm. 7.50

Modern Equipment
Horn Gramophone, inscribed:
His Master's Voice. 104mm. 26.00
Radio operator, inscribed:
Listening in. Some colouring.
Found lustre. 80mm. 60.00
Telephone, upright. 105mm. 13.00

Miscellaneous
Bishop chess piece. 70mm. 16.00
Ashtray, semi circular with
colour transfer of a cigarette.
95mm long. 12.50
Cigarettes, octagonal holder.
64mm. 4.00
Matches, octagonal holder. 64mm. 4.00
Pastry cutter, clover shaped.
90mm long. 10.50
Thimble. 43mm. 10.50

Miniature Domestic
Cheese Dish, 1 piece. 50mm. 5.50
Cheese Dish and cover, horseshoe
shaped. 45mm. 12.50

Wil-Wat China

For mark see *Crested China*, p. 297.

Trademark used for a retailer by Alfred B. Jones and Sons Ltd, Grafton China Works, Longton. (Usual trademark Grafton).

Monuments
The Monument, Laceby. 150mm.   21.75

Traditional/National Souvenirs
Leaking Boot, Cleethorpes (Statue of boy, boot joined to hand by string). 156mm.   50.00

Animals
Fish, straight, with open mouth. 100mm long.   3.50

W and R

For mark see *Crested China*, p. 297.

Trademark used for a London wholesaler by Hewitt and Leadbeater, Willow Potteries, Longton. (Usual trademark Willow Art).

Ancient Artefacts
Lincoln Jack. No. 34. 52mm.   2.25

Seaside Souvenirs
Lighthouse, not named. 110mm.   4.75

Animals
Cat, sitting, badge on chest. 72mm.   12.50
Cat, standing, chubby. 70mm.   10.50
Elephant, walking. No. 113. 52mm.   13.00
Pig, standing. 85mm long.   10.00

Birds
Swan posy holder. 65mm long.   4.75

Great War
Soldier with rifle, inscribed: *Our brave defender*. 132mm.   40.00
Monoplane with moveable propeller. 150mm long.   55.00
Battleship, impressed: *HMS Lion*. 140mm long.   22.50
Tommy's Steel Helmet. 75mm dia.   22.50

Home/Nostalgic
Grandfather Clock. Inscribed: *Make use of time. . .* 125mm.   10.50

Comic/Novelty
Billiken, not named. 73mm.   4.00

Alcohol
Beer Bottle. 42mm.   7.50

Transport
Car, open 4 seater. 114mm long.   30.00

Footwear
Ladies Riding Shoe with square toe. 115mm.   11.00

Miscellaneous
Hand holding tulip. 80mm.   4.00

Miniature Domestic
Coffee Pot with lid. 69mm.   7.50

W.R. & S.

For mark see *Crested China,* p. 298.

Trademark used by William Ritchie and Co.
Ltd, 24,26 and 28 Elder Street, Edinburgh. (Usual trademark Porcelle).

Seaside Souvenirs
Whelk Shell. 100mm.   3.00

Great War
Nurse. *A Friend in Need.*   40.00
Bell Tent. 74mm.   10.50

Hats
Top Hat. 45mm.   5.50

Wy Not? Crest China

For mark see *Crested China*, p. 298.
Mark can also be found as Wy Knot.

Trademark used for a wholesaler by Hewitt
and Leadbeater, Willow Potteries,
Longton. (Usual trademark Willow Art).

Ancient Artefacts
Loving Cup, 3 handles. 39mm.   3.00
Winchester Leather Jack, not
   named. 50mm.   2.25

Buildings — White
Knaresborough Castle. 95mm.   70.00

Monuments
Bunyan's Statue. 163mm.   19.50
Lord Byron's Monument. 165mm.   40.00

Historical/Folklore
Bunyan's Chair. 90mm.   10.50
Bunyan's Cushion. 100mm long.   16.00
Burn's Chair, Dumfries. 83mm.   7.50
*James V Chair at Stirling Castle,
Model of*. 102mm.   7.50
*Mary Queen of Scots Chair, Edin-
burgh Castle, Model of*. 75mm.   6.50
*Sir Walter Scotts Chair, Abbotsford,
Model of*. 85mm.   7.50
Skull, inscribed: *A Prehistoric
Skull. No. 171*. 60mm.   7.50

Traditional/National Souvenirs
Lancashire Clog, with yellow
   buckle. 88mm long.   4.75
Welsh Hat. 57mm.   4.75

Animals
Cat, sitting, blue bow. No. 62.
   2 sizes: 60mm.   10.00
          75mm.   12.50
Cheshire Cat, inscribed:
   Still Smiling. 88mm.   7.50
Dog, sitting, badge on chest.
   80mm.   12.50
Dog, Collie, standing. 85mm.   12.50
Elephant, walking. 52mm.   13.00
Mouse (very fat, often described
   as a guinea pig). 62mm.   13.00
Teddy Bear. 75mm.   8.50

Great War
Nurse, inscribed: *A friend in need*.
   130mm.   40.00
Sailor, inscribed: *Our brave
defender*, and carrying a flag on
his chest instead of a crest. The
flag transfer is inscribed: *Good
Luck. The boys in blue*. 130mm.   75.00
Soldier, inscribed: *Our brave
defender*. Only example known
has Union Jack on chest and in-
scribed: *Bravo!. Kitchener's Army*.
(A Willow Art decoration).   75.00
Battleship, 4 funnels.
   127mm long.   19.00
Red Cross Van, red crosses on
   side. 84mm long.   23.00
Field Gun. 120mm long.   17.00
Field Gun with screen. 115mm.   18.50
Pickelhaube. 50mm.   16.00
Kit Bag, 74mm.   15.00
Tommy's Steel Helmet. 76mm long.   22.50
Kitchen Range. Inscribed: *Keep
the Home Fires Burning*.
   78mm long.   12.50

Home/Nostalgic
Book. 58mm.   5.00
Grandfather Clock. 124mm.   10.00
Iron and Trivet. 70mm long.   8.50
Shaving Mug. 55mm.   5.50

Comic/Novelty
Billiken. 70mm.   4.00

Miscellaneous
Hand holding a tulip. 81mm.   4.00

Miniature Domestic
Cheese Dish and cover. 50mm.   6.50

Unmarked Models

Many models found unmarked are recognisably pieces from the major firms which for some reason escaped from the pottery without the trademark. Some factories, such as Grafton, did not mark pieces with firing flaws, but most firms did not mark all their perfect ware. However, Grafton pieces usually bear their painted stock numbers. Models with no crest could well be travellers samples. Unmarked models of known origin are not listed below. Many models in the original listings in earlier Price Guides have turned out to be Savoy. Certain shapes did not have enough room on the base to carry a factory mark. Possible factories have been put in parenthesis where known. A trained eye can tell which pottery made an unmarked piece in most cases.

There are however quantities of unmarked crested china which cannot be attributed to any one manufacturer. This china could have been made by several firms known to have made crested wares but do not appear to have used a trademark. These firms include:

George Proctor and Co., High Street, Longton.

Barkers and Kent Ltd, The Foley Pottery, Fenton.

Biltons (1912) Ltd, London Road Works, Stoke-on-Trent.

C.J. Bisson and Co, 82 Liverpool Road, Stoke-on-Trent.

As these firms were earthenware manufacturers the models would tend to be reasonably heavy.

Many German firms also manufactured crested china for the English souvenir market and chose not to use a trademark, especially after the Great War. German wares tend to be somewhat whiter and of poorer quality than British made wares. These include:

Max Emanuel, The Mosanic Pottery, Mitterteich, (usual trademark Mosanic).

Moschendorf, Hof, Bayern (usual trademark PM and Rex).

Hutschenreuther, Probstzella, Thuringia

(Trademark P).

Klösterle, Carlsbad (usual trademark Union K).

However, many of the models listed below are known to have been produced by Wilhelm Kutzscher and Co., Schwarzenberger Porzellanfabrik, Schwarzenberg, Saxony, now in East Germany (usual trademark, St George China, Impero, Saxony and Princess).

Generally, pieces which have neither factory mark nor inscription are less desirable than those which do and are worth slightly less. This is not as important with rare items or with medium range wares.

Values for pieces with firing defects and therefore not finished off, i.e. misshapen, having no crest or colouring are about half to three-quarters of the full value.

Parian/Unglazed

Brandenburg Gate, Berlin. 62mm.	90.00
Cartmel Priory Church.	
100mm long.	40.00
St Pauls, stone coloured.	
87mm long. (probably Savoy)	100.00
Solomons Temple (Grinlow Tower). Inscribed: *Erected on the site of a Historic Barrow.*	
85mm.	37.50
York Minster, West Front.	
128mm.	25.00

Ancient Artefacts

Winchester Bushel. 102mm dia.	8.75

Buildings — Coloured

Abbot Reginalds Gateway and old Vicarage Evesham.	
130mm long.	75.00
Abel Fletchers, Bell Hotel.	
120mm long.	47.50
Birthplace of Andrew Carnegie.	
83mm long.	60.00
Craigwell House, Bognor.	
115mm long.	75.00
Canterbury Weavers, The. No. 141.	82.50
Dan Winter's Cottage, where the first orange Lodge was formed in Co. Armagh, Ireland.	
A Money Box. 128mm long.	40.00
Fair Maids House, Perth. 80mm.	70.00
The Feathers Hotel, Ludlow. 112mm.	75.00

Gabled House, not named.
Nightlight. 135mm long. 75.00
The Keep, Hawarden. Unglazed.
140mm long. 82.50
Hampton Court Palace. 80mm. 55.00
Harlow, Ye olde Village Shoppe.
124mm. 110.00
Harvard House, with long in-
scription: *Restored by Marie*
Carelli. . . 145mm. 90.00
Irish Cottage, Money Box.
110mm long. 30.00
Ledbury, Old Market House.
97mm long. 65.00
Market Harborough Old Grammar
School.
2 sizes: 126mm. 75.00
150mm. 85.00
Mowcop Castle, Staffs. Unglazed
on oval base. 130mm long.
(Tunstall Pottery). 75.00
Knaresborough Castle. 50.00
Old Falcon Tavern, Bideford on
Avon. 115mm. 75.00
Old Lantern Chapel, Ilfracombe.
74mm long. 25.00
Pete's Cottage, Isle of Man.
57mm long. 65.00
Plas Newyd House, impressed:
The House of the Ladies of
Llangollen. 115mm long. 72.50
Priory Church, Christchurch.
Unglazed. 223mm long. 125.00
Pump Room and Baths. Trefriw
Wells, plus long inscription.
95mm long. 100.00
St Pauls Cathedral, unglazed.
145mm long. 100.00
Shakespeare's House.
2 sizes: 65mm long. 15.00
157mm long. 25.00
Shanklin, IoW, The Old Village.
98mm long. 100.00
Stokesay Castle, Gate House.
116mm long. 95.00

Buildings — White
Archway, wooden door, large
iron hinges, steps up to door.
105mm. 16.00
Battle Abbey Gateway. 96mm. 18.00
Beverley, North Bar. 90mm. 18.50
Blackpool Tower with buildings,
impressed: *The Tower of Black-*
pool. 120mm. 15.00
Birmingham Town Hall.

95mm long. 20.00
British Government Pavilion B.E.E.
Wembley 1924-5. 60mm. 30.00
Castle, (unknown). 76mm. 45.00
Conduit, Uttoxeter Market Place.
120mm. 30.00
Cottage, single storey. 66mm. 8.75
Folkestone, Parish Church. AD1138.
106mm long. 40.00
Guildford, The Castle. 100mm. 30.00
Old Home of the Right Hon. D. Lloyd
George Esq. MP Llanstymdwy near
Criccieth. 76mm long. 47.50
Mickelgate Bar, York. 98mm. 20.00
Ripon Cathedral, West Front.
80mm long. 31.50
Rowton Tower, Chester.
88mm long. 26.00
St Albans, Clock Tower (very
small) 74mm. 15.00
St Tudno's Church, Llandudno
with open pillars. 52mm. 60.00
Scarborough Castle Ruins.
75mm long. 25.00
Windmill, fixed sails. 80mm. 10.50
Windmill on stilts on square
base, fixed sails in form of
scent bottle. 78mm. 15.00
York Minster, West Front.
114mm. 25.00

Monuments
Ashington Boer War Memorial.
138mm. 40.00
Bradlaugh's Monument, Northampton.
2 sizes: 110mm. 40.00
140mm. 45.00
Brixham Clock Tower. 120mm. 21.50
Cleethorpes Clock Tower. 136mm. 24.00
Captain Cook's Monument. 135mm. 21.75
Hall Cross, Doncaster.
2 sizes: 156mm. 22.50
185mm. 27.50
Larg's Tower, inscribed: *Battle of*
Largs Memorial. 166mm. 14.50
Margate Surf Memorial with
inscriptions. 144mm. 24.75
The Metal Man, Tramore. 150mm.
(Saxony). 52.50
Parnells Memorial. 165mm. 67.50
St Winifreds Statue, Holywell.
135mm. 25.00
Skegness Clock Tower. 120mm. 10.00
Swanage Globe.
2 sizes: 54mm white. 7.50
65mm coloured. 14.00

Historical/Folklore

Bass Rock, in relief on square plaque. 125mm long.	26.00
Baby in wraps, perhaps Moses in bullrushes. 66mm long.	11.00
Banbury Lady on Horse. 130mm.	20.00
Auld Brig O'Doon, Ayr. Picture in relief on wall plaque. 125mm long.	23.50
Burns Cottage, interior of, in relief on rectangular plaque. 125mm long.	22.00
Exterior of *Burn's Cottage,* in relief on plaque. 128mm long.	22.00
Bust of General Booth, can be found inscribed: *Salvation Army.* 75mm.	24.00
Charles Dickens, bust. 110mm.	20.00
Edwardian Lady carrying black cat and basket. 106mm.	24.50
If named *Mary Bull*	29.50
Execution Block. 100mm long.	5.50
Giant's Causeway. *Wishing Chair.* 105mm.	40.00
Idol or grotesque imp or lucky charm. 90mm long.	11.00
Jacobean Font at Newport, IoW. Model of. 70mm.	11.00
Knaresborough Dropping Well. 77mm.	22.50
Knight's Helmet and Visor, with reclining animal on top. 80mm.	17.50
Mother Shipton, fully coloured. 110m.	30.00
Sanctuary Chair, Beverley Minster. 68mm.	15.00
Scold's Bridle, bust of old woman wearing bridle, with story of gossiping women. Can be found coloured. 64mm.	
White.	30.00
Coloured.	40.00
Skull. 44mm.	8.75
Sword in scabbard, ornate. 135mm.	35.00
Ulphus Horn, Original in York Minster, Model of. 110mm long.	25.00
Viking or Saxon King standing on 3 stepped base, axe in hand and scrolls in the other. 150mm.	40.00
Dick Whittington and cat, figure with very large sitting cat holding shield. 100mm.	40.00

Traditional/National Souvenirs

John Bull, bust. 75mm.	8.00
John Bull, standing, no dog. 120mm.	17.00
Bust of General Booth.	34.00
Bolton Trotter. 132mm long.	4.75
Bolton Trotters, two joined as a pair. 107mm long.	10.50
A Plate o' Bolton Trotters, Three pigs trotters on a plate.	11.00
Cheddar Cheese, Model of, with inscription: *This famous cheese has been made in and around Cheddar for centuries, and to this day no country in the world has been able to equal it.* 60mm dia. (Grafton).	11.00
Jersey Milkmaid. 80mm.	30.00
Lancashire Clog. 112mm long.	5.50
Lincoln Imp, on pedestal. 110mm.	6.50
Melton Mowbray Pie, with pastry roses and leaves. 55mm.	16.00
Bust of Burns, glazed. No. 589.	14.50
Gretna Priest, inscribed: *The famous Gretna Priest from the celebrated Blacksmiths shop, Gretna Green.* 118mm. (Saxony).	30.00
Highland Mary, statue. 150mm.	20.00
Scotsman playing bagpipes on pedestal. 138mm.	40.00
Tam-o'shanter, sitting in chair. 130mm.	20.00
Jug with thistle pattern in relief. 51mm.	3.00
Miniature Toby Jug Welsh Lady, coloured. 42mm.	14.50
Welsh Lady in chair. 100mm.	16.00
Welsh Hat, very tall. 70mm.	8.00
Dutch Girl, bust, flowers in relief on base.	14.00
Two Lady grape treaders with skirts rolled up, standing in barrel of grapes. 105mm. (Saxony).	35.00

Seaside Souvenirs

Canoe. 110mm long.	5.50
Lighthouse. 100mm.	5.50
Lighthouse Salt, Pepper and Mustard. 160mm. No. M282.	7.50
Lighthouse, tiny. 70mm. (Grafton).	6.00
Beachy Head Lighthouse. 124mm.	5.50
Cabin Trunk. 60mm long.	4.50
Un-named Rock, no crest, original could be off the Devon coast. 40mm.	12.50
Lifeboatman on rock base. 120mm. (Carlton).	30.00
Fisherman holding rope. 113mm.	17.00
Mermaid with fish. 84mm.	23.50

Waves, group of. 95mm long.	7.50
Shell. 110mm long.	3.00
Whelk Shell. 84mm long.	3.00
Suitcase, closed. 80mm long.	3.50
Yacht. 128mm.	10.00

Countryside

Axe in Tree Stump. 75mm.	10.50
Butterfly with open wings and wire legs. 90mm long. (German).	15.00
Four bar gate with stile and milestone. 96mm long.	6.50
Tree Trunk spill holder, with 2 sheep in front. 75mm.	12.00
Tree Trunk spill holder, with 2 sheep and lady with sickle. 75mm.	12.00

Animals

Bear, playing a Mandolin. (German)	24.75
Bull's head cream jug. 78mm.	9.00
Camel kneeling on rectangular base. 122mm long.	22.00
Kitten, standing.	16.50
Black Cat, sitting up, no crest. yellow/orange, comical face. *Good Luck* in orange. 133mm.	16.00
Cat, angry with arched back, coloured face. 70mm.	14.00
Cat on Drum. 90mm. (Saxony).	22.50
Cat, in holdall, can be inscribed: *Good Morning* or *Good Night*. 55mm long. (Saxony).	22.50
Cat, with toothache, bandage round jaw. 95mm.	19.00
Cat, dressed, with toothache, ruff around neck, bandage around head, left paw raised. 105mm.	19.00
Cat, singing from long sheet of music. 65mm. (Saxony).	22.50
Cat, reading from book. 74mm. (Saxony).	22.50
Cat, sitting, looking up, gilded face. 67mm.	8.50
Cat, sitting, coloured face. 100mm.	8.00
Cat, sitting, comical, right ear down, left ear up. 120mm.	9.50
Cat, Egyptian, with long ears. 90mm long.	30.00
Cat, thin and foreign looking, sitting. 70mm.	8.75
Cat, long necked. 115mm.	6.50
Cat, posy bowl.	11.25

Cat and Rabbit, in high Boot, inscribed: *A jolly place for a jolly couple*. 83mm. (Saxony).	21.75
Cat, angry with grotesque face, standing on tall legs with tail wrapped round them. 96mm.	21.75
Cat, furry kitten with open mouth. 90mm.	9.00
Cat and kitten either side of posy bowl. 105mm long.	11.00
Cat and Kitten, sitting by open square box on ashtray base. 72mm.	23.00
Cat, sitting, left paw raised. 75mm.	10.00
Cat standing drinking from jug, inscribed: *Mothers favourite*. 70mm long. (Saxony).	22.50
Cat, Manx. 90mm long.	16.00
Cat, Manx, standing drinking from jug, sometimes inscribed: *Mothers favourite*. 70mm long. (Saxony).	24.50
Cat with mouse. 77mm.	24.50
Cat, standing, hands on hips, tail forming third leg. 86mm.	19.00
Cat scent bottle, two-piece. 90mm.	40.00
Cheshire Cat, 90mm.	6.50
Cheshire Cat, long neck, looking left, 1 green eye, 1 winking red eye. 115mm.	10.50
Cow lying down, with gold horns, inscribed: *The Jersey Cow*. 108mm long.	21.50
Cow standing, gold horns, inscribed: *The Jersey Cow*. 108mm long. (Pair with above).	21.50
Cow cream jug. 125mm long.	14.00
Dinosaur jug. 85mm long.	5.50
Dog, Bulldog, extremely thin, sitting. 95mm long.	16.00
Dog wearing dress and overcoat, green colouring on hat. 92mm.	30.00
Standing Chauffeur Dog, goggles on cap, smoking pipe, wearing long overcoat. 84mm.	40.00
Dog, Bulldog. 110mm long.	13.00
Dogs, two bulldogs, one seated and the other standing. 57mm. (Saxony).	21.50
Dog, Bull Terrier, sitting next to a bucket. 80mm.	19.50
Dogs, two Pharos Hounds, on oblong base. 76mm long.	65.00

Dogs, two, and cat in basket. 70mm.	21.50
Dog, Pug, lying down. 96mm long.	22.50
Dog, Spaniel with droopy ears. 60mm.	11.00
Dog, King Charles Spaniel, wearing ribbon, lying on cushion. 82mm long.	20.00
Pair of Spaniels in top hat. 82mm.	19.00
Dog, probably a Retriever, lying on oblong base. 120mm long.	22.00
Dog, sitting Labrador puppy. 70mm.	11.25
Donkey, inscribed: A Malvern Donkey. 95mm long.	25.00
Elephant, gigantic, with gold tusks. Trunk raised. 130mm.	35.00
Elephant, Indian, standing. 100mm long.	20.00
Elephant, standing, trunk looped up. 80mm long.	13.00
Elephant, circus, with front feet on stool. 102mm.	82.50
Elephant heads, 2 on vase as handles. 76mm.	7.50
Elephant No. 346. 50mm.	13.00
Two Elephants on Toboggan going down hill. 70mm.	30.00
Elephant with Hunters and two Indian Bearers. 95mm.	35.00
Giant Frog, with huge open mouth. 80mm.	15.00
Frog with bead eyes. 72mm.	10.00
Frog cream jug. 100mm long.	5.50
Fish salt pot, with black markings to face. 108mm long.	4.50
Fish with open back for pin cushion. 118mm long.	3.00
Fish, gilded tail. 112mm long.	3.00
Guinea Pig. 60mm long.	16.00
Kangaroo. 95mm.	70.00
Lambs (two) by hollow tree trunk spill holder. See countryside.	
Lion, walking. 135mm.	13.00
Lion, on rectangular base. 116mm.	8.00
Lion, wearing coat and trousers holding telescope. 132mm.	75.00
Mouse playing Banjo. 90mm.	28.00
Pig, hairy, standing with holes in nostrils. Inscribed: The pig that won't go. 85mm long.	12.50
Pig sitting on haunches, Pepper Pot. 70mm.	16.00
Pink Pig posy holder.	12.00
Polar Bear on ashtray base. 82mm.	25.75
Shetland Pony inscribed: A Native of Shetland. 80mm.	21.50
Rabbit, crouching. 65mm.	6.50
Large Rabbit, crouching. 90mm long.	10.50
Rabbit on sledge. (Saxony).	24.00
Rabbits, 2 arm in arm on wide base. 72mm wide.	25.00
Rabbits, 2 cuddling on ashtray. 54mm.	18.50
Rhino, very grotesque. 155mm long.	30.00
Seal with ball on nose. 73mm.	14.50
Squirrel, large, in shape of milk jug. 90mm.	10.00
Tortoise pin box and lid. 2 sizes: 80mm long.	7.50
128mm long.	10.50

Birds

Blackbird on perch. 118mm long.	10.50
Canary on a perch. 110mm long.	10.50
Chick, yellow, hatching from egg, salt cellar. 60mm.	11.00
Chicken, very plump, on circular base. 60mm.	7.00
Cockerel, pepper pot. 71mm.	6.50
Crested Tit posy holder. 80mm long.	5.50
Duck ashtray, some colouring. 95mm long.	20.00
Duck, ewer with handle. 130mm long.	7.50
Duck pepper pot. 77mm.	6.50
Ducks, 2 with coloured beaks and feet on oval stand. 185mm. (an enormous model).	40.00
Duckling, airing wings. 69mm.	16.50
Duck, circular base, some colouring. 95mm.	14.00
Duckling with brown beak and feet, wings raised, beak upwards and open, on circular base. 85mm.	16.00
Duck posy bowl. 120mm long.	6.00
Eagle on rock, colour on beak and feet. 130mm.	17.00
Egg. 65mm upright.	3.00
Fledgling birds, 2 sitting on base sharing one open beak. (Grotesque).	7.00
Goldfinch on Rock. 105mm long.	16.00
Hen, brooding. 65mm long.	5.50
Hen and Cockerel on circular base. 82mm.	14.00
Hens, two on circular base. 80mm.	14.00

Kingfisher. 60mm.	30.00
Owl on three books. 121mm.	25.00
Parakeet, fully coloured on plinth. 215mm.	25.00
Pelican. 100mm.	12.00
Pigeon with puffed up chest, standing on ashtray base. 75mm.	15.00
Stork, nesting beside chimney pot with baby in nest. 100mm.	23.00
Swan, head back. 72mm.	6.50
Swan trinket box and lid. 69mm.	7.00
Warbler on tree stump. 130mm.	26.00

Great War

Cossack, standing figure on rectangular base. 126mm.	75.00
Jack Ashore, boy sailor on round base, coloured face. 153mm.	65.00
Zeppelin, finely detailed posy holder. 130mm long.	19.00
Bugle. 70mm. (Willow Art).	12.50
Military Cap ashtray, crest inside hat. 126mm long.	8.75
Peaked Cap. 60mm.	8.75
Llandudno War Memorial, not named. 183mm.	55.00
Margate War Memorial. 190mm.	55.00
Matlock War Memorial. 155mm.	100.00
Otley Churchyard, War Memorial Cross. 123mm.	75.00

Home/Nostalgic

Anvil on base. 58mm.	5.50
Armchair padded and three-legged. 66mm.	11.25
Armchair, padded with blue forget-me-nots around back rest. 62mm.	12.50
Ornate French Chair.	12.50
Armchair, upholstered. 85mm.	8.50
Basket with coloured fruit. 85mm. (Carlton).	21.50
Bellows box and lid. 120mm long.	9.50
Boy, feeding birds, standing next to a large basket on a base. 80mm.	30.00
Butter churn. 65mm.	3.00
Cake slice pin box and lid. 138mm long.	13.00
Flat Iron, box style, possibly a money box. 65mm.	6.00
Folded blankets.	19.50
Girl in nightdress standing on square base. Inscribed: *Morning*. 125mm.	27.50
Girl sitting on horse by tree trunk. 110mm.	25.00
Grandfather clock. 129mm.	9.00

Hip Bath. 90mm long.	7.50
Housekeeper/cook, wearing mob cap and apron, carrying keys and a ladle. 120mm. (Saxony).	40.00
Kettle on primus stone. 78mm.	6.00
Mantle Clock. 94mm.	9.00
Photograph Frame, cardboard backing. 94mm. (Gemma).	10.00
Ring. 64mm dia.	17.50
Umbrella. 38mm. (Arcadian).	16.00
Watering Can, oval shaped with no rose on spout. 87mm.	6.00
Watering Can. 77mm.	5.50

Comic/Novelty

Artist's easel on stand. 60mm.	2.25
Baby in Bootee. 80mm long.	10.50
Baby on rug, naked. 130mm long.	50.00
Bathing Belle poking head out of change tent. 80mm. (Carlton).	40.00
Bean Pod, open. 125mm long.	16.50
Biscuit. Impressed *Huntley & Palmer* coloured biscuit. 53mm dia.	26.50
Girl on stool with dog on floor (beige lustre). 108mm.	25.00
Cook, holding wooden spoon. 115mm.	34.50
Clown playing Banjo, some colour. 120mm.	30.00
Jack in the Box with open lid. 92mm. (Florentine).	14.50
Edwardian Child pepper pot. 84mm.	10.50
Hand bell, double faced, old/young woman. Coloured and inscribed: *Nature has endowed women with so much power that the law gives them very little. Dr. Johnson*. 107mm.	28.00
Edwardian Lady holding cat and basket.	25.00
Man in the Sun. 100mm.	47.50
Monk, carrying lantern and basket. 2 sizes: 114mm.	17.00
135mm. (Saxony).	17.00
Pillar Box, miniature. 58mm.	10.50
Pillar Box. 70mm.	8.00
Shaving Mug. 37mm.	5.50
Shaving Mug, angular handle. 44mm.	5.50
Suitcase, gilded straps. 57mm.	4.00
Tomato pepper pot on leaf base. 42mm.	10.50
Vaulting Horse, square looking bulldog with legs joined by	

poles. 80mm long. Some
colouring. (Saxony).   13.00
Washer Woman, holding basket
of washing. 118mm. (Saxony).   40.00
Womans Head on Turtle trinket
box. 80mm long.   16.00
Womans Head tea pot, some
colouring. 66mm.   12.50
Woman carrying case and bottle.   25.00

Cartoon/Comedy Characters
Crested faced man white or
fully coloured. 80mm.   25.00
coloured.   40.00
Felix, standing Cat on oval base,
no colouring. 87mm. (This is a
really nice Felix.)   65.00
Mrs Gamp. 114mm.   44.50
The Sprinter. Comic figure with
cork-screw legs — wound up
for action. 100mm.   75.00
Sunny Jim bust. 85mm.   40.00
Bust of Man with walrus
moustache, button nose and
large ears. Comical character
— identity unknown! 80mm.   45.00

Alcohol
Man in Bowler Hat, sitting,
hold ing beer glass.
Bottle, inscribed: *Lacon's*
Fine Ales. 90mm.   30.00
Champagne Bottle in Ice Bucket.
80mm.   11.00

Sport
Footballer, with ball, no
colouring. 130mm.   70.00
(Savoy range advertised a
coloured version of this model)
Football, leather. 55mm.   6.00
Golf Ball, pepper pot on circular
base. 50mm dia.   6.50
Golf Caddie, holding golf bag.
Hand in front of mouth as if
laughing at players. 65mm.   65.00
Rugby Ball. 74mm long.   7.50
Tennis Court Liner in form of a
wheelbarrow. 90mm long.   20.00
Tennis Racquet with single ball
attached. 135mm long.   14.00
Tennis Racquet, detailed strings.
118mm long.   16.00
Trophy. 100mm.   10.50

Musical Instruments
Drum set with cymbals and
drumsticks. 65mm. (Saxony).   10.50

Harp. 93mm.   5.50

Transport
Aeroplane with pilot, size varies,
usually 100mm long. (Almost
certainly German).   30.00
Bust of Bleriot, inscribed: *Messieur*
Bleriot. 1st man to cross the
Channel in an Aeroplane. June
25th 1909. 90mm.   85.00
Car, vintage, with open top and
hood folded back. 90mm long.
Poor quality.   13.00
Car with chauffeur. 85mm long.   30.00
Hot Air Balloon, square basket.
65mm.   23.00
Petrol can impressed: *Motor*
Spirit. 67mm.   13.00
Sleigh, ornate. 105mm long.   32.00
Tram (Trolley Bus) 100mm long.   135.00
Charabanc 18 seater with driver.
120mm long.   33.00

Modern Equipment
Cash Register. 44mm. (Saxony).   16.00
Typewriter inscribed: *My little*
typewriter. 44mm. (Saxony).   16.00
Identical model to the above.
Gramophone, square.
No horn. 55mm.   15.25

Hats
Boater, Straw. Unglazed.
107mm long.   8.25
Chauffeur's Large Peak Cap.
125mm long.   12.00
Fireman's Helmet vase. 48mm.   21.00
Knight's Helmet forming pin
box and lid. 80mm.   21.00
Opera Hat. 36mm.   20.00
Top Hat, very wide brim. 60mm.   4.75
Top Hat, with antlers across
brim. 65mm.   12.50
Top Hat, with umbrella across
brim. 65mm.   12.50
Top Hat match striker, not
glazed. 42mm.   4.75
Top Hat match striker, inscribed:
The Rapid Patent Silk Hat
Ironing Machine. 45mm.   12.50
(Obviously an advertising item)
Trilby. 96mm long.   15.00

Footwear
Dutch Sabot. 70mm long.   4.50
Boot with Spat. 80mm long.   7.50
Riding Boot with Spur. 90mm.   13.00

Ladies heeled Shoe, frilled
tongue. 107mm long.   7.50

Ladies Shoe, gilded heel
and toe. 150mm long.   11.00

Ladies Shoe, frilled tongue
and edge. 145mm long.   12.50

Ladies Boot, pressed eyelet
holes.

2 sizes: 83mm long.   9.00
          105mm long.   11.00

Sabot with turned up toe.
93mm long.   4.00

Shoe with side fastening.
80mm long.   9.00

Miscellaneous

Bridge Trumps: 60mm.

  Heart   5.50
  Diamond   4.75
  Spade   4.75
  Club   4.75

Gourd. 70mm.   7.00

Horseshoe. 66mm.   3.00

Loving Cup, 3 handled, with
lithophanes of King Edward,
Queen Alexandra, King George
or Queen Mary. 39mm.   36.50

Lithophane match holder/striker
with lithophane of King
Edward VII. 43mm.   32.50

Puzzle Jug. 70mm.   4.50

Miniature Domestic

Candle Snuffer cone. 45mm.   4.00

Cheese Dish and cover.
64mm long.   4.75

Cheese Dish and cover, inscribed:
Cheshire Cheese. 78mm long.   10.50

Cheese Dish and fixed cover.
64mm long.   4.75

Dressing table set comprising:
two scent bottles and
stoppers, three rouge pots
and lids, ring tree, all on rectangular tray. 155mm long.   Set 25.00

Kettle and lid. 80mm.   7.50

Teapot and lid. 75mm.   6.50

Miniature coffee set comprising:
coffee pot and lid, sugar basin,
milk jug, two cups and saucers
on rectangular tray.
155mm long.   25.00

Miniature tea set comprising:
teapot and lid, sugar basin,
milk jug, two cups and saucers
on rectangular or circular tray.   25.00

Country of origin

For mark see *Crested China*, p. 299.

British Manufacture

Some models are found with a simple
British Manufacture stamp, rather than
marked. These include arks, anvils,
cottages, footballs, grandfather clocks,
lighthouses, petrol cans, parian straw
boaters, pillar boxes, propellers, puzzle
jugs and top hats. These often have
tranfer views rather than crests. They are
remarkably similar to the products of the
Corona factory which they probably are.

Buildings — white

Cottage. 70mm long.   7.00

Gateway. 170mm.   19.50

Historical/Folklore

Mary Queen of Scots' chair. 74mm.   6.50

Noah's Ark. (sometimes listed
as a houseboat) 90mm long.   4.75

Ye Olde Chertsey Bell, with
coloured wooden base.
88mm.   25.75

Traditional/National Souvenirs

Cheddar Cheese, inscribed *Prime
Cheddar Cheese,* coloured
yellow. 52mm.   12.00

Cheddar Cheese, model of, with
verse and flowers. 60mm dia.   11.00

Lancashire Clog. 85mm long.   5.50

Welsh Hat, blue band. 58mm.   4.75

Seaside Souvenirs

Canoe. 110mm long.   6.00

Yacht. 128mm.   10.00

Lighthouse. 100mm.   5.50

Whelk Shell. 84mm long.   4.00

Suitcase, closed. 80mm long.   4.00

Animals

Bulldog. 110mm long.   13.00

Cat, angry with arched back,
coloured face. 70mm.   12.50

Cat with long neck. 112mm.   7.50

Cat sitting, bow on neck. 96mm.   12.00

Manx cat. 90mm long.   16.00

Cat sitting, coloured face. 100mm.   10.50

Labrador, sitting. 85mm. 10.50
Bull's head cream jug. 78mm. 9.00
Elephant, standing, tiny. 44mm. 13.00
Fish, gilded tail. 112mm long. 3.00
Fish vase. 90mm long. 5.00
Pig, hairy, standing with holes in
nostrils. Inscribed: *The
pig that won't go.* 85mm long. 10.00
Rabbit, crouching. 65mm. 6.50
Seal with ball on nose. 73mm. 16.00
Tortoise. 70mm long. 6.50

Birds
Egg. 65mm upright. 4.50
Fledgling cream jug. 64mm. 5.50
Brooding Hen. 65mm long. 5.50
Crested tit posy holder. 80mm long. 5.50

Home/Nostalgic
Anvil. 58mm. 6.50
Armchair with padded arms.
62mm. 14.50
Baby in Bootee. 80mm long. 11.00
Basket with coloured fruit. 85mm. 13.00
Grandfather clock. 129mm. 9.00
Pillar Box. 70mm. 9.50
Shaving Mug. 37mm. 5.50
Shaving Mug, angular handle.
44mm. 6.50
Suitcase, gilded straps. 57mm. 4.00

Comic/Novelty
Clown playing Banjo, some
colour. 120mm. 30.00
Jack in the Box with open
lid. 92mm. 16.00

Sport
Football. 55mm. 6.50

Transport
Petrol can impressed: *Motor
Spirit.* 67mm. 13.00
Propeller. 140mm long. 21.75

Modern Equipment
Gramophone, square.
No horn. 55mm. 15.25

Hats
Parian Straw Boater. 110mm long. 8.25
Top Hat. 45mm. 5.50

Footwear
Sabot with turned up toe.
93mm long. 4.75

Miscellaneous
Puzzle Jug. 70mm. 4.50

Miniature Domestic
Kettle and lid. 80mm. 7.50
Cheese Dish and cover. 64mm long. 4.75
Cheese Dish and fixed cover.
64mm long. 4.75

German or Foreign

For mark see *Crested China,* p. 304.

Austria and Czechoslovakia can also be
found.
These marks were used by the German
firms listed under unmarked wares. The
models with impressed numbers would
appear to be made by Max Emanuel.
(Usual trademark Mosanic), as he was
the only German manufacturer known to
use stock numbers and registered
numbers. Foreign, Austria or Czechoslovakia would be used after the Great
War due to the unwillingness of the
British to buy anything German. Nearly
all of these models can be found in
various shades of lustre, mostly
yellow/brown, usually with the lucky
white heather decoration.

Ancient Artefacts
Loving cup, 3 handled. 38mm. 3.00
Irish Bronze Pot. 50mm. 3.00
Southwold Jug. No. 4687. 40mm.
(lustre). 3.00

Buildings — coloured
Robert Burn's Cottage Nightlight.
130mm long. 30.00

Buildings — white
Bandstand. 2 sizes:
No. 3921. 75mm. 8.00
No. 3972. 90mm (lustre). 11.00
Birmingham Town Hall.
95mm long. 20.00
Blackpool Tower. No. 3484.
130mm. 10.00
Blackpool Tower cruet set (Tower
is salt pot, buildings either side
pepper and mustard — very
vulgar and therefore rather
appealing). 135mm. 7.50

Clock Tower. No. 7727.   7.50
Cottage. No. 7208. 65mm long.
(lustre).   6.50
Dunster Yarn Market. 24932.
95mm long.   26.00
Margate Clock Tower. No. 7213.
153mm.   8.50
Scarborough Clock Tower.
No. 3560. 138mm.   8.50
St. Winifred's Well, Holywell.
No. 4195. 60mm.   20.00
Windmill, fixed sails. No. 7223.
90mm.   12.50
Windmill, fixed sails, with hoist
and rope. No. 4167. 110mm.   12.50
Whitby Abbey, Ruin. No. 4169.
175mm.   50.00

Monuments
Banbury Cross.
2 sizes: No. 6895. 135mm.   13.00
           No. 3295. 150mm.   13.00
           or No. 4245.

Historical/Folklore
Cinderella's Coach. No. 5800.
96mm. (Lustre).   27.50
Mary Queen of Scot's Chair, not
named. No. 3604 or No. 3404.
73mm.   4.50
Ripon Hornblower. No. 4196.
with inscription. 123mm.   13.00

Traditional/National Souvenirs
Blackpool Big Wheel.
2 sizes: No. 7534. 80mm.   10.50
           No. 3561. 90mm.   10.50
Burns Cottage, interior.   21.00
Coronation Chair. No. 3583. 97mm.   5.50
Coronation Coach, (inkwell).
85mm.   27.50
Lancashire Clog. No. 3587.
2 sizes: 125mm long.   4.75
           180mm long.   7.50
Leaking Boot, Cleethorpes.
(Statue of boy holding boot,
moulded to chest).
No. 4592. 130mm.   21.50
3 Legs of Man in Lifeboat —
not glazed.   13.00
Highland Mary Statue. 138mm.   20.00
Souter Johnny, unglazed, beige.
115mm.   20.00
Mussolini, Bust, in uniform on
rectangular base. 130mm.   50.00
Rare.

Welsh Lady, standing figure.
No. 8498. 140mm.   18.00

Seaside Souvenirs
Ark. No. 7193. 90mm.   4.75
Bathing Hut with bather sitting
outside. No. 5668. 70mm long.   20.50
Bathing Hut. No. 6026. 60mm.   7.50
Canoe, flag at back and girl
inside. No. 5174. 140mm long.   12.50
Canoe, paddle and flag. No. 5175.
150mm long.   9.00
Canoe, girl with a 2 bladed paddle
but *no* flag. No. 3174.
140mm long.   12.50
Canoe, Indian. 104mm long.   5.50
Coracle tied to Stump. No. 1284.
90mm.   5.50
Gondola. No. 5660. 132mm long.
Can appear coloured
(add £6.00) No. 3803   16.00
Liner on back of oval ashtray.
80mm. If coloured add £8.00.   12.50
Rowing Boat with rudder.
No. 5126. 130mm long.   10.00
Yacht. No. 3482. 103mm.   9.00
Yacht. No. 4132. 113mm.   9.00
Yacht with waves. No. 4422.
105mm.   9.00
Yacht, full sail on waves.
No. 4438. 85mm.   10.50
Anchor, beige. 75mm.   7.00
Fisherman behind ship's wheel.
125mm.   24.00
118mm.   12.00
Fisherman's Creel. No. 7192.
60mm.   3.50
Lifeboatman, standing figure.
3 sizes: No. 6528. 105mm.   17.00
           No. 3562. 128mm.   17.00
           No. 7200. 122mm.   17.00
Lighthouse. No. 1585. 80mm.   3.00
Lighthouse. No. 11223. 110mm.   3.50
Lighthouse. 150mm.   4.00
Beachy Head Lighthouse, black band.
2 sizes: 100mm.   5.50
           145mm.   7.50
Lighthouse (Beachy Head), yellow
rust lustre. No. 6474. 130mm.   6.50
Corbiere Jersey Lighthouse.
No. 751. 100mm.   16.00
Margate Surf Boat Memorial,
yellow rust lustre. No. 3562.
125mm.   20.50
Shell dish, black edging.
145mm long.   3.50

Cockle shell dish. 115mm long.	4.00
Crab, Pin Box, in orange lustre.	
No. 2191. 80mm long.	10.50
Lobster in relief on one side of	
large Dutch Sabot. Lobster	
coloured red. 105mm long.	9.00
Boy on Lobster. No. 4426.	
100mm long.	11.00
Boy in trunks on diving board.	
No. 5799. 110mm long.	19.00
Boy in skiff holding ice cream.	
No. 4446.	13.00
Girl on rubber duck in sea.	
No. 5179. 85mm.	19.50
Girl wearing a hat on a donkey.	
No. 4170. 110mm.	13.00
Girl riding a donkey. No. 4840.	
115mm.	13.50
Boy riding a donkey. No. 4840.	
115mm. Pair with above.	13.50
Mermaid on a shell. No. 4430.	
100mm long.	10.50
Bathing Beauty on Shell.	12.50
Luggage Trolley, loaded.	
80mm long.	25.00
Binoculars. 73mm.	8.50

**For Bathing Beauties see under
Comic/Novelty.**

Countryside

Butterfly vase. 45mm.	6.00
Milkmaid holding churn. 124mm.	16.00
Shepherd and Lamb by hollow	
tree trunk. No. 846A. 75mm.	12.00
Shepherdess and Lamb by hollow	
tree trunk. No. 846B. 75mm.	12.00
Stile with milestone, with	
heart and initials. 100mm.	6.50

Animals

Cat with arched back. No. 8922.	
65mm.	9.50
Cat in bandages, sitting. 90mm.	19.00
Cat, black on ashtray. No. 5002.	
92mm long.	14.50
Cat, Cheshire. No. 6622. 70mm.	5.00
Cat, sitting. No. 6623. 55mm.	6.00
Cat, standing on hind legs,	
comical. 85mm.	40.00
Cat in long skirt and blouse with	
tie, carrying tennis racquet.	
100mm. Rare.	60.00
Cat on trinket box. No. 5678,	
No. 5679 & No. 5819.	
88mm long.	11.50
Cats, one large and one small	

either side of a cauldron.	
105mm long.	17.00
Cat posy bowl, detailed fur.	
No. 4394. 115mm.	11.25
Cat, grotesque with long neck,	
overpressed; _Luck_ in orange.	
No. 3402. 132mm.	7.00
Cat, singing, holding song sheet,	
left paw on top of music.	
65mm.	22.50
Cat and Rabbit in High Boot.	
95mm.	21.75
Cat and Rabbit in pair of Boots.	
83mm.	21.75
Cat with paw on Rat.	35.00
Cat on back of Boot, mouse on	
toe. No. 4720. 110mm long.	15.25
Black Cat on orange or blue chair.	
No. 1925 or No. 7287 or 7887.	
Good luck in relief. 68mm.	23.00
Black Cat in orange basket.	
No. 6231. 69mm.	15.00
Dog, Pointer with coiled metal	
tail. 135mm long.	15.00
Dog in kennel. No. 3479.	
70mm.	7.50
Dog in bandages, sitting. 90mm.	19.00
Dog, Scottie, wearing Tam-	
o'shanter. 74mm.	7.50
Dog, Terrier, standing. No. 6630.	
74mm long.	6.50
Pug Dog sitting with top hat	
matchholder. No. 3477. 78mm.	13.00
Dog's head spill holder. 46mm.	8.50
Dog with dead hare in mouth,	
on rocky base, plaque. 140mm.	30.00
Dog with paw on Rat. 72mm.	35.00
Dog, puppy sitting. 70mm.	9.00
Dog, puppy on chaise-longue.	
No. 5894. 84mm long.	24.50
Dog standing, Chauffeur, smoking	
pipe wearing hat with glasses	
and long overcoat. 85mm.	40.00
Dog sitting by Top Hat match-	
holder. 76mm. No. 3417.	21.00
Dog Coal Hod, some colouring.	
80mm.	15.25
Dog Mustard Pot and Spoon.	
80mm.	10.50
Dog, two Bullterriers sitting	
together. 80mm wide.	21.50
Black Dog on pink padded French	
Chair. No. 6590. 65mm.	15.00
Donkey, ears laid back, standing	
on oval base, in harness.	
88mm long.	12.50

Donkey and tree stump.
No. 3486. 90mm. 9.00
Donkey, standing inscribed:
Carisbrooke Donkey. 88mm long. 22.00
Elephant sitting, posy holder.
No. 4391. 120mm long. 7.50
Elephant with foot on ball.
No. 3682. 95mm long. 30.00
Elephant standing, head raised.
No. 6620. 75mm long. 13.00
Elephant, trunk raised. No. 6629.
85mm long. 13.00
Fish, very ornate. 110mm long. 3.00
Fish. No. 6476. 180mm long. 3.00
Fish, open mouthed. No. 6475.
143mm long. 2.50
Fish Pepper Pot, black facial features.
110mm long. 9.50
Fox, standing, wearing dress.
85mm. 40.00
Frog, yellow/green on white
oval base. 60mm. 12.00
Frog on shell, the frog is usually
green on a lustre shell.
No. 4450. 110mm long. 12.00
Two Goats standing by open tree
trunks. 50mm. 12.50
Hare, sitting. 74mm. 8.50
Horse's head and horse shoe,
ashtray. No. 3925. 44mm. 5.50
Jaguar, open mouthed,
crouching on oval base.
No. 934. 125mm long. 40.00
Lion on base. Left and right
facing found. Obviously sold
as a pair as they have the same
No. 4166. 90mm long. 8.75
Lion on a plinth. No. 4155. 115mm. 8.00
Monkey, sitting. No. 7198. 82mm. 10.50
Three Wise Monkeys on wall.
No. 7195. 80mm. 10.00
Pig, standing. No. 3566. 95mm. 10.00
Pig, standing, posy holder, pink.
135mm long. 16.00
Pig, sitting up with front trotters
on hips! Pink snout. 87mm. 40.00
Pig, gilded, peering over rim of
cup. 55mm. 9.50
Polar Bear. No. 4439. 90mm. 30.00
Rabbit in clothes on sledge.
90mm long. (Saxony). 30.00
Seal on rectangular base.
No. 4452. 127mm long. 10.00
Shetland Pony. 100mm long. 19.00
Snail. No. 5178. 112mm long.
(lustre). 11.00

Tortoise trinket box. No. 6625.
85mm long. 10.50

Birds
Egg Shell, empty. 60mm long. 3.00
Bird on rock, head looking right.
80mm. 12.00
Can be found fully coloured. 20.00
Chicken, red comb. No. 6621.
80mm. 6.00
Chickens, two and flowers on
vase. Can be found with a lustre
finish or with chickens, flowers
and ladybird coloured on white
ground. No. 5806. 120mm. 7.50
Cock and two chickens on slope.
No. 5807. 95mm long. Some colouring. 15.50
Duck, fully coloured, on lemon
lustre trinket box and lid.
75mm long. 11.00
Duck jug. 130mm long. 4.50
Duck ashtray. No. 5695.
110mm long. 7.50
Duckling pepper pot, coloured.
80mm. 5.00
Duckling wearing hat, carrying
umbrella, on leaf shaped base.
Yellow lustre on mauve base.
No. 11448. 85mm. 12.50
Fledgling, blue with orange beak
on ashtray base. 14.00
Goldfinch on rock. Coloured. 23.50
Owl on three books. No. 937.
100mm. 21.75
Owl on tree stump, with
inscription. 115mm. 12.50
Squawking parrots, facing one
another. 100mm. 16.00
Parrot. No. 6626. 75mm long. 8.00
Peacock on oval ashtray. No. 4934.
80mm long. 15.00
Pelican, drooping beak. 92mm. 9.00
Penguin pepper pot. 82mm. 11.00
Pheasant, blue on yellow/brown
ashtray. No. 4934. 60mm. 13.00
Seagull posy holder. No. 4445.
120mm long. 7.75
Swan on water. No. 4169.
82mm. 6.50
Swan posy bowl, yellow beak.
93mm. 4.75
Swan posy bowl. No. 3486.
81mm long. 4.75
Turkey posy holder. No. 1361.
90mm. 9.00

Great War

Monoplane with pilot. No. 7207. 100mm long.	30.00
Monoplane with gold fixed prop. 76mm long.	15.25
Monoplane in orange lustre. 110mm long.	16.00
Ambulance, Red Crosses on sides. No. 3916. 80mm long.	22.00
Tank with forward facing guns and curved exhaust pipe on roof. No. 8424. 110mm long.	50.00
Tank, small, no wheels.	40.00
French Soldier's Cap. 60mm long.	40.00
Cenotaph with inscription. 2 sizes: No. 6725. 110mm.	4.50
No. 6726. 148mm.	5.50
Clacton on Sea War Memorial. No. 6999. 125mm.	14.50
Great Yarmouth War Memorial. 110mm.	16.00
130mm.	22.50
Matlock Bath War Memorial, often poor quality. 3 sizes: No. 6655. 120mm.	13.50
No. 4194. 140mm.	15.00
No. 3924. 160mm.	16.00
Southsea War Memorial. No. 6660. 120mm.	18.00
Worthing War Memorial. No. 6776. 2 sizes: 108mm.	13.50
155mm.	15.50

Home/Nostalgic

Anvil. No. 6618. 2 sizes: 60mm.	4.50
85mm.	5.50
Armchair. No. 6095. 76mm.	5.50
Armchair, upholstered. No. 6812. 74mm.	8.50
Basket of coloured Fruit. No. 3918. 85mm.	13.00
Bath on four splayed feet. No. 5188. 115mm long.	8.75
Book, brass bound and open. No. 8470. 52mm.	4.00
Book, open, with heart in relief on front cover. 50mm. No. 8470.	10.50
Box Iron. No. 5671. 90mm long.	7.50
Carpet Bag, open top. 86mm.	4.50
Coffee Table, central stem. 60mm.	4.00
Chair, ornate. No. 3567. 105mm.	12.50
Chair, padded high back. No. 6095. 70mm.	8.50
Fireplace, *There's No Place Like*	

Home. No. 2275. 65mm.	10.00
Grandfather Clock, inscription. *Make use of Time.* No. 3401. 140mm.	7.50
Grandmother Clock. 88mm.	5.50
Clock with rope columns.	6.00
Ornate Mantle Clock.	10.50
Mantle Clock with side wings.	6.00
Mantle Clock. No. 4810. 100mm long.	10.00
Policeman's Lamp. 70mm.	5.00
Pail with handle down. No. 5185. 65mm.	3.00
Pedestal. No. 6905. 83mm.	2.00
Post Box. No. 6496. 75mm.	7.50
Post Box, oval, inscribed: *Letters.* 88mm.	14.00
Sack of Meal. No. 1645. 80mm.	8.75
Sewing Machine, treadle. No. 5439. 72mm.	14.50
Shaving Mug. 2 sizes: 30mm.	5.50
40mm.	5.50
Sofa, ornate. 70mm long.	10.50
Stool, blue lustre. 53mm.	4.00
Watering Can. No. 4427. 90mm.	5.50
Wheelbarrow. No. 51277. 135mm long.	6.00

Comic/Novelty

Baby on Scottie Dog's back, holding flag. 90mm long. No. 7148.	16.00
Boy with begging pug dog. No. 7062. 75mm.	20.00
Boy Scout with dog. 100mm.	25.00
Girl Guide with Cat. 103mm.	25.00
Bride and Groom in large Shell. No. 5795. 105mm.	14.00
Cupid with wings standing at curtained window, his and her shoes on ledge. 90mm.	22.50
Boy on Swing, standing. No. 5809. Some colouring. 110mm.	14.50
Girl on Swing, standing. No. 5808. 110mm.	14.50
Boy, Tennis Player match holder. No. 3414. 80mm.	16.50
Girl, Tennis Player match holder. No. 3414. 80mm. (pair).	16.50
Boy with Flag. No. 5798. 110mm.	10.50
Girl with Flag. No. 5798. (pair).	10.50
Child sitting on red and white Dog, holding flag. 80mm. No. 3148.	16.00

Girl on horse wearing hat.	
No. 4428. 125mm.	13.00
Child in fez, riding elephant.	
No. 7498. 80mm.	30.00
Boy in swimsuit leaning against	
globe. No. 5797. 115mm.	14.00
Boy dressed as Bell Hop with	
Globe. No. 5197. 98mm.	11.00
Girl dressed as Bell Hop with	
Globe. No. 5194. 98mm. (pair).	11.00
Boy dressed as Bell Hop, saluting,	
sitting on suitcase. 75mm and	
97mm. No. 5804	18.00
Girl dressed as Bell Hop, sitting	
on suitcase. No. 5804.	
75mm long. (pair).	18.00
Boy bathing dog in a tub.	25.00
Girl with pigtails sitting on side	
of oval wooden Tub, holding	
two kittens. Cat on other side.	
85mm. Pair to the above.	25.00
Boy, footballer spill holder, fully	
coloured. 80mm.	17.00
Boy feeding birds by basket.	11.00
Dutch Boy with Wheel barrow.	
No. 5803. 95mm.	16.00
Dutch Girl with Wheel barrow.	
No. 5803. 95mm. (pair).	16.00
Dutch Girl, fully coloured.	
No. 7062.	35.00
Two Children skiing on down-	
hill slope. No. 5805. 95mm.	21.75
Two Children on Sledge on slope.	
No. 5802. 95mm.	21.75
Two Children with a Wheelbarrow	
on slope. No. 6381. 90mm.	17.00
Jester. 75mm.	6.50
Pierrot standing by open bag.	
No. 3315. 90mm.	8.50
Pierette standing by open Bag.	
No. 3315. 90mm. (pair).	8.50
Pierette reclining on trinket box.	
No. 3498. 110mm.	17.50
Pixie on oval base. 60mm.	9.00
Policeman, fully coloured at front.	
No. 7083. 84mm.	25.00
Sack of Money, with figure 500,000	
impressed in seal. No. 1645.	13.00
Sultan sitting on bowl. No. 4834.	
100mm.	10.50
Waiter in tailcoat, fully coloured,	
no crest. No. 7061. Height	
unknown.	30.00
Coal Truck. No. 3915. 75mm.	8.75
Coal Truck. No. 3916. 65mm long.	8.75

Twenties Flappers
Found decorated in two styles —
white ware with clothes edged in
rust brown and the face and hair
coloured, or yellow/rust or other
shaded lustre. Value the same.

Bathing Beauty on ashtray.	
No. 4424. 95mm long (lustre).	12.50
Bathing Beauty on square	
ashtray. 110mm long.	12.50
Bathing Beauty on triangular	
ashtray. No. 2578.	
2 sizes: 75mm.	12.00
90mm.	12.00
Bathing Beauty diving through	
waves on lustre dish.	
88mm long.	19.50
Bathing Beauty on oyster	
ashtray. No. 4172.	
75mm. (lustre).	12.50
Bathing Beauty on lustre shell,	
figure coloured. No. 4174.	
70mm.	12.50
Bathing Beauty on shell. No. 4173.	
90mm long. (lustre).	12.50
Bathing Beauty reclining on oyster	
ashtray. No. 4027. 80mm.	14.00
Bathing Beauty sitting on oyster	
shell. 80mm.	14.00
Bathing Beauty on slope — pair of	
girls facing different ways both	
with same No. 5801. Different	
poses. 102mm. (lustre).	17.50
Bathing Beauty sitting outside	
ridge tent. 60mm.	20.50
Bathing Beauty resting on Globe.	
105mm.	11.00
Bathing Beauty peeping out of	
Bathing Hut. 104mm.	17.50
Bathing Beauty on Turtle.	
No. 4451. 100mm long. (lustre).	12.50
Flapper on Stool with Scottie	
dog. No. 5672. 108mm. (lustre).	16.00
Girl in Basket Chair. 115mm.	
White.	12.50
Coloured.	20.00
Girl in Basket Chair. No. 8902.	
74mm. (lustre).	13.50
Girl on horseback. No. 4428.	
105mm.	12.50
Girl on horseback on oval base.	
128mm.	11.50
Girl with parasol in Basket Chair.	
2 sizes: No. 4165. 120mm.	17.50
No. 4074. 104mm.	17.50

Sunbather with parasol, reclining. 17.50
Girl in slacks on beach ball.
115mm. 15.00
Girl in sleeveless dress on sea
shell. No. 4430. 85mm. (lustre). 14.00

Cartoon Characters
Bonzo salt pot, inscribed:
I'm Salt, some colouring
and in lustre. 80mm. 14.00
(This is a very true likeness of
Bonzo, exactly like the drawings
of him).

Alcohol
Toby Jug. No. 6608. 63mm. 8.25

Musical Instruments
Grand Piano. No. 4168.
85mm long. 14.50
Upright Piano. No. 7134. (lustre).
70mm. 12.50
Horn Gramophone. No. 7196.
42mm. 19.50

Transport
Girl in Car. No. 5774.
100mm long. (lustre). 26.00
Girl driving a van with gladstone
bag and bundle on top.
No. 5794. 85mm long. 26.00
Hot Air Balloon, square basket.
90mm. 25.00
Motor Car. No. 3917.
75mm long. (lustre). 16.00
Motor Car, open tourer.
No. 1912. 92mm long. 16.00
Ornate Sleigh. 32.00
Passenger Monoplane.
85mm wide. 30.00
Petrol Can, impressed: *Motor
Spirit*. No. 7214. 67mm. 11.50

Modern Equipment
Binoculars. No. 5187. 75mm. 8.75
Cruet Set Binoculars, in lustre.
70mm. 4.50
Folding Camera. No. 5182.
75mm. 21.50
Flat Iron. 8.00
Horn Gramophone. No. 3563.
70mm long. 19.50
Radio with horn. No. 5180.
70mm. 19.00

Footwear
Ankle Boot, open top.
105mm long. 6.50

Ladies Boot. No. 1835. 70mm. 7.50
Dutch Clog. No. 2079. 70mm long. 4.75
Ladies Slipper. 150mm long. 7.50
Ladies 18th Century Shoe.
84mm long. 7.50
Ornate Ladies Shoe. No. 3322.
115mm long. 10.50

Miscellaneous
Artist's Easel and brushes.
No. 4841. 65mm. 2.50
Club, card suit indicator. No. 3919.
80mm. 8.00

Miniature Domestic
Coffee Pot and lid. No. 3432.
65mm. 5.50
Cheese Dish and cover, traditional
shape. No. 3403. 74mm. 4.75
Cheese Dish and cover, flat
sloping top. No. 3043.
70mm long. 7.50
Kettle and lid. (lustre)
78mm. 7.50
Tea Pot and Lid, wide base.
45mm. 7.50
Tea Pot and Lid. No. 4806.
65mm. 5.50
Toast Rack. 74mm long. 7.00

Numbered Domestic Items
Inkwell with stopper — bound
with metal for thermometer.
No. 02169. 100mm long. 8.25
Heart shaped trinket box.
No. 5098. 70mm wide. 4.00
Two handled vase. No. 5682.
65mm. 2.25

ILLUSTRATED SECTION

In the following pages will be found illustrations from virtually every theme and all major factories.

Any similar item from another factory will be worth approximately the same as one shown here.

By using this easy-to-use section, one should be able to determine an idea of correct retail price.

All prices exclude VAT and are for pieces in perfect condition.

Index to Illustrations

Unglazed/Parian busts	323
Buildings	325
Monuments	330
National/Traditional Souvenirs	332
Seaside Souvenirs	336
Animals and Birds	340
Great War	349
Home/Nostalgic	358
Comic/Novelty	363
Alcohol	366
Ancient Artefacts	367
Sport	**368**
Musical Instruments	370
Transport	371
Footwear	373
Miscellaneous	374
Miniature Domestic	375

Arcadian George V £35.00

Arcadian Joseph Chamberlain £40.00

Arcadian Lloyd George £40.00

Arcadian Edward VII in Trilby £56.50

Grafton Roberts £47.50

Arcadian Kitchener £55.00

Arcadian Joffre £47.50

Arcadian Edward VII £35.00

Swan Queen Alexandra £35.00

Willow Burns £20.00   Willow Scott £17.50   Carlton Wordsworth £23.00

Grafton George V £45.00

Shelley Kitchener £34.50

Carlton Ruskin £30.00

Grafton Lloyd George £45.00

Grafton Kitchener £40.00

Arcadian Albert King of the Belgians £65.00

Shelley Burns £24.50

Swan Queen Mary £35.00

Swan George V £35.00

Shelley Sir John French £40.00

Carlton Edward VII £55.00

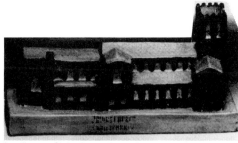

Leadbeater Christchurch Priory Church £125.00

Gretna Blacksmith's Shop £30.00

Carnegie's Birthplace £60.00

Willow Old Curiosity Shop £65.00

Foreign Burns' Cottage £30.00

Carlton Oxford Tom Tower £28.00

Willow Pevensey Old Mint House £130.00

Willow Canterbury Cathedral £40.00

Crofters Cottage £30.00

Saxony Largs Memorial £14.50

Willow Taunton Tudor House £40.00

Glastonbury Tor £40.00

Willow Art Old Ostrich Inn Colnbrook £115.00

Arcadian Westminster Abbey £30.00

Willow Lancaster Castle £32.00

Milton Feathers Hotel Ludlow £60.00

Willow Ann Hathaway's
Cottage £30.00

Willow Upleatham Church
£26.00

Regency Clifton Bridge £40.00

Tuscan Newquay Look-out
£40.00

Royal Arms China
Thatched Cottage £10.50

Willow Worcester Cathedral £40.00

German Windmill,
Fixed Sails £12.50

Foreign Irish Cottage £30.00

Arcadian Wimborne Minster £47.50

Saxony
St. Tudno's
Church £40.00

Willow Art Godalming
Town Hall £110.00

Carlton Wembley Stadium £35.00

Arcadian Portsmouth
Town Hall £40.00

Burns' Cottage Interior £21.00

Carlton Forth Bridge £30.00

Willow Chatham Town Hall £65.00

Foreign Thatched Cottage
Money Box £30.00

Arcadian The Globe
Swanage £19.50

Alexandra St. Paul's £21.50

Grafton Toll Gate House £40.00

House of the Ladies of Llangollen
£72.50

Guildford Castle £28.00

Willow Windsor Round
Tower £18.50

Grafton Smallest
House in
Wales £24.50

Knaresborough Castle £50.00

Carlton Dutch Cottage,
Canvey Island £82.50

Foreign Lantern Hill
Chapel Ilfracombe £25.00

Arcadian Kent
Hopkin £27.50

Willow Art First & Last House
£16.00

Wilton Ann
Hathaways Cottage
£15.00

Arcadian Brick Cottage
£6.50

Willow Monnow Bridge £30.00

Alexandra Tower Bridge £29.00

Arcadian Boston Stump £47.50

Norfolk Crest
Shakespeare's House £10.00

Swan Tower Bridge £29.00

Arcadian Big
Ben £13.00

Grafton Southampton
Bargate £20.00

Carlton the Alderley
Beacon £50.00

Willow Abbey Gate,
Bury St. Edmunds £57.50

Brit. Man. Brick
Cottage £7.00

Podmore Lincoln Cathedral £19

Carlton Arundel Castle
Keep £47.50

Carlton Ripon
Market Cross
£13.00

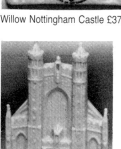

Willow Nottingham Castle £37.50

Saxony Skegness
Clock Tower £7.50

Savoy Portsmouth Town Hall £47.50

Carlton
Lighthouse £10.50

Carlton Paignton
Tower £75.00

Carlton Hastings Castle £22.00

Grafton Bath Abbey £19.50

German Bandstand
£8.00

Victis Shanklin Old Village £75.00

Botolph Big
Ben £13.00

Saxony Llandudno Church
£40.00

Arcadian Marble Arch £13.00

ork Micklegate Bar
18.00

Arcadian Windmill
£19.50

Arcadian Rochester
Castle £37.50

Willow Canterbury
West Gate £26.00

Devonia Drake
Statue £13.00

Saxony Fisherman's
Memorial
Southend £16.00

Thistle Burns
Statue £18.50

Saxony Captain
Scott Memorial
£21.75

Willow Surf Boat   Lifeboatman
Memorial £22.50   on Rocky
                    Base £16.00

Arcadian King
Alfred's
Statue £30.00

Clarence Crest,
Baron Burton
Statue £20.50

Willow Hull
Fishermen's
Memorial £16.00

Willow Laceby
Memorial
£25.00

Willow Queen
Victoria Statue,
Blackburn £35.00

Willow Edith
Cavell Statue
£12.00

Arcadian Richmond
Market
Cross £16.00

Willow Flodden
Cross
£20.00

Willow C.S.Rolls
Memorial
£30.00

Devonia Art
Derry's Clock
Plymouth £16.00

Willow Gibbet
Cross,
Hindhead
£10.50

Willow Ruskin
Memorial £21.75

Willow Florence
Nightingale
Statue £15.50

Willow Bunyan
Statue £19.50

Willow Grimsby
Hydraulic Tower
£23.00

WHH and S.
Plymouth Armada
Memorial £30.00

Willow Isaac
Newton Statue
£22.00

Carlton Fisherman
'Son of the
Sea' £30.00

Arcadian Maiwand
Memorial
Reading £14.50

Shelley Rufus
Stone £5.50

Corona Ruskin
Memorial £12.50

Carlton Queen
Eleanor's Cross
Northampton £56.50

Boy Scout and his Dog £25.00

Arcadian Bust of Judge £14.00

Shelley Lincoln Imp £18.00

Carlton Jenny Jones £35.00

Arcadian Bust of Peeping Tom of Coventry £16.00

Alexandra Burns and Highland Mary £30.00

Gemma Coronation Chair £4.50

Regis Mary Queen of Scots Chair £6.50

Suffragette Handbell £35.00

Unmarked Bust of General Booth £34.00

Carlton Ripon Hornblower £16.00

Saxony John Bull and his Dog £19.50

Wy-Not? Crest Burns' Chair £7.50

Savoy Cornish Pasty £7.50

Shelley Pat's Hat and Dudeen No. 154 £17.00

Willow Archbishop of Canterbury's Chair £10.50

Willow 'Alas Poor Yorick' Skull £7.50

Grafton Prime Cheddar
Cheese £7.50

Carlton Cheddar
Cheese (Wedged)
£5.50

Arcadian English Folksong
Bride and Chest £40.00

Willow Souter
Johnny £30.00

Carlton Crown
£21.50

Grafton Welsh
Lady Toby
Jug, Coloured
Ethnic Series
£30.00

Shelley Seated Welsh Lady £57.50

Arcadian Bust of John Bull £22.50

Arcadian Coal Miner's
Lamp '1836' £16.00

Kingsway   Regis Dutch Arcadian Mother
Dutch Girl   Boy £12.00   Shipton £13.00
£12.00

Arcadian
Coaching
Hat £7.50

Carlton Biddenden
Maids £40.00

Arcadian Lincoln
Devil £12.00

Carlton
Yorkshireman
£30.00

Carlton Caveman
with Club £82.50

Willow Daniel
Lambert £47.50

Shelley Legs of Man
No. 351 £19.50

Willow Art
Tam O'Shanter £30.00

Arcadian 'Colleen' on
Ashtray £56.50

Carlton Tam O'Shanter
£24.50

Carlton Ulphus
Horn £27.00

Arcadian Irishman on
Shamrock Ashtray
£56.50

Arcadian Welsh
Ladies Tea
Party £35.00

Lucky Charm £11.00

Podmore Chester Imp £30.00

Edwardian
Lady, Cat and
Basket £24.50

Tall Welsh Hat £8.00

Kingsway Handbell
£6.00

Grafton
President
Wilson's
Grandfather's
Chair £14.50

Saxony Gretna
Priest £30.00

Arcadian Henry V
Cradle £40.00

Podmore Bunyan's
Chair £10.50

Shelley Sir Walter
Scott's Chair
No. 325 £12.50

Willow Scott's Chair £7.50

German French
Chair £12.50

Arcadian High Backed
Chair £5.50

Willow James V
(Stirling) Chair £7.50

Willow Burn's (Dumfries)
Chair £7.50

Shelley Bunyan's
Chair £13.00

Tuscan Coronation
Chair £7.50

Carlton Old Arm
Chair £12.50

Crown Rocking
Chair £19.50

Rialto Carved
Chair £12.50

Foreign Upholstered
Armchair £8.50

Carlton Armchair £7.50

Saxony Lloyd Loom
Chair £12.50

Foreign Padded
Armchair £8.50

Grafton Whelk Shell £6.50   Shelley 'Sheringham Whelk' £16.00

Swan (RNLI) Fish Collection Box £40.00

Botolph Bather and Bathing Machine £14.50

Arcadian Fish £4.00

German Girl on Seaside Donkey £13.50

Florentine 'Manx' Lifebelt £16.00

Shelley Lifeboat No. 323 £12.50

Foreign Coracle (Tied to Stump) £5.50

Brit. Man. Houseboat (Ark) £4.75

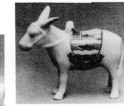

Arcadian Donkey £23.00

Carlton Motor Boat on Waves, with Driver £20.00

Arcadian 'Plaice' Ashtray £7.50

Carlton Fishing Boat £29.50

Willow Blackpool Big Wheel £12.00

Grafton Oyster Shell (Coral Legs) £5.50

Saxony 'Sea Waves' £7.50

Botolph Whelk Shell £3.00

Arcadian Scallop
Inkwell £10.50

Florentine Bathing
Chair £10.50

Willow Blackpool Tower £13.00

Excelsior Laxey Wheel
£40.00

Foreign 'Bathing Belle'
on Globe £11.00

Lighthouse
Miniature
£6.00

Arcadian Fish Basket £5.50

Grafton Girl on Sand with Bucket
and Spade £75.00

Grafton
Eddystone
Lighthouse
£7.50

German Yacht on Sea
£9.00

Coronet Punch
and Judy £50.00

Foreign Frog on Whelk Shell
£12.00

Arcadian Lifebelt £8.75

Arcadian Curled Fish £6.50

arlton Bathing Belle
50.00

Foreign Sunbather
on Shell £12.50

Sunbather with Parasol £35.00

Gemma Lighthouse
£5.50

Shelley Fish Basket No. 186 £7.50

Arcadian Bathing Machine £7.50

Arcadian Lighthouse £7.50

Grafton Lighthouse £7.50

Clock Tower £7.50

Swan Fish Basket £5.50

Grafton Boy on Sand with Toy Yacht £75.00

Whelk Shell £3.00

Foreign Bell-Hop on Suitcase £18.00

Carlton Bandstand £14.00

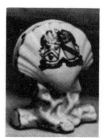

Willow Art Shell Hatpin Holder £7.00

Foreign Liner £20.50

Shelley Scallop Shell No. 166 £6.00

Podmore Margate Clocktower £10.50

Willow Beachy Head Lighthouse £7.50

Dainty
Lighthouse
£5.50

Brit. Man.
Lighthouse
£5.50

Milton
Octagonal
Lighthouse
£5.00

Grafton
Lighthouse
(Black Band)
£11.50

Queens
Lighthouse
(Oval Rock)
£5.50

Carlton
Lighthouse
'Sailor Beware'
£10.50

Willow
Lighthouse
£4.75

Arcadian
Beachy
Head
£7.50

Saxony
Beachy
Head
£6.50

Beachy
Head
Lighthouse
£6.50

Saxony
Beachy Head
(Banded)
£9.00

Saxony The Needles
Lighthouse £19.50

Shelley
Pharos
Lighthouse
No. 73 £9.00

Carlton
Flamborough
Head
Lighthouse
£25.75

Shelley Motor Boat on Waves No. 353 £19.50

Kingsway Lifeboat £8.25

Willow Paddle Steamer £82.50

German Mother Hen
and Chicks £15.50

German Parakeet
and Cockatoo £16.00

Willow
Canary £13.00

Podmore
Penguin
£11.50

Ugly Duckling £16.50

Carlton Chick
in Egg £5.50

Grafton Hen £17.50

Arcadian Cock o'th'
South £14.50

Savoy Duck £7.00

Carlton Turkey on
green base £21.50

Arcadian Duck/Rabbit £22.00

Florentine Pig £10.00

Arcadian Black Cat
on Yacht £60.00

Seagull on Rock £12.5

Arcadian Peacock £20.00

Arcadian Pelican £30.00

Canary on Perch £10.50

Arcadian Sussex
Pig £12.50

Corona Mouse
eating Nut
£19.00

Clifton Chick
Hatching £5.50

Coronet Swan Posy Holder £4.75

Carlton Owl (with Mortar Board) £14.50

Carlton Sitting Hen £6.50

Arcadian Cockerel £14.50

Arcadian Parrot £10.50

Gemma Swan £5.50

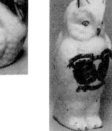
Arcadian Owl (Verse) £10.50

Florentine Frog Cream Jug £5.50

Florentine Kingfisher Cream Jug £5.50

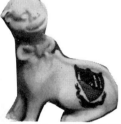
Arcadian Cheshire Cat £8.75

Alexandra Cat in Boot £14.50

Unmarked Tortoise Pin Box £7.50

Grafton Cheshire Cat (smiling) £11.00

Devonia Labrador £12.50

Wilton Cat on Pouffe £16.00

Arcadian Angry Cat Arched Back £12.50

Arcadian Black Cat in Well £47.50

Arcadian Black Cat with Bottle £40.00

Arcadian Black Cat on Jug £45.00

Arcadian Black Cat operating Radio £70.00

Arcadian Black Cat on Pouffe £19.50

Corona Large
Cat with ruff
£17.50

Kitten and Rabbit
in Boots £21.75

Florentine Pekingese in Cradle
£10.50

Carlton Puppy in Slipper £30.00

Savoy Dog Cream Jug
£13.00

Florentine Puppy
(Large/Sitting) £10.00

Florentine Spaniels
in Hat £17.00

Foreign Cat on Pin Box
(Beige Lustre) £11.00

Gemma Manx Cat £17.00

Carlton Ape
with orange
face £19.50

Gemma Pug £22.50

Shelley Bulldog
in Kennel £12.00

Saxony Cat,
Playing Mandolin
£22.50

Grafton
Monkey
£13.00

Arcadian Black Cat
on vertical
Horseshoe £40.00

Arcadian Black Cat on
Horse Shoe Pin Box
£27.50

Gemma Dog and Fly
£22.50

Saxony Puppies
and Kitten in
Basket £22.50

Arcadian Black Cat
Climbing Milkchurn
£40.00

Carlton Puppy and Horn Gramophone 'His Masters Voice' £70.00

Savoy Diminutive Cat £10.00

Carlton Dog with Banjo £26.00

Sylvan Cat on Pouffe £10.50

Grafton Bulldog Standing £13.00

Alexandra Bulldog Standing £15.00

Willow Art Cat with Bow £12.50

Carlton Scottie wearing Tam O'Shanter £11.00

Gemma Dog Lying £24.50

Boxer £10.50

Norfolk Crest Dog wearing Medallion £13.00

Grafton Terrier £26.00

Spaniel on Cushion £20.00

Arcadian Bill Sykes Bulldog £12.50

Arcadian Long-Necked Cat £8.75

Gemma Comical Cat £20.00

Carlton Cat Wearing Black Top Hat £13.00

Foreign Cat
Singing £24.50

Gemma Egyptian Cat £30

Cat Sitting £13.00

Carlton Pup One
Ear Raised £8.25

Arcadian Pup One
Ear Raised £7.50

Grafton Cat Scent
Bottle £40.00

Brit.Man.Sitting Cat £12.50

Saxony Military Cat
(Bandaged) £19.00

Cat (Imperial Bazaar)
Sitting £13.00

Saxony Pair of Bulldogs
(1 Piece) £21.50

Wilton Terrier £16.00

Arcadian Sitting Dog
£10.50

Kingsway Scottie
Wearing Glengarry
£10.50

Carlton Scottie
Begging £17.00

Arcadian Spaniel
on Cushion £8.25

Carlton Kitten,
Blue Bow
£12.00

Carlton French
Bulldog £9.00

Willow Art Dog
Standing £16.00

Leadbeater Dog
Sitting £10.50

Arcadian Small Cat
£10.00

Willow Scottie
Wearing Glengarry
£12.50

Arcadian Three Wise
Monkeys £10.50

Grafton Bear and
Ragged Staff £19.50

Grafton Snail £13.00

Grafton Seal £17.50

Willow Monkey
holding Coconut
£17.00

Carlton Black Cat on
Oval Base £21.50

Shetland Pony £21.50

Arcadian Cod £4.00

Grafton Frog Sitting £20.50 Arcadian Lion £12.50

Arcadian Tortoise £6.50

Arcadian Crab £8.25

Arcadian Teddy Bear
95mm £10.50

Arcadian Small
Teddy Bear
70mm £8.50

Arcadian Rabbit
£6.50

Willow Art
Rabbit, Raised Ears
£6.50

Polar Bear Ashtray
£25.75

Kingsway Wise
Old Owl £10.50

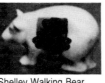

Shelley Walking Bear
No. 67 £35.00

Shelley Scottie
No. 506 £40.00

Carlton Duck on
Green Base £21.50

Grafton Labrador Puppy £19.00

Arcadian Squirrel £15.00

Saxony Frog Candlestick £16.50

Corona Bear (Large and Furry) £12.00

Queens Indian Elephant £15.00   Albion Toad £10.50

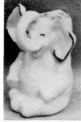

Pearl Arms Elephant Cream Jug £7.50

Arcadian Frog £6.50   Griffin Camel Kneeling £13.00

Grafton Fish Open Mouth £8.25

German Lion £10.50

Savoy Clara Cluck Candlesnuffer £19.50

Foreign Goldfinch on Rock £23.00

Corona Swan Posy Holder £4.75

Foreign Rabbit on Sledge £30.00

Grafton Dog on Ashtray Swains Studdy Series £25.00

Arcadian Standing Pony £21.50

Brit. Man. Chick Jug £5.50

Kitten £16.50

Arcadian Yellow Chick on Egg £16.00

Grafton Spaniel £11.50

Willow Mouse £16.00

Willow Long-Eared Hare £9.00

Florentine Polar Bear £30.00

Shelley Sitting
Fox No. 62
£50.00

Carlton Stork
£20.00

Shelley Long Cat No. 381 £35.00

Carlton Cat
Pepper Pot
£10.50

Arcadian Black
Cat on Swing
£65.00

Willow Standing
Polar Bear £40.00

Arcadian Three Black Cats on Sledge
£95.00

Nornesford
Chick £7.50

Dainty Swan
Posy Holder
£4.75

Savoy Owlet
£15.00

Albion Manx Cat £16.00

Swan Pig £8.25

Willow Collie £12.50

Foreign Pink Pig Posy Holder £12.00

Grafton Calf £20.00

Foreign Pharos Hounds
(Two on Base) £65.00

Shelley Camel No.64 £19.50

Queens Grotesque
Animal £10.00

Grafton Red Fox and Pheasant
No. 434 £60.00

Saxony Eagle
on Perch £17.00

Grafton Duck, Open
Posy Holder £7.50

Savoy Mouse £14.50

Willow Sitting Doe
£30.00

Gemma Cat
in Bowl
£25.00

Arcadian Rabbit
or Duck £22.00

British Manufacture
Fish Vase £5.00

Frog
Huge Open
Mouth £15.00

Willow Crouching
Lion £19.50

Carlton Turkey,
Coloured
£31.50

Standing Donkey
'We are Two' £22.50

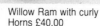

Willow Ram with curly
Horns £40.00

Grafton Sitting
Comic Cat
(Yellow Bow)
£30.00

Crown Brooding
Hen £6.50

Grafton Duck Swimming
No. 377 £19.00

Savoy Walking Lion £21.00

Saxony Swan Open
Winged Posy Holder £4.75

Carlton Monkey
£39.50

Savoy Giant Frog £21.50

Dainty Sitting
Pup £10.50

Arcadian Chic
Salt Pot
£4.75

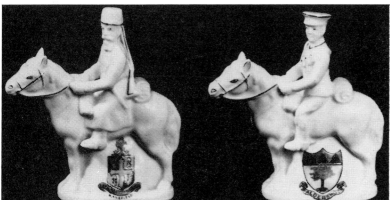

Arcadian Russian Cossack on Horseback £145.00

Arcadian British Cavalry Soldier on Horseback £145.00

Arcadian Sentry in Box £75.00

Arcadian Nurse £47.50

Arcadian Nurse and Wounded Tommy £85.00

Arcadian Machine Gunner £30.00

Arcadian Sailor £75.00

Willow Art Pot on Stove £9.00

Arcadian Bust of British Territorial Soldier £30.00

Grafton The Bomb Thrower £125.00

Arcadian Bugler Boy £135.00

Arcadian Standing Soldier £87.00

Arcadian Observer
Balloon £47.50

German Monoplane
with Pilot £30.00

Arcadian Monoplane £55.00

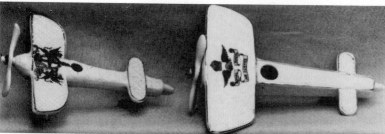

Carlton Monoplane £55.00

Willow Monoplane £55.00

Savoy Model of
British Motor
Searchlight £145.00

Savoy Monoplane £60.00

Arcadian Bi-Plane £100.00

Arcadian Nurse
Cavell £11.00

Shelley Zeppelin £65.00

Arcadian Monoplane with coloured
roundels £75.00

Swan British Aerial
Torpedo £30.00

Carlton Biplane with coloured roundels
£175.00

Arcadian Bury St.
Edmunds Bomb £1

Grafton Battleship £40.00

Corona Submarine
E.4. £16.00

Carlton Battleship HMS Warspite £60.00

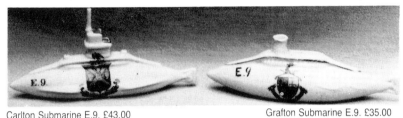

Carlton Submarine E.9. £43.00

Grafton Submarine E.9. £35.00

Alexandra Torpedo £47.50

Corona British Airship £20.00

Savoy
Scottish
Soldier
£110.00

Swan HMS Queen Elizabeth £30.00

Corona 'Lusitania' £75.00

Carlton RMS Lusitania £75.00

Grafton HMS Iron Duke £85.00

Savoy Submarine E.1. £40.00

Carlton HMS Humber Monitor £55.00

Willow Liner converted
to Troopship £90.00

Savoy Battleship HMS Lion £56.50

Arcadian
Hair Brush
Grenade
£130.00

Arcadian Torpedo Boat
Destroyer £19.50

Carlton HMS Queen Elizabeth £57.50

Carlton Minesweeper £60.00

Carlton H.M.S. Australia £65.00

Shelley Submarine E.9.
£40.00

Willow Art Airship
Beta £40.00

Carlton Battleship. HMS Tiger £55.00

Carlton
Munitions
Worker £80.00

Arcadian Sailor
winding Capstan
£82.50

Arcadian Bust of
a Sailor £30.00

Swan Tommy's Hut £40.00

Savoy Armoured Car £80.00

Shelley Armoured Car
No. 329 £40.00

Grafton Motor Tractor
as used on
the Western Front
£170.00

Arcadian Tommy driving Steamroller over the Kaiser
£435.00

Arcadian
Sheringham
Bomb £82.50

Carlton Vickers Tank £215.00

Coronet Tank £21.50

Willow Tank with Trailing Wheels
£14.50

Arcadian Tank 160mm long
£22.00

Carlton Fiat Tank
£300.00

Savoy Tank £30.00

Grafton Tank £24.50

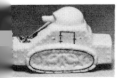

rcadian Armoured Car
30.00

Grafton Desert Gun £52.50

Corona Renault Tank £65.00

Shelley Red Cross
Van £26.50

Corona Red Cross
Van £23.00

Savoy Two-Piece Machine Gun £120.00

Savoy Howitzer £27.50

Carlton Field Gun with
screen and sight hole £28.00

Arcadian Howitzer £16.00

Willow Art Field Gun with screen £18.50

Swan Field Gun with screen £18.50

Grafton Mills Hand
Grenade with Pin
£22.00

Grafton 'French 75' £47.50

Arcadian Trench Mortar £10.50

Shelley Howitzer £35.00

Arcadian Field Gun £17.00

Carlton Machine Gun £30.00

Arcadian Despatch Rider £43.50

Arcadian German Aerial Torpedo £30.00

Grafton Water Bottle £13.00

Aynsley Hand Grenade with Flames £30.00

Carlton German Incendiary Bomb £20.00

Swan Bullet Clip £13.00

Corona Shell £4.00   Willow Kitbag £15.00   Grafton Cannon Shell £5.25   Arcadian Sandbag £13.00   Swan Anti-Aircraft Shell £17.50

Arcadian Canister Bomb £13.00

Arcadian Field Glasses £13.00

Arcadian Mills Hand Grenade £13.00

Arcadian Anti-Zeppelin Candlestick £14.00

Carlton Cannon Shell £5.00   Shelley Shell £11.00   Swan Jack Johnson Shell £8.00

Swan Trench Dagger £40.00

Aynsley Bell Tent £23.00

Shelley Tent and Soldier with Concertina £75.00

Carlton 'Shrapnel Villa' Dugout £34.50

Arcadian Trench Lamp £10.50

Porcelle Glengarry £16.00

Arcadian Territorial Officer's Peaked Cap £10.00

Aynsley Forage Cap £25.00

Corona Torch £10.50

Corona Peaked Cap £10.00

Savoy French Trench Helmet £40.00

Arcadian Tommy's Steel Helmet £22.50

Carlton Forage Cap £14.50

Willow German Pickelhaube £17.50

Foreign French Infantry Helmet £40.00

Aynsley Colonial Hat £18.00

Aynsley High Boot £22.00

Willow Nurse Edith Cavell Norwich Memorial £25.00

Arcadian Dover War Memorial £65.00

Aynsley Pith Helmet £21.00

Arcadian Folkestone War Memorial £60.00

Arcadian [Patrol Mer £22.00

Shelley Marianne
No. 406 £105.00

Arcadian Gurkha
Knife £20.00

Shelley Tank with Trailing
Wheels No. 400 £16.00

Shelley 'Black Watch'
Dog in Kennel
No. 316 £15.25

Arcadian Battleship £15.50

Swan Capstan
£10.00

Carlton Searchlight
£30.00

Carlton Douglas
War Memorial
£75.00

Foreign Southsea
War Memorial £18.00

Patriotic
Bottle with
Black Watch
Private and
Decoration
£20.00

Carlton Scottish
Soldier with
Rifle £135.00

Willow The Cenotaph £5.50

Shelley Bust of
Admiral Sir John
Jellicoe £43.50

Carlton Field Gun £17.00

Carlton Bust of
Sailor 'HMS
Dreadnought'
£30.00

Arcadian
Standing
Jovial Sailor
HMS Lion'
£5.00

Corona Peace
Clock £56.50

Carlton Brighton War Memorial
£100.00

Peaked Cap £10.00   Savoy Donner Blitzer Tank £45.00

Willow Ornate Hand
Mirror £20.00

Gemma Rocking
Chair £12.50

Arcadian Three-
Legged Stool £5.50

Willow Art
Grandfather
Clock £10.50

Foley Bellows
£10.50

Carlton Warming
Pan £8.75

Grafton Winged
Armchair £15.25

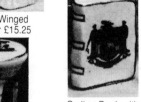

Arcadian Cradle £6.00

Brit.Man.Suitcase
£4.00

Florentine Flat
Iron £8.50

Carlton Book with
Gilded Clasp £5.00

Arcadian Woven Straw
Basket £4.00

Foreign Tiny Basket £2.00

Three Legged
Stool £3.00

Gemma Four-Legged
Stool £5.50

Victoria Broomhead £15.25

Willow Coal Scuttle
£4.50

Wilton Grandfather
Clock £10.50

Arcadian Narrow
Grandfather
Clock £10.50

Carlton Expanding
Suitcase £4.00

Carlton Square
Sundial £7.50

Arcadian Alarm
Clock £19.50

Arcadian Gramophone
Cabinet £40.00

Shelley Valise No. 58 £6.50

Gemma Bucket £4.00

Gemma
Grandmother
Clock £5.50

Tuscan Crusty
Bread Loaf £15.00

Willow Dressing Table
Mirror £12.00

Gemma Ornate Mantle
Clock £10.50

Gemma Helmet Coal
Scuttle £5.50

Arcadian Dustpan £8.00

Florentine Cradle on
Rockers £6.50

Carlton Shaped
Clock £16.00

Carlton Time
Glass £10.00

Crown Circular
Sundial £5.00

Willow Sundial
£10.50

Shelley Handbag
No. 184 £12.50

Foreign Mantlepiece
Clock with Side
Wings £6.00

Queens Narrow
Grandfather
Clock £22.50

Cyclone
Suitcase £4.75

Foreign Clock with
Rope Columns £6.00

Podmore
Grandfather
Clock £10.50

Brit. Man.
Grandfather
Clock £9.00

Carlton
Grandfather
Clock £10.50

Brit. Man.
Grandfather
Clock £9.00

German
Grandfather
Clock £7.50

Brit. Man.
Grandfather
Clock £9.00

Arcadian
Grandfather
Clock £10.50

Porcelle
Grandfather
Clock £10.50

Shelley 14th
Century Clock
No. 307 £16.00

Florentine
Pillar Box 'I can't
get a Letter
so send you
the Box' £9.50

Shelley Victorian
Pillar Box No.
157 £19.00

Willow 'GR' Post
Box £17.00

Willow Grandfather
Clock £10.50

Savoy Sundial £8.7

Arcadian Sundial 'Life's
but a Walking
Shadow' £5.50

Warwick Sundial
£10.50

Willow Art
Anvil £5.50

Signal Anvil £4.50

Florentine Sofa £10.50

Arcadian Village
Pump with
Trough £7.50

Foley Water Pump
No. 51 £9.00

Kingsway
Hammerhead Match
Holder £11.00

Arcadian Umbrella
£14.50

Coronet Carboy
£3.00

Triood Sloping
Desk Top £7.50

Shelley 'Ancient Lights' Lantern £12.50

Willow Book
£5.00

Savoy Kennel £6.50

Willow Fish Basket £6.50

Shelley Garden Roller No. 358 £12.50

German Oval Post
Box £14.00

Gemma Wheelbarrow £6.00

Premier Coal
Scuttle £4.00

Foley Cradle £10.50

Arcadian 'GR' Miniature Post Box £13.00

German Open Carpet Bag £4.50

Shelley Milk Churn No. 46 £7.00

Botolph Policeman's Lamp £4.75

Shelley Sundial £16.00

Grafton Axe in Tree Stump £10.50

Arcadian Fireplace 'There's No Place Like Home' £12.50

Wall Plaque Ayr-Brig O'Doon £23.50

Arcadian Devonshire Dumpling £10.50

Foley Kennel No. 49 £7.50

Gemma Garden Trug £3.50

Willow Watering Can £5.50

Arcadian The Old Armchair £7.50

Willow Chest and Lid £7.50

Arcadian 'Ally Sloper' £40.00

Podmore Mr. Pussy Foot £30.00

Carlton 'Bonzo' Dog £30.00

Arcadian Bust of Harry Lauder £30.00

Carlton Winkie the Gladeye Bird £15.00

Swan Clown £17.00

Grafton Chinese God Fu Hing £40.00

Arcadian Girl in Egg £16.00

Carlton John Citizen 'Housing Unemployment, Taxes' £82.50

Foreign Boy Feeding Birds £11.00

Podmore Wilfred Wilfred £35.00

Carlton Jester £14.50

Arcadian Black Boy and Crocodile £110.00

Arcadian Black Boy in Bed with Spider £56.50

Arcadian Black Girl making Ink in Bath £65.00

Arcadian Black Boy playing Banjo £85.00

Florentine Baby on
Rock £16.00

Foreign Sailor Boy
and Flag £10.50

Peeping Tom Bust
£20.00

Monk with Lantern
£17.00

Arcadian Baby Boy
in Wash Bowl £45.00

Arcadian Baby Girl
by Hip Bath £85.00

Willow Art Mermaid
on Rock £20.00

Arcadian Black
Boy in
Egg £24.00

Arcadian Jester £8.25

Victoria Fat
Screw £20.00

Arcadian Black Boy and
Girl on Log £75.00

Arcadian Black Boy
with Pumpkin £100.00

Arcadian Sailor and
Parrot Mustard £36.50

Willow Man in the
Moon £19.50

Flapper with
Feet in Pool £65.00

Cyclone Schoolboy
on Scooter £16.00

Arcadian Japanese Girl £34.00

Foreign Mermaid £10.50

Arcadian Sailor Toby £47.50

Arcadian Fat Lady weighing on Scales £33.00

Savoy Fat Policeman £70.00

Grafton Dutchman Holding Cheese £17.00

Botolph Pillory £17.00

Willow RSM Pepper Pot £47.50

Shelley Matches No. 190 £17.00

Carlton Boy Blowing Bubbles £75.00

Arcadian Sailor Toby Jug £45.00

Wilton Tramp and Tankard etc. £85.00

Grafton Baby £16.00

Cyclone Baby Bath £11.00

Victoria 'Jack-in-the-Box' £16.00

Brit. Man. Baby in Bootee £11.00

Arcadian Policeman on Point duty £25.00

Arcadian Jovial Policeman 'Stop' £28.00

Carlton Baby 'Mothers Darling' £75.00

Regency Cigarette Case £13.00

Arcadian Soda
Syphon £10.00

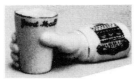

Carlton Hand and Glass £7.50

Arcadian Scotch and Soda £12.50

Carlton Drunkard by
Lamp Post £56.50

Grafton
Soda
Syphon
£12.00

Carlton Jovial
Monk £16.00

Podmore Beer Barrel £4.50

Arcadian Toby Jug £8.25

Grafton Drinker in
Beer Barrel £30.00

Arcadian Tankard
Overflowing £4.75

Willow Art
Beer Barrel £3.00

Willow Bottle and Tankard
on Horseshoe £12.50

Savoy Barrel and stand
two-piece £7.50

Grafton Champagne Bottle £7.50
Willow Scotch Bottle £7.50
Arcadian Miniature Corked Bottle £4.75

Arcadian Man with
Tankard £25.00

Arcadian Jovial Monk
with Glass £12.50

Shelley Beer Keg
No. 48 £5.50

Arcadian Man climbing Beaker £34.50

Arcadian 'Nap Hand' Beer Labels on Ashtray £45.00

Carlton Drinker and Barrel £55.00

Florentine Champagne Bottle in Bucket £7.50

Shelley Hanley Chinese Vase No. 80 £4.75

Shelley Celtic Ancient Jar No. 200 £4.00

Shelley Salamis Lampshade No. 130 £7.00

Shelley Gastrica Bottle No. 138 £4.75

Shelley Tibet Sacred Vase No. 209 £4.00

Shelley Phoenican Water Jar No. 207 £6.00

Shelley Cyprian Vase No. 206 £4.00

Shelley Cleopatra's Vase No. 114 £7.50

Shelley Eastern Olive Jar No. 208 £4.00

Shelley Indian Wine Vessel No. 303 £8.75

Shelley Celtic Water Bottle No. 205 £4.50

Arcadian Winchester Bushel £13.00

Gemma Policeman's Lamp £4.50

Gemma Puzzle Tankard £8.50

Shelley Roman Vestal Lamp No. 149 £7.50

Carlton Merthyr Vase No. 382 £3.00

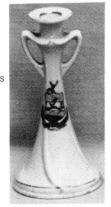

Shelley Altar Candlestick No.306 £9.50

Willow Thames Punt £75.00

Panorama
Footballer Trophy
'RN Accountants'
£100.00

Carlton 'Put and Take'
Ashtray £65.00

Carlton Boy Jockey
on Ashtray £21.50

Grafton Footballer
£80.00

Grafton Girls on Punt £40.00

Carlton Golfer on Ashtray £85.00

Arcadian
Cricket
Bat £40.00

Grafton Tennis
Player Suzanne
Lenglen £85.00

Brit. Man. Canoe £6.00

Carlton Cricket
Batsman on
Ashtray £95.00

Arcadian
Caddie
and Golf
Clubs £55.00

Arcadian Chess
Rook £4.00

Sussex
Chess
Knight
£8.25

Corona
Chess
Knight
£8.25

Corona
Chess
Bishop
£16.00

Heraldic Chess
King £19.50

Alexandra Chess
King £19.50

Arcadian Golf Club £10.50

Kingsway Golf Ball £5.50

Arcadian Yacht £12.50

Victoria Yacht in Full Sail £10.50

Shelley Golf Ball on Tee No. 215 £7.50

Small Football £6.50

Carlton Roller Skate £22.00

Large Football £6.50

Shelley Tennis Racquet and Balls No.194 £14.00

Botolph Tennis Racquet £7.50

Norfolk Cricket Cap £22.00

Florentine Boxing Glove £30.00

Arcadian Tennis Racquet £7.50

Grafton 'The Colonel' £30.00

Carlton Jockey on Racehorse £75.00

Swan Cricket Bag £9.00

Savoy gilded Golf Club £10.50

Foreign Jockey Cap £20.00

Civic Cricket Bag £8.00

Large Rugby Ball £7.50

Arcadian Billiard Table, Cue and 3 Balls £95.00

Willow Lute £35.00

Wilton HMV Horn
Gramophone £26.00

Devonia Bagpipes £15.00

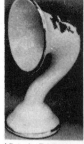

Victoria Radio
Horn £18.00

Victoria Upright Piano
(Open Lid) £12.50

Florentine Grand Piano £14.50

Arcadian Tambourine
£7.50

Arcadian Harp £6.50

Shelley Bugle £30.00

Willow Guitar £10.50

Saxony Harp £6.50

German Ornate Grand Piano £14.50

Saxony Tiny Horn
Gramophone £19.50

Florentine Box
Gramophone £15.25

Arcadian Banjo £9.50

Arcadian Upright Piano
(Closed Lid) £13.50

Foreign Ornate Sleigh £32.00

Carlton Motor Cycle
and Sidecar £75.00

Foreign Coronation Coach
Inkwell £27.50

Carlton Gondola £14.50

Foreign Girl in Car Laden
with Luggage £26.00

Arcadian Taxi-Cab
EH 139 £56.50

Arcadian
Petrol Pump
Attendant
£40.00

Foreign Hot
Air Balloon
£25.00

Arcadian Motor
Spirit Can
£13.00

Villow Coal Truck £16.00

Carlton Stephenson's
Locomotion No. 1 £85.00

Carlton Locomotive £70.00

Carlton Coal Truck
'Black Diamonds' £16.00

Florentine Saloon
Car £30.00

Florentine
Charabanc with Driver £30.00

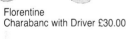

Podmore Charabanc
XL 100 £27.50

Arcadian Charabanc 7734 £33.00

Shelley Coupe No. 360 £265.00

Savoy Red Cross Van
£40.00

Shelley Open Top Motor Car
No. 361 £145.00

Carlton Saloon Car DN 999 £56.50

Dadat-Limoges Open Car £30.00

Grafton 'Dreadnought'
Charabanc £55.00

Botolph Saloon Car £30.00

Swan Open Tourer EH 139 £30.00

Botolph Red Cross
Van EH 139 £23.00

Diamond Ambulance £40.00

Foreign Bisque Open
Top Car £16.00

Caledonia Open 4-Seater Tourer £30.00

18-Seater Charabanc £28.00

Carlton Luggage Trolley £40.00

Foreign Open Tourer
Chauffeured £30.00

Carlton Open Sports Car
DN 999 £30.00

Foreign Sabot
(Colour/Chain/Flowers) £10.50

Arcadian Large
Boot £16.00

Saxony Ladies
Boot £8.25

Arcadian Slipper
Wall Pocket
£7.50

Side Fastening
Boot £5.50

Grafton Oriental
Slipper £6.50

Florentine Bootee £20.00

Foley Dutch Sabot £7.50

Temple Oriental Slipper £6.50

Gemma Ladies Shoe,
Frilled Tongue £7.50

Edwardian Shoe
£11.00

Shelley Highboot
£16.00

Porcelle Ankle
Boot £4.75

German Boot £11.00

German Ladies Boot £12.50

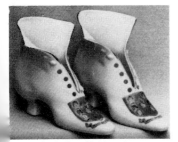

Saxony Ankle Boot £9.00 each

Corona Lancashire Clog £4.75

Grafton Boot
with Puttees
£21.75

Saxony Shoe
with Eyelets
£7.50

Willow Tiny Clog
£4.75

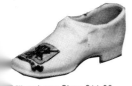

Willow Long Shoe £11.00

Pair Carlton Lancashire Clogs £15.00

Carlton Cash Register £20.00

Talbot Gas
Cooker £8.25

Foreign Camera £21.50

Impero
Saxony
Washerwoman
with Basket
£25.00

Carlton Dice Pin
Box £13.00

Foreign Lamb
and Shepherdess
£13.00

Arcadian rectangular
Haystack £5.50

Arcadian
Bishop's
Mitre £6.50

'Spade' £3.00

Podmore Hand
Holding
Tulip £3.50

Carlton Beehive £7.50

Carlton Stick
Telephone £16.00

Carlton Closed
Pine Cone £4.00

Unmarked German Stile,
Gate & Milestone £6.50

Carlton Campfire £11.50

Willow Art Lincoln Imp £8.50

Willow Art Wheelbarrow £10.50

Gemma Pierced Dish £4.00

Gemma Coffee Pot £7.50

Gemma Meat Dish £8.75

Carlton Saucepan £7.50

Carlton Cylinder Vase £2.25

Fairy Ware Teapot £7.50

Gemma Puzzle Teapot £16.00

Grafton Mustard Pot & Lid £5.50

Gemma Kettle £7.50

Swan Puzzle Teapot £4.75

Gemma Diamond Shaped Teapot £14.00

Gemma Hot Water Jug £7.50

Gemma Miniature Cup and Saucer £5.50

Clifton Bagware Cup and Saucer £4.00

Shelley Persian Cafeterre £10.50

Arcadian Bird Series Sugar Bowl £8.00

Tuscan Lemon with Open Top £6.50

German Shaving Mug £3.00

Arcadian Shaving Mug £5.50

Shelley Shaving Mug £7.50

Gemma Shaving Mug (Green) £10.50

Arcadian 'Hair Pins' Oval Box £5.50

Florentine Hair Brush (Moulded Bristles) £10.50

Carlton Circular Pot with Curved Lid £4.00

Robinson and Leadbeater Oval Box and Lid £4.00

Florentine 'Trowel' Box and Lid £14.50

Carlton Rectangular Pin Box and Lid £4.00

Arcadian Heart Shaped Pin Box and Lid £4.00

Rectangular Box and Lid £4.25

Carlton Swedish Kettle £3.00

Carlton Bottle £6.50

Gemma Square Teapot £12.00

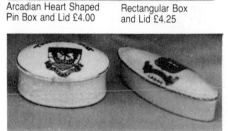

Arcadian Oval Trinket Box and Lid £4.75

Oval Box and Lid £4.00

German Teapot £10.00

Gemma Moustache Cup £6.50

Gemma Cup and Saucer £4.50

Pearl Arms Coffee Pot £7.50

Ornate Butterfly Vase £6.00

Grafton Cruet Happy & Sad £25.00 Pair

Wilton Ashtray £12.50

Gemma Cheese Dish £4.75

Arcadian Cheese Dish £7.50

Gemma Shaving Mug £3.00

Coffee Pot £7.50

Carlton Kettle 'Polly Put . . . £12.50

Grafton Hereford Kettle £5.50

Gemma Teapot £7.50

Florentine Teapot £7.50

Carlton Pepper & Salt £6.50 Pair

Cyclone Coffee Pot £7.50

Arcadian Turquoise Kettle £5.50

Silver Rimmed Tankard £7.00

Arcadian Comical Teapot £22.00

Shelley Teapot £16.00

Gemma Cheese Dish & Lid £14.00

Crown Devon Sauce Boat £20.00

Gemma Shaving Mug £5.50

Arcadian Flower Vase £4.00

Carlton Cheese Dish and Cover £7.50

Foreign Cheese Dish and Cover, One-Piece £4.75

Fenton Cheese Dish and Cover £6.50

William Henry Goss

The story of the Staffordshire family of Potters who invented Heraldic Porcelain

Lynda & Nicholas Pine

In this first ever biography of the man who is credited with inventing heraldic porcelain and his family who worked with him and at times against him, the authors tell the story of Goss china in fascinating detail.

From a promising start as a literary student, William Henry Goss used the important contacts he made in London to carve himself a career in the pottery industry in Stoke-on-Trent. At first, he produced a limited, expensive range of parian busts and figurines, but with the entry of his sons Adolphus and later Victor and Huntley into the business, production switched to the small white models bearing colourful coats of arms for which the firm became famous.

The authors recount the stories of Godfrey, who ran away to New Jersey with a factory paintress, began a pottery there and founded the American branch of the family; the surprising Falkland Islands connection, still continuing today; why William refused to speak to his wife for the last twenty years of his life and how he came to have four homes all at the same time.

The history of the three periods of production is complemented by fascinating chapters on how the porcelain was both manufactured and sold through agencies in virtually every town in the country.

The book is illustrated with over 350 photographs and maps, includes much material not previously published and comprehensive family trees.

As the story unfolds you can discover:

- The beginnings of William's potting career. Why did he decide to become a potter?

- How the romantic young William became an obstinate and pedantic father and eventually a near recluse.

- Why William did not speak to his wife for the last 20 years of his life - and how he came to have four homes all at the same time.

- His amazing generosity towards his friends and work force and his unbelievable meanness and cruelty towards his wife and children.

- How William viewed his two sons Adolphus and Victor as rivals.

- Who *really* invented heraldic porcelain, and how it was manufactured and marketed.

- The three periods of Goss manufacture and how the trade developed leading eventually to mass popularity nationwide.

- The amazing Falkland Islands connection, how Port Stanley and the Upland Goose Hotel came to be so-named and the exciting story of how the Goss family came to emigrate to those barren islands - and the dreadful fate that befell them.

- Why youngest daughter Florence married a bewhiskered Bostonian millionaire older than her father.

- The truth about the rumour that second son Godfrey got a factory girl 'into trouble' and was banished to America. Why did Godfrey emigrate to America? and did he start a US Goss factory?

260mm x 217mm 350 Illustrations 5 Family Trees 256 pages. Bibliography and Glossary.

CRESTED CHINA

By Sandy Andrews

This title, first published in 1980, is the first and only serious and comprehensive reference work ever attempted on this subject – although written in a readable lighthearted style.

A large, lavish production with hard cover and coloured dust jacket, it contains 304 pages. Over 750 illustrations – 90 in full colour – are included, depicting over 1000 pieces from all factories and showing items from every possible theme with special emphasis on animals, buildings and Great War crested china.

Particulars of well over 4000 pieces are given with their dimensions and relevant details where thought to be of interest. This is the first attempt at a complete listing of all the pieces made by every factory. The history of and all known information about over 220 factories is provided, and a mass of other exciting facts answer all the questions that collectors have been asking for years such as 'Why does the same piece appear with a different factory mark?' 'Why do some pieces have no crest, factory mark or name?' 'Why are some pieces numbered?'; etc, etc.

In addition to all this information, over 270 line drawings of factory marks are shown to aid identification, the majority of which are not in any of the usual 'mark books'.

The story of crested china, how the trade expanded, and some of the colourful characters involved in it is told for the first time. A chapter on the W.H. Goss factory with illustrations of pieces from all periods of that factory's life, throws important new light on the later period and what happened during the Goss England, or Third Period about which there is often confusion.

The book is not a price guide, although indications of rare items are given, but a lasting profusely illustrated reference work which is recommended to all crested china enthusiasts.

303mm × 220mm. 304 pages. Cased. 753 illustrations. £19.95.

Available from bookshops everywhere or by post direct from Milestone Publications. Descriptive leaflets on this and all other titles connected with Goss and crested china are sent on request.

The Concise Encyclopaedia and Price Guide to Goss China

Nicholas Pine

Now in its fifth edition, this latest guide has much fresh information including numerous new pieces, many announced for the first time. A well illustrated domestic section clarifies this area of the factory's wares and improved layout and explanations make this chapter easier to understand and pieces easier to locate.

The dimensions and inscription for every piece are given and the Historic Models and Special Shapes section contains the correct matching arms for each model — all separately priced. The very latest revised prices are given right through the book which is also a now virtually complete descriptive listing of every piece of Goss ever produced.

The guide is the standard work on Goss china and is used by the leading dealers and auctioneers.

The prices given form the base prices of pieces to which the values for particular arms or decorations should be added.

The work is well illustrated and is superbly bound in hardcover with colour jacket. It is a pair with **The 1989 Price Guide to Crested China** and the sequel to **Goss China Arms Decorations and Their Values** by the same author.

The Major Features of the Concise Encyclopaedia and 1989 Price Guide to Goss China include:

- Every chapter revised and updated incorporating thousands of detail amendments to previous editions.
- 1200 illustrations — including both common and rare items.
- Every model now illustrated — even the rare Haamoga Amaui from Tonga and the newly discovered Letchworth Roman Urn.
- All pieces designated into first, second and third periods.
- The original inscription on every piece given.
- Every correct matching arms recorded and priced.
- Dimensions given for each piece and variation.
- Over 2500 pieces listed.
- A complete chapter on factory marks with 30 illustrations encompassing every known mark — with dates.
- An informative history of W.H. Goss and Goss China and many notes for collectors.
- Additional chapters on Goss Postcards, Goss Cabinets, The Goss Records and The League of Goss Collectors.

215mm × 155mm. 1200+ illustrations. 384 pages.

Goss & Crested China Ltd. are the leading dealers in Heraldic China

We have been buying and selling for over twenty years and our experienced staff led by Lynda and Nicholas Pine will be able to answer your questions and assist you whether you are a novice or an experienced collector.

A constantly changing attractively priced stock of some 5,000 pieces may be viewed at our Horndean showrooms which includes Goss cottages, fonts, crosses, shoes, lighthouses, models etc. and the full range of crested ware including military, animals, buildings etc. covering all the other manufacturers.

Visitors are welcome to call during business hours of 9.00-5.30 any day except Sunday. Those travelling long distances are advised to telephone for an appointment so that they may be sure of receiving personal attention upon arrival, but this is not essential.

Most of our business is by mail order and we publish *Goss & Crested China*, a monthly 32 page illustrated catalogue containing hundreds of pieces for sale from every theme and in every price range. The catalogue is available by annual subscription; please turn over for details of this and the Goss & Crested China Club.

In addition, if you specialise, we will be pleased to offer you particular pieces or crests from time to time as suitable items become available. Please let us know your wants as with our ever-changing stock we will probably have something to suit.

Our service is personal and friendly and all orders and correspondence are dealt with by return. You will find us fair and straightforward to deal with, as we really care about crested china and this is reflected in our service.

Finally, we are just as keen to buy as we are to sell and offers of individual items or whole collections are always welcome. These will be dealt with by return and the very highest offers will be made.

Goss & Crested China Ltd,
62 Murray Road,
Horndean,
Hampshire
PO8 9JL

Telephone: Horndean (0705) 597440
Facsimile: Horndean (0705) 591975

Would you like to join

The Goss & Crested China Club

Exclusively for collectors and customers of Goss & Crested China Ltd. Membership will provide answers to questions such as:

How do I find the pieces I am looking for?

What is a fair price?

Where can I obtain information about Goss China and Goss collecting?

Where can I exchange or sell pieces I no longer require?

Join the Goss & Crested China Club without delay and receive the following benefits:

FREE Specially designed enamel membership badge.

FREE Membership card and number.

FREE Telephone and postal advice service.

FREE Information on books about heraldic china collecting.

FREE Valuation service for your collection.

FREE Especially favourable Club members part-exchange rates for pieces surplus to requirements.

FREE Without obligation search-and-offer service for any items or decorations that you seek.

FREE Invitations to Club open days.

EXCLUSIVE Club Members only special offers to be announced periodically.

Membership is free and is available to subscribers to *Goss & Crested China* the club's monthly catalogue of pieces for sale.

To join, just send £9.00* annual subscription to Goss & Crested China Ltd, 62 Murray Road, Horndean, Hampshire PO8 9JL, and you will receive a membership application form with your first copy of the catalogue. Upon receipt of the completed form, you will be sent your enamel badge, membership card and full details of the club's special offers and services.

For Airmail outside of Europe add £6.00.

Other titles available from
Milestone Publications

Please send for full catalogue

William Henry Goss. The story of the Staffordshire family of Potters who invented Heraldic Porcelain.
Lynda and Nicholas Pine.

Goss China Arms, Decorations and their values
Nicholas Pine

Crested China. The History of Heraldic Souvenir Ware
Sandy Andrews

The 1989 Price Guide to Crested China including revisions to **Crested China**
Nicholas Pine

Take Me Back To Dear Old Blighty.
The Great War through the eyes of the Heraldic China Manufacturers
Robert Southall

The Goss Record War Edition (1916)
reprinted

Let's Collect Goss China
Alf Hedges

Goss and Other Crested China
Nicholas Pine

In Search of the Better 'Ole The Life, The Works and The Collectables of Bruce Bairnsfather
Tonie and Valmai Holt

Parian Ware
Douglas Barker

Discovering Heraldry
Jacqueline Fearn

Goss & Crested China. Illustrated monthly catalogues listing items for sale. Available by Annual Subscription. Details upon request from 62, Murray Road, Horndean, Hants. PO8 9JL.